JUDGES

JUDGES

A Theological Commentary for Preachers

Abraham Kuruvilla

CASCADE *Books* • Eugene, Oregon

JUDGES
A Theological Commentary for Preachers

Copyright © 2017 Abraham Kuruvilla. All rights reserved. Except for brief quotations in critical publications or reviews, no part of this book may be reproduced in any manner without prior written permission from the publisher. Write: Permissions, Wipf and Stock Publishers, 199 W. 8th Ave., Suite 3, Eugene, OR 97401.

Cascade Books
An Imprint of Wipf and Stock Publishers
199 W. 8th Ave., Suite 3
Eugene, OR 97401

www.wipfandstock.com

PAPERBACK ISBN: 978-1-4982-9822-3
HARDCOVER ISBN: 978-1-4982-4823-5
EBOOK ISBN: 978-1-4982-9823-0

Cataloguing-in-Publication data:

Names: Kuruvilla, Abraham.

Title: Judges : A Theological Commentary for Preachers / Abraham Kuruvilla.

Description: Eugene, OR: Cascade Books, 2017 | Includes bibliographical references and index.

Identifiers: ISBN 978-1-4982-9822-3 (paperback) | ISBN 978-1-4982-4823-5 (hardcover) | ISBN 978-1-4982-9823-0 (ebook)

Subjects: LCSH: Bible. Judges—Commentaries. | Bible. Judges—Homiletical use.

Classification: LCC BS1305.53 K8 2017 (print) | LCC BS1305.53 (ebook)

Manufactured in the U.S.A. 04/20/17

To
John
for pointing me
to some of the best stories
I've ever read

"God made man because he loves stories."
Elie Wiesel
The Gates of the Forest

CONTENTS

Preface . ix
Abbreviations . xi

Introduction . 1

Pericope 1   (Jdg 1:1—2:5): Failure and Indictment . 26
Pericope 2   (Jdg 2:6—3:11): Paradigm and Exemplar . 46
Pericope 3   (Jdg 3:12-31): Ehud (and Shamgar) . 65
Pericope 4   (Jdg 4:1-24): Barak (and Deborah) . 85
Pericope 5   (Jdg 5:1-31): Song of Deborah . 105
Pericope 6   (Jdg 6:1—7:22): Gideon: Panic and Pride . 125
Pericope 7   (Jdg 7:23—8:32): Gideon: Power and Perversion . 146
Pericope 8   (Jdg 8:33—10:5): Abimelech . 165
Pericope 9   (Jdg 10:6—12:15): Jephthah . 186
Pericope 10   (Jdg 13:1—14:20): Samson: Favored but Feckless . 207
Pericope 11   (Jdg 15:1—16:31): Samson: Spirited but Slack . 226
Pericope 12   (Jdg 17:1—18:31): Micah, Levite, Danites . 246
Pericope 13   (Jdg 19:1-30): The Powerful and the Powerless . 266
Pericope 14   (Jdg 20:1—21:25): Israel *vs.* Israel . 284

Conclusion . 303

Bibliography . 307
Index of Ancient Sources . 313
Index of Modern Authors . 315
Index of Scripture . 317

PREFACE

After completing a commentary on Ephesians, with delight I turned my attention again to narrative—this time to the book of Judges, the stories of which have captivated me all my life. But this was a troubling book to study and write about. The darkness of the accounts, especially in the latter parts of Judges, was saddening and heavy. All those leaders, with such great potential, chosen by God and gifted with his Spirit, frittering away their calling, squandering their divine opportunities—how could their stories not grieve the people of God, not to mention God himself?

Painful though the reading and writing was, it strengthened my own resolve to attend more carefully to the call of God in my own life, in the spheres in which he has placed me to lead, as he has each and every one of his children. So this commentary goes out with the hope that all of God's people—God's leaders in some fashion or another, to some degree or another, in some arena or another—will endeavor to become godly leaders after God's own heart, by taking the words of Judges and applying them, in the Spirit's power, to their own lives.

> We must beseech God insistently, day and night, to make us understand why the Scripture was given, that we may apply the medicine of the Scripture, every man to his own wounds. If not, we remain idle disputers, and brawlers about vain words, ever gnawing upon the bitter bark outside, and never reaching the sweet pith inside. —William Tyndale, "Prologue to the Pentateuch"

May our consumption, digestion, and assimilation of the "sweet pith" be for the glory of God, for the furtherance of his kingdom, and for the edification of his people! Let's go . . . and lead, God's way!

Abraham Kuruvilla
Dallas, TX
Feast of Tyndale 2016

ABBREVIATIONS

1QM	*War Scroll*
Aqht	Aqhat Legend
ANET	*Ancient Near Eastern Texts Relating to the Old Testament* (Pritchard)
ARM	*Archives royales de Mari*
b.	Babylonian Talmud
B. Bat.	Baba Batra
Jub	Jubilees
L.A.B.	*Liber antiquitatum biblicarum* (Pseudo-Philo)
Meg.	Megillah
Naz.	Nazir
Sanh.	Sanhedrin
T. Reub.	*Testament of Reuben*
Yebam.	Yebamot

INTRODUCTION

Theology, Goals, Prolegomena

"Let those who love Him be like the rising of the sun in its strength."
Judges 5:31b

THE GOAL OF PREACHING is to bring to bear divine guidelines for life from the biblical text upon the situation of the congregation, to align the community of God to the will of God for the glory of God. This is the preacher's burden—the translation from the *then* of the ancient text to the *now* of modern listeners, with authority and relevance. This commentary is part of a larger endeavor to help the preacher make this move from text to praxis.[1]

THEOLOGY

Elsewhere it was proposed that the critical component of the ancient text to be borne into the lives of the modern audience was the *theology of the pericope*, what the author is *doing* with what he is saying in the text.[2] This is what moves the people of God to valid application, for pericopal theology is the

---

1. For more on this concept of preaching, see Kuruvilla, *Privilege the Text!* and idem, *A Vision for Preaching*.

2. While acknowledging its more common connotation of a portion of the Gospels, I employ "pericope" here to demarcate a segment of Scripture, irrespective of genre or length, that forms the textual basis for an individual sermon with a discrete theological thrust. Also, for the purposes of this commentary no particular distinction will be made between the divine and human authors of the biblical text.

ideological vehicle through which divine priorities, principles, and practices are propounded for appropriation by readers.³ The goal of any homiletical transaction, thus, is the gradual alignment of the church, week by week, to the theology of the biblical pericopes preached. Pericope by pericope, the various aspects of Christian life, individual as well as corporate, are progressively brought into accord with God's design for his creation: faith nourished, hope animated, confidence made steadfast, good habits confirmed, dispositions created, character molded, Christlikeness established.⁴

All such discrete units of pericopal theology together compose a holistic understanding of God and his relationship to his people, with each individual quantum of pericopal theology forming the weekly ground of transformation of the lives of God's people into Christlikeness. In a sense, this week-by-week and sermon-by-sermon alignment to the call of each pericope is an imitation of Christ. This is at the core of the theological hermeneutic followed in this commentary, a *christiconic* hermeneutic specifically geared for preaching.⁵ Because the children of God are called to conform to the image of Christ, preachers everywhere are, in turn, called to discern the theology of the pericope—i.e., the facet of Christlikeness depicted therein—and apply it to the widely diverse situations of believers across the globe, across millennia, and across cultures, to enable them to emulate the perfect Man, their Lord Jesus Christ.⁶ In other words, while pericopal theology describes *what* Christ looks like, sermon applications based on pericopal theology tell us *how* we can begin to look more like him in our own particular circumstances. Unfortunately, the importance of the pericope and its theology—what the author is *doing* with what he is saying—and its employment in sermons for the edification of God's people, have generally been neglected by Bible scholars. This work seeks to correct that misdirection.

GOALS

This commentary is part of a long-term endeavor to rectify the neglect of the pericope and its theology. Its goal is essentially this: to develop the

---

3. See Kuruvilla, *Text to Praxis*, 142–90; and idem, "Pericopal Theology," 3–17.

4. Adapted from Tertullian, *Apology* 39.

5. After all, God's ultimate design is to conform his children into the "image" (εἰκών, *eikōn*) of his Son, Christ (Rom 8:29). See Kuruvilla, *Privilege the Text!* 238–68; and idem, "Christiconic Interpretation," 131–46.

6. It is into the likeness of Christ's perfect *humanity* that God's people are being transformed, not his *deity*, of course. And, needless to say, such growth in Christlikeness can only be accomplished in the power of the Holy Spirit (see Kuruvilla, *Privilege the Text!* 204–7).

theology of each pericope of Judges for preachers so that they may be able to proceed from this crucial intermediary to a sermon that provides valid application (i.e., application that is both authoritative and relevant). There is, thus, a twofold aspect to the homiletical transaction: the exposition of the theology of the pericope, and the delineation of how the latter may be applied in real life.

The first move, from text to (pericopal) theology, draws meaning *from* the biblical text with authority; the second, from theology to praxis, directs meaning *to* the situations of listeners with relevance. The advantage of employing pericopal theology as the intermediary between text and application is that its specificity for the chosen text makes possible a weekly movement from pericope to pericope, without the tedium of repetition of themes, but with a clear progression and development of distinct theological ideas as one preaches through a book. In sum, the theology of the pericope (a crystallization of which is labeled "Theological Focus" in this commentary) functions as the bridge between text and praxis, enabling the move from the *then* to the *now* for valid application. The resulting transformation of lives reflects a gradual and increasing alignment to the values of God's kingdom and thus an increasing approximation of Christlikeness, as pericopes are sequentially preached. So, a pericope, as a quantum of the biblical text, is more than *informing*; it is *transforming*. Sermon by sermon and pericope by pericope, God's people are being conformed into the image of Christ by the power of God's Spirit (Rom 8:4, 29)—a christiconic hermeneutic.

This commentary, as with the others in this series, adopts a synchronic approach that deals with the final form of the text as we have it, construing it as a meaningful, coherent, canonical unit of theological worth. I take it that a biblical author writes purposefully, creating a text with intention, each part of it contributing to the overall theological agenda of the book. Each of the narratives in Judges "has a literary integrity apart from circumstances relating to the compositional process, the historical reality behind the story, or the interpretive agenda of the reader" and that privileging the pericope and its literary features will reveal its thrust, the theology of the pericope.[7] This, of course, is not to deny the relationship between the pericope and

---

7. Bowman, "Narrative Criticism," 17.

the larger narrative it is part of. As with pearls and the necklace they make up—pearls are carefully chosen by color, grade, shape, and size to create the necklace—pericopes, too, are diligently selected and linked to create the larger account. Pericopes, thus, are interpreted by the arc of the broader text they create and, in turn, the trajectory of the overall text is determined by the theological thrusts of the individual pericopes it comprises. It is a "both ... and ... " situation, a dual polarity true of any interpretive endeavor: the parts determine the whole and the whole determines the parts.

This work does not intend to lead preachers all the way to a fully developed sermon on each pericope; rather, it seeks to take them through the first move—from text to (pericopal) theology: the *hermeneutical* aspect of sermon preparation. Though that is the primary focus, the commentary does provide two "Possible Preaching Outlines" for each pericope, to advance preachers a few more steps closer to a sermon. However, they are left to work out the second move from theology to sermon/application (the *rhetorical* aspect of sermon preparation) on their own, providing appropriate moves-to-relevance, specific application, illustrations, etc., all of which can only be done by the shepherd who knows the flock well. Beyond a few general guidelines, it is impossible for a third party to determine what exactly specific application looks like for a particular audience. That is a task between the preacher, the Holy Spirit, and the congregation. Therefore, this is not a "preaching" commentary, in the usual sense. Rather it is a "theology-for-preaching" commentary, i.e., a work that seeks to undertake an extremely focused interpretation of the text, one that moves the preacher from text to pericopal theology, en route to a sermon. In that sense, this is a "theological" commentary.

Commentaries were described by Ernest Best as "the backbone of all serious studies of scripture."[8] Therefore, it is hoped that not only preachers, but all interested laypersons, Sunday School teachers, and others who teach Scripture will find this commentary—a small vertebra in that spinal column—helpful. For that matter, if application is the ultimate goal of Bible study of any kind and at any level, a work such as this promises to be useful even for those making their own way through Judges. Which brings me to another point: while a working knowledge of Hebrew will be very handy for the reader, Hebrew terms and phrases (and the rare Greek ones), wherever referred to in the commentary, have been both transliterated and translated, in order to enable those not as facile with the original language to use this work efficiently.[9]

---

8. Best, "The Reading and Writing of Commentaries," 358.
9. With the goal of maximizing size-to-benefit ratio, this commentary will not

Needless to say, in all sermonic enterprises, quality and depth and intensity of preaching go only so far towards accomplishing the spiritual formation of listeners. Augustine (*De doctrina christiana* 4.27.59) noted wisely: "But whatever may be the majesty of the style [of the preaching], the life of the speaker will count for more in securing the hearer's compliance," not to mention the divine work of the Spirit in the hearts of listeners. Therefore, this commentary is submitted with the prayer that preachers, the leaders of God's people, will pay attention to their own lives first and foremost, as they work through Judges, seeking to align themselves to God's call in each pericope of the book, thus becoming, in the power of the Spirit, a leader more Christlike.

PROLEGOMENA

The judges too, each when he was called,
   all men whose hearts were never disloyal,
who never turned their backs on the Lord—
   may their memory be blessed!
May their bones flower again from the tomb,
and may the names of those glorious men live again in their sons.

(Sir 46:11–12)

For all his enthusiasm, Jesus Ben Sira never mentions the name of a single judge, though he is keen to present other "glorious men" of Israel by name in preceding chapters (44:1—45:26). Perhaps that tells us something.

> [T]he judges described in [the book of Judges] are anything but stirring, patriotic heroes. Rather, they represent almost caricatures of what a hero and leader should be, and they lead Israel from a unified nation cementing its covenant relationship with God, as in Josh 24, to a nation becoming an independent group of jealous tribes who compete with one another, steal priests from one another, and eventually decimate one whole tribe of their people and have to resort to a desperate measure to repopulate the tribe.[10]

---

repeat matters discussed extensively in standard works on Judges—historical criticism, redaction criticism, and textual criticism—unless they are immediately relevant to the theological interpretation of the pericope at hand. Abundant information on all of this may be unearthed from standard commentaries on the book. See, for instance: Chisholm, *Judges and Ruth*; Block, *Judges, Ruth*; Webb, *Judges*; Butler, *Judges*; Younger, *Judges, Ruth*; Boling, *Judges*; and Schneider, *Judges*.

10. Butler, *Judges*, 82.

As one traverses the book, it is not only the judges who become increasingly misguided, but the Israelites themselves become progressively more culpable. With Othniel, there is no mention of any unilateral tribal action—a perfect situation with the whole nation operating as one unit. With Ehud, the Ephraimites are mustered for war (Jdg 3:27), with no obvious input from Yahweh. With Barak, Zebulun and Naphtali are called in (4:10), but an entire chapter is given over to excoriate non-participating tribes (Judges 5). With Gideon, the Abiezrites, Manasseh, Asher, Zebulun, and Napthali are summoned (6:34–35), but the throng is culled by Yahweh to just a few hundred (7:4–8); a second rallying of troops, primarily of Ephraim (7:24) turns out to create a brouhaha, with this tribe protesting their late call into battle (8:1–3), though Gideon negotiates his way out of trouble. Not so with Jephthah: he gathers troops from Gilead and Manasseh (11:29), and later from Ephraim (12:1). This time also the Ephraimites are unhappy, but Jephthah shows no hint of diplomacy; instead, he slaughters them (12:2–6). With Samson, there is almost no national or tribal action (resembling the story of the first judge, Othniel) with one unfortunate exception: the Judahites turn Samson over to the Philistines (14:10–13)! And after the judges have passed from the scene, the Israelites plunge into an immoral cauldron of idolatry and brutality, and slaughter an entire tribe in a civil war (Judges 19–21). This book is, thus, quite negative: it begins bleakly, continues darkly, and ends horribly.

While it is easy to assume that the term "judges" deals with judicial functionaries, the verb "to judge" (שפט, *shpt*) does not always indicate such a responsibility. The legal and forensic functioning of "judges" in the OT is seen in their non-military activities depicted in Exod 18:13, 22, 26; Deut 16:18; 17:9, 12; 19:17–18; 21:2; 25:1–2; 1 Sam 4:18; 7:6, 15–17; 2 Sam 15:4; 1 Kgs 3:9, 28; 2 Kgs 15:5.[11] In Judges, the function of these God-raised leaders is best as seen as *military* judge-deliverers, as indicated in 2:16–17: "And Yahweh raised up judges who delivered them from the hands of those who plundered them."[12] Block therefore suggests that the "judging" by these deliverers—the "major judges" of the book—is more likely that of "leading"

---

11. Such a non-military role is Deborah's portfolio (Jdg 4:4), one of adjudication and arbitration. See Pericope 4 (Jdg 4:1–24).

12. "Judge" as a regular verb or as a participle shows up in 2:16, 17, 18, 19; 3:10; 4:4; 10:2, 3; 11:27; 12:7, 8, 9, 11, 13, 14; 15:20; 16:31. For judges as deliverers (ישע, *ysh'*, "to deliver"), see 2:16; 3:9, 15, 31; 6:14, 15; 8:22; 10:1; 13:5. They are always raised up by Yahweh (or his agent). Yahweh himself is also acknowledged as the one who "delivers" Israel in 2:18; 6:36, 37; 7:7; 10:12, 13.

or "governing," especially in a militaristic fashion to overcome the primary problem facing their people: enemy oppression.[13]

Structure

The Body of the book of Judges (Jdg 3:7—16:31) is flanked by Prologues I and II (Jdg 1:1—2:5 and 2:6—3:6) and Epilogues I and II (17:1—18:31 and 19:1—21:25)[14]:

Judges 1	Socio-political decline	**Prologue I**
Judges 2	Religious decline	**Prologue II**
Judges 3–16	Major and minor judges	**Body**
Judges 17–18	Religious collapse	**Epilogue I**
Judges 19–21	Socio-political collapse	**Epilogue II**

The account of the judges in the Body is carefully structured, with twelve judges that directly or indirectly represent the twelve tribes of Israel. The order of the judges more or less follows a south-to-north sequence of tribes: Othniel (Judah), Ehud (Benjamin), Shamgar (perhaps Simeon, from his southern center of operations against the Philistines), Barak (Napthtali, but Deborah operated in Ephraim, 4:5), Gideon (half tribe of Manasseh), Tola (Issachar), Jair and Jephthah (Gilead, representing Gad and Reuben, and perhaps the other half tribe of Manasseh east of the Jordan, too), Ibzan and Elon (the latter was from Zebulun, so the former, from Bethlehem in the north, was likely to have hailed from Asher). Then we see Abdon, the Ephraimite, at a textual location where one might have expected Barak, the Naphtalite. Thus it appears that Barak and Abdon have effectively swapped seats, serving the narrator's theological agenda, with Deborah's presence in the Barak story lending it a quasi-Ephraimite flavor.[15] After Abdon comes the last judge, Samson (Dan). "[T]his hypothesis becomes even more compelling when one considers how the arrangement of the twelve judges [in

---

13. Block, *Judges, Ruth*, 23-24. Less clear is how the "minor judges" perform their "judging": 10:3; 12:8–9, 11, 13, 14. No military, or for that matter, forensic responsibility is explicitly assigned to these.

14. Pericope divisions assign Prologue I (Jdg 1:1—2:5) to Pericope 1; Prologue II (Jdg 2:6—3:6) to Pericope 2 that also includes the story of the first judge, Othniel (3:7–11); Body (Jdg 3:7—16:31) to Pericopes 3–11, though 3:7–11 is part of Pericope 2; Epilogue I (Jdg 17:1—18:31) to Pericope 12; and Epilogue II (Jdg 19:1—21:25) to Pericope 13 (Jdg 19:1–30) and Pericope 14 (Jdg 20:1—21:25).

15. The Barak-Abdon switch also confirms that Barak is the judge, i.e., military deliverer, of Judges 4, not Deborah. See Wong, *Compositional Strategy*, 244-46.

the Body] seems to reflect the same south-to-north geographic trajectory introduced in the prologue of the book in Judges 1."[16]

Each of the judge stories follows a paradigmatic structure described in Pericope 2 (Jdg 2:6—3:11), in 2:11–19. It comprises Israel's evildoing, punishment, groaning, Yahweh's raising up of a deliverer, and his support for that individual, Israel's deliverance, the land's rest, and the judge's demise (see below).[17] But things begin to fall apart quite rapidly. Except for the consistent evildoing of the Israelites at the beginning of each account of the major judges, the shape of the paradigm governing the judge stories progressively disintegrates. Other than Othniel's story—he was the model judge—the rest of the stories do not strictly adhere to the pattern. The deviations are important clues to the theologies of the individual pericopes.

On the other hand, the accounts of the minor judges do not follow this standard cyclical scheme set forth in 2:11–19; besides, their reports are abbreviated, without much narrative development.[18] Yet there seems to be a "minor judge paradigm" unique for those accounts, comprising: tribe/clan/family lineage, years of service (in rounded numbers), evidence of peacefulness (amidst times of turmoil/transition), and the death and burial of the judge.[19] All in all, it seems that the minor judges have been added to bring the total number of major and minor judges to twelve. Even if each does not unambiguously represent one of the twelve tribes of Israel, the numerical symbolism points to the fact that all of Israel was affected by the crises of that age. And thus all of God's people of all time are being addressed in this book.

Williams's arrangement of the twelve judges in a twelve-segmented circle with four quadrants is intriguing[20]:

---

16. Ibid., 241 (also see 239–41).

17. Also see Neh 9:27–28 that recognizes this cyclical nature of the narrative.

18. Their longevity in service, ranging from seven to twenty-three years, makes them hardly minor in real-life importance; they are minor only in the narrator's theological agenda.

19. Beem, "The Minor Judges," 150–51.

20. Figure below from Williams, "The Structure of Judges 2:6—16:31," 81.

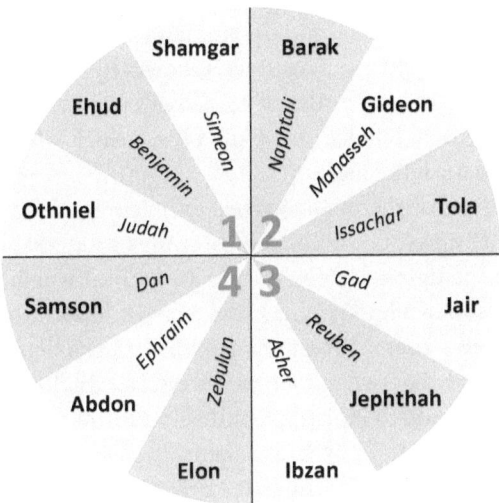

The twin sons of Joseph, Ephraim and Manasseh are opposite each other, as also are Reuben and Benjamin, the oldest and youngest of Jacob's sons—each is the middle item in its quadrant. With two exceptions, every major judge is opposite a minor judge. With the Ehud-Jephthah exception, one might note that Jephthah's account in 10:6—12:7 is sandwiched by minor judge accounts on either side, 10:1–5 and 12:8–15. Besides, with Jephthah's years of service and death and burial details provided in 12:7, resembling the format of the minor judges around him, Jephthah almost becomes a minor judge himself.[21]

Another indication of careful structuring is that the Spirit of Yahweh comes upon one judge in each quadrant: Othniel, Gideon, Jephthah, and Samson (Samson, the summation of the series, receives the operations of the Spirit *four* times: 13:25; 14:6, 19; 15:14). Of note, the land finds rest only after each major judge in quadrants 1 and 2: Othniel (3:11), Ehud (3:30), Barak (5:31), and Gideon (8:28). It also appears that the role of women seems to be going from Yahwistic to anti-Yahwistic as one proceeds through the book. Quadrant 1 (by extrapolation) has Achsah, Othniel's wife (she

---

21. Williams also notes that both Ehud and Jephthah deal with the offspring of Lot: Ehud with Moab, and Jephthah with Ammon. Both send messages or messengers to the oppressing enemy king (3:19–20; 11:12–14), and both are involved with Ephraimites (3:27; 12:1–6). Incidentally, the middle judge of each quadrant has some connection with Ephraim: besides Ehud who leads them and Jephthah who slaughters them, Gideon placates them, and Abdon represents them (ibid., 81–82). The Shamgar–Ibzan exception to the major-minor combination is not easily explained, other than that they appear to be the most obscure of the twelve.

is actually found in 1:12–15), eagerly seeking land promised by Yahweh. Quadrant 2 has Deborah, Jael, and the woman who killed Abimelech—heroines of their day, all of them. Quadrant 3, however, has a passive daughter of Jephthah who becomes a victim of her father's vile oath and his tendency to manipulate Yahweh. Finally, Quadrant 4 has Delilah who betrays a judge to the Philistines for filthy lucre.[22]

The first three of the major judges, Othniel, Ehud, and Barak, come from acceptable backgrounds. The last three major judges, however, have a less-than-stellar pedigree: Gideon's father was a Baal worshiper (6:25); Jephthah was the son of a harlot (11:1); and Samson hailed from the apostate tribe of Dan (13:2). These three show failures and character flaws that are far more significant than what their predecessors exhibited: Gideon, in his hubris, spurs the nation to idolatry, Jephthah performs a human sacrifice in an attempt to manipulate Yahweh, and Samson, enslaved to his sensual passions, abandons the calling of Yahweh entirely. The activities of this final trio are also marked by brutal vengeance: Gideon against the Succothites and Penuelites (8:4–9, 13–17); Jephthah against the Ephraimites (12:1–6); and Samson, rather randomly, against the Philistines (15:3, 7–8; etc.). Gideon's and Jephthah's actions against their own fellow-Israelites, and the Judahites betrayal of Samson to the Philistines (15:9–13) bespeak an internal fracturing that, not surprisingly, culminates in the bloody civil war of Epilogue II (Pericopes 13 and 14: Jdg 19:1–30 and 20:1—21:25).[23]

Chronology

The timeframe of the book of Judges spans the death of Joshua and the transition to a monarchy in the time of Samuel. From the chronological notations given in 3:8 (8 years); 3:11 (40 years); 3:14 (18 years); 3:30 (80 years); 4:3 (20 years); 5:31 (40 years); 6:1 (7 years); 8:28 (40 years); 9:22 (3 years); 10:2 (23 years); 10:3 (22 years); 10:8 (18 years); 12:7 (6 years); 12:9 (7 years); 12:11 (10 years); 12:14 (8 years); 13:1 (40 years); and 15:20 (20 years), a total of 410 years is obtained for the days of the judges. Adding the wilderness

---

22. See ibid., 82.

23. Younger, *Judges, Ruth*, 38. Each of the two at the center of the list of six major judges, Barak and Gideon, has a second protagonist—Deborah and Abimelech, respectively. And, incidentally, the stories of these two judges also have a named pair of enemy kings/leaders: Jabin and Sisera (in Barak's account), and Zeeb and Oreb, and Zebah and Zalmunnah (in Gideon's account). Abimelech's story, essentially a continuation of Gideon's, also has two named antagonists: Jotham and Gaal. After the third major judge comes the Song of Deborah taking up a whole chapter (Pericope 5: Jdg 5:1–31). This puts the hymn in the structural center of the book of Judges, with three major judges preceding (Othniel, Ehud, and Barak), and three major judges following (Gideon, Jephthah, and Samson). All this further confirms the careful structuring of the book.

wanderings, the conquest, the remaining years of Joshua, the judgeships of Eli and Samuel, and the careers of Saul and David, would yield an Exodus-to-Solomon span of over 600 years. This figure is dissonant with the 480 years between the Exodus and Solomon's fourth reigning year (966 BCE) noted in 1 Kgs 6:1.[24] Chisholm's solution to this problem is based on a parallel structure that is observable in the Body of the book (Jdg 3:7—16:31):

A		**Israelites' evildoing (Othniel; 3:7)** "prevailed over" enemy; land's rest after Othniel (3:10–11)
	B	**Israelites' *continued* evildoing (Ehud, 3:12)** "subdued" enemy; land's rest after Ehud (3:30)
	B	**Israelites' *continued* evildoing (Barak, 4:1)** "subdued" enemy; land's rest (after Barak?) (4:23; 5:31)
A'		**Israelites' evildoing (Gideon, 6:1)** "subdued"; land's rest (8:28; after Gideon, but not after Abimelech)
	B'	**Israelites' *continued* evildoing (Jephthah, 10:6)** "subdued"; but no land's rest after Jephthah (11:33)
	B'	**Israelites' *continued* evildoing (Samson, 13:1)** no subduing; and no land's rest after Samson (13:1)

The pattern is obvious in the two panels *ABB* and *A'B'B'*, with *BB* and *B'B'* each noting the Israelites' *continued* evildoing, signified by יסף, *ysp*. This verb "consistently indicates or implies temporal sequence when it is collocated with an infinitive construct in the Former Prophets," and so its omission has implications for the chronological sequence of events in the book.[25] So Chisholm speculates that *ABB* and *A'B'B'* are chronologically concurrent, thus permitting some consolidation of time to approximate the 480 years of 1 Kgs 6:1. He estimates the period of the Judges as running from 1336–1130 BCE.[26]

---

24. Block, *Judges, Ruth*, 59–61; and Chisholm, "The Chronology of the Book of Judges," 247–48. The table is modified from ibid., 251. Of course, the number 480, equivalent to twelve generations of forty years each, may be an artificial and theological construct, rather than chronological and historical. Likewise, the timespans in Judges: the years of judgeship and lengths of enemy oppression appear precise (3:8, 14; 6:1; 9:22; 10:2, 3, 8; 12:7, 9, 11, 14), whereas the periods of the land's rest are noted as multiples of forty (3:11, 30; 5:31; 8:28), another generational index perhaps (Block, *Judges, Ruth*, 63).

25. Chisholm, "In Defense of Paneling," 376. Notice also the progressive "rest-lessness" of the land and Israel's increasing failure to subdue its enemies, as one proceeds through the book.

26. Chisholm, "The Chronology of the Book of Judges," 251–52. This scheme

In any case, the preacher must remember that these are *behind-the-text* speculations. What is important *for preaching*—and that is the concern of this commentary—is the way things, people, and situations are depicted by the inspired narrator to portray a world *in front of the text*.[27] While not concocting data out of thin air, the textual presentation of what happened is a narratological choice based on the theological agenda of the author—the thrust of the text, the theology of the pericope. It is this pericopal theology that must be discerned, preached, and applied.

In Judges, the Jebusites live with the sons of Benjamin in Jerusalem "to this day" (1:21); the city that the man from Bethel built is named Luz "to this day" (1:26); Gideon's altar to Yahweh, named "Yahweh is Peace," is still in Ophrah "to this day" (6:24); the thirty sons of Jair had thirty cities in Gilead called Havoth-jair even "to this day" (10:4); the hollow place in Lehi where Samson miraculously found water was named by him as Enhakkore, and it is still in Lehi "to this day" (15:19); and the place where the Danites camped at Kiriath-jearim is called Mahaneh-Dan "to this day" (18:12). Besides, 18:30 mentions the captivity of Israel (between 734–721 BCE; the unauthorized Danite shrine persisted until 734 BCE), and it is asserted that there was no king in Israel "in those days" of the judges (17:6; 18:1; 19:1; 21:25). All of these notations indicate editorial work on the book at different times and periods. In addition, the reference to "king" in 17:6; 18:1; 19:1; and 21:25 may suggest that Judges achieved its final form after the monarchical period of Israel. Both Epilogues I and II (Pericope 12: Jdg 17:1—18:31; and Pericope 13: Jdg 19:1–30 and Pericope 14: Jdg 20:1—21:25) have random, wandering, unemployed Levites. Webb thinks this places those events after the separation of the northern kingdom of Israel from the southern kingdom of Judah, either when Jeroboam I appointed non-Levites as priests (1 Kgs 12:31), or when Hezekiah's reforms (or Josiah's) involved the closure of a number of shrines (2 Kgs 19:1–4; 23:1–20).[28] But "[t]he simple fact of the matter is that we are not in a position to reconstruct the history of the text's literary evolution with any degree of confidence."[29]

---

would render Jephthah's declaration that Israel had occupied trans-Jordan for 300 years (11:26) inaccurate: Chisholm calculates that Jephthah was operating only 185 years after the Israelite conquest of 1406 BCE. Seeing Jephthah's address as "purely rhetorical," Chisholm is conducive to viewing this as Jephthah's error (in addition to this judge's mislabeling of Chemosh as the god of the Ammonites: see Pericope 9 [Jdg 10:6—12:15]). See ibid., 254. More likely, Jephthah was being hyperbolic; rather than rounding the 185-year gap to 200 years, he tacked on another century for good effect.

27. For more on this notion, see Kuruvilla, *Privilege the Text!* 39–43.
28. Webb, *Judges*, 420.
29. Chisholm, *Judges and Ruth*, 55.

Provenance

The Prologues establish the Israelites' God as Yahweh, the one with a relationship to the patriarchs (Jdg 2:1, 10, 12, 17, 20, 22; 3:4), the one who had delivered them from the bondage of Egypt (2:1, 12; also see 6:8, 13), the one who had made a covenant with them at Sinai (2:1, 20; 5:5). But it is the Israelites' evildoing that is prominent in Judges. Besides the text's explicit statements to that effect (2:11; 3:7, 12; 4:1; 6:1; 10:6; 13:1), the Israelites also fail to drive out the Canaanites according to Yahweh's desire (1:18–36); they fail to pass on their faith in Yahweh to a future generation (2:10); they refuse to join in Yahweh's military enterprises (5:15b–17, 23); they attack Yahweh's deliverer who seeks to destroy a Baal altar (6:28–30); they play harlot after Gideon's ephod (8:27); they replace Yahweh with Baal-berith (8:33); they turn over the Spirit-directed deliverer to the enemy (15:11–13); they manufacture sacred idols for private cults (17:1–13); a whole tribe sponsors paganism (18:14–31); brutality and immorality reign unchecked (19:1–30); and, finally, the entire nation is plunged into a civil war (20:1—21:25).[30] The judge-deliverers that God raises go from bad to worse (except for Othniel who fits the paradigm of 2:11–19 precisely): Ehud is deceptive, Barak is fearful, Gideon is arrogant (and his offspring, Abimelech, ungodly and ruthless), Jephthah is manipulative, and Samson is profligate. Yet despite the despicable infidelity shown by his people, and the deplorable example set by his leaders, Yahweh remains, time and again, gracious and willing to intervene on behalf of his people and deliver them (2:16, 18; 3:9–10, 15; 4:6–7, 23; 6:11–12, 14, 16, 34, 38, 40; 7:2, 7, 9, 22; 11:29, 32; 13:3–5, 25; 14:6, 19; 15:14, 19).

Block speculates that the prophetic message of Judges would have been most appropriate for the protracted and pernicious reign of Manasseh (790–739 BCE; see 2 Kgs 21:1–18; 2 Chr 33:1). This regent reconstructed pagan cultic installations and "worshipped all the host of heaven and served them" (2 Kgs 21:3), not to mention the altars he raised to them in Yahweh's temple (21:4–5)—not very different from the Israelites in the days of the judges (Jdg 2:3, 11–13, 17, 19; 3:6–7; 6:25–32; 8:27, 33; 10:6–16; 17:1–13; 18:14–20, 30). Indeed, Manasseh, like Jephthah, engaged in child sacrifices, and involved himself in demonic practices—"great evil in the sight of Yahweh, provoking him to anger" (2 Kgs 21:6). As did Abimelech, Manasseh, too, was a brutal tyrant who "shed much innocent blood" that "filled Jerusalem from one end to another." And, as the nation followed Gideon, so, under the aegis of Manasseh, Israel was plunged into sin, doing more evil

---

30. Block, *Judges, Ruth*, 39.

14   *Introduction*

than the nations around (21:6, 9), and failing to listen to the warnings of God through his prophets (21:10–15).³¹

Purpose

The book is gory, with bloodletting without remit. There is the assassination of Eglon (Jdg 3:21–25); the killing of Sisera (4:21); the execution of Oreb and Zeeb (7:25) and of Zebah and Zalmunnah (8:21); the murder of sixty-nine of his siblings by Abimelech (9:5); the assassination of Abimelech (9:53–54); the sacrifice of Jephthah's daughter (11:39); Samson's suicidal exertions (16:30); and the murder of the Levite's concubine (19:27). That adds to seventy-nine specific individuals killed. But it is the large-scale killings that are shocking: ten thousand Canaanites and Perizzites "struck down" by the Judah-Simeon coalition (1:4); "about" ten thousand Moabites killed by Ehud and his army (3:29); six hundred Philistines struck down by Shamgar (3:30); 120,000 Midianites killed by Yahweh (7:22; 8:10); the burning alive of "about" a thousand in Shechem (9:49); 42,000 Ephraimites felled by Jephthah (12:6); Samson's killing of thirty Philistines (14:19), later another thousand (15:15), and finally three thousand more (16:27, 30); 22,000 Israelites killed by Benjamin on one day (20:21) and 18,000 on another (20:25); and 25,100 Benjaminites killed by Israel (20:35). That comes to a total of 242,730 in numbered military casualties alone. Whew! It is certain that the defeats of Canaanite armies and cities—and some internecine warfare by Israel—involved killing as well, but no victim tallies are given (1:4, 5, 8, 9–10, 17, 18, 25; 3:10; 4:15–16, 24; 8:12, 17; 9:43, 45; 11:32; 12:4; 15:8; 18:27; 21:10). In addition, there might have been more wars fought by Israel as suggested in Yahweh's reproach of his people in 10:11–12 that lists some defeated people groups not mentioned elsewhere in Judges.³² Altogether, roughly a quarter of a million people perish in Judges!³³ No wonder there

---

31. Ibid., 66–67.

32. Among the more violent incidents in the book are the mutilation of Adonibezek (1:6), the disembowelment of Eglon (3:21–22), the skull-splitting of Sisera (4:21), the slaying of the Midianite kings (8:21), the head-crushing of Abimelech (9:53), and the burnt sacrifice of Jephthah's daughter (11:39). The gouging out of Samson's eyes (16:21) and the dismemberment of a concubine's corpse (19:29) may be included in this bloody catalog of violence.

33. Of note, quite large numbers are noted throughout Judges. "It is doubtful that such large numbers can be taken at face value in light of demographic analysis of ancient Palestine by modern archaeologists," with population estimates for Israel between the twelfth and eleventh centuries BCE ranging from 50,000 to 75,000, and for Canaan in the same period ranging from 50,000 to 150,000 (Chisholm, *Judges and Ruth*, 110 n.2). Perhaps the large numbers in the book are hyperbolic. More likely, אלף, *'lp*, usually translated "thousand," refers not to a fixed number but to a contingent of troops

is weeping by the nation at the beginning (2:4), and there is weeping by the nation at the end (20:23, 26; 21:2). Webb is right: "Judges does not simply give us raw violence, but interpreted violence. The challenge for those of us who read it as Scripture is not whether we can identify with the violence, but whether we can identify with the theology that frames and interprets it."[34] Authors always *do* things with what they say and the burden of the interpreter is to figure out what they are *doing*, even with all the slaughter and mayhem—the thrust of the text, the theology of the pericope. It is this entity alone that can guide the reader to valid application that is aligned to the intent of the author(s).

O'Connell notes the pervasive influence of Deuteronomic phraseology and ideology in Judges.[35] Explicit condemnation of Israel for failing to uphold Yahweh's covenant occurs in 2:1–3, 11–19; 2:20—3:6; 3:7; 6:7–10, 25–26; 8:27; 9:56–57; 10:6–16, 30–31, 39; 14:1, 7, 8–9; 15:1; 16:17; 17:1–13; 18:31; 19:22–27; 21:1–23. The assessment, when all is said and done, is abysmally negative, and Israel becomes her own enemy, led by her leaders into a spiraling catastrophe, each judge worse than the one preceding. So this is ultimately a book on leadership, or rather, the lack thereof.

> The book of Judges is concerned with seeking an answer to a straightforward question, "Who is going to lead Israel?" The book begins with this question (Jdg 1:1) and a variation is repeated towards the end (Jdg 20:18). . . . The stories in the book are less about battles and the reasons for them than they are about such issues as how the various judges attained their office, what individuals did in order to express their leadership, what judges' relationships were with the deity, their reasons for fighting, how much power they wielded before and after their major battle/s, and what other actions they carried out which impacted their relationship with the Israelite deity and set the stage for the next generation. The book begins with Othniel, the model judge, and ends with Samson, who is so negatively

---

numbering far less than a thousand. However in Jdg 20:10, אלף clearly means "thousand." Also difficult to reconcile with this understanding of אלף as a contingent is the "twenty-five *thousand* [אלף] and a hundred," in 20:35. "[N]o workable solution to the problem of the large numbers has so far been found, and the advantages of leaving them as they are outweigh any gains involved in changing them. They cannot be changed without upsetting their relationship to other numbers, and they serve an important rhetorical purpose that is lost if they are altered" (Webb, *Judges*, 74; see his discussion in ibid., 71–74). For the purposes of this commentary, the traditional numbering will be followed.

34. Ibid., 61.
35. O'Connell, *The Rhetoric of the Book of Judges*, 20–25, 57.

evaluated that he not only dies in battle with foreigners, but his death leads to anarchy in Israel. These poles, Othniel and Samson, highlight the steadily decreasing worth of the judges over time, and at the same time, the downward spiral of all Israel.[36]

Evildoing and the recurring cycles of ever worsening leadership take over the structure of the book.[37] All this, despite the graciousness of God in intervening in each chaotic iteration to raise up a deliverer to defeat the oppressing enemy. Finally, Judges culminates in horrible idolatry and a horrific civil war, in an age of godlessness and leaderlessness, when "everyone did what was right in his own eyes" (21:25).

Though the book is about the misdeeds of God's leaders, it is also entirely applicable to the lives of God's people, for the latter are only as good as the former are. God's leaders draw God's people to their level, explaining the higher standards for leadership throughout Scripture. But those criteria, whether they be in Judges or elsewhere, are appropriate for God's people to adopt, for God desires that all his people be like his leaders, emulating their holiness, faith, and zeal for him. Besides, all of God's people are leaders in some arena or another, to some degree, in some fashion. Therefore it behooves *all* believers to take the lessons of the book of Judges to heart.

Canaanization of Israel

Within the first three chapters of the book that make up the Prologues (I and II: Jdg 1:1—3:6), the seed of the Israelites' Canaanization is sown and quickly takes root: they fail to drive out the native peoples—2:1–5 and 2:6—3:6 are clear in labeling this a spiritual failure and covenantal violation. From that point, the descent is spiral with a cyclical repetitiveness (2:11–19) that worsens with each iteration of the judge stories (2:17–19), and it is rapid,

---

36. Schneider, *Judges*, xiv.

37. It must be noted that no judge is entirely bad—a fact true of most humans. That is, no doubt, why the writer of Hebrews lauds Gideon, Barak, Samson, and Jephthah, among other OT worthies (Heb 11:32; also see 1 Sam 12:11 that mentions Jerubbaal, "Bedan" [likely Barak], and Jephthah as "deliverers"). That does not necessarily vitiate the generally negative assessments of these individuals in the book of Judges. Of these characters, the writer of Hebrews notes in subsequent verses that "they conquered kingdoms, . . . and routed foreign armies" (Heb 11:33–34). Surely these intrepid individuals, warts and all, did exercise faith of some sort, in some way, to some degree. "The narrator's use of the Old Testament text in this regard is neither strained nor improper," and neither do those illustrative citations in the NT contradict the (negative) pictures painted in Judges (Chisholm, *Judges and Ruth*, 78).

occurring within a generation or two (2:10). Yahweh is forgotten (2:6–10; 3:7), and exogamy with the Canaanites deals the final coup (3:6).[38]

From there on, in the Body of the book (3:7—16:31), it is one disaster after another, each judge progressively worse than the one preceding, and leading the nation deeper into the abyss. Until the judgeship of Gideon, the land finds rest at the end of each cycle; after him, this never happens again. By the time of Samson, even the standard practice of the Israelites crying out to Yahweh in despair when under oppression disappears: the Israelites seem to have become strangely content under a foreign thumb. This last judge shows no involvement with the rest of Israel and even gets himself killed—a first for the book. Towards the end, then, the judges themselves become the problem!

The scope of the Israelites' idolatry also expands as time goes on, with 10:6 laying out God's indictment of his people for having gone after Baals, Ashtaroth, and the gods of Aram, Sidon, Moab, Ammon, and the Philistines—*seven* species of false deities. They just kept on adding to their sacrilegious pantheon. In parallel, Yahweh's rebuke testifies to his having delivered Israel from *seven* people groups/nations: Egyptians, Amorites, Ammonites, Philistines, Sidonians, Amalekites, and Maonites (10:11–12).[39] And with this, the otherwise paradigmatic deliverance by Yahweh, a fixture of each cycle thus far, transforms into a stinging rebuke (10:14).

The final chapters composing the Epilogues (I and II: Jdg 17:1—21:25) show the depth to which Israel has fallen: gross idolatry, failure of the priesthood, utter immorality, and a bloody civil war attest to the almost total Canaanization of God's people. No more was the enemy external; it was entirely within. Israel was collapsing from its own internal moral bankruptcy. "The spiritual condition of the people inhabiting the land of Canaan at the end of the settlement period is the same as it had been at the beginning. It had made no difference that a new group of people [Israel] now occupies the land."[40] The dangers of those godless and leaderless times are ever present in every age.

Thematic Parallels: Prologues and Epilogues

There are significant parallels and links between the different sections and narrative pericopes in Judges, reinforcing the charitable assumption of

---

38. Block, "Echo Narrative Technique," 338.

39. Yahweh's deliverances from the Egyptians, Amorites, and Maonites are otherwise not encountered in Judges, causing the reader to suspect that Israel's malfeasance went well beyond what is described in the book.

40. Ibid., 341.

reading that "a single creative mind stood behind the present form of the book, and that each constituent narrative is to be read as an integral part of the larger whole."[41]

Links between the Prologues and Epilogues include: the selection of Judah to lead military campaigns (foreign in 1:2; but domestic in 20:18)[42]; battles as חרם (*kherem*, "holy war"; 1:17; and 21:11[43]); "inquiring" of Yahweh (1:1 and 20:18, 23, 27[44]); treatment of women (1:11–15; and 19:1–30; 21:1–25); idolatry (1:11—3:6; and 17:1—18:31); references to Jebusites (1:21 [×2]; 3:5; and 19:11) and to Jerusalem (1:7, 8, 21 [×2]; and 19:10)[45]; "struck . . . with the edge of the sword" (of enemies: 1:8, 25; but of fellow-Israelites: 18:27; 20:37, 48[46]); corporate weeping at a cultic site before Yahweh (2:4; and 20:23, 26; 21:2[47]); "covenant" (2:1, 2, 20; and 20:27[48]); links to Moses (1:16, 20; 3:4; and 18:30); and "giving" of "daughters" as "wives" (1:12, 13; 3:6; and 21:1, 7, 18).[49] Interestingly, the cultic centers, Jerusalem, Bethel, and Shiloh are mentioned only in the Prologues and Epilogues (Jerusalem: 1:7, 8, 21; 19:10; Shiloh: 18:31; 21:12, 19, 21; and Bethel: 1:22, 23; 2:1 [possibly with a pseudonym, Bokim]; 20:18, 26, 31; 21:2, 19), with the exception of Bethel in Jdg 4:5. All of this indicates careful textual construction, subservient to the theological intent of the narrator/editor/redactor.

---

41. Wong, *Compositional Strategy*, 23. Much of what follows in these sections on thematic parallels is taken from ibid.

42. The choice of Judah for leadership in the civil war in Epilogue II (particularly Pericope 14: Jdg 20:1—21:25) seems quite unnecessary, since the tribe plays no distinguishing role in the ensuing battles; neither is Judah ever mentioned again. It appears to have been added simply to link the Epilogue with the Prologue.

43. The only occurrences of the root חרם in the book.

44. No other act of "inquiring" of Yahweh occurs in the book (but see 13:18; 18:5). For that matter, the inquiries of 20:18, 23, 27 are the only instances in the OT where such a seeking of advice from Yahweh is made regarding a battle against *fellow-Israelites* (ibid., 34 n.17).

45. These are the only references to these peoples and this place in Judges.

46. These are the only occurrences of the phrase in Judges.

47. These are the only instances of corporate grief expressed by "weeping" in the book; 2:4 and 21:2 have the only occurrences of "lifted up their voices and wept." The first lament takes place at Bokim, the second at Bethel. If it is true that Bokim is a pseudonym for Bethel (see Pericope 1: Jdg 1:1—2:5), then the two events are linked further.

48. The only mentions of "covenant" in Judges.

49. The only times such giving in marriage is noted in the book. All these instances (except for 3:6, which deals with exogamy) are pledges preceding a war—Caleb taking Kiriath-sepher (1:12), and the Israelites decimating Benjamin (21:1–24). But in the first case, the result is "blessing" (1:15); in the second, a "curse" (21:18) (ibid., 43–44; also see Pericope 1).

In sum, the events in the Prologues and in the Epilogues are "practically two sides of the same coin. While one records Israel's failure to do what was right, the other records Israel's success in doing what was wrong, and both resulted in a diminishing of national fortune"—things were going from bad to worse.[50]

Thematic Parallels: Prologues and Body

Prologue I (1:1—2:5) and II (2:6—3:6) also have substantial links with the Body of Judges (3:7—16:31). The most obvious connection is the paradigm of 2:11-19 that forms the skeleton of each of the subsequent judge narratives: evildoing (2:11); punishment by being given into the hands of enemies for a certain number of years (2:14 [×2]); groaning of the Israelites in distress (2:18); Yahweh's raising up of judge-deliverers (2:16, 18); Yahweh's support for those leaders (2:18); deliverance of Israel from the hands of enemies (2:16, 18); and the land's rest for a number of years and the judge's death (2:19). This cycle repeats in the story of each succeeding judge (see Pericope 2: Jdg 2:6—3:11).

In Prologue I, the sequence of activities shows two movements: a general *geographic* and directional trajectory that heads from south to north, based on tribal location, and a second moral and *spiritual* trajectory that describes the decreasing success of the tribes in their attempts to take over lands allotted to them.[51]

The *geographic* structuring in the narrative of Prologue I (Pericope 1: Jdg 1:1—2:5), with a south-to-north organization of tribal activities, is as follows: Judah, Simeon, Benjamin, Zebulun, Asher, Naphtali, and Dan (1:2-36). This reflects the arrangement of the judges in the Body, from Othniel (Judah) in the south to Samson (Dan) in the north (see above). But the whole scheme is "too neat to be an accurate reflection of actual historical reality. For historical reality is almost inevitably messy, and therefore does not readily lend itself to orderly schematisation."[52] Besides, the unsuccessful undertakings of Dan to appropriate land actually took place in their original location in the *south* (Josh 19:40-46); but in Prologue I, they have been placed at the end of the schema, in the *north*, which is where they ended up quite successfully (Jdg 18:1-31). This idiosyncrasy (but in furtherance of the author's theological agenda) is visible also in the story of Samson: the

---

50. Ibid., 41.

51. The moral and spiritual aspects of the tribes' failures are clearly noted in Prologue I (see 2:1-5), and what would subsequently happen with the judges in the Body is foreshadowed in Prologue II (see 2:11-19).

52. Ibid., 152.

sequence of judges from south to north (Judah to Dan) implies Samson's northern center of operations, but the actual cities in which he was active were in the south—Zorah, Eshtaol, Gaza, Ashkelon (see Pericope 10: Jdg 13:1—14:20 and Pericope 11: Jdg 15:1—16:31). He even had to deal with the southern Judahites (15:10–13). Thus a dischronology is created here, likely to connect Prologue I and Body (Pericopes 10 and 11) to serve a theological agenda—the author was *doing* something with what he was saying.[53]

But what primarily links these trajectories in Prologue I to the Body is that the same *spiritual* route in the former is taken by the narrator in arranging the narratives of the judges in the latter. In Prologue I, from Judah to Dan things go from bad to worse, the result of spiritual failure (2:1–5), a pattern subsequently reflected in the Body—from Othniel to Samson. As the commentary shows, each judge story depicts a situation worse than that of the one it follows. A progressive deterioration of morality and spirituality is evident in the accounts as one proceeds through the Body (adumbrated in 2:19): decreasing faith in Yahweh, increasing self-interest of the judges, diminishing participation of the tribes with each military campaign against oppressing enemies, increasing brutality against fellow-Israelites[54], and Yahweh's mounting frustration with his people's recalcitrance and recidivism.[55]

---

53. Another dischronology: In 1 Sam 12:9–11, the order of the judges mentioned is Jerubbaal, "Bedan" (likely Barak), and Jephthah; in Heb 11:32, it is Gideon, Barak, Samson, and Jephthah. In other words, the layout of the Body (the story of the judges, 3:7—16:31, that has Barak, Gideon, Jephthah, and Samson, in that order) may not necessarily be in chronological sequence. Dischronology is also observable elsewhere: a grandson of Moses, Jonathan, Micah's domesticated Levite-priest, is in action in Epilogue I (Pericope 12: Jdg 17:1—18:31; see 18:30), and a grandson of Aaron, Phinehas, in Epilogue II (specifically Pericope 14: Jdg 20:1—21:25; see 20:28). Thus the events of the Epilogues likely occurred soon after Joshua's time. The placement of those events towards the end of the book of Judges serves the narrator's theological purpose—he is *doing* something with what he is saying. So the reader's interest, for application purposes, ought to be not *behind* the text, upon chronologies, histories, and such, but upon the theological thrust projected *in front of* the pericope.

54. Barak: verbal rebuke of non-participating tribes (5:15b–17, 23); Gideon: diplomacy with Ephraimites (8:1–3), but cruelty towards Succothites and brutality towards Penuelites (8:4–9, 13–17); Jephthah: slaughter of Ephraimites (12:1–6).

55. Yahweh personally raises up Othniel and Ehud (3:9, 15); then he sends a representative to do so for Barak (4:4–7); subsequently, he first sends a prophet to rebuke his people, accusing them of disobedience, before the angel of Yahweh raises up Gideon (5:7–10, 11–24); later, in a direct and irate remonstrance, he completely refuses to help the Israelites in the Jephthah narrative, accusing them of forsaking him (10:11–14). (Nevertheless, in all the narratives, Yahweh graciously deigns to help his people in distress.) This corresponds to the Israelites' increasing disloyalty to, and unconcern for, Yahweh: they cry, desperate for release from oppression, in the narratives of Othniel, Ehud, Barak, Gideon, and Jephthah (3:9, 15; 4:3; 6:6; 10:10), but not in the story of Samson, where Israelites seem to be content with living under a foreign hand, and this

This makes the iterations of each narrative not a cycle, but rather a retrogressing spiral, sliding into an abyss of national disaster in the Epilogues.⁵⁶ Altogether, there is dissolution.

Thematic Parallels: Epilogues and Body

The events of the Epilogues are characterized by wanton brutality and profligacy. But the echoes between these stories and those in the Body are deliberate. "[B]y showing that the bizarre acts in the epilogue have all found precedents in the lives of the judges, the narrator has managed to cast the judges in a very uncomplimentary light."⁵⁷ The judges in the Body are no better than the characters in the Epilogues.

Micah's and the Danites' idolatry reflects the sad situation at the end of Gideon's judgeship (Pericope 7: Jdg 7:23—8:32). Interestingly, אֵפוֹד (*'epod*, "ephod") as a cultic object in its six occurrences in Judges has a uniformly negative connotation. Five of these occur in Epilogue I (Pericope 12: Jdg 17:1—18:31): 17:5; 18:14, 17, 18, 20; the only other instance is in 8:27, of Gideon's manufacture of this illicit sacral item. The fact that the mentions of ephod are somewhat unnecessary for the story of Micah and the Levite, there being other incriminating cultic objects, makes it likely that אפוד is a deliberate attempt to link the narrative of Epilogue I with the Gideon story.⁵⁸

The audacious violations of the law and of propriety perpetrated by the Levite in Epilogue I (Pericope 12: Jdg 17:1—18:31) are comparable to Samson's misdemeanors (Pericope 10: Jdg 13:1—14:20 and Pericope 11: Jdg 15:1—16:31). The former include: wandering away from an appointed Levitical town (17:7, 9); seeking employment away from the main sanctuary (17:8, 9; 18:4); idiosyncratic relationship with patron (17:10-12); engagement in idolatry (18:20); and taking on the title of a priest, though he was not a descendant of Aaron (18:30). Samson's reckless malpractices include: amorous inclinations towards Philistine women, even marrying one of them (14:1-4, 10-18; 16:1, 4), and then abandoning her (14:19-20); neglect of his Nazirite vow (14:5, 8-9, 10, 19; 15:8, 15; 16:17); and his wanton violence throughout the narrative.⁵⁹ The Levite of Pericope 12 was associated

---

for forty years (13:1). Indeed, though they started out worshiping only the Baals and the Ashtaroth (2:13), by the time of Jephthah, they had aligned themselves not only to these false gods, but also to a number of other pagan deities, forsaking Yahweh completely (10:6).

56. "Forsaking" Yahweh is also a theme introduced in Jdg 2:12, 13, 21 that shows up again in 10:6, 10, 13, the only instances of the verb in Judges.

57. Ibid., 139.

58. See ibid., 87–88.

59. See ibid., 89–96.

with the Danites; Samson, of course, was a Danite. Thus both this Levite and the Danite judge succeed in flouting the regulations and stipulations that defined their divine callings.

Even the Danites' exploits in Epilogue I reflect those of the Danite, Samson, in Pericopes 10 and 11. Both narratives are linked to Zorah and Eshtaol (13:2, 25; 16:31; and 18:2, 8, 11) and Mahaneh-dan (mentioned only twice in Scripture: 13:25 and 18:12); departing Zorah and Eshtaol, both Samson and the Danites "see" either an attractive woman or a secure city (14:1 and 18:7), and attempt to persuade either parents or fellow tribesmen to take action based on this "seeing" (14:2 and 18:9); Samson decides what is "right in my eyes" (14:3), and Epilogue I points out that every Israelite was doing what was "right in his own eyes" (17:6).[60]

The story of the other Levite, in Epilogue II (Pericope 13: Jdg 19:1–30 and Pericope 14: Jdg 20:1—21:25), is also linked to Samson's story: the idea of prostitution is present in both (16:1; and 19:1–2); both Samson and the Levite seek to win back their spouses from whom they have been separated—both men arrive at the houses of their fathers-in-law (15:1; and 19:2–3); both spouses meet a violent death (15:6; and 19:27), caused, directly or indirectly, by men seeking relations with them (15:1; and 19:25); and both Samson and the Levite seek revenge (15:3, 7; and 19:29—20:7).[61]

There are also likely parallels between Epilogue II (especially Pericope 14: Jdg 20:1—21:25) and the story of Ehud (Pericope 3: Jdg 3:12-31): the left-handedness of Ehud the Benjaminite (3:15, "bound in the right hand") and that of the Benjaminite warriors (20:16, also "bound in the right hand") are the only two instances in the OT of this obscure term[62]; and the relatively rare gentilic terms describing the tribal affiliation of Ehud (3:15: בֶּן־הַיְמִינִי, ben-haymini) and that of the Gibeahites (19:16: בְּנֵי יְמִינִי, bne ymini).[63]

---

60. A specific refrain that there was no king in Israel in those days, a shortened version of the narrator's comment in 17:6 and 21:25, brackets the Danites' campaign (18:1; 19:1). The omission of "doing right in his own eyes" in 18:1 suggests that the concrete illustration of that axiom was the Danites' "rape" of Laish, just as the actualization of that axiom in 19:1 was the brutal rape and murder of the Levite's concubine (ibid., 99 n.59). Of course, the ophthalmic deficiencies of Samson drive his entire story. See ibid., 97–99; and Pericope 12 with Pericopes 10 and 11.

61. See ibid., 103–9.

62. This description of the seven hundred Benjaminite warriors in 20:16 seems rather incidental, for these fighters, their lefthandedness, and their slings play no role in the ensuing war with the Israelites. Instead, it is "sword" that occurs frequently (20:15, 17—Benjaminite swordsmen; and 20:25, 35, 37, 46, 48—Israelite swordsmen), making it quite likely that the description of their leftie "stonesmanship" was introduced as a deliberate link to the only other left-handed Benjaminite in Judges, Ehud.

63. See ibid., 112–24.

The near-annihilation of the Benjaminites by the rest of Israel in Epilogue II (especially Pericope 14) is striking for its internecine character: Israel vs. Israel, brother against brother (20:23, 28; 21:6). God's people had become their own enemies exacting חֵרֶם upon their own. But note the links with Gideon's punishment of an Israelite town, Penuel, that had refused to render him aid in his pursuit of two Midianite kings: Gideon later kills the Penuelites (8:17). This is particularly remarkable since the judge, soon thereafter, tells the captured kings that he would have saved their lives had it not been for their having killed his siblings (8:19). In other words, Gideon had been harsher with his fellow-Israelites, than he would have been with foreign enemy rulers (Pericope 7: Jdg 7:23—8:32). Also note the parallels between the Benjaminite massacre in Epilogue II (specifically, Pericope 14) and Jephthah's treatment of Ephraimites (Pericope 9: Jdg 10:6—12:15). Jephthah diplomatically negotiates with the king of Ammon (11:12-28) but shows no patience for, and offers no bargain to, his fellow-Israelites from Ephraim: instead he slaughters 42,000 of them (12:1-6). Thus the Israelites against the Benjamintes, Gideon against the Penuelites, and Jephthah against the Ephraimites, all show the same brutal and homicidal tendencies against fellow-Israelites.[64]

Other links between the Benjaminite massacre of Epilogue II (specifically, Pericope 14) and the Jephthah story (Pericope 9) can be detected as well. The civil war had left six hundred Benjaminite men without wives. The resulting fraudulent and duplicitous dealings of the Israelites became a black mark on Israel's treatment of women. The crime of gang rape of a single woman led to authorized corporate kidnaps and rapes of six hundred virgins (four hundred from Jabesh-gilead and two hundred from Shiloh). This was similar to Jephthah's sacrifice of his only daughter. Both were the result of foolish vows/oaths (11:39; and 21:1, 7, 18, but using different words: שׁבע, *shb'*, and נדר, *ndr*).[65] Just as the victim in Jephthah's story was a "daughter" (11:34, 35, 40) and a "virgin" (11:37, 38) who "did not know a man" (11:39), so also the female victims of the civil war in Epilogue II were "daughters" (21:21 [×2], making the elders of Israel father figures, akin to Jephthah) and "virgins" (21:12), who "did not know a man" (21:12). Jephthah's daughter came out to greet him with "dancing" (11:34); the kidnapped and raped daughters of Shiloh were also "dancing" (21:21).[66] These parallels

---

64. See ibid., 125–30.

65. Wong notes that the two words are synonymous (see Num 30:2; Ps 132:2; the former of these even has the phrase "all that came out of his mouth," identical to "that which came out of your mouth," Jdg 11:36). See ibid., 133–34.

66. These are the only two instances in Judges of the phrase "did not know a man" and of the noun "dancing" (another closely related verb, "to dance," is found in 21:23).

make the construction far from random, and appear to be deliberate, linking Epilogue II and Pericope 9 together.[67]

In conclusion, there is a clear skein of links between the Epilogues and the Body of Judges, demonstrating that what happens with God's leaders (Body: Israel's judges) is replicated—with greater intensity and in worse fashion—by God's people (Epilogues: leaderless Israel). Even the anonymity of most of the actors in the Epilogues points the reader to the possibility that they could be "Everyman," a universalization of the failures of specific individuals in a community where "everyone does what is right in his/her own eyes" (see 17:1; 21:25). God's leaders had left nefarious examples for God's people to follow in the Body. The rest was (chaotic) history in the Epilogues, "the worst of the judges served up in one concentrated dose"![68]

Theological Focus of Judges

Each pericope of Judges contributes a slice or a quantum of theology to the broad theological focus of the entire book. Those pericopal segments of theology are: uncompromising faithfulness to God, maintenance of godly traditional values, and reliance on divine strategies for success results in divine blessing (Pericope 1: Jdg 1:1—2:5 [Prologue I]); personal experience of God produces unwavering commitment to him (Pericope 2: Jdg 2:6—3:11 [Prologue 1; Othniel]); integrity in life, driven by reverence for God and reliance upon him, receives divine approbation (Pericope 3: Jdg 3:12-31 [Ehud]); reverencing of God by fearless faith characterizes godly leadership (Pericope 4: Jdg 4:1-24 [Barak]); participation in the endeavors of God, with God, keeps one in the realm of his blessing (Pericope 5: Jdg 5:1-31 [Song of Deborah]); refusal to take prideful credit for divine action results in blessing (Pericope 6: Jdg 6:1—7:22 [Gideon-1]); godliness is expressed in the rejection of self-glorifying pursuits (Pericope 7: Jdg 7:23—8:32 [Gideon-2]); an illicit thirst for power brings about the fitting retribution of God (Pericope 8: Jdg 8:33—10:5 [Abimelech]); ungodly manipulation of God for selfish purposes can lead to tragic loss of blessing (Pericope 9: Jdg 10:6—12:15 [Jephthah]); rejection of Yahweh's interests in favor of selfish passions leads only to trouble (Pericope 10: Jdg 13:1—14:20 [Samson-1]); disdaining of one's divine calling can lead to destruction (Pericope 11: Jdg 15:1—16:31 [Samson-2]); godless leadership brings about godlessness in society (Pericope 12: Jdg 17:1—18:31 [Epilogue I]); immoral unconcern for the weak and defenseless marks a godless and leaderless community

---

67. See ibid., 132–35; and Pericope 14 (Jdg 20:1–21:25) with Pericope 9 (Jdg 10:6—12:15).

68. Ibid., 140.

(Pericope 13: Jdg 19:1–30 [Epilogue II-1]); continued ungodliness only leads to more evildoing, greater havoc, and a hopeless future (Pericope 14: Jdg 20:1—21:25 [Epilogue II-2]).

A summative theological focus of the entire book of Judges may be discerned as follows:

> *Maintenance of godly traditional values, personal experience of God* (Prologues), *and manifesting virtues of godly leadership* (Body)—*integrity in life* (Ehud), *fearless faith* (Barak), *participation in the endeavors of God* (Song of Deborah), *giving God credit for his work* (Gideon-1), *rejection of self-glorifying pursuits* (Gideon-2) *and the thirst for power* (Abimelech), *avoiding manipulation of God* (Jephthah), *maintaining devotion to God and his interests* (Samson-1), *faithfully cleaving to one's call* (Samson-2)—*result in a godly society and provide hope for the future* (Epilogues).

And as God's leaders and God's people actualize these thrusts in their lives, conforming to Christlikeness pericope by pericope and sermon by sermon by the power of the Spirit, the Father's kingdom is, in a sense, being established. This is the goal of preaching, and of preaching the book of Judges in particular. A grand task, indeed!

PERICOPE 1

Failure and Indictment

Judges 1:1–2:5

[Failure of the Conquest; God's Indictment]

SUMMARY, PREVIEW

Summary of Pericope 1: The first pericope of Judges (1:1—2:5) comprises Prologue I of the book. It sets the sociopolitical stage of the rest of the narrative, depicting the failure of God's people to live in uncompromising godliness and to trust him for success. The consequence of this failure is a progressively worsening state of coexistence with the native Canaanites; these defeats culminate in a divine indictment.

Preview of Pericope 2: The next pericope (Jdg 2:6—3:11) is made up of Prologue II of the book and the story of Othniel. It details the religious decline of the Israelites, the unfaithfulness of the new generation after Joshua who did not know or experience God firsthand. A cycle of evildoing, punishment, and deliverance is described. Othniel, the first judge, is the parade example of a godly leader: his narrative follows the paradigm for the judge stories precisely and, with divine aid, he becomes the deliverer of Israel.

1. Judges 1:1–2:5

THEOLOGICAL FOCUS OF PERICOPE 1

1 Uncompromising faithfulness to God manifest in behavior distinct from that of unbelievers, maintenance of godly traditional values, and reliance on divine strategies for success results in the enjoyment of divine blessing (1:1—2:5).

    1.1   Failure of uncompromising obedience to divine commands precludes the enjoyment of divine blessing.

    1.2   Faithfulness to God involves behavior distinct from that of unbelievers, maintenance of godly traditional values, and abandonment of reliance on human strategies for success.

OVERVIEW

The Prologues (I: Jdg 1:1-2:5 and II: Jdg 2:6—3:6) and the Epilogues (I: Jdg 17:1—18:31 and II: Jdg 19:1—21:25) are structured around the Body (Jdg 3:7—16:31) as follows[1]:

Judges 1	Socio-political decline	Prologue I
Judges 2	Religious decline	Prologue II
Judges 3–16	Major and minor judges	Body
Judges 17–18	Religious collapse	Epilogue I
Judges 19–21	Socio-political collapse	Epilogue II

Joshua, the one who had begun to lead the Israelites so successfully against the Canaanites, and who was God's agent for assigning land to the various tribes, was now gone. At his departure he had exhorted his people to follow after Yahweh, and not after the gods of the Canaanites—an apostasy that would jeopardize the Israelites' taking over of the Promised Land (Joshua 22–24). Would they heed the words of this worthy one? An era had concluded with the death of Joshua. A new beginning was at hand, and with it the challenge of finding godly leaders. This is the burden of the book of Judges.

---

1. Prologue I comprises Pericope 1 (Jdg 1:1-2:5); and Prologue II, Pericope 2 (Jdg 2:6—3:11)—this also includes the Othniel narrative (3:7–11). Epilogue I comprises Pericope 12: Jdg 17:1—18:31; and Epilogue II, Pericope 13: Jdg 19:1-30 and Pericope 14: Jdg 20:1—21:25.

There appears to be a clear demarcation between Jdg 1:1—2:5 and 2:6—3:6: the first pericope is more narratival and descriptive, dealing with the sociopolitical decline of Israel, while the second pericope is more sermonic and evaluative, dealing with the religious decline of God's people. Besides, Joshua's death, noted in 2:6–9, seems to be starting a fresh unit, as also did the first pericope with a mention of that valiant one's demise (1:1).[2] In Judges 1, there are almost verbatim repeats of the central themes of Joshua:

JUDGES	JOSHUA
1:10–20	15:13–14
1:11–15	15:15–19
1:21	15:63
1:27–28	17:11–13
1:29	16:10
1:34	19:47

Indeed, a similar recapitulation occurs in Joshua 1 duplicating the central themes of Deuteronomy, after the death of the hero of that book, Moses.

> [T]he question in Joshua was not *whether* Israel under Joshua would occupy the land but how much or how little they would occupy; that they would indeed occupy the land had already been decided during Moses' lifetime, as narrated in Deuteronomy 9–10. The Book of Judges goes a step further. Now the question is not how much or how little land Israel would occupy during the period of the judges, but *why* they had not been able completely to drive out the inhabitants of the land. The Book of Judges, like Joshua, briefly recapitulates the previous book before interpreting it further.[3]

One notices that the opening of Judges (1:1) resembles that of Joshua (1:1) and of 2 Samuel (1:1); in these cases, a leader dies and a new one takes over. But in the case of Judges, no new leader is on stage. This is concerning: What would happen to a rudderless nation? Rather than an individual, we

---

2. However, the sequence of *waw*-consecutive verb forms that commence Judges 2 moves undisturbed throughout 2:1–23. While this—as well as the similarities between the divine speech in 2:20–22 and the angelic utterance in 2:1–3 ("fathers," "covenant," "obey/listen," and "drive them out" are shared)—may incline one to treat chapter 2 as an integral whole, the notion of a pericope that is espoused here is more pragmatic: separating 1:1—2:5 from 2:6—3:6 (and including the account of Othniel, 3:7–11 to comprise Pericope 2), enables the preacher to derive fairly distinct theological thrusts from each of the two pericopes, keeping the resulting sermons also distinct.

3. Polzin, *Moses and the Deuteronomist*, 148.

see a tribe designated to lead: "Judah shall go up," said Yahweh (Jdg 1:2). But down the road, it would be the same tribe that would lead in the tragic civil war (20:18). From the failures of the first chapter to the catastrophe of the last chapters, the nation is leaderless, faithless, and ultimately, godless!

This first pericope is carefully structured[4]:

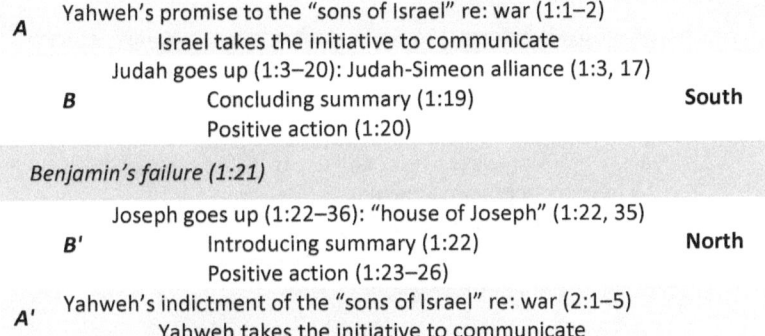

Judah and Joseph[5] (*B, B'*) conduct parallel wars, around which are placed Yahweh's promise to the "sons of Israel" regarding the war in 1:21—a prospective view (*A*), and, at the other end, Yahweh's indictment of the "sons of Israel" (the only two occurrences of the label in this pericope)—a retrospective view (*A'*, 2:4). The first time the "sons of Israel" are seekers of divine guidance; the second time they are subjects of divine grievance.

One also gets the sense of a geographic layout in the narration, a south-to-north arrangement commencing with Judah and concluding with Dan: Judah + Simeon, Benjamin, Joseph, Manasseh, Ephraim, Zebulun, Asher, Napthali, Dan. While this pericope mostly focuses on a human perspective of the war—a socio-political decline—the next (Pericope 2: Jdg 2:6—3:11), takes a divine perspective, providing reasons for the general failure of Israel's military effort—a religious decline.

One notices that Benjamin stands alone in 1:21 as an orphan in the "house of Joseph." This may well be an allusion to Epilogue II (especially Pericope 14: Jdg 20:1—21:25) where, again, Benjamin's isolation shows up—the victim of Israel's civil war. The insularity here in 1:21 is underscored by an unusual word order: "And the Jebusites [inhabitants] . . . were not driven out [verb] by the sons of Benjamin [tribal name]"; this is unlike the descriptions in 1:27, 29, 30, 31, 33, where the order is verb-tribal

---

4. From O'Connell, *The Rhetoric of the Book of Judges*, 62.
5. "House of Joseph" (1:22, 23, 35) is a league that indicates the northern tribes.

name-inhabitants.[6] Another reason for Benjamin's isolation may also be its geographic location between the major tribes of the south and the north.

1. Judges 1:1–2:5

> **THEOLOGICAL FOCUS 1**
>
> 1 Uncompromising faithfulness to God manifest in behavior distinct from that of unbelievers, maintenance of godly traditional values, and reliance on divine strategies for success results in the enjoyment of divine blessing (1:1—2:5).
>
> 1.1 Failure of uncompromising obedience to divine commands precludes the enjoyment of divine blessing.
>
> 1.2 Faithfulness to God involves behavior distinct from that of unbelievers, maintenance of godly traditional values, and abandonment of reliance on human strategies for success.

NOTES 1

1.1 *Failure of uncompromising obedience to divine commands precludes the enjoyment of divine blessing.*

There is an adumbration of danger right at the start. A comparison of Josh 1:1 with Jdg 1:1 immediately strikes the reader: the passage of the prior leader (Moses) in Josh 1:1 is juxtaposed to the appointment of the leader of the next generation ("Joshua, Moses's servant"). But in Jdg 1:1, there is no subsequent leader waiting in the wings when Joshua exits. Besides, in Josh 1:1, Yahweh took the initiative to give directives; in Jdg 1:1, he is strangely silent, until the Israelites take the initiative. Things do not look good!

The living arrangements between the Israelites and Canaanites as this pericope progresses are revealing. Initially, with the endeavors of the Judah-Simeon alliance, we are not told of Canaanites living among the Israelites; then from Benjamin to Zebulun, the Canaanites are found living with the Israelites; the situation worsens with Asher and Naphtali: here it is the *Israelites* who are living among the Canaanites; in the final phase, they are themselves displaced, unable to occupy the valley. Far from a conquest, this is an "anticonquest"[7]:

---

6. Ibid., 60–61.

7. Block, *Judges, Ruth*, 83. This is certainly a stylized and schematized arrangement of reality that is rarely so neat. But, of course, such author's *doings* serve a theological agenda.

1:3–21	Canaanites not said to be living with the Israelites Israelites fail in the valley (1:21)
1:21–30	Canaanites living with/among the Israelites (1:21, 27, 29, 30)
1:31–33	Israelites living among the Canaanites (1:32, 33)
1:34–36	Canaanites oppress Israelites (1:34) Israelites not allowed in the valley (1:34)

In sum, this pericope portrays a failed project to take over Canaan.

> Unlike most ancient military reports, the aim of this document is not to celebrate the achievements of the generation of Israelites that survived Joshua but to lament their sorry response to the divine mandate to occupy the land and to eliminate the Canaanites. Although the author delays sermonizing on the subject (cf. 2:1–5; 2:6—3:6), the structure of the chapter declares that this military failure accounts for the disastrous history of the nation in the next two or three centuries, as it is reported in the remainder of the book.[8]

And so while there is a seeking of God at the beginning of this pericope (1:1–2), there is, unfortunately, a weeping before him at the end (2:4–5; see below).

The verb "go up" (עלה, ʿlh, in the militaristic sense of "go against") is a key word in this pericope (1:1, 2, 3, 4, 16, 22; 2:1; it does not occur at all in the next pericope). Of all these uses of עלה, only those indicating the key movements of Judah, Joseph, and the angel of Yahweh (1:4, 22; 2:1) are emphasized by location at the head of the sentence, at the commencement of the appropriate section (1:4–20; 1:22–36; 2:1–5). Certainly some of this upward movement is related to geography (for there is a "going down," ירד, yrd, as well, in 1:9), but it also serves as a link: the consequence of all the (failed) "goings up" in 1:1–36 is the ominous "going up" of the angel of Yahweh from Gilgal to indict the Israelites (2:1).

One also notices that in these "goings up" in Judges 1, Yahweh is associated only with the movements of two tribes (1:4, 19, with the Judah and Simeon alliance; and 1:22, with the house of Joseph—a broad south-north division of the nation[9]); both these campaigns at least begin

---

8. Ibid., 83–84.

9. As the father of Ephraim and Manasseh, whose descendants formed the two largest northern tribes (Gen 41:50–52), "Joseph" was a convenient designation for all the northern tribes (see Josh 18:5; Ezek 37:15, 19; Zech 10:6).

well. Judah's war is initially successful, but later meets with failure (1:19, 21—with the failure of Benjamin against Jerusalem; also see 1:8). Joseph's war, though gainful, is suspect from the very start: despite a victory at Bethel/Luz, the informant from Bethel is allowed to go free in exchange (1:24–26), and he promptly rebuilds the destroyed city. A litany of incomplete "successes" and outright failures then follows (1:27–36). All of these miscarriages in Judges 1 form the basis for Yahweh's indictment of Israel in 2:1–5. The same "sons of Israel" who had sought Yahweh's counsel in 1:1 are now rebuked by him, for they were disobedient, making covenants with foreigners and not destroying their altars (2:2). Therefore, Yahweh announced, he would not completely drive out the land's inhabitants who would end up as thorns to the Israelites (and their gods as snares; 2:3).[10] Of course, Yahweh would be faithful to keep his covenant and Israel *would* possess the land, as he had promised the "fathers" (2:1). The question is *why* they failed to possess it now.

There was Moses who was unlike any other prophet in Israel, whom Yahweh knew face to face (Deut 34:10); then there was Joshua, "Moses's servant" (Exod 24:13; Num 11:28; Josh 1:1), one attested by Yahweh as having his Spirit (Num 27:18; also Deut 34:9), and who followed Yahweh fully as his servant (Num 32:12; Jdg 2:8). Now Joshua had died. Who would be the next godly servant to lead Israel? Yahweh's choice of a tribe, Judah, rather than an individual, is surprising. But then again, the Israelites did not ask him for a leader, only for a tribe to lead the battle. Indeed, a note of hesitancy is introduced into the Israelites' question in Jdg 1:1 that literally reads: "Who will go up for us, against the Canaanites, first, to battle them?" Did Israel need to know *who* would go up? And why "first," which has the limited sense of a beginning—"Who will . . . start to battle"? "Victory is relativised from scratch," only a commencement of operations is envisaged by the Israelites.[11] Commitment and confidence is thereby shown to be shaky. This, when the divine utterance is unambiguous: "Behold! I have given [perfect tense in Hebrew] the land into his [Judah's] hand" (1:2). Though Judah conducts the most successful military exercises in this pericope, no longer in Judges will Judah appear in a leadership role before 20:18. There, Judah leads an utterly failed enterprise that becomes the conflagration of a civil war.

And why did Judah decide to include Simeon (1:3)?[12] The specificity of God's assurance that he had given the *land* into Judah's hands (1:2) is con-

---

10. See Deut 7:1–5, 16, 25–26 for Yahweh's similar warning to the exodus generation.

11. Marais, *Representation in Old Testament Narrative Texts*, 75.

12. Perhaps it was because Simeon's land allotment was within that designated for Judah (Josh 19:1–9)?

sistently maintained in the narrative, despite Judah's unilateral co-opting of Simeon into its martial endeavors: Judah conquers peoples *and* lands (1:4, 5, 8, 9, 10, 11, 18, 19), but Judah + Simeon conquers only peoples (1:17)—and besides, even in this particular battle against the Canaanites of Zephath/Hormah, Simeon is not described as doing any fighting.[13] All this renders Judah's initial forays suspect.

Judah's ascent in 1:3–7 ("going up," 1:3, 4) and descent in 1:9–18 ("going down," 1:9) bookend its efficacious exploits in Jerusalem (1:8), making its engagements a stark contrast with the failed project of Benjamin (1:21). But that is not to say Judah was entirely successful—they were not, presumably because their foes had "iron chariots" (1:19). If Yahweh was with Judah as 1:19 claimed he was, why were iron chariots too hard to defeat? The nine hundred iron chariots of Jabin, king of Canaan, would turn out not to be a problem for deity (4:3, 13, 15; see Pericope 4).[14] Besides, Joshua had declared that iron chariots would not create obstacles for the Israelite conquest (Josh 17:16–18). Even in the literary structure of Jdg 1:19 and 1:20, Judah's attenuated "successes" are underlined, with the failure of Judah contrasted with the success of one Judahite, Caleb; the paronomasia is obviously disparaging of the tribe's endeavors.

1:19	"… were not able to drive out	the inhabitants of the valley …."
		אֶת־יֹשְׁבֵי הָעֵמֶק
		'et-yoshbe ha'emeq
1:20	"… drove out	the three sons of Anak."
		אֶת־שְׁלֹשָׁה בְּנֵי הָעֲנָק
		'et-shloshah bne ha'anaq

---

13. Klein, *The Triumph of Irony*, 23–24. "Hormah" is a play on חָרַם (*kharam*, "utter destruction"). On "utter destruction," see Deut 2:34; 3:6; 7:2; 20:17; Josh 2:10; 6:17–21. While the issue of such violence may need to be addressed some time in one's pastoral ministry, my recommendation for the preacher is not to get bogged down by it in the pulpit. Employing another occasion to deal with it (Sunday School class? Adult Bible Fellowship?), or even writing a white paper on the topic, would be a better alternative. In a sermon, the preacher needs to maintain focus on the theological thrust of the text. As Younger notes, "[חָרַם] was not concerned with the eradication of . . . particular cultural preferences. But it was deeply concerned with the eradication of the Canaanite religion: its gods/idols, altars, rituals, divinatory practices, uses of magic, worldview, and so on" (*Judges, Ruth*, 77).

14. Not to mention the chariots of Pharaoh (Exod 14:23–28; 15:4; also see Josh 11:4–9) that were no match for Yahweh's might. Drews suggests that it was the iron tires attached to wooden rims that are being referred to here. The weight of fully iron-clad chariots was likely too prohibitive for any kind of martial use; besides, the widespread use of iron occurs only later in history ("The 'Chariots of Iron,'" 19–20).

The contrast between 1:20 and 21 also vividly portrays another failure[15]:

A   "... he [Caleb]
   B   *drove out* from there
      C   the three sons of Anak.
      C'   But the Jebusites, the inhabitants of Jerusalem,
   B'   they did *not drive out*
A'   —the sons of Benjamin."

In keeping with Moses's promise (Josh 14:6-15), Caleb was successful in "driving out" the Anakites and capturing Hebron.[16] However, though Jerusalem was in territory allocated to Benjamin (Josh 15:8; 18:28), they were unsuccessful in "driving out" the Jebusites who lived there; in fact, these peoples lived there *with* the Benjaminites "to this day."[17]

The remainder of the account (Jdg 1:22-36) describes the continuing failure of the Joseph league: the two Joseph tribes proper, Manasseh (1:27-28) and Ephraim (1:29), then Zebulun (1:30), Asher (1:31-32), Naphtali (1:33), and finally Dan (1:34-35).[18] Perhaps these continued failures were the result of the precedent set at Bethel (1:22-26). In any case, the tribes do not evict the land's inhabitants (1:26-35), but cohabit with them, even subjecting them to slavery and feudalism ("forced labor," 1:28, 30, 33, 35).[19] The inability to "drive out" the inhabitants of various parts of the Promised Land is repeatedly noted (1:19, 21, 27, 28, 29, 30, 31, 32, 33). Indeed, the

15. Webb, *Judges*, 110.

16. Thus Caleb's success (1:20) is enclosed on either side by failures: Judah's (1:19) and the Benjaminites' (1:21).

17. That Jerusalem shows up again in 1:21 makes it likely that the Judahites' exertions described in 1:8 were against the Jebusite fortress on the southern hill of the city; the Benjaminites likely directed their attention to the citadel further north.

18. Issachar's absence is inexplicable, though Chisholm notes that this may be to reduce the more complete number seven (= tribes involved in the inheritance lists in Joshua 18-19) to an incomplete six (= tribes involved in Judges 1: Judah, Joseph [= Ephraim + Manasseh], Zebulun, Asher, Naphtali, and Dan) (*Judges, Ruth*, 135-36). Reuben and Gad lived outside the boundaries of the Promised Land, where the Amorites had already been taken care of (Numbers 21). Levi, of course, did not have a land inheritance.

19. The subjection to "forced labor" was permitted by Yahweh, but only of the inhabitants of those cities not given to the Israelites as an inheritance (Deut 20:11, 16-18; also see 7:1-2). Those allotted to Israel—depicted in Judges 1—were to be utterly destroyed. So the notations of "forced labor" are disconcerting. Was this some sort of compromise the Israelites had made with the Canaanites in exchange for their lives? Was there an economic criterion factoring into their (dis)obedience to divine command?

Amorites, in a climactic paragraph at the end of Judges 1, begin to "oppress" (לחץ, *lkhts*) the Israelites instead (1:34), an ominous development and a foreshadowing of what would happen with recurring and tragic frequency: 2:18; 4:3; 6:9; 10:12 (all have the root לחץ). And moreover, the only nation whose borders are mentioned is that of these Amorites (1:36)—it is not the attacking nation that is expanding its borders: "a final sardonic comment on the chapter as a whole!"[20]

Interestingly, while 1:27 states that Manasseh "did not drive out" the Canaanites, Josh 17:12 notes that Manasseh "was not able to drive out" these inhabitants (17:18 mentions their iron chariots, too). The theological purpose of the narrator of Judges is to suggest that this failure was inexcusable, more due to lack of desire than lack of ability.[21]

Naphtali's failure to "drive out" the inhabitants of Beth-shemesh and Beth-anath (Jdg 1:33), is particularly poignant: those towns were named after Canaanite deities, Shemesh and Anath. Pagan religiosity and culture remained completely untouched by the Israelite campaigns. In any case, the absence of any mention of Yahweh in the later military undertakings of this pericope, unlike in Jdg 1:2, 4, 19, 22, is also telling.

The relatively minor failures of Judah's campaign thus led into the major failures of the operations of the house of Joseph. Our curiosity is aroused about the cause of all these failures—only one such adversity was given a reason (1:19), leading one to suspect an intentional and widespread abrogation of responsibility, rather than any external cause thereof. We find the real answer only in 2:1–5—there was a *spiritual* reason for the Israelites' lack of military success. These failures, we are told there, stemmed from an illicit covenanting with the inhabitants of Canaan, noted in 1:22–26. Despite the assured presence of Yahweh as the house of Joseph went against Bethel, the campaign was a failure—not only did a Hittite family go free (1:25), the destroyed city was also rebuilt as Luz (1:26): the people and their culture had rebounded (see below). This was clear disobedience to divine will that no covenant be made with the local peoples: Israel was to destroy them utterly (Jdg 2:2; Deut 7:1–2, 16). This covenantal failure, snowballing over generations, would ultimately result in an abandonment of Yahweh for the gods of the land (Jdg 2:2; 10:6–14; also see Deut 7:4–5, 25–26).

Compromise and disobedience are always disastrous. In sum, the degradation of the nation had begun immediately after the demise of Joshua. This pericope begins with the most positive of the tribes (Judah) and ends with the most negative (Dan). Almost the same sequence of tribes

---

20. Ibid., 128.
21. Olson, "The Book of Judges," 744.

is followed in the sections on individual judges (Jdg 3:7—16:31), with this progressive dissolution expressly detailed.

1.2   *Faithfulness to God involves behavior distinct from that of unbelievers, maintenance of godly traditional values, and abandonment of reliance on human strategies for success.*

There are three anecdotal interpolations in what is otherwise the account of a military campaign: 1:5–7 (featuring Adoni-bezek); 1:12–15 (featuring Achsah); and 1:23–26 (featuring the house of Joseph and Bethel). This section will examine these further, along with the summarizing indictment of the Israelites in 2:1–5.

Adoni-bezek is the first individual Canaanite mentioned in Judges; in fact, he is the first named leader we encounter in the book. It is significant that this defeated foe recognizes the truth that actions have consequences, something the Israelites fail to see time and again, as the rest of Judges will describe. Upon reading 1:4–7, one might be justified in wondering how Israelites could so mutilate a human, albeit an enemy (mutilation *after* death is seen in 2 Sam 4:12). Certainly, there was retribution being visited on the king for his past misdeeds (Jdg 1:7), but those evidently were not misdeeds directed against the Israelites. In other words, the Israelites were doing exactly what their Canaanite enemy had done, but without provocation, except for the fact that he was an enemy ruler. This was not a tit-for-tat, at least not for any mutilation or gross violation Adoni-bezek had perpetrated against the Israelites. There is also the oddity of Adoni-bezek being allowed to live post-mutilation till he was taken to Jerusalem. If he was not to be killed immediately, why was he mutilated? In fact, the text does not even tell us that he was later executed by the Israelites, but simply that "he died there" (1:6, 7). In contrast, the original Jerusalemites were utterly destroyed by the Israelites (1:8). The treatment of Adoni-bezek sounds like the beginning of the "Canaanization" of Israel, further suggested by the subsequent degradation of its military endeavor, cohabitation with Canaanites, and involvement in idolatry found in rest of this pericope (see above). In the large scheme of the book, Adoni-bezek, the Canaanite who killed seventy kings, foreshadows Abimelech, the only other "king" in Judges, an Israelite, who also killed seventy (9:5).[22] This Israelite "Adoni-bezek" turned out to be worse than his Canaanite counterpart, killing in cold blood his own broth-

---

22. Adoni-bezek is not explicitly called a "king," but his name (Adoni-bezek = "Lord of Bezek") suggests he was, as also does the description of his enemies as "seventy *kings*." It is likely deliberate that Abimelech is the only one labeled "king" in Judges (9:6), crowned entirely by human initiative with no input from deity whatsoever.

ers, with retribution also mentioned twice in his story (9:24, 56, as opposed to only once in 1:7): Adoni-bezek's thumbs and toes for those of the seventy kings he had killed; and Abimelech killed by a stone for the seventy siblings he had killed on a stone. "[H]e [Abimelech] may have even out-Canaanised the Canaanites."[23] Israel was not just in Canaan now; Canaan was in Israel!

Another anecdotal "interpolation" occurs in 1:12–15. In Joshua, Kiriath-arba/Hebron was given to Caleb in Joshua's day (Josh 15:13; and see 14:6–15); in Judges, it is Judah that gets Hebron, and this *after* Joshua's day (Jdg 1:10–11).[24] In Joshua, Caleb was the one who defeated the three Anakites, Sheshai, Ahiman, and Talmai (Josh 15:14–15); in Jdg 1:10 it is Judah who does so.[25] The very presence of the similarly named Anakites in these early days of Judges is itself reflective of the dogged persistence of these peoples and the failure of the Israelites to drive them out until now. While a victory is described here, there is a hint that these Canaanites as a whole are hard to dislodge from the Promised Land. Judah proceeds to attack Kiriath-sepher, and Caleb promises to give his daughter to the one who captures it (1:11–12). Othniel, Caleb's nephew, performs the honors, captures a town, and wins a wife (1:13).

Achsah, Caleb's daughter, however, is not satisfied with Kiriath-sepher—she calls it the "land of the Negev" because of its desert-like nature (1:15). Hence the request to her father by this enterprising lady for additional "springs of water," which is granted.[26] This episode might be a priming of the pump for another father-daughter story later in Judges 11—a pejorative account of the father who also made a vow before a battle and sacrificed his daughter (Pericope 9: Jdg 10:6—12:15). Here, however, the father finds his daughter a valiant husband (1:12–13), and rewards her initiative and resourcefulness with what she requested him for—a blessing

---

23. The verbs used for "recompense" are different, שלם, *shlm*, in 1:7 and שוב, *shub*, in 9:56–57, but Wong notes that the verbs are used in parallel elsewhere in the OT (Exod 21:34; Deut 32:41; Ezek 33:15; Joel 3:4) (*Compositional Strategy*, 205, 206). See Pericope 8 (Jdg 8:33—10:5). The interpolation of the Adoni-bezek cameo, that does not seem to fit the rest of the movement of Prologue I, indicates the likelihood that his story was deliberately intended to adumbrate the narrative of Abimelech and depict the latter as worse than his Canaanite counterpart.

24. Note the singular as the verb "*he*, Judah, went" in Jdg 1:10, 11, whereas plural verbs indicate the subject "sons of Judah" in 1:8, 9.

25. Reconciling these with Josh 10:36–37; 11:21–22 is not easy; there it appears that Joshua wiped out the Anakites in Hebron. Perhaps the Judges 1 account (and perhaps the Joshua 14–15 narratives) is a flashback, included here for theological purposes, rather than chronological completion.

26. "She charmed him [her father] to ask for a field" (1:14). Chisholm observes that "she 'buttered' her father up (as daughters are apt to do!)" (*Judges and Ruth*, 125).

(1:14–15).²⁷ It also is a preparation for the presentation of Othniel as the first and paradigmatic judge in 3:7–11. Incidentally, all of the characters in this anecdote are Kenizzites—descendants of Kenaz an Edomite leader (Gen 15:19; 36:11, 15, 42; Jdg 1:13)—who joined up with the Israelites (Num 32:12; Josh 14:6, 14).²⁸ So much so, Caleb is the proud face of the tribe of Judah, an exemplar of a Yahweh-worshiper. Thus the endogamy practiced is also subtly being held up, in contrast to the Israelites' interest in non-Israelite women, pointed out in Jdg 3:6 and exemplified in the stories of Gideon (who had a Canaannite concubine) and Samson (who went after Philistine women all his life).²⁹

But the key aspect of this cameo is the contrast it makes with the story of fathers and daughters in Epilogue II (particularly Pericope 14: Jdg 20:1—21:25). The giving of daughters as wives is mentioned six times in Judges, each time with the words "give," "daughter," and "wife" in proximity: 1:12, 13; 3:6; 21:1, 7, 18. Except for 3:6, the others deal with Israelite endogamy, and are all found in Prologue I (Pericope 1: Jdg 1:1—2:5) and Epilogue II (specifically, Pericope 14: Jdg 20:1—21:25), as part of a war narrative: Caleb, a tribal leader, finding a wife for his daughter; and the Israelite leaders finding wives for the depleted Benjaminites. Pre-war pledges also characterize each of these stories, the first a "blessing" to "give" a daughter as wife (1:12, 13, 15), the second a "curse" "not to give" daughters as wives (21:1, 18). "[W]hile Caleb's pre-war promise to give his daughter in marriage to the one who succeeds in taking Kiriath Sepher seems to represent a wise move that merged concern for the fulfillment of YHWH's promise with concern for his daughter's welfare, the pre-war oath of Israel's leadership not to give their daughters in marriage to any Benjaminite seems to represent a rash and foolish decision made out of muddled thinking and excessive vindictiveness."³⁰ The contrast between a benevolent father in Judges 1 and malevolent fathers in Judges 19–21 is obvious (see both Pericope 13: Jdg 19:1–30 and Pericope 14: Jdg 20:1—21:25). Caleb not only gives his daughter to an intrepid warrior of his own tribe (endogamy), he also acquiesces to her enthusiastic request. The other fathers not only are involved in curses, the negligence of their daughters, and the murder of most of the men in an Israelite tribe, they also resort to deceptive and highly questionable practices to procure females for the remaining Benjaminite males. The contrast

27. There are several other equally zestful women in Judges: Deborah (4:4–14), Jael (4:17–22), and the woman of Thebez (9:53–54).

28. The Kenaz in Jdg 1:13 was another individual—Caleb's brother.

29. The maintenance of covenantal purity through endogamy was an established tenet of Israelite life (Exod 34:16; Deut 7:3–4; Josh 23:12).

30. Ibid., 45.

is also being made of a leader of the Joshua generation who appreciates and respects women, and leaders of the Judges generation who oppress and objectify and murder them. The former is keen on fulfilling the promises of Yahweh in the land and is concerned for, and protective of, his daughter's (and her husband's) welfare, unlike the latter who are rash, self-focused, and vindictive. The presence of this anecdote in Judges 1, then, points to the well-disposed, magnanimous, and bountiful nature of the leaders in a prior generation of Israel.[31]

So here is the first woman in the book of Judges, a remarkable lady keen on obtaining the best for her inheritance, family, and posterity within the community of Israel! She is asking for more than a gift; she wants land, the tangible sign of divine blessing in the OT. And thus "Achsah emerges as an image of ideal Yahwist womanhood," and becomes the standard by which all other women in the book will be judged.[32] This sense of fruitfulness in the presence of Yahweh depicted for the first time in Judges—by a woman—is significant; unfortunately this prosperity will only decline and drop henceforth as the book of Judges unfolds.

The third anecdotal "interpolation" in Pericope 1 deals with the capture of Bethel by the Joseph league (and their failure to keep it—it was rebuilt as Luz, a Canaanite city), and is described in greater detail than are the other campaigns of 1:22–36. The presence of Yahweh with the house of Joseph is noted in 1:22, and we anticipate another relatively successful takeover as in 1:4–20. In retrospect, one sees that unlike in 1:4, where Yahweh "gave" the victory, here we are only told that Yahweh was with the Israelite army. And that is borne out in the *human* strategy that the latter engages in, in their taking of Bethel. Besides, in 1:4–20 and in 1:22–36, an individual Canaanite is highlighted: Adoni-bezek and the Bethel informant, respectively. The former, a named ruler, is found, fought against, pursued, caught, mutilated, transferred, and probably killed (1:5–7). The latter, an anonymous man, is seen, spoken to, negotiated with, and shown חֶסֶד (*khesed*) and freed, family and all. And he promptly rebuilds Luz (1:24–26). The presence of Yahweh with the house of Joseph should have rendered all humanly contrived strategies unnecessary; indeed, there was to be no covenant made with the Canaanites (2:2; also see Deut 7:2). Tragically, there is no mention of Yahweh being present with the campaigns of any of the other tribes after this fiasco.

---

31. Ibid., 42–45. In another parallel, Achsah "descends" from a donkey (1:14); the raped concubine "ascends" one (19:28)—these are the only two women in Judges on donkeys. Both women, for different reasons, leave their husbands and go to their fathers. One is blessed; the other raped and murdered. The father of one is benevolent, that of the other is malevolent (see Pericope 13: Jdg 19:1–30).

32. Klein, *The Triumph of Irony*, 26.

The house of Joseph, in their campaign to take Bethel, may have been attempting to imitate Joshua's takeover of Jericho with the help of a native Canaanite (Joshua 2; see below for a comparison of the two events). However, the differences are significant (shaded below): in the earlier account Rahab took the initiative to ask for חֶסֶד, with a proclamation that was Yahwistic through and through, acknowledging his preeminence and his great deeds (Josh 2:9–13)—she had converted![33] So much so, after a divinely accomplished victory over Jericho, Rahab and her family were noted to be residents of Israel thenceforth: "to this day" (6:25).[34] In the present case, there is no indication that the informant made any Rahab-like alliance with the Israelites, or with Yahweh. And the man's final action of rebuilding Luz (which also stands "to this day," Jdg 1:26), becomes a scandalous symbol of the unwise covenanting of the house of Joseph with a foreigner. It was as if the hostilities and capture of Bethel by the Israelites had never taken place—the city had merely been transferred from one site to another—"the spirit of Luz lived on."[35]

Campaign against Jericho (Joshua 2, 6)	Campaign against Bethel (Judges 1)
Yahweh's presence (Josh 6:27)	Yahweh's presence (Jdg 1:22)
Spying activity (Josh 2:1)	Spying activity (Jdg 1:23, 24)
Canaanite: Rahab, a harlot (Josh 2:1)	Canaanite: Anonymous man (Jdg 1:24)
Rahab acknowledges Yahweh (Josh 2:9–13)	No acknowledgment of Yahweh by man
Agreement to "do" חֶסֶד (Josh 2:13–14)	Agreement to "do" חֶסֶד (Jdg 1:24)
Israelite spies aided to exit (Josh 2:15–21)	Israelite army aided to enter (Jdg 1:25)
City divinely taken (Josh 6:1–21)	City humanly taken (Jdg 1:25)
Rahab and family spared (Josh 6:22–25)	Man and family spared (Jdg 1:25)
Rahab continues in Israel (Josh 6:25)	Man moves to Hittite land (Jdg 1:26)
Curse on rebuilding Jericho (Josh 6:26)	Man rebuilds Luz (Jdg 1:26)
Rahab lives in Israel "to this day" (Josh 6:25)	Luz continues "to this day" (Jdg 1:26)

A slavish imitation of a past strategy of success, without comprehension of that event's critical elements, is futile. What was necessary here was an

---

33. In fact, the formulation "do חֶסֶד unto . . . " is found only in these two accounts in Joshua and Judges (Josh 2:12 [×2], 14; Jdg 1:24), making the construction of this text in Judges a deliberate allusion to the one in Joshua.

34. Again, there is verbal correspondence in the "sending" away of Rahab and her family after the city was destroyed "with the edge of the sword" (Josh 6:21, 23), and the "sending" away of the anonymous Bethelite and his family after their city was struck "with the edge of the sword" (Jdg 1:25).

35. Wong, *Compositional Strategy,* 152–53. Table modified from Webb, *Judges,* 117.

understanding of God's work, his power, and *his* strategy for success—and a cooperation with that work, that power, and that strategy.

The final section of this pericope, 2:1–5, gives the reaction of God to the compromising and self-reliant attitudes and actions of his people. Judges 2:1–5 is a hinge between the failed conquest ("anticonquest") of Judges 1 and the following "literary soliloquy" of the narrator in 2:6–23 (see Pericope 2: Jdg 2:6—3:10).[36] It links to the previous section with the angel's "going up" (2:1; the verb shows up also in 1:1, 2, 3, 4, 16, 22), and to the following pericope as well, with the impactful words of Yahweh's angel: the reference to "covenant," the accusation of "not listening to My voice," and Yahweh's resolution "not to drive [the nations] out before" Israel are found in both 2:1–3 and 2:21.[37] In other words, the paradigm of 2:11–19 (see Pericope 2) and the pattern of the rest of the judge-narratives (built on this framework) are all based on what happened here in Pericope 1.

The angel's message takes a forensic form: reminder of Yahweh's past deeds and promise (2:1b)[38]; reminder of Yahweh's demands (2:2a); an accusation (2:2b); the call for an explanation (2:2c)[39]; and a warning of punishment (2:3). The structuring of 2:1–5 places the accusation of disobedience and demand for an explanation at the center of the chiasm.

A   Angel of Yahweh; Bokim (2:1a)
    B   "And he [angel of Yahweh] said"; "you"; "fathers" (2:1b)
        C   "'and I said'"; relationships: Yahweh-Israel and Israel-nations (2:1c–2a)
            D   Disobedience and interrogation (2:2bc)
        C'   "'and I also said'"; relationships: Israel-nations and Israel-gods (2:3)
    B'   "the angel of Yahweh spoke"; "all the sons of Israel"; "the people" (2:4)
A'   Bokim; Yahweh (2:5)

---

36. Block, *Judges, Ruth*, 109.

37. The verbs for "drive out" are different: גרשׁ, *grsh*, in 2:3 and ירשׁ, *yrsh*, in 2:21. But Wong notes that they are synonymous; see Exod 33:2 and Josh 3:10; Josh 24:18 and Jdg 11:23; and Pss 44:3 and 80:9 (*Compositional Strategy*, 148n22).

38. While it is not certain what Yahwistic covenant is referred to in 2:1, it is likely to have been a promise to the nation to give them the Promised Land (Lev 26:42–44; and see Gen 24:7; 26:3; Exod 13:5, 11; 32:13; 33:1; Deut 6:10, 18). While binding upon Yahweh, the extent of the takeover of the land, how much, when, and in what manner, were all contingent on the behavior of the human partners to the covenant (see Jer 11:4–5, as well as the various iterations of the promises to the patriarchs in Genesis, that see a ratcheting up of the items of fulfillment with obedience, especially in Gen 22:16–18) (see Kuruvilla, *Genesis*, 261–62).

39. "What is this you have done?" is formulaic in the OT and indicates "a major breach of proper relations between parties" (see Gen 3:13; 12:18; 26:10; 29:25; Exod 14:11; Jdg 8:1; 15:11) (Niditch, *Judges*, 47).

The past history of Israel's conquest had a significant place marker, Gilgal, where the crossing of the Jordan was commemorated as the first major place of worship (Josh 4:1–24; 5:9). Now with the notice that Yahweh's angel was *leaving* Gilgal to come to Bokim, the reader is alerted to the change of circumstances—from Joshua's day of celebrated victory to this day of mourned defeat.[40] This angel of Yahweh may well be "the captain of the host of Yahweh" that Joshua had encountered at Bethel (Josh 5:13–15), another not-so-subtle reminder of how much things had changed between then and now.[41] Now Yahweh's agent was "going up" to provide a divine verdict on the "goings up" of the Israelites. So, before a single judge shows up on the scene, in the very first pericope of the book, the status of God's people before him is starkly diagnosed: they have been disobedient! For the rest of the book, there will only be cause for weeping (Bokim = "place of weeping/weepers"). Thus, in a sense, Judges commences with weeping (2:1, 4, 5) and concludes with weeping (21:2): "the book of Judges introduces the history of Israel as a story to weep about."[42]

Yahweh's rebuke is stinging: It is not so much that Israel had failed to drive out the inhabitants of Canaan, but that they, forgetting their covenant God, had made covenants with the Canaanites, and not destroyed their cultic sites: they had disobeyed the explicit commands of Deut 7:1–5, 16, 25–26 (see Jdg 2:1–2).[43] In fact, it was because of their disobedience that God was refusing to drive out the Canaanites before the Israelites, that otherwise would have been accomplished by God himself (2:3). "In other words, the process of dispossession and occupation would have been completed in due course if the Israelites had fulfilled their obligations to Yahweh, but now their disobedience has put the completion of the Conquest in

---

40. In fact, that place was called "Gilgal" because Yahweh had "rolled away" (גלל, *gll*) the reproach/disgrace of Egypt and changed the fortunes of Israel (Josh 5:9). Was another change of fortunes on the way here?

41. It is possible that Bokim is a pseudonym for Bethel: an "oak of weeping [בכות, *bakuth*]" was located near Bethel (Gen 35:8). In fact the LXX at Jdg 2:1 has the angel coming "to Bokim and Bethel, that is, the house of Israel." In Judges 20–21, the final part of the book (Pericope 14: Jdg 20:1–21:25), weeping takes place at Bethel (20:26). Besides, Gilgal and Bethel are often linked: see Hosea 4:15; Amos 4:4, 15; 5:5. Bethel also has the status of a place of rebuke in prophetic literature (1 Kgs 13:1–3; 2 Kgs 23:15–20; Amos 7:10–17). Though why the real name of the place should be camouflaged in this pericope is unclear; perhaps Bethel in the narrator's day was a holy city, prompting the writer to soften the blow of indictment. See Block, *Judges, Ruth*, 112; Spronk, "A Story to Weep About," 91–92; and Amit, *Hidden Polemics*, 119–28.

42. Spronk, "A Story to Weep About," 87. In between these two lachrymal events, there is also weeping in 11:37; 14:16; 20:23, 26.

43. The accusation that Israel had not torn down the altars of the Canaanites (2:2) is rather unexpected; we had not heard any mention of cultic activity in Judges 1. Presumably all this anti-Yahwism was concurrent with the failed conquest.

jeopardy (2:3)."⁴⁴ Moreover, the Canaanite gods would ensnare the Israelite people (Exod 23:32–33; 34:11–15; Num 33:55; Deut 7:16; Josh 23:13).

After the mourning and sacrificing, "[o]ne expects to read of Israel breaking their alliances with the native population and launching a vigorous military campaign against the pagan altars and those who worship there. But the text is silent. Through the smoke of the weeping Israelites' sacrifices, one can still see the outlines of the pagan altars."⁴⁵ Nonetheless, the contrition exhibited by the Israelites in Jdg 2:4–5 is hopeful (the only time it happens in conjunction with sacrifices in all of Judges) but, as it turns out, this change of heart is only transitory: the Israelites' apostasy only worsens as the next pericope will show and the rest of the book will depict.

SERMON FOCUS AND OUTLINES

THEOLOGICAL FOCUS OF PERICOPE 1 FOR PREACHING[46]

1 Faithfulness to God manifest in uncompromising godliness and reliance on God brings blessing (1:1—2:5).

Of the three narrative "interpolations" in this pericope—1:5–7 (featuring Adoni-bezek); 1:12–15 (featuring Achsah); and 1:23–26 (featuring the house of Joseph and Bethel)—it might be best to bypass the Achsah story with a brief mention, in the interests of time: the contrast is with the mistreatment of women in the Epilogues, and that, I believe, is the primary function of the cameo here.

---

44. Younger, *Judges, Ruth*, 74. Yahweh expands the apostasy of the Israelites and the intensity of his threat in the next pericope.

45. Robert B. Chisholm, personal communication.

46. In the view of preaching espoused in this commentary, the exposition of the theology of the pericope (represented as a statement by the "Theological Focus"), with all the power and potency of the text, is the critical task of the homiletician. Needless to say, the preacher must also provide the congregation with specifics on how the theological thrust of each pericope may be put into practice so that lives are conformed to Christlikeness in the power of the Spirit, for the glory of God.

Possible Preaching Outlines for Pericope 1[47]

I. Background[48]
   Thrust of the book of Judges: leadership
   God's people: only as good as God's leaders
   All of God's people are leaders in some fashion, to some degree
   Structure of book: Prologues I and II; Body; Epilogues I and II
   Leadership change in Israel; silence of Yahweh (1:1)
   Move-to-relevance: God's leaders today; God's people as leaders today[49]

II. Failures
   Judah's inclusion of Simeon (1:3)
   Iron chariots and Benjamin (1:19–21); yet Caleb's success (1:20)
   Joseph's abortive effort (1:22–26)
   Failure of the rest of the tribes (1:27–36)
   Move-to-relevance: Our failures

III. Consequences
   Worsening of situation with Canaanites (1:3–21, 21–30, 31–33, 34–36)
   Indictment by God (2:1–3)
   Move-to-relevance: Consequences for the church and the Christian

IV. *Live godly!*[50]
   How we lose divine blessings today with an ungodly lifestyle
   Start to live godly: repentance (weeping: 2:4–5)[51]

---

47. One must see the points in these outlines as "moves," rather than static chunks of information dumped on the unwary listener. See Kuruvilla, *Vision for Preaching*, 71–89. The outlines provided are deliberately skimpy; they are intended merely to be suggestions for further thought—rough-hewn stones to be polished by the preacher. It is nigh impossible to prescribe an outline without knowing the particular audience it is to be used for, and therefore this commentary will refrain from micromanaging homiletics for the preacher. Some equally abbreviated suggestions for development are provided below each main point.

48. Since this is the first pericope/sermon on Judges, reviewing the background state of affairs is helpful, including a statement of the overall theme of the book: leadership, and how this impacts the people of God.

49. Moves-to-relevance are critical in every major move of the sermon, relating the theological thrust (or portions thereof) to the listeners and their circumstances.

50. Outlines in this commentary will have an imperative of some sort as a major outline point—the application. The specificity and direction of that imperative is between the Holy Spirit, the preacher, and the audience.

51. Corporate repentance may be a good first step of commitment to live in uncompromising godliness.

A Problem–Solution–Application outline is given below[52]:

I. PROBLEM: Loss of Blessing
   Worsening of situation with Canaanites (1:3–21, 21–30, 31–33, 34–36)
   Indictment by God (2:1–3)
   Move-to-relevance: Consequences for the church and the Christian
II. SOLUTION: Uncompromising Godliness[53]
   Judah's inclusion of Simeon (1:3)
   Iron chariots and Benjamin (1:19–21); yet Caleb's success (1:20)
   Joseph's abortive effort (1:22–26)
   Failure of the rest of the tribes (1:27–36)
   Move-to-relevance: Our failures
III. APPLICATION: *Live godly!*
   How we lose divine blessings today with an ungodly lifestyle
   Start to live godly: repentance (weeping: 2:4–5)

---

52. This age-old rhetorical scheme is easy to organize and manipulate; perhaps the reason is because we tend to think that way. There might very well be a hardwiring in our brains for a Problem–Solution–Application sequence.

53. Of course, the portion of text employed here depicts the negative: the *un*solution, if you will (or the cause of the problem)—what the Israelites did to merit the loss of blessing.

PERICOPE 2

Paradigm and Exemplar

Judges 2:6–3:11

[Israelites' Infidelity; Spiral of Failure; Othniel's Example]

REVIEW, SUMMARY, PREVIEW

Review of Pericope 1: In Jdg 1:1—2:5, the background of sociopolitical decline for the rest of the book of Judges is set. The people of God fail to live in uncompromising godliness, and to trust God for success. As a consequence, there is a progressively worsening state of coexistence with the native Canaanites, drawing an indictment from God.

Summary of Pericope 2: The second pericope of Judges (2:6—3:11) comprises Prologue II of Judges and the Othniel story. It details the religious decline of the Israelites, the unfaithfulness of the new generation after Joshua who did not know or experience God firsthand. Their infidelity spirals downward with each iteration of the judge stories, creating a paradigm for these failures, as well as for the divine punishment that ensues. Othniel, the first judge, is the parade example of a godly leader: his story follows the paradigm precisely and, with divine aid, he deliverers Israel.

Preview of Pericope 3: The next pericope, Jdg 3:12–31, depicts the second major judge in the series, Ehud. His duplicitous words and deceptive actions are subtly deprecated in his story. Finally, the cameo of Shamgar makes this minor judge a foil for the major judge who lacks integrity. With the implicit disapproval of Ehud's actions and the approval of Shamgar's, integrity in leadership forms the thrust of this pericope

2. Judges 2:6–3:11

THEOLOGICAL FOCUS OF PERICOPE 2

2 Personal experience of God produces unwavering commitment to him, with minimizing of self so as to give him glory (2:6—3:11).

　　2.1　Failure of uncompromising obedience to divine commands precludes the enjoyment of divine blessing.

　　　　2.1.1　*Failure to experience God firsthand dilutes commitment to him.*

　　　　2.1.2　*Forsaking the true God and following other idols have disastrous consequences.*

　　2.2　Faithful commitment to God gives him the glory and minimizes self (3:7–11).

OVERVIEW

Judges 1:1—3:6 constitutes the Prologue of the book of Judges, comprising Prologue I (Pericope 1: Jdg 1:1—2:5) and Prologue II (part of Pericope 2: Jdg 2:6—3:11, that also includes the Othniel story, 3:7–11). This corresponds to the two-part epilogue of the book: Epilogue I (Pericope 12: Jdg 17:1—18:31) and Epilogue II (Pericope 13: Jdg 19:1–30 and Pericope 14: Jdg 20:1—21:25).

Judges 1	Socio-political decline	**Prologue I**
Judges 2	Religious decline	**Prologue II**
Judges 3–16	Major and minor judges	**Body**
Judges 17–18	Religious collapse	**Epilogue I**
Judges 19–21	Socio-political collapse	**Epilogue II**

O'Connell observes that "[t]he high concentration in 2:11—3:6 of phraseological parallels to biblical passages that focus upon covenantal adherence (particularly Josh 23-24, Deut 4-11 and 31:14-29)" are indicators of the narrator's concern in this pericope to view Israel's conduct as essentially covenantal malfeasance (i.e., religious decline), as opposed to the primary interest of Pericope 1 (1:1—2:5) which was to depict Israel's failure to conquer the land (i.e., socio-political decline).[1] There is concern for the conquest of the land in Pericope 2 (2:6, 21, 23; 3:1, 3), but that does not appear to be its focus; rather, the failure to occupy the land and the continuing presence of the enemy in Canaan seem to be symptoms of a disease: covenant disloyalty. Unfortunately, under the leadership exhibited by the various judges in this book, a strong commitment to Yahweh's covenant will never materialize—the calamitous story of Judges. Indeed, a glance at Prologues I and II clue us in to the reason: Prologue I begins with the cult: 1:1-2, Israel seeking Yahweh's guidance; Prologue II ends with the cult: 3:5-6, but unfortunately with Israel serving other gods.

In sum, while Pericope 1 reports events from a human point of view–socio-political decline—most of Pericope 2 relates matters from a divine point of view—religious decline. The first is more linear in arrangement and historical in nature; the second, more cyclical in arrangement and theological in nature, particularly 2:11-19, that creates a repeatable paradigm that resonates through the rest of the book.[2] In Pericope 2, the story shifts back to Joshua's demise already noted in 1:1 (and reported in Josh 24:28; see Jdg 2:6-10). From this starting point, 2:6—3:6 paints "a panoramic temporal overview of the entire period covered by the Book of Judges. In sweeping temporal terms, a cyclical sequence is presented [2:11-19] which explains not only the incidents of Judges 1 but *all* the events to follow in the book."[3] After this flashback to Joshua's death and burial (2:6-10),[4] there is a description of the cycle of disobedience, discipline, and deliverance (2:11-19, the paradigm), followed by the report of Yahweh's censure (2:20-23), and a narratival summary reflecting the divine diatribe and the people's covenantal failure (3:1-6). The text then provides the account of the first judge in the book, Othniel (3:7-11), that precisely fulfills all the elements of the

---

1. O'Connell, *The Rhetoric of the Book of Judges*, 117.
2. Younger, *Judges, Ruth*, 84-85.
3. Polzin, *Moses and the Deuteronomist*, 151.
4. Judges 2:6 begins with a *wayyiqtol* verb, usually indicating a sequential order of the narrative, but that need not always be the case: see 2:23; 3:16; 5:1; 8:4 (referring back to 7:25), 29; 9:42; 11:4 (referring back to 10:9); 12:4; 16:3; 20:36; 21:6, 24; etc., for exceptions. It is best to see 2:6 as a flashback. See Chisholm, *Judges and Ruth*, 152 n.9.

paradigmatic cycle of 2:11–19.[5] In any case, the outlook is bleak for the Israelites and this period of the judges.

2.1. Judges 2:6–3:6

> **THEOLOGICAL FOCUS 2.1**
>
> 2 Personal experience of God produces unwavering commitment to him, with minimizing of self so as to give him glory (2:6—3:11).
>
>   2.1 Failure to experience God firsthand and forsaking him have disastrous consequences (2:6—3:6).
>
>   *2.1.1 Failure to experience God firsthand dilutes commitment to him.*
>
>   *2.1.2 Forsaking the true God and following other idols have disastrous consequences.*

NOTES 2.1

2.1.1 Failure to experience God firsthand dilutes commitment to him.

The narrative could easily have moved from 2:5 to 2:11, from repentance to regression, from contrition to corruption. Instead, we have a sort of detour in 2:6–10 to establish a theological point. Judges 2:6–10 is almost identical to Josh 24:28–31, but it weaves the story in its own way for a different theological purpose—a case of the author *doing* things with what he is saying. The death of Joshua had already been noted in Jdg 1:1, to introduce the military failures of the Israelite conquest. Now the restatement of the hero's demise in Pericope 2 explores the theological underpinnings of these Israelite debacles.

---

5. Judges 3:7–11 remains distinct from 2:6–3:6, for it introduces the first of the judges; it forms part of the Body of the book (3:7—16:31). But Othniel's account adheres perfectly to the paradigm of the cycle depicted in 2:11–19 and is therefore included within Pericope 2 (Jdg 2:6—3:11). As was noted in the Introduction, "pericope," as I see it, simply designates a preaching text, irrespective of size or genre. The distinction made between pericopes is more pragmatic than technical. A pericope generates a theological thrust for a sermon sufficiently distinct from the theological thrust of the pericope preceding and following. In other words, a pericope is a unit of text upon which a sermon with a discrete theological idea can be preached.

	Generation before		Death of Joshua		Generation after
Judges	2:6	2:7	2:8	2:9	2:10
Joshua	24:28	24:31	24:29	24:30	—

As seen above, Joshua 24:31 is shifted forwards in the Judges report (making it Jdg 2:7), to which 2:10 is added (that has no parallel in Joshua 24).[6] This distinguishes the generation *before* (2:7) the death of Joshua (2:8–9)[7] from the generation *after* (2:10). Another change worthy of note: Josh 24:31 uses the verb "know" to describe the generation before Joshua's death—they *knew* the deeds of Yahweh.[8] Judges 2:7 changes that to "see"—this earlier generation did not just know the "great deeds of Yahweh," they had actually *seen* them![9] Judges 2:6 also has "*the sons of Israel went* each to his inheritance *to possess the land*" (Josh 24:28 simply has "each to his inheritance"). These additions in Jdg 2:6 underscore the responsibility of the Israelites: they had to *go* and *possess the land*—that was the intent of Joshua's dismissal and, indeed, the goal of the entire conquest.

Unfortunately, as was detailed in Pericope 1, the post-Joshua generation *went* but did not *possess the land* for, as Jdg 2:10 declares, they did not "know Yahweh, or the deeds which he had done." This is the most significant change from Josh 24:28–31—the addition of the notice in Jdg 2:10 regarding the generation *after* Joshua's death and their ignorance of Yahweh and his

---

6. The LXX maintains an identical order of verses between Josh 24:28–31 and Jdg 2:6–9 but, like the MT, it adds 2:10.

7. A further nuancing: The generation of Joshua includes those elders who outlived him (2:7), those who had seen Yahweh's great work. These, of course, die only after Joshua (2:10a). It is the subsequent generation that is the problem (2:10b). The term "gathered to one's fathers" (2:10a), employed of Joshua's generation, is idiomatic for death and burial, but in this instance it may also connote integral union and solidarity in faith with the generations that preceded them (i.e., *before* Joshua). This is, of course, in contrast, to the subsequent generation (i.e., *after* Joshua) that was ignorant of God and his work (2:10b). Did the generation of Joshua's time contribute unintentionally to this loss of collective memory of Yahweh and his deeds? "In one generation true religion, the religion of Josh 24, vanished from the promised land. . . . A generation that does not teach its children, as Josh 4:6, 21 advised, would lose its children to false religion" (Butler, *Judges*, 42).

8. The verb "know" shows up in 2:10: the generation after Joshua did *not* "know" Yahweh or his deeds.

9. And emphasizing what the previous generation had *seen*, the narrator of Judges also adds "great" to describe the work of Yahweh (2:7; the adjective is missing in Josh 24:28). There are, in addition, a few stylistic alterations of conjunctions, a minor difference in the name of Joshua's burial place, etc., between the Joshua and Judges accounts.

work. And what they did in their abysmal ignorance—and kept on doing—is the burden of 2:11—3:6, and indeed, of the rest of the book of Judges. Strikingly, in "all" the days of Joshua, and in "all" the days of the elders of his day (2:7), "all" that generation (2:10) had *seen* "all" the great work of Yahweh on behalf of Israel (2:7). But now there was a new generation indifferent to Yahweh and his deeds (2:10). What a contrast! Since "knowing" in Hebrew has deeper connotations than simply cognition, and includes covenantal relationships and loyalty thereto (for e.g., Gen 18:19, between God and man; Gen 4:1 [with Mal 2:13–16], between man and wife), "'not knowing' involves more than lacking information; it is a refusal to accept the obligations entailed in a [covenant] relationship."[10] Thus, Jdg 2:6–10 is not primarily about Joshua; it is about the new, post-Joshua generation of people and their deplorable failure to follow Yahweh as their predecessors had done.[11] Had it been otherwise, had they followed Yahweh wholeheartedly, "Israelite history would have taken a completely different course, the events described in the rest of the book would never have happened, and the Book of Judges would never [have] been written."[12]

The only named human in this pericope (excluding the Othniel account, 3:7–11) is Joshua, the exemplar, "the servant of Yahweh" (2:8; also in Josh 24:29), a term also used of Moses (Exod 14:31; Num 12:8; Deut 34:5; Josh 1:1; etc.). In contrast to him are the Israelites, "who did not know Yahweh or the deeds which He had done" (Jdg 2:10), and who "played harlot after other gods and bowed down to them" (2:17), corrupt and stubborn (2:19). The other actant here is, of course, divine: Yahweh. This one is in turn angry (2:14), moved to pity (2:18), and angry again (2:20), with the evil engagements of his people. This cycle of emotions parallels the cycle of wickedness of the Israelites: doing evil and following other gods (2:11–13), groaning about their punitive afflictions (2:18), returning again to evil and to other gods once their oppression has been alleviated (2:19). The first clues of apostasy were seen in Pericope 1, but it is highlighted in 2:11—3:6, so that the bulk of Pericope 2 declares "the author's fundamental thesis: the nation of Israel has been thoroughly Canaanized; this accounts for and is fundamental to the darkness demonstrated in the rest of the book."[13]

And the result? Yahweh had once promised to give Canaan "into the hands" of the Israelites (Josh 6:2; 10:8; 11:6); he had once begun to give

---

10. Webb, *Judges*, 138.

11. The mention of Joshua's 110 years (2:8) also subtly underscores the lengthy service of Yahweh that this leader of an earlier generation performed, making the rapid failure of the following generation all the more striking and painful.

12. Block, *Judges, Ruth*, 118.

13. Ibid.

the land "into the hands" of the Judah-Simeon alliance (Jdg 1:4). But alas, that was only a partial success (see Pericope 1: Jdg 1:1—2:5). Now we are told in 2:14 that Israel was given/sold "into the hands" of their enemies by Yahweh himself, the result of their unfaithfulness to him (2:11-13). It was no longer a coexistence of Israelites with Canaanites, the latter—divinely ordained enemies—were oppressing the former. All because of a "failure of the community to keep alive its memory of Yahweh's gracious saving acts. . . . All that follows in the book is a consequence of Israel's loss of memory" (2:10) and a lack of firsthand experience of God.[14]

2.1.2 *Forsaking the true God and following other idols have disastrous consequences.*

Judges 2:11–19 forms the paradigmatic layout of what will be discovered in each of the six major judge accounts.[15]

---

14. Ibid., 122–23.

15. Modified from Gillmayr-Bucher, "Framework and Discourse," 691–93; and Greenspahn, "The Theology of the Framework of Judges," 388. Yahweh "selling" his people into the hands of their enemies also finds mention in 11:21; 15:12, 18. And the "giving" of enemies into Israel's "hands" is also mentioned in an oracle (1:2), prophetic speeches (4:3, 14), a divine utterance (7:7), a dream sequence (7:14, 15), altercations (8:3, 7), a recital of history (11:21), a vow (11:30), and in a plea (15:18). The presence of the Spirit of God, as we shall see again, is not an indicator of Yahweh's approval of the subsequent actions of the judge so imbued; it merely reminds the readers that God is acting, whether the judge knew it or not. One also must remember that, outside of Othniel's story—he was the model judge—the rest of the stories show deviations from this paradigm, the shifts and alterations themselves being clues to the theologies of the individual pericopes.

Paradigm	Othniel	Ehud	Barak	Gideon	Jephthah	Samson
2:11 Evildoing	3:7	3:12 (×2) Continues	4:1 Continues	6:1	10:6 Continues	13:1 Continues
2:14 (×2) To enemies for X years	3:8 Sold 8 years (3:7)	[3:12] [—] 18 years (3:14)	4:2, 9 Sold 20 years (4:3)	6:1 Given 7 years (6:1)	10:7 Sold 18 years (10:8)	13:1 Gave 40 years (13:1)
2:18 Groan	3:9 Cry	3:15 Cry	4:3 Cry	6:6, 7 Cry	10:10 Cry	[—]
2:16, 18 Judge raised	3:9	3:15	[4:4, 6?]	[6:14?]	[—]	[13:2–25?]
2:18 Yahweh's support	3:10 "Spirit"	 [—]	[4:6–7?] [—]	6:16, 34 "with ..." "Spirit"	11:29 "Spirit"	13:25; 14:6, 19; 15:14 "Spirit"
2:16, 18 Fate of enemies	3:10 Given	3:30 Subdued	4:23 Subdued	8:28 Subdued	11:32, 33 Given Subdued	 [—]
2:19 Land's rest Judge	3:11 40 years Dies	3:30; 4:1 80 years Dies	5:31 40 years [—]	8:28, 32 40 years Dies	12:7 Dies	16:30 [Dies]

That 2:11–19 describes a paradigm or a pattern is clear: "everywhere they went" (2:15), "when[ever] Yahweh raised" (2:18; the temporal sense of כִּי, *ki*), and "when[ever] it came about that the judge died" (2:19; the temporal sense of בְּ, *b*).[16] The structure of 2:11–14a, the opening indictment of the Israelites, is illuminating:

		Wayyiqtol Verbs
A And the sons of *Israel* did evil in the sign of *Yahweh* (2:11a)		*and ... did evil*
B and they *served* the *Baals* (2:11b)		*and they served*
C and they forsook *Yahweh* ... (2:12a)		*and they forsook*
and they went after other gods		*and they went after*
D ... and they bowed		*and they bowed*
... and they angered *Yahweh* (2:12b)		*and they angered*
C' And they forsook *Yahweh* (2:13a)		*and they forsook*
B' and they *served* Baal and the *Ashtaroth* (2:13b)		*and they served*
A' And the anger of *Yahweh* burned against *Israel* ... (2:14a)		

---

16. In addition, Chisholm notes the sequence of *weqatal* forms in 2:18 ("[Yahweh] raised," "[Yahweh] was with . . . ," where one might have expected *wayyiqtol* forms), and a customary imperfect followed by a *weqatal* in 2:19 ("they *returned* and *acted corruptly*")—all evidences of the narrator describing a pattern or a custom (*Judges and Ruth*, 149 n.5).

Notice the interweaving of the names of deities that literarily demonstrates the Israelites' syncretism: "Yahweh" in *A, C, D, C', and A'*; and "Baal(s)"/"gods"/"Ashtaroth" in *B, D, B'*. "Israel" is symmetrically found in *A* and *A'*. Chisholm observes that the eight *wayyiqtol* verbs in 2:11-13 that depict Israel's evildoing forms a pattern: one (2:11a, summary) and seven (2:11b-13, details), suggesting a comprehensive and thoroughgoing apostasy.[17] So the central element, *D* (2:12b), though stunning, is not surprising. It was not simply a memory lapse that the Israelites suffered, in forgetting Yahweh and his great deeds (2:10); neither was it merely an inadvertent straying from the straight and narrow. Rather, it was a deliberate going after other gods *and worshiping them*![18] This was treason!

Not knowing Yahweh firsthand, Yahweh is only "the God *of their fathers*" to the current generation (2:12)—suggesting distance. But the false gods they were running after now were "the gods *of the peoples who were around them*" (2:12)—suggesting greater proximity.[19]

> The Canaanites, "the inhabitants of the land" (1:32–33), were practiced at working the land and attributed their success to the worship of these gods. The new generation of Israelites, who had known only desert life, had no such skills, but their survival now depended on adapting to their new situation as quickly as possible. What else could they do but learn from their Canaanite

---

17. Ibid., 153. Amos 1–2 has, in a similar fashion, seven judgment oracles against the nations and Judah, followed by an eighth specifically against Israel.

18. We find out in 2:19 that these depravities were the result of "stubbornness"—deliberate and rebellious acts of evil. The note in 2:17 about Israel neglecting the "commandments of Yahweh" is particularly stinging, in light of the efforts of Joshua in the previous generation to instill in his people the importance of abiding by the word of God (Josh 1:7-8; 23:6-8, 14-16; 24:26-27). The succeeding generation, then, had not only forgotten ("not known") Yahweh and his deeds (Jdg 2:10), they had forgotten his *words*, too!

19. "Baals" in 2:11 is a generic term indicating "all false divinities, powers, or numina, of either sex." "Baal and the Ashtaroth" in 2:13 are more specific, indicating the male and female components of these false gods (Sasson, *Judges 1–12*, 190). In the OT, "Baal" is often in the plural and with the article ("*the* Baals," 2:11) or with a localizing suffix (Baal-gad, Josh 11:17; Baal-hazor, 2 Sam 13:23; etc.; also see Baal-berith, Jdg 8:33; 9:4). Therefore, "Baal" is essentially a common noun, even when singular where it is likely a shorthand for Baal-*X* (where *X* = a particular place). On the other hand, "Yahweh" is always used as a personal name, and never with the article, or with a place-suffix. "In other words, according to the biblical writers the Canaanites, in contrast to Israel, worshiped many different 'Baals'"—a pluralism of deities (Webb, *Judges*, 142). The "Astharoths" (singular "Ashtoreth," a distortion of Astarte) were consorts and female counterparts of the Baals, often associated with sacred prostitution (2 Kgs 23:7). The gendering of these deities indicated their importance to fertility, particularly of land and livestock (though Baal was primarily a storm god).

neighbors? It was the way of "common sense" and "necessity." It was not the way of Yahweh, however; it was the triumph of pragmatics over principle, and a failure to trust the God who had proven himself capable of meeting their needs in the wilderness, and would surely have done so again in the land he had given them if only they had trusted him to do so. But they did not; they abandoned him . . . .[20]

In the chiastic scheme shown above, first, human actions are depicted (2:11–13): "did evil," "served" (×2), "forsook" (×2), "went after," "bowed," and "angered."[21] Then divine actions, in response to the human ones, are described (2:14–15): "burned," "gave," "sold," "was against." "Doing evil in the sight of Yahweh" (2:11a) frequently indicates idolatrous practices in the OT: Deut 4:25; 9:18 (referring to the golden calf episode); 17:2–3; 31:29 (where "work of your hands" = idols); and Jdg 2:11; 3:7; 10:6 (though the element occurs in all the narratives in Judges, only here is evildoing specifically linked to idolatry). In several of these references, one also finds the verb "angering" with Yahweh as the subject (Jdg 2:12), also frequently linked with the idolatrous practices of his people (see Deut 4:25; 9:18; 31:29; 32:16, 21). Of course, doing "evil in the sight of Yahweh" is equivalent to each Israelite doing what is "good in his own sight" (Jdg 17:6; 21:25). And so Yahweh's disgust and outrage at the progressively increasing Canaanization of his people is depicted in the repeated statement: "and the anger of Yahweh burned against Israel" (Jdg 2:12b, 14a; also 2:20a, and later in 3:8; 10:7), bespeaking deity's emotional and personal involvement with his people. A direct discourse, later in 2:20–22, opens a window into Yahweh's deep concern. Thus the whole scheme of punishment "is not caused by an automatic deed-consequence nexus." Rather, it is a sequence of Israelites' deed → Yahweh's intense emotion → Israelites' punishment. In other words, Yahweh has strong feelings towards, and an abiding personal involvement with, his people.[22] His giving the Israelites—and selling them—into the "hands" of their enemies (2:14) is equated with the "hand" of Yahweh being against them for evil (2:15): the people fall from the divine "hand" into the human "hand."[23] And, with the native hostile characters mentioned in 3:3, the entire topography of the Promised Land is seen to be filled with belligerents inimical to Israel's and Yahweh's interests: the Philistines in the

20. Ibid., 143.
21. Also see 2:19 for the Israelites' "going after," "serving," and "worshiping."
22. Gillmayr-Bucher, "Framework and Discourse," 691.
23. This was not a surprise for the Israelites, for the text makes it clear that this return of evil for evil (tit for tat) was "as Yahweh had spoken and as Yahweh had sworn to them"—they had been warned (2:15; see Deut 6:14–15; 7:4; 28:15–37; 31:16–21).

southwest,[24] the Sidonians in the northwest, the Hivites in the northeast, and the Canaanites in the southeast. The Israelites are in for a tough time, surrounded by enemies!

When the Israelites "groan" or "cry" to Yahweh, an immediate response from the latter takes place only in 2:18; 3:9; and 3:15 (see paradigm above). In the rest of the narratives, the reader is in suspense: Will Yahweh act? Clearly the relationship between God and his people deteriorates with time. Indeed, the entire paradigm, first set in 2:11–19 and then exemplified perfectly in Othniel (3:7–11), crumbles as the narration proceeds in the rest of the Body of Judges. Exum's observation is perceptive:

> Although we are led to expect a consistent and regular pattern, what happens is that the framework itself breaks down. Rather than attributing it to careless redaction, I take it as a sign of further dissolution. The political and moral instability depicted in Judges is reflected in the textual instability. The framework deconstructs itself, so to speak, and the cycle of apostasy and deliverance becomes increasingly murky.[25]

Yahweh's lack of response to the burden of his people in later narratives is because the Israelites' "cry" does not necessarily include repentance.[26] The "groaning" (and later "crying") of the Israelites in 2:18 reflects their weeping (and sacrifices) in 2:4–5—neither had any indication of being accompanied by repentance. Though שוב, *shub,* "turn back" (frequently denoting repentance in the OT) occurs in 2:19, that did not constitute repentance towards Yahweh. It was actually the other way round—a deeper plunge of the Israelites into apostasy, their "return" to *idolatry.* It was as if they had repented of Yahwism! "Indeed one could reasonably argue that the cries so described have no spiritual or theological component, but are simply 'the loud and agonized "crying" of someone in acute distress, calling for help and seeking deliverance.'"[27] This sense of "crying" sans repentance explains the repeated cycle of evildoing in Judges: they "continued to do evil" in

---

24. The mention of "Philistines" in 3:3, a puzzling addition, for these were one of several of Sea Peoples who came from Anatolia and the Mediterranean in the twelfth to eleventh centuries. and, according to 1:17–18, 34–36, in the days of Judges, Canaanites were occupying those cities that would only later be part of Philistine territory; perhaps the scene of 3:1–6 is set at a time later than 1:1–36.

25. Exum, "The Centre Cannot Hold," 412.

26. See Lam 2:18 and Isa 19:20 (repentance is seen only in 19:22). "Crying" is often paralleled with "wailing" (Isa 14:31; 65:14; Jer 25:34; etc.), and it also used in connection with the Israelites' murmuring and complaining in Exod 15:25; 17:4; Num 11:2.

27. Greenspahn, "The Theology of the Framework of Judges," 392 (citing Hasel, "זעק, *zā'aq,*" 4:115).

3:12; 4:1; 10:6; 13:1), they had *never* stopped! That, of course, makes God's compassion even more remarkable as, time and again, he sends deliverers/judges to relieve his people from their enemies (2:18; 3:9, 15; 4:6–7; 6:12, 14, 16; 13:3–5).

The rest of the book details how everything falls apart from this point, each leader worse than the previous one. This spiral downwards is visible even here at the beginning. Earlier, in 2:12, the Israelites were said to have "gone after" (הָלַךְ אַחֲרֵי, *halak 'akhare*) false gods; here, in 2:17, they have "lusted after" (or "played harlot after," זָנָה אַחֲרֵי, *zanah 'akhare*) those gods: they had gone from bad to worse![28] In fact, they were "turning aside *quickly*" from the obedient ways of their fathers (2:17), each succeeding generation "being *more* corrupt" than the previous (2:19), with a greater intentionality about their apostasy—"they did not abandon their practices or their stubborn ways" (2:19).[29] Unfortunately, Yahweh's compassion and deliverance (2:18) has no lasting effect on his people.

The last portion of Pericope 1, 2:1–5, is reflected in this pericope, in 2:20–22: both mention "covenant" (2:1, 2, 20), "fathers" (2:1, 20, 22) "obey/listen" (שׁמע, *shmʻ*, 2:20), and "not drive out" (גרשׁ, *grsh*, in 2:3; and ירשׁ, *yrsh*, in 2:21). But while in the earlier pericope, Yahweh spoke directly *to* his people through his angel (2:1–5), here in 2:20–22, he only speaks *about* them rather obliquely. The distancing is obvious. Besides, earlier, Yahweh only reminded Israel of his threat not to evacuate the inhabitants of the land (2:3); here, in 2:22, he actually decides to make good on that threat, declaring that he will "not drive out . . . any man from the nations" (2:21), not even one! It appears, from the language of 2:21—"I, also, for my part, will no longer drive out" Israel's enemies—that, since "the nation has transgressed

---

28. The metaphor of harlotry, is appropriate here: the relationship between Yahweh and Israel is frequently described in terms relating to marriage (Exod 34:15–16; Lev 17:7; 20:5–6; Deut 31:16; Pss 73:27; 106:39; Ezek 6:9). Unlike adultery, harlotry implied "habitual illicit behavior," for ill-gotten gains, and with a multiplicity of partners. One must also consider the fact that the Canaanite deities were "lusty young fertility gods," and that their cultic system often had erotic rituals and cultic prostitution. In a book whose narrative characters themselves frequently consort with prostitutes (Jdg 11:1; 16:1; 19:2) this metaphor is even more apt. See Younger, *Judges, Ruth*, 91n20; also Block, *Judges, Ruth*, 129; Butler, *Judges*, 47.

29. The phrase "turning aside quickly" occurs elsewhere in the OT only in Exod 32:8 and Deut 9:12, 16, in the context of apostasy. There is also a subtle change in the particles following the verb "to serve," from Jdg 2:11b (*B*, above) to 2:13a (*B'*): עבד את (*'bd 't*, "service *of*") becomes עבד ל (*'bd l*, "service *to*). Sasson observes that, judging from 1 Sam 4:9, the latter may suggest that the Israelites had become victims of their idolatry, in bondage to false deities—a worsening of their already sorry state (*Judges 1–12*, 190). The very posture they adopt, "bowing themselves down [or 'giving service'] to them" (Jdg 2:12) indicated the depth of their enslavement and perversion.

My covenant" (2:20), Yahweh, too, was going to hold off on his promise of giving his people success in the conquest. This announcement of the divine intention to leave Israel's opponents in the Promised Land also had other goals besides chastisement (2:6–21): it would be a "test" of Israel's adherence to Yahweh's covenant and his commandments—keeping the way of Yahweh and walking in it (2:22; also 3:4)—and it would also be a "test" of Israel's capacity for war (3:1–2). But these are not all disparate tests/purposes: it is obvious that all of these are wrapped into the single goal of God: to have his people walk in his ways.[30]

As Prologue II concludes with 3:5–6, we run into a couple of surprises: it is said that the Israelites "*served* [עָבַד, *'bd*] their gods," i.e., *all* the gods of the peoples just mentioned: Canaanites, Hittites, Amorites, Perizzites, Hivites, and the Jebusites (3:5)![31] This was a wholesale defection from Yahweh to harlotry! Talking of which, we are also surprised to spot another new datum regarding the apostasy of the Israelites: their intermarriage with the inhabitants of the lands (along with a repeated affirmation that they served other gods, 3:6)—the first time such an accusation of exogamy is brought against God's people in Judges. That was a clear violation of warnings given in Exod 34:16; Deut 7:3–4; and Josh 23:12–13. By these unsanctioned unions, societal structures would be destroyed, religious affections diluted, and Yahwistic passions adulterated. According to Chisholm, this is "the missing piece in the puzzle that explains how the compromises of Jdg 1:1—2:5 led to the outright paganism of 2:6—3:6 . . . for close alliances of this type pollute the covenant community and inevitably lead to compromise and sin."[32] One might picture the causal relationships that link Prologues I and II this way.[33]

---

30. Thus we come up with an inexplicable relationship between cause and effect: the Israelites' role in *not* removing the nations (1:1–36) was itself the cause of God *not* removing the nations (2:6–23). How divine sovereignty is linked to human responsibility is a question far beyond the capacity of any human's portfolio. Nevertheless, considering a cyclical sequence might help give this some sense: God in his foreknowledge keeps enemies in the land in Joshua's time (2:23); Israelites fail to drive them out (1:1—2:5); they cohabit with them and fall into apostasy (2:6—19); God refuses to drive out the nations any further (2:20—3:6), etc.

31. This business of serving false gods gets progressively worse as one proceeds through Judges: there is suspicion about idols in Ehud's day (3:19, 26); Gideon's father had an altar to Baal and an installation to Asherah that he sponsored (6:25); Gideon himself created an ephod, causing Israel to succumb to the lures of false gods (8:27); the situation was horrible in the time of Jephthah with a pantheon of gods in Israel's cupboard (10:6–8). And of the nefarious affairs of Micah, his mother, his Levite, and the Danites (in Judges 17–18), the less said, the better!

32. Chisholm, *Judges and Ruth*, 162.

33. Webb, *Judges*, 150.

3:5	Israelites *living* among the Canaanites	**Prologue I: 1:1–2:5**
	3:6a Israelites *intermarrying* with Canaanites	
3:6b	Israelites *serving* Canaanite gods	**Prologue II: 2:6–3:6**

Intermarriage is thus the "middle term" that demonstrates the sequence: living → intermarrying → serving. This particular sin had not been mentioned thus far; instead, what we found was the *endogamous* marriage of Othniel and Achsah, the former being the first and exemplar judge of the book (3:7–11). But the Israelites fail to follow that perfect model and lapse into harlotry, in more ways than one (2:2, 11–13, 17, 19; 3:6).

Thus Prologue I/Pericope 1 (Jdg 1:1—2:5) appears to take place before the apostasy of the Israelites. The consequence of living with the Canaanites was intermarriage, that led to the Israelites' subsequent infidelity to Yahweh. So Prologue II (2:6–3:6) is a "narrative abstract, an outline" of this progressively increasing unfaithfulness that is detailed in the remainder of the book and is contemporaneous with the accounts of the judges (Body: Jdg 3:7—16:31).[34] All that to say, forsaking God has its consequences.

2.2. *Judges 3:7–11*

THEOLOGICAL FOCUS 2.2

2   Personal experience of God produces unwavering commitment to him, with minimizing of self so as to give him glory (3:7–11).

   2.2   Faithful commitment to God gives him the glory and minimizes self (3:7–11).

NOTES 2.2

2.2   Faithful commitment to God gives him the glory and minimizes self.

The final part of Pericope 2 is the narrative of the first judge, Othniel (3:7–11). His story is launched with a formulaic report, "And the sons of Israel did what was evil in the sight of Yahweh" (3:7; also seen in the paradigm in 2:11, replicated at the beginning of the narratives of each of the major judges: 3:12; 4:1; 6:1; 10:6; 13:1). It is likely that Othniel is part of the post-Joshua generation; his label as the son of Caleb's "younger brother" (in 1:13

---

34. Ibid., 154.

and 3:9), emphasizes this generational distinction.³⁵ And thus the stories of the judges begin, with a new generation on stage.

In its details, Othniel's account corresponds precisely with the paradigm set up in 2:11–19:

Othniel	Paradigm
3:7	2:11–13 (Israel's evildoing)
3:8	2:14 (Israel sold into hands of enemy)
3:9a	2:18 (Israel's cry)
3:9b	2:16, 18 (Judge raised up for Israel)
3:10a	2:18 (Yahweh's support for the judge)
3:10b	2:16, 18 (Enemies given into Israel's hands)
3:11	2:19 (Land's rest and judge's death)

All of the stereotypical language is closely followed; there is no indication of any heroic personal action on the part of Othniel. Othniel's account does not resemble a narrative as much as it does a "pattern-fulfillment description."³⁶ No other account will follow the paradigm of 2:11–19 as closely and as unambiguously as does the Othniel narrative, the shortest one of the stories of the major judges. Othniel is depicted as an ideal judge in a far-less-than-ideal age—when the post-Joshua generation did "what was evil in the sight of Yahweh" (3:7).

Othniel, as far as we are told, has no flaws, no character deficiencies, and no idiosyncrasies that cripple him, unlike the judges who follow. In the other judge accounts, there is always mention of a personal detail of the judge in question that appears to render that individual an unlikely choice for leader: Ehud's left-handedness, Barak's timidity, Gideon's indecision, Jephthah's pedigree, and Samson's promiscuity. But not for Othniel—he, apparently, is blemishless, unless one counts his Kenizzite status: he is of foreign blood, but becomes firmly entrenched in the tribe of Judah.³⁷ "[A]lthough for the first time there is a particular enemy and a particular judge, there are no plot expansions or developments: no dialogue, no reported speech of any kind, no dramatization of events, no scenic presentations, no descriptions of any character flaws, and so on. . . . Nothing distracts the reader from the

---

35. Othniel is simply labeled the son of Caleb's "brother" in Josh 15:17.

36. Butler, *Judges*, 56–57.

37. Or perhaps Othniel's "deficiency" is that he was the son of a "*younger* brother" (1:13; 3:9). "In a society strongly influenced by primogeniture, the likelihood that the offspring of a younger (literally 'smaller' with implications of 'unimportant') brother will become the leader of the elder's descendants warrants attention" (Klein, *The Triumph of Irony*, 34).

clear message of God's intervention through the deliverer . . . he raises up."[38] Thus any future deviation from the paradigm and its parade example, Othniel's account, will be significant. "It is almost as if the narrative immediately presents us with an example of what the coming story about the judges will *not* look like."[39] So all we have in 3:1–7 is a verbally frugal, narratively skeletal story of a man faithful to his God, bringing about good for his people. Perhaps that *is* the best kind of leader, the one without flashy pyrotechnics or glaring flaws. If only all the judges had been like Othniel, responsibly setting things straight, zealously striving for Yahweh, warring in the might of Yahweh's Spirit, and bringing about rest for the land. But, alas, 3:12 shows us what happens after this worthy judge: "And the sons of Israel continued to do evil in Yahweh's sight." After Othniel, each judge account seems to be disintegrating, at least from the perspective of the paradigm, losing elements therefrom or, as in most cases, adding more insalubrious details of the evildoing of the Israelites, the turpitude of the judge, the oppression of the enemies, and the deplorable state at the demise of the particular leader.

Despite the strict adherence to the paradigm, 3:7 does introduce yet another new facet of the Israelites' evildoing: "they *forgot* Yahweh their God." This failure of memory, of which they had been warned in Deut 6:12 and 8:11, seems to have been the cause of all their transgressions—evildoing and serving Baals and the Asheroth (hinted also in Jdg 2:10–11: this new generation did not know Yahweh or his deeds, and that led them to evildoing and serving Baals). "To forget the Lord involves neglect of his covenant demands, ingratitude for his blessings, and a self-sufficient attitude. This in turn opens the door to idolatry."[40] It seems that forgetting Yahweh made them remember Baals! Because the Israelites "served" the Baals and Asheroth (3:7), they were made to "serve" the king of Mesopotamia, Cushan-rishathaim (3:8).[41] The impact of his name and its etymology echoes in this brief narrative: "Cushan-rishathaim" occurs twice in 3:8 and twice in 3:10 (also repeated is "king of Mesopotamia," 3:8, 10); "Othniel," too, occurs only twice in the cameo (3:9, 11). But one notices that "Yahweh" occurs seven times in just five verses. So this narrative turns out to be primarily not about Othniel, but about Yahweh, himself. Indeed, in no other judge narrative is the role of God so clearly depicted; no other story does Yahweh permeate as fully as he does this one.

38. Younger, *Judges, Ruth*, 100.
39. Polzin, *Moses and the Deuteronomist*, 156.
40. Chisholm, *Judges and Ruth*, 168–69.
41. "Cushan-rishathaim" is likely to have been a pseudonym, for it could mean "Cushan-the-Twice-Wicked" (רִשְׁעָתַיִם, *rish'atayim*, being the dual form of רֶשַׁע, *rsh'*, "wickedness").

Yahweh's support, an element of the paradigm, also shows up in an unusual way for the first time: "And Yahweh's Spirit came upon him" (3:10). In the paradigm, this is reflected in the notice that "Yahweh was with the judge" (2:18), but the coming of the Spirit upon Othniel (and on some of the other judges) indicates a dramatic and dynamic involvement of Yahweh with his chosen deliverer.[42] Underlining this support are textual clues: Othniel's actions (in *wayyiqtol* verbs) is three times preceded by God's primary action:

	God's Action	Othniel's Action
3:9bc	Yahweh raised up a deliverer ...	"And he delivered them—Othniel ..." וַיּוֹשִׁיעֵם, *wayyoshi'em*
3:10ab	Yahweh's Spirit came upon him ...	"And he judged Israel" וַיִּשְׁפֹּט, *wayyishpot*
3:10de	Yahweh gave ... into his hand ...	"And his hand *was strong* over ..." וַתָּעָז, *watta'az*

Othniel sets the standards by which all other judges must measure themselves. Othniel places the tribe of Judah at the head of the list of deliverers just as it stood at the head of the list of tribes who would go up to conquer for Yahweh (1:1–2). Othniel lets God remain in center stage. Othniel delivers Israel after only eight years of oppression. Othniel does nothing to intrude his own personality, his fears, his doubts, or his greed into the narrative.... The book of Judges should reflect a boring string of framework narratives like this. Instead it has to add the many stories of disobedience and ego.[43]

While the role of all the judges was to deliver their people (a notion introduced in the paradigm in 2:16, 18), only the first two judges, Othniel and Ehud actually are labeled "deliverers" (as a noun: 3:9, 15; the verb form is used of other judges, both major and minor: 3:31; 6:14, 15; 8:22; 10:1; 13:5). This sets these two apart from the ones who followed them. The unraveling has commenced!

The result of Othniel's leadership is four decades of rest for the land—and this after a single-sentence report of a battle against one who was "doubly wicked"! The attainment of rest was a major goal of the conquest as Josh

---

42. However, this does not necessarily reflect on the particular judge's uprightness or the moral probity of his subsequent actions, Samson being a case in point.

43. Butler, *Judges*, 66.

11:23 and 14:15 indicate. But this is possible only when the leader is raised and empowered by God and aligns himself to divine purposes, eschewing self-aggrandizement, faithlessness, and fear. "Othniel, who lives in Israel after the death of Joshua and the elders who outlived Joshua, models true judgeship for all who follow him in that position. There never is another Joshua, a survivor of a faithless generation, and there never is another Othniel, a survivor of a faithful generation."[44] His faithful commitment to deity glorifies God and minimizes himself.

SERMON FOCUS AND OUTLINES

THEOLOGICAL FOCUS OF PERICOPE 2 FOR PREACHING[44]

2 Personal experience of God produces unwavering commitment to him and gives him glory (2:6—3:11).

The negative side of "personal experience of God" is what is depicted in this pericope—the failure to experience God firsthand. Did the prior generation have a role in this? Were they negligent in some way? This pericope does not address the issue, but specific application could conceivably go in that direction: those who have experienced God firsthand are responsible to teach the next generation to do so themselves. Or the application could be an exhortation to the people of God to experience God personally, firsthand, themselves: perhaps this includes remembering the deeds of God in one's own life (or in the corporate life of the church), etc.

Possible Preaching Outlines for Pericope 2

I. Forgetting God
   Failure to experience God firsthand: new generation (2:6–10)
   Missing the blessings of God: the cycle/spiral of failure (2:11–19)
   Divine punishment (2:20—3:6)
   Move-to-relevance: How God's people forget him; the consequences
II. Following God
   Importance of experiencing God firsthand: old generation (2:6–10)

---

44. Hamilton, *Handbook on the Historical Books*, 113.

45. In the view of preaching espoused in this commentary, the exposition of the theology of the pericope (represented as a statement by the "Theological Focus"), with all the power and potency of the text, is the critical task of the homiletician. Needless to say, the preacher must also provide the congregation with specifics on how the theological thrust of each pericope may be put into practice so that lives are conformed to Christlikeness in the power of the Spirit, for the glory of God.

       Othniel's parade example: minimizing self (3:7–11)
       Move-to-relevance: The blessings of God for following him[46]
 III. *Experience God!*
       How we can experience God firsthand
       How we can teach the next generation to do so

A rearrangement of the outline above gives us this:

  I. LESSON: Forgetting God vs. Following God
       Failure to experience God firsthand: new vs. old generation (2:6–10)
       Missing the blessings of God: the cycle/spiral of failure (2:11–19)
       Divine punishment (2:20—3:6)
       Move-to-relevance: How God's people forget him; the consequences
 II. EXAMPLE: Othniel
       Othniel's parade example: minimizing self (3:7–11)
       Move-to-relevance: The blessings of God for following him
III. APPLICATION: *Experience God!*
       How we can experience God firsthand
       How we can teach the next generation to do so

---

46. That God is pleased with the obedience and righteousness of his people is an essential biblical concept. See Kuruvilla, *Privilege the Text!* 253–58.

PERICOPE 3

Ehud (and Shamgar)

Judges 3:12–31

[Ehud's Lack of Integrity; Shamgar the Foil]

REVIEW, SUMMARY, PREVIEW

Review of Pericope 2: In Jdg 2:6—3:11 (Prologue II and the Othniel story), the religious decline of the Israelites is detailed—the infidelity of the post-Joshua generation of Israelites. Things spiral from bad to worse, creating a paradigm that reflects this descent in each of the subsequent judge stories. Othniel, the first judge, however, is a parade example of a godly leader, whose story follows the paradigm precisely. With divine aid, he becomes Israel's deliverer.

Summary of Pericope 3: The third pericope of Judges (3:12–31) depicts the second major judge in the series, Ehud. His duplicitous words and deceptive actions are subtly deprecated in his story: his left-handedness is suspect; his meticulously planned skullduggery is disfavored; he is equated to Joab, and with excrement. And, finally, the cameo of Shamgar makes this minor judge a foil for the major judge who lacks integrity. With the implicit disapproval of Ehud's actions and the approval of Shamgar's, integrity in leadership forms the thrust of this pericope.

> **Preview of Pericope 4:** The next pericope, Jdg 4:1–24, is the story of Barak. Raised up by God's representative, Deborah, he refuses to fulfill his commission unless she go with him into battle, despite God's unambiguous promise of triumph. As a result of his faithless fear, Barak loses out on the honor of victory and the capture of the enemy general, Sisera, being preempted in the latter's execution by another woman, a non-Israelite, Jael.

3. Judges 3:12–31

THEOLOGICAL FOCUS OF PERICOPE 3

3 Integrity in life, driven by reverence for God and reliance upon him, receives divine approbation (3:12–31).

    3.1   God who remains ever faithful to his people is worthy of their reverence.

    3.2   Unilateral, self-reliant strategies show a lack of dependence upon deity.

    3.3   Duplicity in life, demonstrating a lack of integrity, receives God's disapprobation.

    3.4   God uses those who avoid self-reliance, duplicity, and disdain for deity.

OVERVIEW

This pericope follows the standard paradigm of 2:11–19 and simulates the ideal model of Othniel (3:7–11), though with some critical differences (see below).

Paradigm	Othniel	Ehud
2:11 Evildoing	3:7	3:12 (×2) Continues
2:14 (×2) To enemies for X years	3:8 Sold 8 years (3:7)	[3:12] [—] 18 years (3:14)
2:18 Groan	3:9 Cry	3:15 Cry
2:16, 18 Judge raised	3:9	3:15
2:18 Yahweh's support	3:10 "Spirit"	[—]
2:16, 18 Fate of enemies	3:10 Given	3:30 Subdued
2:19 Land's rest Judge	3:11 40 years Dies	3:30; 4:1 80 years Dies

Pericope 3 is carefully structured, centered on the assassination of Eglon by Ehud[1]:

    A   Negative introduction: defeat; "smite" (3:12–14)
        B   Gift "in his hand" (3:15–17)
            C   Ehud and idols (3:18–19)
                D   Assassination (3:20–22)
            C'   Ehud and idols (3:23–26)
        B'   Yahweh gives enemies "into your hands" (3:27–28a)
    A'   Positive conclusion: victory; "smite" (3:28b–30)

In this story, there is plenty of suspense, tension, intrigue, caricature, and "scatological humor."[2] Block calls it "a literary cartoon" that is "polemical and coarse."[3]

---

1. Dorsey, *The Literary Structure of the Old Testament*, 109.
2. Alter, *Art of Biblical Narrative*, 40.
3. Block, *Judges, Ruth*, 156.

3. Judges 3:12–31

THEOLOGICAL FOCUS 3

3 Integrity in life, driven by reverence for God and reliance upon him, receives divine approbation (3:12–31).

    3.1   God who remains ever faithful to his people is worthy of their reverence.

    3.2   Unilateral, self-reliant strategies show a lack of dependence upon deity.

    3.3   Duplicity in life, demonstrating a lack of integrity, receives God's disapprobation.

    3.4   God uses those who avoid self-reliance, duplicity, and disdain for deity.

NOTES 3

3.1   God who remains ever faithful to his people is worthy of their reverence.

Deviations from the model judge's account—the Othniel story—point to the less than stellar nature of the second judge, Ehud. Both leader and people evidence a lack of reverence for Yahweh.

In the Othniel and Ehud stories, there is, in each case, a single enemy king (Cushan-rishathaim and Eglon, respectively), though in the first account, Cushan-rishathaim is never the subject of a verb and so does not act, at least not literarily. Eglon, on the other hand, is active and vocal in this pericope, symbolic of his active oppression of the Israelites (3:14, 17, 19)—an oppression they deserved as punishment from God for their infidelities and evildoing. Things are quickly beginning to slip and slide away from the relative perfection of the Othniel account.[4]

Right at the start, we are told *twice* that Israel "did evil in the sight of Yahweh" (3:12). Indeed, in its first iteration in that verse, the text declares: "And the sons of Israel *continued* to do evil in the sight of Yahweh"—they

---

4. As in the Othniel account, in this narrative, too, there is only one Israelite character, Ehud. In contrast, in the accounts of the rest of the major judges, besides the protagonist judge, there is always one or more Israelite character speaking (or being spoken to) on the narrative stage: Deborah (Barak: Judges 4–5); Joash, Ephraimites, leaders of Succoth, Penuelites, and Jether (Gideon: Judges 6–8); elders of Gilead, Jephthah's daughter, and the Ephraimites (Jephthah: Judges 10–12); Samson's parents, Judahites (Samson: Judges 13–16). The multiplicity of actants and speakers, pulling one way and another—usually farther away from a Yahwistic center—reflects the progressive breakdown of the societal and religious fabric of the Israelites.

had never stopped doing evil, it seems, after they first engaged in it in 3:7. And unlike the preceding Othniel narrative, in the Ehud account there is no mention of the Israelites being "sold" into the hands of the enemy; instead we are told that Yahweh "strengthened" (חזק, *khzq*) Eglon, the king of Moab, against Israel (3:12). The verb occurs in the exodus stories, to describe God "hardening" (חזק) Pharaoh's heart (Exod 4:21; 9:12; 10:20, 27; 11:10; 14:4, 8) and that of the Egyptians (14:17). That is, of course, not a good sign.

The result of Yahweh "strengthening" the hand of the king of Moab was that Moabites "took possession" (ירש, *yrsh*) of the city of the palm trees (Jdg 3:13).[5] Once Yahweh had prohibited the Israelites from infringing upon Moabite territory, land he had given those peoples (Deut 2:9). Now the Moabites were encroaching upon land allotted to the Israelites, and with Yahweh himself behind that invasion. Evildoing has its consequences. "Taking possession" (or "driving out," also ירש), was exactly what the *Israelites* were supposed to do, and at which they had failed (see ירש in Jdg 1:19, 20, 21, 27, 28, 29, 30, 31, 32, 33; and 2:6, 21, 23).[6] Countering his own "strengthening" of the hand of the Moabite oppressor, Eglon (3:12), Yahweh then "raises up" an Israelite deliverer, Ehud (3:15). But quite surprisingly, for the rest of the pericope, Yahweh does not seem at all involved with the goings on. We are not told that Yahweh "was with the judge" (as the paradigm had it, 2:18), or that his Spirit came upon that individual (as with Othniel, 3:10). And the final victory won by the Israelites is not attributed by the narrator to any work of Yahweh, either (3:29–30).

This virtual absence of Yahweh in the story also raises suspicions about how his people, in particular his leader, regarded him. While one assumes that God's commissioning a deliverer and endowing that judge with the Spirit is a guarantee of the individual's upright behavior and exemplary life, that is not necessarily so: from Othniel to Samson, several of the judges are empowered by God and endued by the Spirit, yet there is a progressive and inexorable deterioration of behavior and morality despite this special divine intervention and/or connection. So too, here, with Ehud; his being "raised up" by Yahweh does not necessarily imply that all his actions were scrupulous and virtuous. Rather, Yahweh's curious absence from the main event of Eglon's assassination (3:16–25), as well as from the dénouement of

---

5. The "city of palm trees" is likely to have been Jericho, or near it (Deut 34:3; 2 Chr 28:15). If so, Eglon had captured a key city that Israel had taken over under Joshua (Joshua 2–6), achieving what even the capable prophet Balaam could not (Numbers 22–24).

6. Also see Josh 1:11, 15; 3:10; 8:7; 13:6; 23:5, 9, for divine utterances that exhorted and promised "possession" (from ירש) of the land.

the story, the routing of the Moabites (3:26–30), give the reader pause and raise suspicions.

In the case of Othniel's victory over Cushan-rishathaim, at the onset of Israel's military engagement with the enemy, the narrator asserted that Yahweh "gave" the enemy king into Othniel's hand (3:10). Here, however, things are more indirect: Yahweh's role in the pericope (for the only time after 3:15) is described in Ehud's voice and not by the narrator, and that as part of Ehud's exhortation to his troops *after* the assassination of the enemy king (3:28).[7] Both in Othniel's story and in Barak's, God's role in the military victory is explicitly noted by the narrator (3:10; 4:23). Here, in Ehud's story, Moab is merely the subject of a passive verb: "Moab was subdued . . . under the hand of Israel" (3:30). So, outside of Ehud's declaration in 3:28, there is no sign of Yahweh or his activity. As we will see, Ehud's self-interest, self-reliance, and duplicity preclude any involvement by deity. Apparently God is not needed in those precincts.

Another structural element underscores the disdain of Yahweh in the story. The mention of "idols" (from פָּסִיל, *pasil*) in 3:19 and 3:26 brackets the heart of the pericope—the story of Eglon's killing. These religious objects were manmade cult images; and Ehud passes by them on his way in to kill, and again as he leaves from his kill. The noun is derived from the verb פָּסַל (*pasal*) meaning to "hew/carve" (Deut 10:1, 3); in the OT פסל/פסיל always indicates hewn/carved idols.[8] Obviously these are anti-Yahwistic: Jdg 2:2, 11–13, 17, 19. Judges 3:6 had already warned of the Israelites' predilection for Canaanite gods and, indeed, 3:12 asserts that such evildoing had "continued' into the time of this narrative. "[T]he twin references to the *pĕsîlîm* articulate the decisive and dramatic core of the adventure. Everything that precedes 3:19–26 is preliminary; everything which follows is anticlimactic."[9] Bookending the critical core of the Ehud story (3:19, 26), one wonders why these idols are markers for the narrative. Where did they come from and what was Ehud doing in relation to them? "Cultic indolence," O'Connell, called it:

> The predominant deuteronomic concern, that of cultic disloyalty, remains implicit in Ehud's failure to remove from the land the twice-mentioned idols that frame the portrayal of Eglon's assassination (3:19aab and 3:26b). This failure to remove the

---

7. This is the only account in Judges in which an enemy king is killed before his army is routed.

8. In Judges, "idols" are found only in 3:19, 26 and 17:3, 4; 18:14, 17, 18, 20, 30, 31. All of the latter set are pejorative labels; obviously that is the denotation of the former set as well.

9. Mobley, *The Empty Men*, 90.

idols characterizes negatively both Ehud (as microcosm) and the tribe whom he delivers (as macrocosm) and ostensibly leads to the religious apostasy that begins the following deliverer account (cf. 4:1).[10]

Even if they were Moabite installations, it would certainly have been a lot easier to sabotage these idols than to assassinate the highest-ranking Moabite official. After all, the command to the Israelites to destroy them was unambiguous (פְּסִיל in Deut 7:5, 25; 12:3; פֶּסֶל in Deut 4:16, 23, 25; 5:8; 27:15).[11] If Ehud accomplished the murder of the king with relative ease, surely he could have done something about the idols.

But, despite this disdain for Yahweh, all is not lost. One must remember that this is only the account of the second judge, the one who immediately follows the paradigmatic model of the first judge, Othniel. So not everything has gone awry yet. Ehud, we will see, "escapes" (3:26 [×2]) after his daring single-(left)handed assassination of Eglon; but, following the attack of the Israelites, none of the Moabites "escapes" (3:29). And as the pericope concludes, Israel succeeds in overthrowing the yoke of the oppressor: though the Moabites "smite" (נכה, *nkh*) Israel at the beginning of the narrative (3:13), in the end they are the ones who are "smitten" (3:29). And, finally, the land is said to enjoy rest for eighty years, an unusually long period, the longest span of rest in Judges (the next closest is forty: 3:11; 5:31; 8:28).

All that to say, evidently Yahweh was at work, even though he seems to have been (literally) absent: there are fingerprints of providence all along.

3.2 Unilateral, self-reliant strategies show a lack of dependence upon deity.

Right at the start of the Ehud story we get a sense that something is not right. Yahweh raises up Ehud, "the Benjaminite, a left-handed man" (3:15). There is an assonant repetition of יְמִינִי, *ymini*, in בֶּן־הַיְמִינִי (*ben-haymini*, "the Benjaminite," literally "son of the *right* [hand]") and in אִטֵּר יַד־יְמִינוֹ (*'itter yad-ymino*, "bound in his *right* hand"), both relatively rare terms. The first, the gentilic or demonymous form of the tribal affiliation, בֶּן־הַיְמִינִי, is unusual and used only in about a dozen out of seventy references to Benjaminites in the OT; elsewhere it is the collective בִּנְיָמִן (*binyamin*, "Benjamin")

---

10. O'Connell, *The Rhetoric of the Book of Judges*, 84.

11. Also see 2 Kgs 17:41; 2 Chr 33:19, 22; 34:3, 4, 7; Ps 78:58; and often in the prophets.

or בְּנֵי בִנְיָמִן (*bne binyamin*, "sons of Benjamin").¹² And the only other use of אֲשֶׁר יַד־יְמִינוֹ in Scripture is in 20:16, where it is used of the Benjaminites who aid and abet wickedness.¹³ So it appears that Ehud is not all "right" (!), and is not what he appears to be or is supposed to be: he is a "son of the right hand" who is "bound in his right hand."¹⁴ His left-handedness may be a subtle disparagement.

> In many cultures, including cultures in the ancient Near East, the left hand is associated with impurity or deviance. The right is the place of honor and sovereignty, virility, strength, goodness; the left the place of vassalage, subservience, evil, and weakness. . . . [T]he left hand may not be used for eating; it is commonly associated with matters of personal hygiene that discourage its use in the preparation or ingestion of food. The left hand is expressly disfavored in ancient Israelite ritual.¹⁵

The sense of Ehud's deficiency is amplified by these negative connotations of left-handedness. In any case, 3:15 ends up depicting Ehud, the left-handed son of right-handers, as an unlikely hero who has a strange whiff about him. "[I]f the point of the wordplay is indeed to highlight a 'falling short' in a core area of one's identity, . . . can one not further extend this sense of 'falling short' and see it as subtly foreshadowing certain of Ehud's actions in the ensuing narrative?"¹⁶ It seems likely, then, that Ehud's subsequent deceptions in this story are subtly being deprecated from the very start.

> Instead of simply highlighting Ehud's left-handedness, the incongruity revealed by the wordplay may carry deeper symbolic significance in portraying Ehud as someone whose actions and choices are liable to fall short of the standard expected of him on

---

12. Wong, *Compositional Strategy*, 114–15.

13. If those Benjaminites fell far short of the expected norm of behavior as Israelites—an incongruity between action and identity that lead to the dreadful civil war (see Pericope 13: Jdg 19:1–30 and Pericope 14: Jdg 20:1—21:25)—then it is fair to say that the same incongruity and improbity is reflected, albeit in a less intense way, in Ehud, the second judge in the series, and another Benjaminite. "[T]he bizarre behaviour of these Benjaminites in Judges 20 is no isolated incident when it comes to Benjaminites. For another Benjaminite, a judge of Israel, no less, had also displayed the same propensity to act in a way that falls short of the expected norm" (ibid., 124).

14. Halpern thinks that that the left-handedness of these Benjaminites was a nurtured deviance, accomplished by literally "binding" the right hand, to give such warriors an advantage over others in a sword-and-shield battle ("The Assassination of Eglon," 35).

15. Miller, "Verbal Feud in the Hebrew Bible," 112–13. See Exod 29:20; Lev 7:32; 8:23.

16. Wong, *Compositional Strategy*, 117.

the basis of who he is. Thus, if the choice of Ehud is surprising, it is surprising not only because his restriction in the right hand obviously fell short of the norm expected of a "son of the right-handers," but also because the tactics he used likewise fell short of the standard expected of a deliverer raised up by YHWH.[17]

The anomaly of a member of a right-handed tribe being a left-handed man seems to be hinting at the theological oddity of a deliverer raised up by Yahweh (3:15) resorting to underhanded tactics.

It is striking that a unilateral human endeavor without any input from deity is undertaken to solve the eighteen-year-long thorny problem that Eglon and Moab posed for the Israelites. Such an attitude, showing independence from Yahweh, is suggested by the phrase in 3:16, וַיַּעַשׂ לוֹ אֵהוּד חֶרֶב (wayya'as lo 'ehud khereb), "Ehud made *for himself* a sword," seeing לוֹ as reflexive, "for himself." There is no inquiry of Yahweh, no input from Yahweh, no imperative from Yahweh. And the sword is *for himself,* not for tribe, nation, or deity. This, in itself, is not necessarily negative, but in light of Yahweh's invisibility throughout the account, it certainly is suspicious.

The judge/deliverer then goes to great lengths to prepare for his lethal meeting with the oppressor-in-chief, ostensibly to present a tribute (3:15, 18). Ehud manufactures a weapon fit/appropriate for the corpulent Eglon (3:17, 22): its length is stressed—a "cubit" long (about 12–18 inches)—"custom-designed for Eglon: short enough to conceal; long enough to do him in."[18]

The hand-motif recurs in this narrative. For starters, as we have seen, Ehud is "a left-handed man" (אִישׁ אִטֵּר יַד־יְמִינוֹ, *'ish 'itter yad-ymino*), and the tribute to Eglon is "sent" (שלח, *shlkh*) "by his hand" (בְּיָדוֹ, *byado*, 3:15). At the climax of the story, Ehud "stretches" (שלח) his "hand" (יָד, *yad*) to consummate his regicide (3:21). The narrative concludes with a statement that Moab was subdued that day under the hand (יָד) of Israel (3:30).[19] The hand of Ehud and the hand of Israel monopolize the story, with but a single mention by Ehud about Yahweh giving the Moabites into the "hand" (יָד) of the Israelites (3:28).

And what of 3:28, itself—was that an unadulterated sign of reliance on Yahweh by Ehud? Thus far, there has been "no hint of any spiritual sensitivity in Ehud's heart nor any sense of divine calling. On the contrary, Ehud operates like a typical Canaanite of his time—cleverly, opportunistically,

---

17. Ibid., 119–20.
18. O'Connell, *The Rhetoric of the Book of Judges,* 89 n.48.
19. There is also the paronomasia of Ehud's sword "thrust" (תקע, *tq'*) into Eglon's belly (3:21), and his "blowing" (also תקע) a trumpet to muster his troops (3:28).

and violently, apparently for his own glory."²⁰ Nonetheless, Ehud's declaration in 3:28, in the perfect tense, that "Yahweh has given your enemies the Moabites into your hands," is significant (see similar assertions in 4:14; 7:14–15: all creditable utterances).²¹ While he has employed deception in his assassination (see below), he is not completely lacking in faith or in knowledge of the Almighty. Remember, the slippage of the judges has only begun with Ehud and, as the first to follow Othniel's perfect footsteps, one does not expect to see him depicted with too much negativity. Both Othniel and Ehud were, after all, raised by Yahweh (3:9, 15—the only two judges who are called "deliverers," using a substantival participle), and both brought rest to the land (3:11, 30).²²

But notice this: While it is quite appropriate that Ehud, after the assassination and the summoning of his troops, orders them, "Follow after *me*" (3:28, where he also invokes Yahweh), one again gets the sense of a self-focused individual.²³ He appears intent on using himself as a model primarily, with his army following him; he supports his exhortation with Yahweh's name only secondarily.

> [T]he subsequent growing concern of the Judges compiler/redactor with the leadership qualities of Israel's deliverers leads one, in retrospect, to inquire whether Ehud's characterization

---

20. Block, *Judges, Ruth*, 171. In Pericope 4 (Jdg 4:1–24), one may say the same about Jael, who also assassinated an enemy leader by deceiving him. But the striking difference between her and Ehud is the total lack of premeditation on her part: her victim came to her door, she improvised on a weapon, and she is depicted as a foil for the faltering and fearful hero, Barak. Ehud, on the other hand, had his tactics all planned out. A better comparison with Ehud—and clearly deliberate on the part of the narrator—is Shamgar (see below). Again, it must be stressed that more than the historical actions of the characters (the *world behind the text*), it is the way in which those actions are depicted—i.e., how the narrative is written, focused, and directed (the *world in front of the text*)—that determines the theological thrust of the text, and therefrom, the application of a sermon on that text.

21. Such an idiom was also used by God himself: Jdg 1:2; 7:9.

22. Chisholm, who advocates the view that Ehud is entirely positive in this narrative, has noted the parallels between Ehud and David: collocations of שָׁלַח יָד and לָקַח חֶרֶב (*shalakh yad*, "sending/stretching the hand," and *laqakh khereb*, "taking the sword," Jdg 3:21; 1 Sam 17:49, 51: the only places they occur together in the OT); Yahweh "giving [the enemy] into your hand" (Jdg 3:28; 1 Sam 17:47); and "falling to the ground" (Jdg 3:25; 1 Sam 17:49). Yet the differences are considerable, primarily David's almost incessant acknowledgement of the role of Yahweh before his killing of Goliath (1 Sam 17:26, 36–37, 45–47), completely absent in Ehud's story, except for the exhortation to his troops in 3:28, *after* the coup has been accomplished. See Chisholm, "Ehud: Assessing an Assassin," 280.

23. With 3:27 placing Ehud in front of his troops, the command in 3:28 is clearly to follow him, Ehud, not the Moabites, who had not yet mustered.

as a self-promoting saviour is an intended nuance. While Ehud claims Yhwh's guarantee of success in 3:28ab on the basis of his foregoing success, there is something implicitly self-authenticating about it, for by no explicit means had Yhwh disclosed this to any character in the story world.[24]

Besides, in the case of Gideon, his sharing of victory laurels with Yahweh is subsequently proven to be born of arrogance and conceit (8:17, 20). So much so, one wonders if the narrator's subtle disparagement is also reflected in the absence of any statement at the end of the narrative that "Ehud judged Israel for X years." Only Gideon shares that dubious distinction. Even Samson has a statement to this effect.

3.3 Duplicity in life, demonstrating a lack of integrity, receives God's disapprobation.

After presenting the Israelite tribute to Moab, Ehud leaves, only to return to the king (3:19). Ehud speaks twice to Eglon, employing a mere six words total: "I have a secret *message* [דבר, *dbr*, also 'thing'] for you, O king" (3:19), and "I have a *message* [thing] from God for you" (3:20). Clearly the utterances were intended to deceive: Eglon expected a "message," but Ehud gave him a "thing" (the sword). Thus "the duplicity of both speeches' use of דבר may play on a key feature of Ehud's sword—its double-edgedness."[25] The tool Ehud fashioned for the assassination was a "sword of (two) mouths," i.e., a two-edged sword (3:16; for an identical Greek term, see Sir 21:3; Heb 4:12; Rev 1:16; 2:12). Berman concludes: "[T]he double-, or multi-edged sword, which we find . . . in the biblical, apocryphal and pseudepigraphal literature, always bears a metaphorical or figurative meaning pertaining to orality. In all but one case, the 'sword of [two] mouths' stands as a trope for the potency of speech."[26] In any case, "sword" and "mouth" are linked frequently: "by edge of the sword" is literally "by the mouth of the sword" (לְפִי־חָרֶב, *lpi-khareb*; see Jdg 1:8; 25; 4:15, 16; 7:22; 18:27; 20:37, 48; 21:10; and elsewhere in the OT). All that to say, there is intentional duplicity here. And so the sword is doubly concealed—physically, under Ehud's cloak (3:16), and verbally, by referring to it as a "message/thing" (3:3:20). The lin-

---

24. O'Connell, *The Rhetoric of the Book of Judges*, 97–98.

25. Ibid., 91 n.52.

26. Berman, "The 'Sword of Mouths,'" 292–93; also see Wong, *Compositional Strategy*, 121–22. "Sword of mouths" is found in Ps 149:6 and Prov 5:4. "Sword" can denote, or be parallel to, speech (Ps 57:5; Isa 49:2): swords open (Ps 37:14; Ezek 21:33); they devour/eat (Deut 32:42; 2 Sam 2:26; 11:25; Isa 31:8; Jer 12:12; 46:14; Nahum 3:15); and are satiated (Isa 34:5; Jer 46:10).

guistic parallels between Ehud's preparation and his assassination of Eglon are also notable[27]:

	Preparation		Assassination
3:15	וַיִּשְׁלְחוּ ... בְּיָדוֹ מִנְחָה *wayyishlkhu ... byado minkhah* "And they *sent* ... tribute by his *hand*"	3:21aα	וַיִּשְׁלַח אֵהוּד אֶת־יַד שְׂמֹאלוֹ *wayyishlakh 'ehud 'et-yad smo'lo* "And Ehud *sent* [out] his left *hand*"
3:16a	וַיַּעַשׂ לוֹ ... חֶרֶב *wayya'as lo ... khereb* "and he made for himself ... a *sword*"	3:21aβ	וַיִּקַּח אֶת־הַחֶרֶב *wayyiqqakh 'et-hakhereb* "and he took the *sword*"
3:16b	עַל יֶרֶךְ יְמִינוֹ *'al yerek ymino* "on his *right thigh*"	3:21aγ	מֵעַל יֶרֶךְ יְמִינוֹ *me'al yerek ymino* "from his *right thigh*"

This was a carefully plotted undertaking, intended to deceive and to kill. The undercurrent of a perfidious plot is detected in the very commencement of the story, with the tribute literally hiding (sandwiching) a plot to murder.

    A   Tribute sent by the hand of Ehud (3:15)
        B   Ehud makes a sword and hides it (3:16)
A'   Tribute presented by Ehud (3:17)

Ehud's use of deception is a significant part of the development of the story: he conceals his weapon on his right thigh, because of his left-handedness (3:16); he makes an innocent first visit to allay suspicion and, subsequently, a second one for his tactical and homicidal operation (3:18, 19); he leaves his weapon in the stout Eglon's belly and lets the man's fat close around it, preventing any blood stains getting on his person (though fecal matter did seep out—the smell of which apparently fooled the king's courtiers, 3:22; see below); and he locks the doors behind him as he makes his escape (3:23) to keep the courtiers out longer.[28] Of course, all of this could be interpreted

---

27. From O'Connell, *The Rhetoric of the Book of Judges*, 91 n.52.

28. Ibid., 91–92. Locking the doors from the outside would have been possible for Ehud, if the lock was of the "tumbler" kind (see Chisholm, *Judges and Ruth*, 188 n.40). In terms of the architecture of the murder location, it is likely that an anteroom ("vestibule," 3:23) separated the inner king's chamber ("roof chamber," 3:20, 23, 24, 25) from an outer servants' waiting area (room? courtyard?). It is also likely, going by the servants' wrong assumption in 3:24, that the king's chamber had a toilet for Eglon's use. Ehud kills the king (3:21–22), exits the king's chamber into the vestibule, locks the

positively as Ehud's actions undertaken with a trust in Yahweh's ability to give him victory.[29] But, again, the absence of Yahweh in these transactions is a hint of pejoration from the narrator's quill.

The action is fast-forwarded from the moment the king rises to greet Ehud the second time around (3:20)—eight *wayyiqtol* verb forms cascade through 3:21–23 as the assassination is accomplished: Ehud stretched, he took, he thrust, the handle entered, the fat closed, he did not draw out, excrement (implied) came out, Ehud came out, closed the doors, and locked them (וַיִּשְׁלַח, וַיִּקַּח, וַיִּתְקָעֶהָ, וַיָּבֹא, וַיִּסְגֹּר, וַיֵּצֵא, וַיֵּצֵא, וַיִּסְגֹּר; *wayyishlakh, wayyiqqakh, wayyitqa'eha, wayyabo', wayyisgor, wayyetse', wayyetse', wayyisgor*)![30] He knows what he is doing—it is intentional, deliberate, and delivered with malice aforethought. "Taken together therefore, the unexpected left-handed 'son of the right-handers' wielding a double mouthed weapon would constitute a fitting symbolic introduction to an incongruously deceptive deliverer who would attempt an assassination with the help of verbal double entendres."[31]

There is yet another argument for seeing Ehud negatively in this story: the parallels between Ehud and Joab—their respective assassinations are remarkably similar.[32]

---

door to the king's chamber behind him (3:23), and exits from the vestibule into the outer servants' area and leaves the palace (3:24a, 26). The courtiers, considering Ehud's business with the king finished, enter the vestibule but are stymied by the locked door (and the smell of excreta) (3:24bcd, 25a).

29. And, no doubt, these positive outcomes were the results of Yahweh's sovereign provision.

30. If the sword was of the kind without a hilt, its going in, handle and all (3:22), is a plausible account.

31. Wong, *Compositional Strategy*, 123.

32. Idem, "Ehud and Joab," 404–5.

EHUD	JOAB
Assassinates Eglon (Jdg 3:15–22)	Assassinates Abner and Amasa (2 Sam 3:27; 20:8–10)
Sword in the *belly* (בטן, *btn*, Jdg 3:21–22)	*Sword* in the *belly* (דמש, *dmsh*, 2 Sam 3:27 [see 1 Kgs 2:32]; 20:10)
Deception involving *speech* (דבר, *dbr*, Jdg 3:19)	Deception involving *speech* (דבר, 2 Sam 3:27)
Carriage of weapon (חגר [*khgr*, girded], מד [*md*, garment], Jdg 3:16)	Carriage of weapon (מד, חגר, 2 Sam 20:8)
Disembowelment (Jdg 3:22)	Disembowelment (2 Sam 20:10)

Scripture clearly is disapproving of Joab's actions: see 2 Sam 3:28–39; 1 Kgs 2:5–6, 31–32. That there was a deliberate attempt to link Joab's killing of Amasa with Ehud's killing of Eglon seems evident. The elaborate details of Joab's attire (2 Sam 20:8) seem to be quite unnecessary, unlike in the case of Ehud where covertness was critical. Also, it is Joab's left hand that delivers the *coup de grâce* (his right hand held Amasa's beard, 20:9), though it would not have mattered to the story had Joab held Amasa's beard with his left hand and thrust the sword in with his right; for Ehud, his other-sidedness helped him smuggle in a weapon. The notice of Amasa's disembowelment (20:10) also seems somewhat adventitious; that of Eglon was crucial to Ehud's escape cloaked in nasty odors. All that to say, Joab's actions seem to have been described with an intentional allusion to Ehud's.

> If Joab's two assassinations are indeed meant to be understood negatively . . . one can infer that there must have been aspects of Ehud's assassination that were also viewed negatively by the author of the Joab accounts. And since the allusions seem to concentrate especially on the use of deception, one can only conclude that this use of deception by Ehud must have been what was viewed negatively by the author of the Joab accounts. . . . [T]his negative view of Ehud's use of deception must have been sufficiently well established among contemporaries of the author of the Joab accounts for him to simply make the allusions without having to worry about his audience missing the point. What this seems to suggest is that a negative view of Ehud's use of deception may have early intra-biblical support.[33]

33. Ibid., 409–10. Chisholm, countering Wong's case, observes that there are similarities between Ehud's assassination of Eglon and Jael's of Sisera (see Pericope 4: Jdg

Thus it all seems to be a conscious attempt to draw parallels between one deception and another, equating the negative evaluation of one with that of the other.

Altogether, Ehud does not fare very well in the narrator's reckoning, and that is cleverly expressed in a carefully constructed text that plays on who and what is going in and out in 3:19–24.

>   A   Courtiers "go out" (יצא, *yts'*, 3:19)
>   B   Ehud "goes in" (בוא, *bo'*, 3:20)
>   C   Sword "goes in" (3:22a)
>   C'   Excrement "goes out" (3:22d)
>   B'   Ehud "goes out" (×2; 3:23a, 24a)
>   A'   Courtiers "come in" (3:24b)

The "going out" and "going in" of courtiers and Ehud, dagger and excrement, are neatly arranged in concentric fashion, centering on the assassination proper: dagger goes in and excrement goes out (*C, C'*, 3:21). Notice that Ehud "goes in" and the sword "goes in" (*B, C*)—the implement and its maker/carrier/user are identified with each other: both "go in." But Ehud is also set in parallel with excrement: *both* "go out" (*C', B'*)! This parallelism between fecal matter going out (3:22d) and Ehud going out (3:23a) indicates the narrator's scatological regard for Ehud's duplicitous activities. Also notice the syntactical and assonant parallels between the two goings out:

3:22d	הַפַּרְשְׁדֹנָה		וַיֵּצֵא
	haparshdonah		*wayyetse'*
	"through the anus/opening"		"and it went out"
3:23a	הַמִּסְדְּרוֹנָה	אֵהוּד	וַיֵּצֵא
	hammisdronah	*'ehud*	*wayyetse'*
	"into the vestibule"	"Ehud"	"and he went out"

4:1–24): both "drive" weapons into their victims' bodies (תקע, *tq'*, 3:21; 4:21); and the demise of these enemies are described similarly: "Behold, their master falling to the ground, dead" (3:25) and "Behold, Sisera falling, dead" (4:25) (*Judges and Ruth*, 196–97). One may rebut this by arguing that, unlike Ehud's act, Jael's was entirely unpremeditated. Nonetheless, the parallels here are valid, and show that Ehud's killing of the foreign king was indeed a welcome end to an oppressive regime. In sum, it is the whole gestalt of the Ehud account that renders this judge in a negative light—but not *entirely* negative; after all, he is but the second judge on the downhill slope of judgeships. In any case, here is a judge who is showing clear signs of not being utterly committed to Yahweh, signs that are muted, but surely present. Then, of course, there is Shamgar who, in my reading, starkly shows up Ehud for his failures (see below).

There seems to be a deliberate effort to create wordplays between the exit of Ehud and the egress of feces![34] "[T]he repetition of the verb ['go out'] in such different contexts, underscored by a cluster of consonance, assonance and word stress in the concluding word of each clause, does warrant attention.... Ironic, the comparison is not honorable to Ehud."[35] No, this is not a very positive depiction of the Israelite deliverer—not at all.

Yet there can be no doubt that this account also mocks both the Moabite king (Eglon = "fat calf"[36]) and his courtiers who are completely taken in by Ehud's sleight of hand. After Ehud's decampment, they fail to enter Eglon's private room, thinking that their lord was relieving himself—the stench of the intestinal detritus seeping out of the stab wound (or the anus, with an involuntary relaxation of the sphincter) no doubt was the cause of this misdirection (3:22, 24).[37] And so Eglon's people "delayed" in

---

34. Barré, "The Meaning of PRŠDN," 8–9. The *hapax legomenon* הַפַּרְשְׁדֹנָה (3:22) has caused considerable confusion. O'Connell's explanation makes the most sense, seeing פַּרְשְׁדֹן as "anus" (from an Akkadian cognate meaning "hole, opening"; Koelher, *et al.*, "פַּרְשְׁדֹן*," 978), with the final ה, *h*, being an ה-locative ("at/through the anus"). Thus וַיֵּצֵא הַפַּרְשְׁדֹנָה would mean "and it went out through the anus." (Of course, the "opening" may as well have been that created by Ehud's sword perforating the descending colon.) But this leaves the subject missing. "[I]n view of the obviousness of the subject and the evocative force of innuendo (both פרשׁ [*prsh*] 'faecal matter' and צאה [*ts'h*] 'filth, excrement' are paronomastically echoed in ויצא הפרשדנה), its ellipsis need hardly offend us. The difficult ויצא הפרשדנה (3:22b) may therefore mean, 'and it [i.e. "excrement"] went out the anus.'" See *The Rhetoric of the Book of Judges*, 93 n.54.

35. Klein, *The Triumph of Irony*, 38–39.

36. The name "Eglon" is, like "Cushan-rishathaim" in 3:8, a label of ridicule; it recalls עֵגֶל, '*gl* = "calf" (see Exod 32:4, 8, 19, 20, 24, 35, for the golden "calf"), or עֶגְלָה, '*glh* = "heifer" (Jdg 14:18), making Eglon calf-like or bovine. No doubt there is a subtle link with עָגֹל ('*gl*, "round/rotund") as well. His corpulence is clearly attested—"very fat" (3:17; the adjective "fat," בָּרִיא, *bari*', is often used of "fat" cattle: Gen 41:2, 4, 5, 7, 18, 20; 1 Kgs 4:23; Ezek 34:20; Zech 11:16). Perhaps Eglon's obesity is also to be linked with the Moabites' eighteen-year-long oppression of the Israelites (Jdg 3:14), as they live off the fat of the land. "Fat" shows up again in the story, with a different word: it envelops the blade of Ehud's weapon thrust into the belly of the "fat calf" (3:22). Subsequently, the defeated Moabites are described as כָּל־שָׁמֵן וְכָל־אִישׁ חָיִל, *kal-shamen wkal-'ish khayil*, "all stout and all valiant men" (3:29). The word שָׁמֵן, like בָּרִיא ("fat") applied to Eglon in 3:17, is an antonym of רָזֶה (*razeh*, "lean") (see Num 13:20 and Ezek 34:20). Webb notes, therefore, that שׁמן "in this context is capable of the same kind of *double entendre* as the word 'stout' in English" (*Judges*, 166). The verb form of the noun also indicates a dulling of heart (Isa 6:10), adding insult to the injury of Eglon and his cohorts here. Physically and mentally, they are no match for Ehud and his crew.

37. The courtiers thought Eglon was "relieving himself" (3:24)—literally: "he was covering his feet" (having dropped his garments?)—an euphemism for excretion. Or, "feet," here may be a euphemism for genitalia (as in Deut 28:57; Isa 7:20).

the vestibule,[38] "till they were embarrassed" (3:25), daring not to disturb their lord in his privy.

Thus, the tribute/offering *to* Eglon (3:15, 17), ends up being a sacrifice *of* Eglon! There is plenty of sacrificial imagery here: the offering itself (מִנְחָה, *minkhah*, 3:15, 17, 18),[39] "to offer" (קָרַב, *qarab*, in the hiphil; 3:17, 18),[40] "to send" (שָׁלַח, *shalakh*, 3:15),[41] and even a cutting implement (3:16, 21, 22), not to mention a "very fat [בָּרִיא מְאֹד, *bari' m'od*]" "calf" (3:17), and all the "fat" (חֵלֶב, *kheleb*) that is dissected out (3:22)![42] That this fattened calf is called "king of Moab" four times (3:12, 14, 15, 17)—even Ehud calls him king (3:19)—only multiplies the irony.[43] Yet for all the skewering of Moab (at least of its king—literally!), there is a clear thread of anti-Ehud polemic detectible.

3.4   *God uses those who avoid self-reliance, duplicity, and disdain for deity.*

The one-verse note about Shamgar (3:31) is a satire in a nutshell. Both the enemy (Philistines) and the preceding hero (Ehud) are discomfited by a number of curious elements that mark his cameo. Most certainly, an oxgoad is a strange weapon with which to do war.[44] That it succeeds in "striking down" (3:31; the verb is also used in 3:13, 29) six hundred Philistines is, well, striking! The one who, ostensibly, is an ox-driver had become a warrior: clearly the man was an amateur, not a professional, at least by his choice of improvised weapon.

Equally odd are the antecedents of Shamgar. He is the son of "Anath" (also noted as such in 5:6), a Canaanite goddess ("Anath/Anat") known to be a violent warrior and the consort of Baal. She was one of the leading deities in the Canaanite pantheon, well attested in Ugarit literature. "Ben Anath" is also found in Egyptian records, in the person of a Syrian sea captain, whom Pharaoh Rameses II rewarded for his services by giving him

---

38. "Delaying" is הִתְמַהְמְהָם, *hitmahmham* (3:26), that contains the reduplication of מָה (*mah*, "what"), so "what?-what?-ing," or "dilly-dallying" or even "hemming-and-hawing."

39. The word מִנְחָה is commonly employed of grain offerings to Yahweh (Lev 2:1–15; 5:13; 6:7–16; etc.). Such an allusion adds to the pejorative depiction of the Moabites as those extracting "tribute" that rightly belonged to Yahweh.

40. See Lev 1:1–15; 2:1–14; etc.

41. See Lev 14:7, 53; 16:10, 21, 22, 26; etc.

42. See Lev 3:3–17; 4:8, 9, 19, 26, 31, 35; etc.

43. But the instant Eglon is killed, his name drops out of the story.

44. The oxgoad was likely an instrument used to train oxen to be docile: a 4–6-foot long wooden pole with a metal point at one end.

one of his daughters in marriage.⁴⁵ Our Shamgar, too, may have been Syrian, a Canaanite who lived among the Israelites and intermarried with them (1:21–36; 3:6).⁴⁶

Shamgar's mini-account is explicitly linked to Ehud's narrative: 3:31 commences with "And *after him* [Ehud]" and tells us that "he [Shamgar] *also* delivered Israel." If he, *also*, like Ehud "delivered" Israel, then Yahweh, who raised Ehud as a "deliverer" (3:15), may well have been sovereignly behind Shamgar's being raised up as a deliverer of Israel, too. Since 4:1 refers back to Ehud again, 3:31 appears to be a deliberate interpolation of Shamgar's story into Ehud's, *before* the formal conclusion of the latter's narrative, causing the reader to take a second look at this man without antecedents, without tribe, without location, and without formal weaponry or army, who "also" manages to "deliver" Israel.

From 10:11 that has Yahweh claiming to have delivered the Israelites from a number of Canaanite peoples *himself*, including the Philistines—3:31 has the only mention of deliverance from this group in Judges prior to 10:11—one may safely assume that Shamgar, the one who struck down six hundred of them, was an agent of the divine.⁴⁷ That he is said to "also deliver" Israel (3:31) seems to be adequate evidence in itself of Shamgar's connections with deity.

In short, here's a foreigner whose genealogy is unknown (unlike Ehud, an Israelite, whose antecedents are pointedly provided: "son of Gera, the Benjaminite," 3:15), who has no specific characteristics of note (unlike the left-handedness of Ehud, 3:15), who, as far as we can tell, is not a leader (unlike Ehud who was appointed by the "sons of Israel" to take tribute to Eglon, 3:15), who does not muster troops to aid his endeavors (unlike Ehud, 3:27–29), who does not speak in the narrative (unlike Ehud and his double-mouthedness, 3:19), who has no fancy weapon (unlike Ehud who, strategizing carefully, fashioned for himself a cubit-long, double-edged sword, that was bound on his right thigh, under his cloak—a detailed description of his

---

45. The same Pharaoh also called another daughter *bint 'Anath* (daughter of Anath).

46. See Danelius, "Shamgar Ben 'Anath," 191. "Shamgar" (שמגר, *shmgr*) includes גר, *gr*, a hint that perhaps he was a "sojourner" (גר, *ger*) and a proselyte. Perhaps this would explain Egyptian inscriptions of the time that indicate the existence of an *'Apiru* ("Hebrew") "troop of *'An[ath]*." Analogous forms of "Shamgar" have been discovered in Nuzi texts (Block, *Judges, Ruth*, 173). "Son of Anath" has also been found inscribed on Phoenician arrowheads as an "honorific military title," rather than as a particular pedigree (Day, *Yahweh and the Gods and Goddesses of Canaan*, 134–35).

47. It is not at all accidental here that Yahweh does not list deliverance from the Moabites in his resume (10:11; that was entirely Ehud's humanly contrived operation, it seems), but includes deliverance from the Philistines (Shamgar's portfolio, 3:31)!

packing arrangements, 3:16), and who, without any obvious planning (unlike Ehud who seems to have meticulously orchestrated his multiple moves, 3:16–23), "also delivers Israel" (*like* Ehud, 3:15, for a change!). "He, *also*, delivered Israel" (3:31) is thus clearly ironic and an intended contrast with the laborious and manipulative (and godless) preparations and equipment of Ehud, not to mention his deceptive transactions. In other words, Shamgar is a *positive* foil for Ehud, a counter to the latter's negative profile—his slipping downward from the Othniel-like norm.[48]

Shamgar's mini-narrative, by the way, is the only *minor* judge account that has a detail about how he went about his martial activity—with an unusual tool. Being the first of the minor judges, perhaps he—like Othniel, the first of the major judges—is a paragon and exemplar of these lesser leaders, though unlike for most of them, we have no clue about Shamgar's biodata, marital status, children produced, death, or legacy.

SERMON FOCUS AND OUTLINES

THEOLOGICAL FOCUS OF PERICOPE 3 FOR PREACHING

3   Integrity, driven by reverence for God and reliance upon him, receives divine approbation (3:12–31).

The Theological Focus of this pericope is stated in the positive, though the example of Ehud is, of course, negative. While the pejorative notes will come through in the sermon, it is probably best to keep the focus positive.

Possible Preaching Outlines for Pericope 3

I.   Ehud's Intrigue
    Israel's evildoing, punishment, idolatry (3:12–15, 19, 26)
    Ehud, the son of the right hand, bound in his right hand (3:15)
    Ehud's duplicitous words and deceptive actions (3:16–23)
    Move-to-relevance: How we tend to act without integrity[49]

II. God's Interpretation
    Yahweh's absence
    Ehud, another Joab

---

48. Another individual who used an unusual weapon is Jael; she, too, is non-Israelite; and she, like Shamgar, is a foil for the Israelite warrior who is the protagonist in her story—Barak.

49. The "Move-to-Relevance" here (and in other outlines) is intended to keep the sermon from becoming a lecture; it serves to connect with the audience, answering their implicit question "Why are we listening to this?" Unless such moves are made often and that question answered, the sermon will remain a detached endeavor for the most part, unrelated to the audience and adrift in a sea of words.

Ehud's "going in" and "coming out" (3:19–24)
Ehud equated with excrement (3:22)
Shamgar's cameo (3:31)
Move-to-relevance: God's approval of integrity
III. Our Integrity: *Lead righteously!*
How to lead with integrity/righteousness[50]

The Ehud story is, in my opinion, a perfect one to setup as a "single-move" sermon that points out the clues to the theological thrust as one goes along in the story. By the end of this creative retelling of the narrative that points out the clues to the theology of the pericope, the theological thrust should be clear to the listener (it may or may not be explicitly stated—that is the preacher's call). One can then move to application.[51]

I. Leader without Integrity
Israel's evildoing, punishment, idolatry (3:12–15, 19, 26)
Yahweh's absence
Ehud, the son of the right hand, bound in his right hand (3:15)
Ehud's duplicitous words and deceptive actions (3:16–23)
Move-to-relevance: How we tend to act
without integrity
Ehud's "going in" and "coming out" (3:19–24)
Ehud equated with excrement (3:22)
Shamgar's cameo (3:31)
Move-to-relevance: God's approval of integrity
II. *Lead with integrity!*
How to lead with integrity/righteousness

---

50. This may be a good time to refocus on the notion that *all* God's people are called to be leaders, to some degree, in some fashion, on some stage—home, office, school, marketplace. . . . Leading with integrity in whatever sphere one is called to, is an essential part of a godly, Christlike life.

51. Far too often, sermons with points/moves/chunks turn out not to be seamless. Chunks create clunks in the preaching, not always, but often. I generally try to make the moves seamless these days; in other words, I attempt to create "single-move" sermons rather than multi-move ones. The application, of course, should be made distinct, so that section may conceivably be a second move, as shown, though that seam could also very well be rendered imperceptible. Needless to say, moves-to-relevance must be made often even in such single-move exercises.

PERICOPE 4

Barak (and Deborah)

Judges 4:1–24

[Barak's Faithless Fear and Loss of Honor]

REVIEW, SUMMARY, PREVIEW

Review of Pericope 3: In Jdg 3:12–31 we have the second major judge in the series, Ehud. His duplicitous words and deceptive actions are subtly deprecated in his story. Finally, the cameo of Shamgar makes this minor judge a foil for the major judge who lacks integrity. With the implicit disapproval of Ehud's actions and the approval of Shamgar's, integrity in leadership forms the thrust of this pericope

Summary of Pericope 4: The fourth pericope of Judges (4:1–24) forms the story of Barak. Raised up by God's representative, Deborah, he waffles in fear and refuses to fulfill his commission unless she go with him into battle, despite God's unambiguous promise to Barak of victory. As a result of his faithless fear, he loses out on the honor of capturing the enemy general, being preempted in the killing of Sisera by another woman, a non-Israelite: Jael. Barak, because of his lack of faith and courage, accomplishes nothing, wins nothing, and loses all.

Preview of Pericope 5: The next pericope, Jdg 5:1–31, comprises the Song of Deborah, a hymn extolling God's victory over his enemies. As the divine warrior proceeds into action, the call of this Song is for God's people to participate in his works, with him. Non-participants—tribes, individuals—are cursed. Participants—tribes, individuals, particularly the non-Israelite, non-male, non-warrior Jael, and even nature itself—are blessed.

4. Judges 4:1–24

THEOLOGICAL FOCUS OF PERICOPE 4

4 Reverencing God by fearless faith results in blessing, for God always remains faithful to his people (4:1–24).

    4.1 The people of God reverence him, avoiding evildoing and pseudo-repentance (4:1–3).

    4.2 God's people live by fearless faith, for God always remains faithful to his people (4:4–16).

        4.2.1 *God's people live by fearless faith.*

        4.2.2 *God always remains faithful to his people.*

    4.3 Fearless faith results in divine blessing (4:17–24).

OVERVIEW

This pericope is carefully structured, with the motif of "hand" linking its various parts.[1]

A   Israelites continue to do evil (4:1)
    B   Sons of Israel oppressed (4:2–3): Yahweh sells Israel into *"hand* of Jabin"
        C   Deborah (4:4–9): "your *hand*"; "in the *hand* of a woman" (4:7, 9)
            D   Barak and Sisera both "call" (4:10–12, 13)
                E   "Yahweh has given Sisera into your *hand*" (4:14a)
            D'   Barak and Sisera both "go down" (4:14b, 15–16)
        C'   Jael (4:17–22): "in her *hand*" (4:21)
    B'   Sons of Israel press Jabin (4:23–24): God subdues; Israel's *"hand* ... upon Jabin"
                          Song of Deborah (5:1–31a)
A'   Land finds rest (5:31b)

---

1. Table modified from Davis, *Such a Great Salvation*, 71. Note that *B* and *B'* are parallel in that in Judges 4, only here do we find Jabin referred to as "king of Canaan" (4:2, 4:23–24 [×3]); he is the "king of Hazor" in 4:17. For more on the "hand" motif, see below.

What is also immediately apparent about the whole Barak-Deborah-Jael complex is that the Song of Deborah (Jdg 5:1–31a) is "interpolated" between the declaration of the defeat of Israel's enemies (4:24) and the paradigmatic end-of-judge-story statement about the land's rest (5:31b). No other judge narrative has such an extended hymn within its structure; in fact, no other narrative story in the OT, besides the account of Exodus 14 that is put into poetry in the Song of Miriam (Exodus 15), has this prose-poetry juxtaposition (see below).

4.1. Judges 4:1–3

THEOLOGICAL FOCUS 4.1

4.1 The people of God reverence him, avoiding evildoing and pseudo-repentance (4:1–3).

NOTES 4.1

4.1 *The people of God reverence him, avoiding evildoing and pseudo-repentance.*

The Israelites have not learnt a whole lot—they are "continuing" to do evil in Yahweh's sight (Jdg 4:1). And so Yahweh sells them into the hand of Jabin, the Canaanite king (4:2), and the Israelites cry in desperation (4:3). Thus the paradigm of 2:11–19 is faithfully followed, but the next two elements are missing in the Barak narrative: the raising of a deliverer/judge and any statement of Yahweh's support for that individual. Nonetheless, there *is* a "judge" so named: Deborah (4:4, 6) and she passes on Yahweh's commission of Barak to fight Sisera and extends deity's standard promise to the deliverer: "I will give him into your hand" (4:6–7).

Paradigm	Barak
2:11 Evildoing	4:1 Continues
2:14 (×2) To enemies for X years	4:2, 9 Sold 20 years (4:3)
2:18 Groan	4:3 Cry
2:16, 18 Judge raised	[4:4, 6?]
2:18 Yahweh's support	[4:6–7?]
2:16, 18 Fate of enemies	4:23 Subdued
2:19 Land's rest Judge dies	5:31 40 years [—]

The narrative of the first judge, Othniel (3:7–11 in Pericope 2: Jdg 2:6—3:11), included the name of the enemy king, Cushan-rishathaim, but he never was the subject of a verb. The second narrative (Pericope 3: Jdg 3:7–31), dealing with the judge Ehud, also had a named enemy, Eglon who, though he was a subject of several verbs (3:19, 20, 24, 25), is never said to have oppressed or afflicted Israel.[2] Not so here, in the third judge story (Pericope 4): "He [Jabin, king of Canaan] severely oppressed the sons of Israel for twenty years" (4:3)—more than Israel's service to Cushan-risthathaim for eight years (3:8), and to Eglon for eighteen (3:14). And it was a "*severe oppression*" under the hand of Jabin's general, Sisera (4:3). Things were clearly going from bad to worse in Israel.

And so, as always, the Israelites cry to Yahweh. The reason for their cry is quite unusual this time: the precipitating factor is the advanced technology of the king of Canaan, his nine hundred iron chariots with which he oppressed Israel severely for two decades (4:3).[3] This is also surprising, given that Shamgar had just demonstrated the relative unimportance of high-tech gear, his choice weapon being an ox-goad that he employed quite successfully to deliver Israel (3:31). And just when we think Yahweh, responding to his people's cries, will raise a valiant deliverer for Israel—according to

---

2. Israel is only said to have "served" the enemy kings thus far (3:8, 14).

3. See below for more on these formidable vehicles of war.

the paradigm—we are sidetracked by the cameo in 4:4–10. The preceding judge stories had Israel's cry of distress immediately followed by Yahweh's provision of a deliverer (3:9, 15). Here, in 4:4–10, Deborah's attempted commissioning of Barak is the detailed substitution for the paradigmatic "and he raised a deliverer"-formula found elsewhere. Indeed, this episode of 4:4–10 becomes a "protested call" account.[4]

4.2. Judges 4:4–16

THEOLOGICAL FOCUS 4.2

4.2 God's people live by fearless faith, for God always remains faithful to his people (4:4–16).

4.2.1 *God's people live by fearless faith.*

4.2.2 *God always remains faithful to his people.*

NOTES 4.2

4.2.1 *God's people live by fearless faith.*

In the two prior narratives (the stories of Othniel and Ehud), after the prelude noting the evildoing of the Israelites, their oppression, and their cry, the first person to be introduced was designated with familial antecedents ("Othniel, the son of Kenaz, Caleb's younger brother," 3:9; and "Ehud, the son of Gera, the Benjaminite," 3:15). Here we literally have: "Deborah, a woman, a prophetess, wife of Lappidoth" (4:4)—her primary characteristic is her gender, then her service to Yahweh, then her spousal affiliation. And 4:4 also begins with an unusual disjunction: "Now Deborah . . . was judging Israel" (subject-verb-object order; a deviation from the normal verb-subject-object word order of Hebrew).[5] The signal is clear: something is different in this narrative—and primarily, it is the gender of the first Israelite on stage in Pericope 4.

Interestingly, only here does לַפִּיד, *lappid* (= "torch"; see Jdg 7:16, 20; 15:4 [×2], 5), have a feminine suffix, making it לַפִּידוֹת, *lappidot*. Perhaps this was her husband's actual name, with a rare feminine ending, but in any case, "Lappidoth" continues the already recurring female focus:

---

4. Block, *Judges, Ruth,* 191.

5. "A woman judging Israel . . . is at least as much an improbability in patriarchal Israel as a younger son [or the son of a younger brother: Othniel] or a left-handed warrior [Ehud]" judging (Klein, *The Triumph of Irony,* 41).

דְּבוֹרָה אִשָּׁה נְבִיאָה אֵשֶׁת לַפִּידוֹת, *dborah 'isshah nbi'ah 'eshet lappidot*. The feminine nouns and suffixes echo relentlessly: "Debo*rah*, a *woman*, a *prophetess*, *wife* of Lappid*oth*."[6] But it does not stop there; we also have a feminine pronoun and a verb suffix: "*She she*-judged Israel" (הִיא שָׁפְטָה אֶת־יִשְׂרָאֵל, *hi' shophtah 'et-yisra'el*). Altogether this is an astonishing seven-fold emphasis on the gender of the individual! With that job description, Deborah also becomes one of only two in the OT who "sat" (ישב, *yshb*) to judge the Israelites (4:5; the other was Moses, Exod 18:13–14).[7]

> Why was a *woman* judging? Were not any men available to accomplish this typically male task? Had the Calebs, Othniels, and Ehuds all disappeared? While the text does not necessarily condemn this state of affairs, the situation is definitely less than ideal and, as we shall see, indicative of a problem that becomes more apparent as the chapter and book unfold.[8]

This focus on her gender points a sly finger at the absence of men to fill such roles.

Though Deborah is called a "judge," she is never titled "deliverer" (as were Othniel and Ehud, in Jdg 3:9, 15, respectively), or said to "deliver" Israel (as do other judges: 2:16; 6:14; 8:22; 12:2; 13:5), or give "deliverance" (as with Samson: 15:18).[9] And unlike the other protagonists raised by Yahweh from relative insignificance, it is noteworthy that only Deborah was "judging Israel" *before* the battle to deliver Israel commenced. Besides, after 4:14b, for the rest of the chapter, Deborah is absent, invisible in the main military action. Instead another female achieves prominence, Jael. Deborah is also ignored in 1 Sam 12:11 LXX and Heb 11:32; both name Barak as the hero.[10]

---

6. If one goes with לַפִּיד, *lappid* = "torch," then "wife [woman] of Lappidoth" might mean "woman of fire/torch." In this case, she might have been unmarried (5:1 does not mention her spouse). That might also explain her rather dynamic initiative, unbecoming—as the rabbis concluded—of a married woman in Israel, ordering a man around (b. Meg. 14b; see below).

7. Isaiah 16:5 and Joel 3:12 have the divine or Messianic Judge seated. There were other female prophets in the OT: Exod 15:20; 2 Kgs 22:14–20 (2 Chr 34:22–28); Neh 6:14; Isa 8:3 (Isaiah's wife); Joel 2:28–29. But only men were to become *judges* (Exod 18:21–22), making Deborah's job description all the more surprising.

8. Chisholm, *Judges and Ruth*, 224.

9. That explains why there is no indication that she is "raised up" by Yahweh. Instead she, as God's representative—a prophetess (4:4)—is the one who raises up Barak, the judge (4:6).

10. The MT has בְּדָן, *bdan*, not Barak, in 1 Sam 12:11; "Bedan" is not mentioned anywhere else in the OT. The LXX and the Syriac Peshitta both have "Barak" instead. These passages deal only with the exploits of Barak's military enterprises and their success

That Barak is the one being portrayed as the judge/military deliverer (after the model of Othniel and Ehud) is clear from the verbs he and Deborah are assigned. Most of the actions performed by Deborah deal with her prophetic office: summoning, sending, speaking (Jdg 4:6, 9, 14). She does "arise," "go," and "go up" (4:9, 10), but only as she accompanies Barak; she does not engage in any unilateral action of her own. Besides, all her deeds are done pre-battle (the battle begins in 4:15). Barak, on the other hand, is the military judge-deliverer: he "calls," "goes down," "pursues," and "enters" (4:10, 14, 16, 22), all in the context of the battle. In the narrative, then, "Deborah functions more like an agent than full-fledged character, and her role seems to be restricted mainly to the conveying of YHWH's will and not much else."[11] The specific mention of Deborah as "judging," though common to a number of minor and major judges (3:10; 10:2, 3; 12:7, 8, 9, 11, 13, 14; 15:20; 16:31), is unique in that the exact nature of her activities is given (4:4–5). Hers was a non-martial and forensic kind of judging, also characteristic of Yahweh himself in 11:27, as well as of Moses in Exod 18:13–16, but unlike that of the military judge-deliverers in the rest of the book.[12]

The focus of this pericope then, is rightly on Barak as the judge-deliverer and on his failure of spirit. And while Deborah is the oracle, the stand-in for, and the prophetess of, Yahweh—she is deity's *"alter ego."*[13] This explains why Deborah, God's spokeswoman, "sends" and "summons" Barak, demonstrating an unusual authority (Jdg 4:6), and why she and her commissioning of Barak shows up in the text-space of the paradigm (of 2:11–19) usually reserved for God's raising up of a military judge-deliverer. So even though the narrative makes no mention of Yahweh's direct support (or that of his spirit) for the judge-deliverer, Deborah's status as intermediary between Yahweh and Barak, makes *her*, indirectly, "Yahweh's support (-in-person)" extended to Barak.

Thus we have come across some unusual deliverers after the judging Israelite deliverer, Othniel (the paragon; 3:10): a non-judging Israelite deliverer, Ehud (the left-hander); a non-judging non-Israelite deliverer, Shamgar (the ox goad wielder); and now a judging Israelite non-deliverer, Deborah (the only female one; 4:4)! Things have come far from Othniel's day.

---

against foreign oppressing enemies. That is not to say this general had no foibles (for which, see below).

11. Wong, *Compositional Strategy*, 243.

12. Also see Exod 18:21–26; Deut 1:16–17; 16:18–20; 17:8–13; 19:16–21; 25:1–3; etc. See ibid., 243–44. It was noted in the Introduction that the sequence of the twelve judges in the book also suggests that Barak is considered the judge in this section.

13. Block, "Deborah Among the Judges," 249. Both Barak and Sisera are failures, and shown to be inferior to their female foils, Deborah and Jael, respectively (see below).

At any event, God is undoubtedly in control here. Through Deborah, he commissions his general, Barak, gives him a strategy and, like a puppeteer, controls the enemy's movements (4:6–7). He commands Barak to "march" (מְשֹׁךְ, *mshk*, 4:6), but declares that it is he, Yahweh, who will "draw out" (also מָשַׁךְ) Sisera and his chariots and his hordes (4:7). And later, in 4:14–16, Yahweh is shown in action, defeating the enemies of Israel. The equivalence of Barak's action with that of Yahweh—both are subjects of מָשַׁךְ—makes the former the favored hero. On the other hand, Sisera is merely an object of Yahweh's action, and thus he is the anti-hero. Both Barak and Sisera will "muster" troops (זָעַק, *z'q*; 4:10. 13), both instigated by Yahweh, one directly (mediated through Deborah), the other indirectly (4:7).[14] With Deborah's charge to Barak in 4:6–7, we recognize that Barak has landed the role of the judge-deliverer that Othniel played in 3:7–11. To Othniel, Yahweh "gave" his enemy, Cushan-rishathaim, "into his hand" (3:10); to Barak came the promise that Yahweh would "give" his enemy, Sisera, "into his hand" (4:7). In the light of this unambiguous promise from deity, and in light of history, there was no reason for Barak to doubt, vacillate, or be fearful—but, unfortunately, this is exactly what he does.

So in Jdg 4:6–7, we find a male tribal leader commissioned by a female prophet to fight the enemy. That, in itself, is odd because Deborah's location "between Ramah and Bethel" (4:5) put her farther from Hazor (the location of Jabin's HQ) than Barak, in Kedesh-naphtali (4:6), would be. She who was farther from the enemy had to prod into action a deliverer who was located closer to the enemy. And he, Barak, is unwilling to execute his commission to fight unless accompanied by the prophet, Deborah (4:8).[15] And so, twice the narrator hastens to mention that Deborah "went"/"went up" with Barak (4:9, 10). He demonstrates an unusual lack of confidence, despite his explicit commissioning by Yahweh and an express confirmation of future victory over the enemy (4:6–7). And twice Deborah has to urge Barak into action, both times with a rhetorical question about Yahweh: "Has not Yahweh . . . ?" (הֲלֹא [. . .] יהוה, *halo'* [. . .] *yhwh*, 4:6, 14). Both these exhortations of the prophetess, that contain the arresting "behold!" point to divine initiative: in the first, Deborah reminded Barak that Yahweh had ordered the military expedition, and that he, Yahweh, would give Sisera and his troops into Barak's hands (4:6–7). In the second, she announces to him that Yahweh has gone out to war before him (4:14). Assuredly, divine power would be his, and divine presence would be with him. Yet Barak is faithlessly fearful.

---

14. Murray, "Narrative Structure," 169.

15. Later, he is unable to consummate victory without the "aid" of another woman, Jael.

Why is Barak fearful and faithless? It is very likely that it was Canaan's possession of those intimidating conveyances of war, iron chariots—nine hundred of them!—that scared Barak (4:3, 13).[16] But did he have reason to be intimidated? Joshua 11 describes the defeat of another "Jabin" and the razing of Hazor.[17] Joshua and his army had burned enemy chariots and disabled opponents' horses: Yahweh had proven—again—to be powerful and incomparable to any manmade weapon or utility (Josh 11:1–11).[18] That century-old evidence of divine might over human paraphernalia should have been uppermost in Barak's mind, steeling his nerve. And this narrative should then have gone from 4:7 (Barak's commission) to 4:10 (implementation of Barak's commission). But, alas, "General Lightning" (the word בָּרָק, *baraq* ["Barak"] means "lightning") blinks in doubt and flickers in fear. He was far from being a flashing bolt of power responding with alacrity to divine directives.

Interestingly, in 4:14, Deborah commands Barak, "Arise!" (קוּם, *qum*), but we never find him "arising." Instead, it is *Deborah* who has already "arisen" (קוּם, 4:9b). This seems to be a strange case of the called person refusing to be raised up by Yahweh. One remembers that an element of the paradigm of 2:11–19 missing here is the "raising up" (also קוּם) of a deliverer by Yahweh (as in 3:9, 15 for Othniel and Ehud, respectively). Now we know why this item is lacking in Barak's story—he, the deliverer, literarily (perhaps even literally) resists his being "raised up." So a woman has to "arise" instead. Therefore, as Deborah declared for Yahweh, it would be a *woman* who would get the glory for this victory against Jabin: "For Yahweh will sell Sisera into the hands of a woman" (4:9). Barak was going to miss out on the blessing of partnering in God's triumph.[19]

---

16. The nature of the "iron chariots" is not entirely clear (already encountered in 1:19). Likely these were wooden structures strengthened with thin iron plates hung along the sides and front; perhaps they had iron-reinforced wheels as well. These contraptions formed the cutting edge of military hardware, making the enemy almost invincible. The number of chariots in 4:3, nine hundred, may well be accurate. In the mid-fifteenth century BCE, Thutmose III is said to have conquered 924 chariots in the battle of Megiddo (*ANET*, 237); Amenhotep II captured 730 chariots on his first campaign, and 1,092 in his second (early fifteenth century BCE; *ANET* 246–47); Ahab of Israel, according to the Assyrians, deployed 2,000 of these units in the Battle of Qarqar (853 BCE; *ANET*, 279).

17. This "Jabin" in Josh 11:1–11 lived about a century before the narrative in Judges 4; "Jabin," then, is likely to have been a dynastic royal title rather than a proper name, like "Pharaoh."

18. Perhaps some of these Canaanites survived and reconquered, rebuilt, and repopulated Hazor. Considering the failure of the Israelites to maintain control over land they took over (Jdg 1:1—3:6, Pericopes 1 and 2), this is hardly surprising.

19. Deborah's faith-filled fearlessness is another matter, not the thrust of the text,

In neither of the two preceding judge stories in Pericopes 2 and 3 has such a commissioning of a diffident deliverer been encountered. In fact, God is not said to have uttered even a word in his raising of Othniel and Ehud as his deliverers (3:9, 15). Here, not only does Yahweh need a personal human representative on the scene to call the deliverer to account face to face, she—*she!*—has to deliver not one, but *two* explicit exhortations to goad the nerveless judge into action (4:6–7, 14), not to mention that her physical presence as God's agent had to accompany this deliverer to buttress his backbone.

Barak's faithless fear is depicted in his disregarding the message of a prophetess of Yahweh (4:4), and in his discounting Yahweh's own promise to deliver the enemy into the hand of Barak (4:7). In fact the very notion of the enemy being given into their hands by Yahweh is employed as a rallying cry by Ehud to his troops (3:28), by Deborah, later, to Barak and his army (4:14), and subsequently by Gideon to his (7:15). At any rate, Barak "goes up" with ten thousand men . . . *and Deborah*. Even though Israel had had success against the same number of enemies (ten thousand, in 1:4; 3:29), having ten thousand on his side was not good enough for Barak: he had to have Deborah with him, too (4:10).

We have briefly examined the motif of "hand" in the narrative (see figure above in the Overview section of this pericope). The story essentially begins with Israel sold into the *hand* of Jabin (4:2) and ends with Jabin pressed by the *hand* of Israel (4:24). In between, we have, so to speak, a change of hands: Yahweh first promises, through Deborah, to give "Sisera" (synecdoche for commander and army) into the *hand* of Barak (4:7), but Barak demurs in fear (4:8). So, then Yahweh declares, again through the prophetess, to sell "Sisera" (here standing for the person of the commander) into the *hand* of a woman (4:9). Later, in 4:14, Deborah asserts that "Sisera" (synecdoche for army) has been given into the *hand* of Barak. Finally, fulfilling the declaration of 4:9, Jael takes a weapon in her *hand* and proceeds to kill "Sisera" (the commander; 4:21).[20] What ought to have been an Othniel-style straightforward campaign completed in three verses—from God selling Israel into foreign hands (3:8), to God giving the foreign oppressor into Israel's hands (3:9–10)—becomes an extended narrative of twenty-three verses that intervenes between God selling Israel into foreign hands (4:2), and God giving the foreign oppressor into Israel's hands (4:24). And in this interposition, "Sisera" keeps changing hands, so to speak—all because of

---

but it surely is impressive.

20. That "Sisera" stands variously for "commander + army," "commander," and "army," is, of course, recognized only in retrospect, but that discovery adds to the literary art of the storyteller (helped by the Holy Spirit, no doubt).

Barak's cowardice, his faithless fear that would cost him honor and divine blessing.

Barak's hesitation and its consequence take center stage in his commissioning by Deborah (4:6–9).

- **A**   Barak summoned from "Kedesh-naphtali" (4:6a)
- **B**   Barak commissioned:
  "Yahweh," "go," "Sisera," "into *your* hand" (4:6b–7)
- **C**   Barak hesitates: "go" (×4; 4:8)
- **B'** Barak's commission qualified:
  "go" (×2), "Yahweh," Sisera," "into the hand *of a woman*" (4:9a)
- **A'** Barak accompanied by Deborah to "Kedesh" (4:9b)

Rather than immediately obeying Yahweh's commission, he stipulates a condition—he asks for a woman to go with him (4:8), afraid and faithless as he is with regard to God's promises in 4:6–7. Barak uses "if" (אִם, *'im*) twice in 4:8 in his reply to his commissioning by Deborah. She uses "surely" (כִּי, *ki*) twice in return, in 4:9. One is tentative, the other sure; one is doubtful, the other confident. The consequence of Barak's fearfulness and faithlessness is that "on the way that you [Barak] are going [a way of hesitation and doubt], it will not be your honor" (4:9). God does not need macho individuals or magnificent implements or any such person or thing. Nor is God's man or woman to be deterred by the seeming power of the enemy. But because of Barak's fearful lack of faith, God would instead work through the most unlikely individual and "sell Sisera into the hands of a woman"—not a warrior, not a leader, not even an Israelite! And the honor and glory of victory would fall out of Barak's hand.

4.2.2   *God always remains faithful to his people.*

Yet for all the lack of nerve and spine in Barak, the situation is not desperate—God is always faithful and keeps his promise (given in 4:6–7, 9, 14) to his people. And the Canaanite army is defeated: "And Yahweh routed Sisera and all the chariots and all the army" (4:15; and see below).[21] Yahweh's action of "routing" (הָמַם, *hamam*, 4:15) is also used of Yahweh's victory over

---

21. We saw this in Pericope 3 (Jdg 3:7–31), too, where, despite Ehud's duplicitous actions, victory was granted Israel. Here, also, we must remember that the moral slide of Israel's judges (and people) had only commenced: Barak was not as bad as those judges who followed him, though with his fearful faithlessness he was several notches below those who preceded him.

the Egyptian armies in the exodus: Exod 14:24; 23:27. Here, as there, it was God who was at work on behalf of his people.

There are other parallels with the exodus event. The two prose narratives that precede lyric accounts (Exodus 14 and Judges 4, preceding Exodus 15 and Judges 5, respectively—the only such pairs in the OT) have a number of similarities: Yahweh's plan is disclosed through a prophet (Exod 14:1–4) or a prophetess (Jdg 4:6–7),[22] and "told" to Pharaoh or Sisera (Exod 14:5; Jdg 4:12); in both there are "riders," "horses," and "chariots" (Exod 14:6, 7, 9, 17, 18, 23, 25, 26, 28; Jdg 4:3, 7, 13, 15, 16), and the chariots are numbered (Exod 14:7; Jdg 4:3, 13); both Israel and Barak hesitated to trust Yahweh (Exod 14:10–12; Jdg 4:7); there is "pursuit" (Exod 14:4, 8, 9, 23; Jdg 4:16, 22) and "fear not" (Exod 14:13; Jdg 4:18); Yahweh "routs" the enemy army in both narratives (Exod 14:24; Jdg 4:15), so that "not even one was left among them" (Exod 14:28)/"not even one was left" (Jdg 4:16); both Egyptians and Sisera "flee" (Exod 14:27; Jdg 4:15, 17), and are found "dead" (Exod 14:30; Jdg 4:22).[23] There are also similarities between the portrayals of Moses and Deborah: both are involved in Israel's defeat of a foe armed with chariots (Exod 14:6; 17:8–9; Jdg 4:9, 13–14); both are prophets (Deut 34:10; Jdg 4:4) and judges (Exod 2:14; 18:13–16; Jdg 4:5); they are part of a divinely orchestrated victory (Exod 14:21, 24–25; Jdg 4:15–16); both stories have Kenites figuring in them (Num 24:21; Jdg 4:11, 17); and leaders in both declare that they will "sing . . . to Yahweh" (Exod 15:1; Jdg 5:3). Thus the victory of the Israelites is made to conform to the archetypal victory of Yahweh in the exodus.[24] God is, indeed, faithful to his people.

The overthrowing of the enemy here in Judges 4 is described with wry humor in a series of contrasts. In 4:10, Barak "calls" his 10,000 men who are "at his foot," while in 4:13, Sisera "calls" all his men and his nine hundred chariots—no going on foot for him[25]:

---

22. But both accounts have prophetesses: Miriam in Exodus 15 who sings; and Deborah in Judges 4 and 5 (where she sings).

23. O'Connell, *The Rhetoric of the Book of Judges*, 134–35. Incidentally, bodies of water overwhelm enemy chariots in both encounters (Exod 14:25–27; Jdg 5:21).

24. Ibid., 137.

25. Whereas Barak's rallying mentions only people (4:10), Sisera's mustering commences with a pointed notation of his battalion of chariots: "And Sisera called all his chariots—his nine hundred chariots—and all the people" (4:13).

4:10	And Barak called ...	—and they went up on foot—	ten thousand men, and Deborah, she went up beside him.	
4:13	And Sisera called	all his chariots, nine hundred iron chariots,	and all the people that were with him	

The situation, however, changes dramatically. In 4:14, Barak "goes down," still with his ten thousand, while in 4:15, Sisera also "goes down," but "from the chariot," and "on foot," all alone![26] The tables have been turned!

4:14b	And Barak went down	from Mount Tabor	with ten thousand men ....
4:13a	And Sisera went down	from the chariot	and he fled on foot.

There are more tables overturning as the battle continues: Barak pursues chariots and army (4:16a); Sisera flees on foot (4:17a)[27]:

4:16a	And Barak	pursued ... chariots ... army	unto Harosheth-hagoyim.
4:17a	And Sisera	fled on foot	to the tent of Jael.

But both are going to lose that which they are running for: Barak loses his prey, and Sisera his life.

In any case, the victory ultimately was God's: "God subdued [כָּנַע, *kana'*] Jabin, king of Canaan [כְּנַעַן, *kna'an*]" (4:23). The assonance, in Hebrew, of "subdue" and "Canaan" is ironic. No one can stand against deity, not even with nine hundred chariots. And Barak should have recognized that. Sadly for him, and for his nation, he did not.

4.3. Judges 4:17–24

THEOLOGICAL FOCUS 4.3

4.3 Fearless faith results in divine blessing (4:17–24).

---

26. That Sisera is alone is specified in 4:16: "all the army" was slaughtered, and "not even one was left."

27. In the poetic account, Israelite troops rush with Barak, "at his foot" (5:15), but Sisera's feet are unmentioned; instead, he falls "between her [Jael's] feet" (5:27 [×2]).

NOTES 4.3

4.3 Fearless faith results in divine blessing.[28]

The long and short of the story is that because of his fearfulness and faithlessness, Barak gets no glory: Jael kills the enemy commander and she is lauded (5:24–27; see below). One might think from the narrative thus far that Barak at least had a role in defeating Sisera's army, and perhaps he did in actuality, but the narrator would have us think otherwise: essentially it is *Yahweh* who "routs" the enemy, chariots and all (4:14–15). Barak's role is simply mentioned in passing: Yahweh had "gone out *before you* [Barak]" (4:14), and and "Yahweh routed Sisera and all his chariots and all his army, with the edge of the sword *before Barak*" (4:15). All the man did, it seems, was watch things happen "before" him![29] Yes, he did pursue the enemy and "all the army of Sisera fell with the edge of the sword" (4:16), but the emphatic statement in 4:15 makes it clear that it was *Yahweh* who was responsible for the victory. And we also have: "Yahweh routed . . . all his army *with the edge of the sword*" in parallel with 4:16: "all the army of Sisera fell *with the edge of the sword*." There is no indication that Barak or his men did the honors: neither chieftain nor army is the subject of any active verb indicating wielding of weapons.[30] Later, with regard to the killing of Sisera, too, all Barak did was watch: "Come, and I will *show* you," said Jael, after she had finished off Sisera, and Barak entered, "and—*behold!*—Sisera, fallen dead with the tent peg in his temple" (4:22).

Heber the Kenite, an Israelite and Jael's husband, apparently broke a covenant with the rest of his clan (4:11; see 1:16, and Num 10:29–32) as he separated himself from them to dwell elsewhere. He seems to have made peace with Jabin, the king of Hazor (Jdg 4:17)—likely another covenant, but this with a Canaanite, Israel's enemy, a violation of Exod 23:32 and Deut 7:2.[31] Perhaps this is the very intent of bringing up Heber in in this narra-

---

28. Several of the Theological Foci in this commentary, the reader may have noticed, are stated in the positive, though the text often provides negative examples. This is one instance: Barak loses the honor of victory (a divine blessing that would have been his) because of his faithless fear.

29. The phrases are: לִפָנֶיךָ, *lipaneka*, "before you," in 4:14, and לִפְנֵי בָרָק, *lipne baraq*, "before Barak," in 4:15. The prepositions in question are related to פָּנִים, *panim*, "face," so literally Barak is watching things happen before his face, literally diminishing his own exertions and participation in the battle.

30. How exactly Yahweh wins the battle the reader will discover only in Pericope 5: Jdg 5:1–31.

31. If "Lappidoth" is indeed the name of Deborah's husband, then just as she supplants him (he never shows up in the narrative), so also Jael supplants her husband, Heber (he, too, never shows up in the narrative).

tive—to indicate his covenant of peace with Jabin, the king of Hazor (Jdg 4:17), thereby implying that Jael, his wife, had courageously broken that covenant to side with Israel and assassinate Sisera (see below).

When Sisera appeared at her tent, Jael "went out to meet" him, invited him in (4:18), and ultimately killed him (4:21). Subsequently, Jael "went out to meet" Barak, invited him in, and presented him with the slain Sisera (4:22). Notice, also, the parallels in 4:22: "And, behold, as Barak pursued Sisera.... And, behold, Sisera fallen dead." These similar descriptions of the activities of Sisera and Barak and their parallel treatments by Jael portray two failed men, fallen into the hands of a woman: "an essential oneness in destiny of Barak and Sisera."[32] Both men have lost their honor, particularly poignant in the case of the Israelite protagonist, Barak, who lost his because of fearfulness and faithlessness, in spite of God's promises, reassurances, and backing.

The command Sisera gives Jael in 4:20 to "stand [עֲמֹד, *'amod*] in the door of the tent" is curious, because the verb is a *masculine* singular imperative. Scholars generally think this needs emendation. But there may be more going on here: not only has Sisera addressed Jael as male with this imperative, it seems as if he has abdicated his own manhood as he orders Jael to deny that there is "any man" inside the tent. Ironically, before anyone came along, Jael would make sure there would, indeed, not be any *living* man inside the tent.[33] But curiously enough, later, in 4:22, Jael rushes out to

---

32. Murray, "Narrative Structure," 172. This "falling" of Sisera in 4:22 also parallels the "falling" of his troops in 4:16.

33. Bal, *Murder and Difference*, 92. Sexual connotations have been mined amply by excited exegetes—Jael the quasi-male and Sisera the emasculated one. The story provides a fertile pit for excavation, particularly in light of a named husband with antecedents and locations who never appears in the story. Elements that hint at some illicit sexuality in the narrative include: "water" (4:15; for its sexual connotations, see Prov 5:15, 16; 9:17; Songs 4:15); the invitation to "turn in" (סוּר, *sur*, Jdg 4:18), similar to that made by the "woman of folly" in Prov 9:17; Jael's "going into" Sisera (idiomatic for sexual contact: Jdg 16:1; Ruth 4:13; 2 Sam 12:14; etc.); only two women do things "secretly" in the OT (בַּלָּאט, *balla't*, in Jdg 4:21) and there is a sexual implication in the story of one (Ruth 3:7); πάσσαλος, *passalos*, "peg" (Jdg 4:21, 22 LXX), has been used as a phallic euphemism in Aristophanes (*Ecclesiazusae* 1020). Of course, it is highly unlikely that the couple in our narrative engaged in sexual relations: the male was in danger of being killed by the enemy, and explicitly noted to be thirsty, exhausted, and sleepy (4:19, 20), not exactly a physiological state conducive to erotic entanglements. But the hints are there, an attempt to link "sex and slaughter," or even an emasculation of the enemy commander, Sisera (Niditch, *Judges*, 66). The assassination with a tent peg is "a grim parody of the sexual act, in which the roles are reversed and Jael acts the part of the man." See Lindars, *Judges 1–5*, 201. Indeed, *L.A.B.* 31:3; *b. Yebam.* 103a; and *b. Naz.* 23b concur, suggesting that a sexual motif operates in the narrative. Needless to say, for preaching purposes, it is best not to make much of this, seeing how tenuous the

tell Barak that indeed, there *was* a man in the tent—"Come and I will show you a *man*": a dead one! This is the first death of a man in Judges that occurs at the hands of a woman. There is another in 9:53–54, where it is made clear that such a demise was humiliating, dishonorable, ignoble. "[T]he whole textual evidence, both in the prose narrative and in the Song [Pericope 5: Judges 5:1–31], may be seen as a play on the rather ridiculous helplessness of *both* male protagonists, Barak and Sisera . . . and on the power of the female figures, who are the only really active figures in the whole narrative."[34] The men—and particularly of interest to us, Barak, because of his faithless fear—lose their honor to women.

Perhaps as an indication of the dishonoring of these two males, Jael's address to both, as she welcomes them into her tent, is almost identical: "And Jael came out to meet . . . and she said to/unto him . . ." (4:18, 22). Interestingly, Jael's first word to Barak, when he appears at her tent, is לֵךְ (*lek*, "go," 4:22), where בֹּא (*bo'*, "come") would have been more natural. But there is a reason for this usage: it was also Deborah's first command to Barak—Yahweh's first reported word to Barak through the mouth of Deborah: לֵךְ ("go," 4:6). There seems to be an intentional narrative design here. Barak had protested this first command ("*go*," 4:6), with four "goings" himself ("if you go . . . , I will go; but if you will not go . . . , I will not go," 4:8). As a result, his commission was altered—he would only defeat the army (if at all that), not capture its commander. Now with the second לֵךְ from Jael (4:22), he is "commanded" to see the man he was pursuing ("*go*")—but that man was already dead . . . at the hands (feet? 5:27) of a woman.[35] In short, we are literarily shown how two men are foiled, "united in a tragic fate: ignominious subjection to the effective power of a woman."[36] Jael had conquered both: taken life from one and honor from the other.

While there are links between Ehud's assassination of Eglon and Jael's of Sisera,[37] the former is marked by intent to kill from the beginning of the

---

argument is, and how little it contributes to the theology of the pericope.

34. Grottanelli, *Kings and Prophets*, 80.
35. van Wolde, "Ya'el in Judges 4," 243.
36. Murray, "Narrative Structure," 173.
37. In both assassination stories, Yahweh is missing; in both there is a promise that "Yahweh has given . . . into your hands" (3:28; 4:14); both commence with the Israelites "going down" "from the hill/mount" (3:27, 28; 4:14), "pursuing" and "subduing" (3:29, 30; 4:16, 23); both homicides are described in gory detail (3:15–26; 4:17–22), while the battles are given but a brief notice (3:27–29; 4:14–16); speech is employed to lull the victim into a vulnerable state; both assassins "take" (לקח, *lqkh*) their weapons in their "hand" (יד, *yd*) and "thrust" (תקע, *tq'*) them into their victims (see 3:21; 4:21); the discovery of the killings is heralded in both cases with multiple uses of "behold!" (3:24–25 [×3]; 4:22 [×2]); the description of the corpses are almost identical ("and, behold, [their

story and the entire plot revolves around that intent, in its planning and its execution, and with Ehud deliberately going after Eglon. In the current case, Sisera's arrival at Jael's tent was almost incidental (humanly speaking), and Jael's killing almost an afterthought. While no doubt, Yahweh sovereignly orchestrated both events for his glory, divine purpose is more proximal and immediate in Judges 4 than in Judges 3: we were forewarned in 4:9 that the man, Barak, would *not* get the honor for this victory—it would go to a woman. One might ask, however, why the violently inclined Jael ends up being lauded as "most blessed" (5:24 [×2]). This is not unlike Rahab's approbation in Joshua 2; yet she had lied to the king of Jericho (Josh 2:3–5). In both cases what is credited is not the lying or the deception (though Jael did not lie outright, even if she did encourage Sisera not be afraid [4:18]), but the Yahwistic faith that those actions manifested.[38] What was meritorious was Jael's loyalty to Israel as she, at great personal risk, threw in her lot with a people her husband had abandoned. While Barak was fearfully and faithlessly unwilling to undertake his divinely ordained commission without Deborah accompanying him, Jael valiantly takes matters into her own hands with no help, even to the extent of abandoning her husband's covenant of peace with Jabin, the Canaanite king: she had become a Yahwist, indeed! The man, Barak, wants a woman to go with him; the woman, Jael, does not particularly care to ally with her husband's interests. In any case, Scripture is silent about Jael's motives, preferring to focus on Barak's failures and the resulting loss of honor and blessing. And so, rather than Barak, the Israelite commander with noble antecedents (4:6), it is Jael, one on the fringes of Israelite society and without any antecedents except for a link to a treacherous husband (4:11, 17), who gets the honor.

Frolov and Frolov calculated that the force needed to send an implement like a tent peg, into the skull, through the brain and its coverings, and back out of the skull to "descend" to the ground (צנח, *tsnkh*, 4:21), would be equivalent to driving a stake through 2–3 inches of concrete—and this

---

master/Sisera] fallen . . . , dead," 3:25; 4:22); and both enemy nations are "subdued" as a result (3:20; 4:23). However, in the Ehud story, the assassination (an expanded narrative) comes first, followed by the defeat of the enemy (a compressed narrative); in the Barak story, it is the other way around, with the compressed narrative of the defeat coming first (4:15–16), and the expanded narrative of the assassination coming afterwards (4:17–22) (Block, *Judges, Ruth*, 201). And, as already mentioned, Ehud's actions were planned and premeditated, whereas Jael's appears to have been improvised on the spur of the moment.

38. As well, the plaudits for the Egyptian midwives who lied (Exod 1:15–21). Here, too, it is not their lying that is credited, but the explicitly noted fact that they "feared God" (1:21).

with one blow!³⁹ That raises the question of who/what "descended into the ground" (4:21). The verb there is third-person feminine singular, the subject of which could be either the "peg" of the tent (יָתֵד, *yated*, a feminine noun) or Jael herself (the only other feminine element in the verse). Notably, elsewhere in the OT צנח occurs only in Jdg 1:14 (repeating Josh 15:18), of Achsah's "descending" or "dismounting." Combined with the impossibility of the peg passing through the temple and skull cavity into the ground, this seems to point to Jael as the one who, after having apparently climbed upon the somnolent, spent Sisera and hammered the peg through his head, is now "dismounting." Such a reading fits the long sequence of *waw* consecutive verbs in Jdg 4:21a that precede her "dismounting": "she took," "she seized," "she went," "she thrust," and now, if one accepts that she is the subject of צנח, "she dismounted." And it also serves to create a pattern of increasing activity on the part of Jael; her homicidal enterprise is broken into three sets of an increasing number of actions—one in 4:18b, three in 4:19b, and five in 4:21a, each set corresponding, respectively, to the three responses of Sisera (4:21b)⁴⁰:

	JAEL		SISERA
4:18b	"she covered"	4:21bα	"and he being sound asleep"
4:19b	"she opened" "she gave to drink" "she covered"	4:21bβ	"and he was exhausted"
4:21a	"she took" "she seized" "she went" "she thrust" "she dismounted"	4:21bγ	"and he died"

The killing of Sisera (4:17–21) is bracketed on either side by a report of Barak "pursuing"—he was "pursuing" *before* Sisera died (4:16), and he was "pursuing" *after* Sisera was dead (4:22). Barak had completely failed in the goal of his "pursuit"; a woman had obtained the honor of dispatching the prey. The man's ridicule is subtly accentuated by the repetition of the scorn that was poured on the courtiers of Eglon who arrived to find their master "behold ... fallen ... dead" (3:25). Barak is no different: he, too, finds Sisera "behold ... fallen dead" (4:22).

Barak fights the enemy, but Yahweh routs them (4:15–16); Barak pursues Sisera, but Jael kills him (4:22). One recalls that Jael's tent was near Kedesh (4:11). So we have a pungent irony: "Barak thus ends where he

39. Frolov and Frolov, "Sisera Unfastened," 59–60.
40. From O'Connell, *The Rhetoric of the Book of Judges*, 120–21.

began, in Kedesh Naphtali, with little to show for his trouble except a junior partnership in a female enterprise."[41]

SERMON FOCUS AND OUTLINES

THEOLOGICAL FOCUS OF PERICOPE 4 FOR PREACHING
4   Fearless faith in God results in blessing (4:1–24).

The issue of God's pleasure at his people's obedience was touched upon in the sermon on Pericope 2 (Jdg 2:6—3:11). Here it is the blessing of God upon those who follow him fearlessly. No doubt, God can accomplish his purposes through anyone, anywhere, even through a stone (Hab 2:11; Luke 19:40). The question is: Do we, his people, want to enjoy the blessings of participating with God in his ventures? If we do, then we had better jump in with fearless faith, as Barak unfortunately failed to do.[42]

Possible Preaching Outlines for Pericope 4

I.   Culpability
  Evildoing by Israel; their oppression and faithlessness (4:1–3)
  Absence of men; raising up of women (4:4–5)
  God's promises and Barak's fear (4:6–16)
  Move-to-relevance: Our faithless fear, despite the promises of God
II. Consequence
  Jael's bold initiative (4:17–21)
  Barak's loss of honor/blessing (4:9, 22)
  Move-to-relevance: Blessing for faithful, fearless partnership with God
III. Commission: *Be faithfully fearless!*
  Specifics on how one can be faithfully fearless[43]

---

41. Sternberg, *Poetics*, 283.

42. The focus here should be on becoming faithfully fearless; the notion of divine blessing that results from appropriate behavior also shows up in the next pericope (Pericope 5: Jdg 5:1–31).

43. Applications need to be more specific than just "Be faithfully courageous!" of course. A way to approach such specificities is to explore "significances"—i.e., specific activities that lead/cause one to becoming faithfully courageous (see Kuruvilla, *Privilege the Text!* 61–65). The preacher should ask: What might be a concrete step for God's people to take towards creating a mindset of faithful courage? For example, in a sermon on this text, I exhorted the congregation to make God their first and last thoughts of the day, to get people into a frame of trusting God's constant presence. Hopefully, such actions as are pastorally recommended—based on the theological thrust of the pericope preached—will become *routine*, incorporated into one's life, so that both the action and the attitude it expresses snowball into habits, and dispositions, and character, ultimately conforming the Christian to the image of Christ (Rom 8:29). Thus, ritual practices

Expanding the above outline and exploding it into the specific characters gives us this[44]:

I. Israel
   Evildoing by Israel; their oppression and faithlessness (4:1–3)
II. Deborah
   Absence of men; raising up of women (4:4–5)
III. Barak
   God's promises and Barak's fear (4:6–16)
   Move-to-relevance: Our faithless fear, despite the promises of God
IV. Jael
   Jael's boldness and Barak's loss (4:17–22)
   Move-to-relevance: Blessing for faithful, fearless partnership with God
V. We: *Live powerfully!*
   Specifics on how one can be faithfully fearless

---

become radical passions, so that, over time, one does not not just think of God the first and last moments in a day, but *all the time!*

44. This alternate outline may be more conducive to shaping it into a "single-move" sermon, as was suggested in the previous pericope, with a seamless transitioning between the depicted characters.

PERICOPE 5

Song of Deborah

Judges 5:1–31

[Non-participants with God Cursed;
Participants with God Blessed]

REVIEW, SUMMARY, PREVIEW

Review of Pericope 4: In Jdg 4:1–24, Barak, the judge, is commissioned by God's representative, Deborah, but he waffles in fear and refuses his military orders, despite God's unambiguous promise of victory over Israel's enemy. As a result of his faithless fear, he loses out on the honor of capturing the enemy leader, being preempted in the killing of Sisera by another woman, a non-Israelite: Jael. Barak, because of his lack of faith and courage, accomplishes nothing, wins nothing, and loses all.

Summary of Pericope 5: The fifth pericope of Judges (5:1–31) comprises the Song of Deborah, a hymn extolling God's victory over his enemies. As he, the Divine Warrior, proceeds into action, the call is for his people to participate with him in his work—the key exhortation of the Song. Non-participants—tribes, individuals—are cursed. Participants—tribes, individuals, particularly the non-Israelite, non-male, non-warrior Jael, and even nature itself—are blessed.

Preview of Pericope 6: The next pericope, Jdg 6:1—7:22, foregrounds Gideon's fear, stemming from his lack of trust in God, and manifest in his reluctant commissioning, nocturnal iconoclasm, unsanctioned troop mustering, and presumptuous testing of God. All this, despite God's assurances regarding his promises, presence, and power in the battle against Midian. The irony of the account is that once God enables Gideon to achieve victory over the enemy, this skeptic turns prideful and takes credit for divine action.

5. Judges 5:1–31

THEOLOGICAL FOCUS OF PERICOPE 5

5   Participation in the endeavors of God, the Ruler of the universe—as he fights for his people, empowering them—keeps one in the realm of his blessing (5:1–31).

  5.1   The Almighty God, Ruler of the universe, fights for his powerless people, empowering those who are aligned with him (5:1–11c).

  5.2   Failure to participate in the endeavors of God with God removes one from the realm of his blessing (5:11d–23).

  5.3   Participation in the endeavors of God with God keeps one in the realm of his blessing (5:24–31).

OVERVIEW

As was shown in Pericope 4 (Jdg 4:1–24), the prose account of Judges 4 is completed only by the addition of 5:31b, that forms the final element of the narrative paradigm set in 2:11–19: the statement of the land's rest. In that sense, the Song of Deborah in Jdg 5:1–31a is an interpolation of sorts.

It was noted in 4:23 that "God subdued *on that day* Jabin the king of Canaan before the sons of Israel." Now 5:1 commences with Deborah and Barak also singing "on that day." In this pericope (Pericope 5: Jdg 5:1–31), Deborah is mentioned four times, but Barak only thrice and all three times with Deborah; each time his name follows hers (5:1, 12, 15). She, however, is the one commanded to lead parentally (5:7) and to sing (5:12).[1] And so,

---

1. That Deborah was the author of this song seems likely: she speaks in the first person, naming herself and labeling her own role as "mother in Israel" (5:7). The leadership of women in songs of victory (e.g., Miriam, a prophetess like Deborah [Exod 15:20; Jdg 4:4] leads a song in Exod 15:20–21; also see Jdg 11:34; 1 Sam 18:6–7) lends credence to Deborah's authorship. But, while it might well be the "Song of Deborah," the argument should not be grounded on the first word, וַתָּשַׁר, *wattashar,* a *wayyiqtol* third person

unlike Judges 4, Judges 5 has a preponderance of first-person grammatical elements: first-person pronoun, אָנֹכִי, *'anoki*, "I" in 5:3 (×2); first-person suffixes, לִי, *li*, "to me," in 5:9, and נַפְשִׁי, *napshi*, "my soul," in 5:21; first-person verbs, אָשִׁירָה, *'ashirah*, "I will sing" (5:3); אֲזַמֵּר, *'azammer*, "I will make melody" (5:3); and שַׁקַּמְתִּי, *shaqqamtti*, "I will arise" (5:7 [×2]).[2] Thus, this is a post-victory song of celebration, albeit with a theological thrust of its own. In other words, we are given "two lenses" with which to gaze at the single incident—Judges 4 and Judges 5—and these lenses direct our focus to two discrete pericopal theologies.[3]

In this way, Judges 4–5 (prose + poetry) resembles Exodus 14–15, the prose + poetic account of another battle of Israel against a fearsome enemy. Both have the protagonist "singing ... to Yahweh" (Exod 15:1; Jdg 5:3); both have male and female singers (Exod 15:1, 20–21; Jdg 5:1); Israel's enemies in both are defeated by a deluge (Exod 15:10; Jdg 5:21); both have "horses" and "chariots" (Exod 15:1, 4, 19; Jdg 5:22, 28), theophanies (Exod 15:5, 10; Jdg 5:21, 22), "right hand" (Exod 15:6; Jdg 5:26), and "divide the spoil" (Exod 15:9; Jdg 5:30); and both songs taunt the enemy with direct quotes (Exod 15:9; Jdg 5:28–30).[4]

The differences between the prose account of Judges 4 and the poetic picture of Judges 5, both refracting the same essential historical event (the defeat of Jabin, king of Canaan), are considerable, with the versified

---

feminine singular, "she sang." "The ancient writer had no alternative in the case of his wanting to report an action by female X plus male Y with the preterite form in front" (as also in Gen 24:61; 31:14; Num 12:1) (Fokkelman, "The Song of Deborah and Barak," 596n3). On the other hand, both Deborah and Barak are addressed in the second person in Jdg 5:12, and in the third person in 5:15. But "the reader must remember that this is not a literary photograph but impressionistic poetry. These extraordinary constructions may be attributable entirely to the text's poetic genre" (Block, *Judges, Ruth*, 215). In any case, it is fair to go with tradition here and assign the Song to Deborah.

2. These instances do not include the implied first person speaking when a second person is addressed: 5:2c, 3, 4, 9, 10, 12, 14, 16, 31a.

3. Ibid., 184. Marais is right: "[M]imesis [an unvarnished representation of history] is not the driving principle behind representation in Old Testament narratives. Perspective ... is that driving force" (*Representation in Old Testament Narrative Texts*, 104). And here we have *two* perspectives on the single event. Of note, Judges 5 is among the OT's toughest texts. "The difficulties ... are legion. The text is evidently to some extent in disorder, so that some verses, or parts of verses, appear to be misplaced.... The poem contains words of uncertain meaning, so that we cannot always tell whether corruption of the text or our own ignorance of the full extent of the Hebrew language is the cause for our perplexity" (Lindars, "Deborah's Song," 166). The LXX simply transliterates words its editors found difficult to translate in 5:7, 16, 21, 22. Indeed, a majority of verses have at least one word with a speculative translation. That the Targumic version of Judges 5 has about five times as many words as does the MT reflects the attempt of the former to clarify the obscurities of the latter.

4. O'Connell, *The Rhetoric of the Book of Judges*, 134–35. Also see Pericope 4 (Jdg 4:1–24).

version providing details absent in the documentary description: the call to song and to bless Yahweh (5:2, 3, 9, 10); Yahweh's procession from Sinai as the Divine Warrior (5:4–5); pre-war conditions in Israel (5:6–8); Deborah as a "mother" (5:7); the lauding of Israel's fighters and volunteers, and the scarcity of their of weapons (5:8–11); a tribal roll call, and the detailing of participants and non-participants (5:13–18; only Zebulun and Napthali are noted in 4:10); the involvement of more than one enemy king (5:3, 19); the divinely orchestrated cosmic victory over Sisera (5:20–21); the cursing of Meroz (5:23 [×2]); the nuances of Jael's assassination (5:24–27: her blessedness [×2], her feeding curds to Sisera, and that in a unique container); the response of Sisera's mother and her ladies-in-waiting (5:28–30); and the closing curse and blessing (5:31a).

Missing in the poetic statement of Judges 5 (but present in Judges 4) are: the details of Jabin's oppression and, in fact, any mention of Jabin at all (4:2, 17, 23, 24 [×2])[5]; the background of Deborah, her prophetic office and judgeship (4:4–5); her commissioning of Barak, and his demurral and its consequences (4:6–9); Heber's distancing from Israel (4:11); the mustering of troops by Barak and Sisera, and Deborah's accompaniment of the former (4:12–14); details of the battle, Sisera's fleeing, and Barak's pursuit (4:15–17); Sisera's arrival at Jael's tent and his seeking protection (4:18–20); Sisera's exhaustion and sleep (4:21); Barak's arrival at Jael's tent and his discovery of the slain enemy (4:22); and the summary of Israel's victory over Jabin, king of Canaan (4:23–24).[6] In any case, "[t]here is no way to decide which one [Judges 4 or Judges 5] is primary. There is no way to decide which one is 'real' or nearest to 'reality'; they are both representations, textual creations, they are texts creating worlds and worlds to which texts refer."[7] In each, the author is *doing* something unique, and the burden of the preacher is to discern the *doing* of the author in the particular pericope.

5.1. Judges 5:1–11c

THEOLOGICAL FOCUS 5.1

> 5.1 The Almighty God, Ruler of the universe, fights for his powerless people, empowering those who are aligned with him (5:1–11c).

---

5. Instead, we are told of "kings," in the plural (5:3, 19 [×2]), likely an attempt to depict the broad defeat of *all* of God's enemies, not just this particular one.

6. Block, *Judges, Ruth*, 181–82.

7. Marais, *Representation in Old Testament Narrative Texts*, 105.

NOTES 5.1

5.1 *The Almighty God, Ruler of the universe, fights for his powerless people, empowering those who are aligned with him.*

Judges 5:2 and 5:9 commence the first two sections of the song, respectively (5:2–8; and 5:9–11c). Both sections begin with a notice of "leaders" (5:2) or "commanders" (5:9); both have "in Israel" (5:2, 9); "bless Yahweh" is seen in both (5:2, 9), each time preceded by a phrase containing נדב (*ndb*, "volunteer") in the *hithpael* and the noun "people"; both 5:3 ("kings") and 5:10 ("riders on donkeys," and "sitters on carpets") address enemies sardonically—they are to "give ear" (5:3) and to "tell" (5:10); and the concluding emphasis in each of these sections is on Yahweh: praises are sung to him (5:3), and his righteousness is recounted (5:11abc).

> [I]t is noteworthy that . . . the explicit call to bless YHWH is linked not so much to the victory itself [which only comes later, 5:18–23, 24–27], but to the demonstration of leadership and the voluntary participation of the people in battle. . . . [They form] a preview of a basic concern of the whole song, a concern that has more to do with the people's willingness to participate during a time of national crisis rather than the simple celebration of victory itself.[8]

Attention is immediately given, at the very start of the Song, to the tight relationship between Israel and its covenant deity, "Yahweh, the God of Israel" (5:3–4). Right from the get-go, Yahweh is praised for Israel's "leaders" and "people" enrolling to fight (5:2). Soon that praise transforms into a taunt of "kings" and "rulers," ostensibly those of the foreign nations who dare to fight Yahweh and his people (5:3). Yahweh's actions are further described in 5:4–5 that is symmetrically constructed:

	Yahweh,	
5:4a	When you went out from Seir, When you marched from the field of Edom,	**Procession**
5:4b	The earth quaked Even the heavens dripped, Even the clouds dripped water, The mountains shook,	
5:5	At the presence of Yahweh, this One of Sinai, At the presence of Yahweh, the God of Israel.	**Presence**

---

8. Wong, "Song of Deborah," 6.

Seir/Edom, south and east of the Dead Sea, is located between Israel and the Sinai, the mountain of God. So here, in 5:4–5, we have the Ruler of the universe setting forth for battle, moving northward to help his people, Israel, against Canaan. "This march to battle is truly a cosmic event: the ground trembles as Yahweh sets out; the clouds unleash a mighty storm; an earthquake shakes the mountains. Such is the might of Yahweh, the divine warrior, as this God prepares for battle."[9] The One of Sinai, the God of Israel, was going to fight for his people.[10] This is a remarkably vibrant picture of Yahweh who, at the very outset, is taking the lead and marching out to battle the foes of his people. The water metaphors are pregnant and anticipatory, for it is water (rain and flooding of the Kishon) that will later devastate the foe, chariots and all (5:21).

The "going out" of Yahweh (יצא, yts', 5:4) is dischronological: his "going out" in the prose account (יצא, 4:14) occurs as the battle is about to be engaged. Here, even before any intimation of war, Yahweh is "going out" and marching forth. So also the foreshadowing in 5:4b–5 of the involvement of cosmic elements, storm imagery, and water in the subsequent battle (5:20–21). All of these adumbrations reinforce Yahweh's supremacy, for such symbolism is usually associated with Baal, a storm-god.[11] This out-of-sync portrayal of the Divine Warrior keeps the reader focused on Yahweh and the deeds that he will perform on behalf of his people, Israel. The picture of Yahweh in his dreadful majesty is immediately followed by the introduction of Deborah into those halcyon days before the battle (5:6–7). Thus the advent of Yahweh and that of Deborah are paralleled. Besides, when Yahweh "marches" in 5:4, in response Deborah ("my soul," i.e., the person of the singer of this Song) also "marches" in 5:21. "The power of Yahweh, mythically described in the theophany, is historically revealed in the actions of an individual, specifically a woman."[12] Indeed, all individuals who are in sync

---

9. Ackerman, *Warrior, Dancer, Seductress, Queen*, 35. Earth + heaven in 5:4b is a "merismatic allusion, hinting at cosmic totality, as in Gen 1:1" (Sasson, *Judges 1–12*, 287).

10. Albright argued that זה סיני, *zeh sinay*, in 5:5 reflects North Canaanite epithets for deity formed with a reflective pronoun to indicate "the One of X": "There can thus be little doubt that *zê-Sînai* is an archaic appellation of Yahweh, 'the One of Sinai'" ("The Song of Deborah," 30). The label also occurs in Ps 68:8.

11. Schwemer, "The Storm-gods of the Ancient Near East," 8–16. Baal is pictured in Canaanite mythology as "Rider of the Clouds," wielding thunder and lightning (Green, *The Storm-God*, 190–96).

12. Coogan, "A Structural and Literary Analysis," 154. On the other hand, the poet pointedly keeps from referring to Deborah as "savior/deliverer" of Israel; instead, she is a "mother" in Israel (5:7). Equally emphatic when referring to Deborah's rising is the narrator's avoidance of the root קום, *qum*, "to rise," the technical verb employed for

with the endeavors of God and with the will of God manifest the power of God. If she could align herself to God's purposes, as also did Israel's "leaders," "commanders," "volunteers," and "survivors" (5:2, 9, 13), then non-participants were not only negligent, but also culpable. Besides, "if YHWH is depicted at the outset as leading the way in battle against the enemy, then there is no excuse for any of His people not to be similarly involved."[13] This is further emphasized in the description of the pre-battle state of Israel in 5:6–8. The situation is dreadful: roads deserted and dangerous, peasantry almost annihilated (5:6–7).[14] There seems to have been a total lack of security, freedom, and order. "[I]f living conditions in the nation were indeed as appalling as what is described, then it almost makes it incumbent upon all in Israel to join in the effort to put an end to the misery brought on by foreign oppression. The refusal of any tribe or city to participate would thus be seen once again as inexcusable in light of the nation's suffering."[15]

The structure of 5:6–7 is quite similar to that of 5:4–5. Both parts begin with temporal clauses ("when . . ." [5:4] and "in the days of . . ." [5:6]), and end with repetitions of "presence" (×2, 5:5) or "arose" (×2, 5:7); the final word in both sections is "Israel" (5:5, 7). Besides, the individuals mentioned at the beginning and ending of each part (Yahweh, 5:4a, 5b; Shamgar/Jael/Deborah, 5:6ab, 7b) are those actively working to deliver Israel.[16] The humans' activities are fully aligned with those of God and are therefore described similarly. A subtle jab at the subsequent non-participation of Israel is again seen, now in the mention of Shamgar, the son of Anath, and of Jael (5:6, 7)—both *non*-Israelites who accomplished great deliverances of the nation with unconventional weapons (3:31; 4:17–22).

In any case, Yahweh chooses "new leaders" (5:8), Deborah, Barak, and Jael, for the developing conflict with the Canaanites.[17] Because Israelites dwelt in unwalled villages, "gates" in 5:8b likely refers to fortified habitations of the Canaanites, now preparing for war. But in their dire circum-

---

the "raising up" of Israel's deliverers (2:16, 18; 3:9, 15; 10:1, 3; also see 7:9). Instead שׁקם (*shqm*, also "to rise," piel) is used twice in 5:7. Appropriately enough, it is Barak, the judge-deliverer, who is commanded to "arise" (קוּם; 5:12, as also in 4:14; Deborah, on the other hand, "rises" on her own accord, 5:7, as also in 4:9).

13. Wong, "Song of Deborah," 16.

14. The "peasantry" in 5:8 indicates village life—it had "ceased" (×2, 5:7), perhaps along with agriculture and trade.

15. Ibid.

16. The whole portion, Jdg 5:4–7, has close resemblance to Ps 68:7–8; this psalm also depicts a warrior God fighting and winning victories for his people.

17. It makes better sense to see אֱלֹהִים, *'elohim* ("God"), as the subject of the action of choosing (5:8a): "God chose new [ones]," taking "new" as substantival: i.e., "God chose new *leaders*."

stances—with cessation of peasantry and avoidance of travel (and possibly of commerce as well) (5:6–7a)—the Israelites had hardly anything to fight with: "not a shield or a spear" (5:8cd). The absence of weaponry in the hands of the Israelites further emphasizes the powerful role of Yahweh in the triumph over the Canaanites.

That 5:2–5 parallels 5:9–11c is evident in their structure, especially 5:2–3 and 5:9–10:

Judges 5:2–3		Judges 5:9–10	
Addressees	**Exhortation**	**Addressees**	**Exhortation**
Israelites leaders people/volunteers	"bless Yahweh"	*Israelites* commanders volunteers/people	"bless Yahweh"
Canaanites kings rulers	"hear" "give ear"	*Canaanites* donkey/saddle riders road travelers	"tell"

Each begins and ends with addresses and exhortations to Israelites (5:2, 9) and to Canaanites (5:3, 10). The Canaanite addressees in 5:10, rather than being the "kings" and "rulers" as in 5:3, are ostensibly the wealthy and the elite: those who ride tawny female donkeys sitting on saddles (blankets?), and road travelers (merchants?).

The "division of flocks" (5:11a) likely indicates a separation for the allocation of water. "Like the post office in many small towns of the prairies, the watering holes served as community gathering places, where gossip was exchanged and significant events celebrated. There the Canaanite travelers stop and listen and join in the celebration of Yahweh's victory," a victory equated to the "righteous deeds of Yahweh," accomplished on behalf of his people.[18]

5.2. Judges 5:11d–23

THEOLOGICAL FOCUS 5.2

5.2 Failure to participate in the endeavors of God with God removes one from the realm of his blessing (5:11d–23).

---

18. Block, *Judges, Ruth*, 229.

NOTES 5.2

5.2 Failure to participate in the endeavors of God with God removes one from the realm of his blessing.

The response of the people of God to the call of war is the subject of 5:11d–17, emphasized by the repetition of the "going down" of "the people of Yahweh" (5:11d, 13)—presumably a march into battle. The "survivors" (5:13) of the two decades of oppression under the Canaanites (4:3) were the ones were volunteering for military service, "going down" to face the "nobles" (the kings and rulers of the Canaanites, 5:3). They may have been merely "survivors," but they were "the people of Yahweh," and nothing else counts! In the entire book of Judges, only in 5:11 and 5:13 are the Israelites called "the people of Yahweh," again underscoring the fidelity of those who participated in the battle, and the narrator's approval of their loyalty to deity.[19]

As was noted earlier, it is curious that rather than describe the period as "the days of Deborah" (or Barak), that season is labeled "the days of Shamgar," and "the days of Jael" (5:6), both non-Israelites—one of them a "son of Anath," with non-Yahwistic antecedents (see Pericope 3: Jdg 3:12–31)—who wielded odd implements to deliver Israel. Clearly there is an implied polemic: Where were Israel's own valiant ones? Though Deborah is mentioned here (5:7), Barak is absent, likely reflecting his diffidence and near *non*-participation in the battle in Judges 4. Here, in Judges 5, the disinterest, indifference, and lack of confidence of Barak that is depicted in prose is extrapolated and applied, in poetry, to others in Israel. The unwillingness of certain tribes to participate in this war against the enemy comes in for strong disapprobation in the Song of Deborah. "Indeed, the prose and hymnic versions together comprise a rhetoric of entrapment by which, having invited Israel's indignation against Barak for halfheartedness toward Yhwh in the prose account, the hymn then augments that indignation, directing it against Israel's halfhearted tribes."[20] In fact, "Israel" echoes in 5:2, 3, 5, 7 (×2), 8, 9, 11, but afterwards "Israel" disappears. The unfortunate "rest of the story" is that many of "Israel" were non-participants in this battle. Indeed, it would be a *non*-Israelite, *non*-warrior, *non*-male, wielding a *non*-weapon, who would perform the decisive action that would clinch the victory for Israel against Canaan!

While the prose account lists only two tribes (Zebulun and Naphtali; 4:6, 10), the poetic depiction in 5:14–17 has a roll call of several more, divided into participants and non-participants. The former included Ephraim,

---

19. See ibid., 230.
20. O'Connell, *The Rhetoric of the Book of Judges*, 101–2.

Benjamin, Machir, Zebulun, and Issachar (5:14–15a); the latter included Reuben, Gilead, Dan, and Asher (5:15b–17; and the cryptic "Meroz" in 5:23).[21] It seems best to include 5:18 with the battle section of 5:19–22. This allows human participation in the battle (by Zebulun and Naphtali, 5:18; also see 4:6, 10), which otherwise would only have a divine hand (5:19–22). If deity were the sole participant in the battle then this would deflate the polemic against non-participants in 5:14–17, and it would be incongruent with the idea of *God's people* "going down" to battle (5:11d–13) and with Deborah's encouragement of the "leaders," "volunteers," and "commanders" (5:2, 9), not to mention with Jael's plaudits (5:24–27). But if 5:18 is included in the battle narrative of 5:18–22, we have 5:18–19 listing two *human* participants fighting (Zebulun and Naphtali), and 5:20–22 noting two *non-human* participants fighting (the stars and torrent of Kishon).

A   Participants: Ephraim, Benjamin, Machir, Zebulun, Issachar (×2) (5:14–15a)
    B   Non-participants: Reuben (×2), Gilead, Dan, Asher (5:15b–17)
        C   Human participants (#2) defeat enemy kings (5:18–19)   BATTLE
        C'   Non-human participants (#2) defeat Sisera and his horses (5:20–22)
    B'   Non-participant Meroz: "curse" (×2) (5:23)
A'   Participant Jael: "most blessed" (×2) (5:24)

This makes 5:14–24 a carefully constructed section at the center of which is a human-divine synergistic defeat of Israel's foes (*C, C'*), flanked by a list of non-participants (*B, B'*), and bounded on the outside by participants (*A, A'*). Such a layout is also nicely balanced in terms of the number "2": *A* and *B* have Issachar and Reuben mentioned *twice*, respectively; *C* and *C'* have *two* each of human and non-human participants, respectively; and *B'* and *A'* have Meroz *twice* cursed and Jael *twice* blessed, respectively. There are crucial consequences for participation and non-participation.

Reuben is accused of "searchings of heart" (5:15–16), despite which that tribe determined to stay at home . . . with the sheep.[22] While the mo-

---

21. Machir (son of Manasseh) likely represents the half tribe of Manasseh located on the west of the River Jordan (Gen 50:23; Num 26:29; though some Machirites did settle on the eastern side of the river: Num 32:39–40; Deut 3:15; Josh 13:31; 17:1). Gilead represents the area east of the Jordan that contained Gad and the other half of Manasseh. Wong thus sees a balance between the two groups: each set represents four and a half tribes: the participants are Ephraim, Benjamin, Machir (= half-Manasseh [west]), Zebulun, and Issachar; and the non-participants are Reuben, Gilead (= half-Manasseh [east] + Gad), Dan, and Asher. See Wong, "Song of Deborah," 9–10.

22. Many mss have חִקְקֵי־לֵב (*khiqqe-leb*, "resolves of heart") in 5:15e; some have חִקְרֵי־לֵב (*khiqre-leb*, "searchings of heart") in 5:15e, as in 5:16d. The latter is preferable, for it maintains the strict parallelism between 5:15de and 5:16cd. On the other hand,

tives for the non-participation of Reuben et al. are not forthcoming from the text, Younger speculates that at least for Dan and Asher it may have had to do with "their economic future, which was dependent on Phoenician commerce and shipping." For those in the Transjordan, their hesitation might have had more to do with distance from the battlefront. In any case, "[a]lthough they are theoretically united by their worship of Yahweh and the covenant with him, the Israelites manifest a serious deficiency of political and military solidarity. The nonparticipant tribes refused to sacrifice their individual interest and well-being for the sake of the nation and are severely rebuked."[23] On the other hand, the participating tribes throw themselves into the fray enthusiastically, behind Barak—"at his feet" (5:15c).[24]

Thus a large chunk of the Song of Deborah highlights those tribes participating in the battle (positively portrayed) and a woman, Jael (also positively portrayed), as well as the non-participating tribes (negatively portrayed) and Sisera's womenfolk (also negatively portrayed). If 5:28–30 is included with 5:11d–27, a clear structure is evident:

Positive: Participating tribes (5:11d–15a)
Negative: Non-participating tribes (5:15b–17)
Positive: Participating tribes (5:18)
Negative: Non-participating tribe (5:23)
Positive: Participating woman (5:24–27)
Negative: Non-participating women (5:28–30)

Twice we are told that the kings "fight" (לחם, *lkhm*, 5:19 [×2]); in response, the stars "fight" twice, too (לחם, 5:20 [×2]). And the instrument of their defeat is the torrent, נַחַל (*nakhal*, ×3 in 5:21)—the assonance with this noun

---

the paronomasia might indicate a sardonic comment on Reuben's determinations.

23. Younger, *Judges, Ruth,* 151–52. Another hint of rebuke of the three non-participating tribes in 5:15b–17 is that descriptions of Issachar and Zebulun in Gen 49:13–14 ("seashore," "ships" and "and sheepfolds") are transferred to Reuben ("sheepfolds"), Dan ("ships") and Asher ("seashore") (Jdg 5:16–17). Perhaps this is a way of showing that these latter non-participating tribes were usurping the privileges and prerogatives of those former tribes that did participate in the current battle, adding to the deprecation of those who opted not to participate. Curiously, Dan, the tribe who "sojourned" (גור, *gur,* or "stayed") in ships, possessed no land on the seacoast (1:34); perhaps they had arrangements with the coastal Phoenicians as clients or hired workers (Webb, *Judges,* 213).

24. "Feet" show up again in 5:27 (×2), describing Sisera's death. This corresponds to the prose account, where also Barak's troops were "at his feet" (4:10), and Sisera's escapade was conducted "on his feet" (4:15, 17).

is unmistakable in the conjugated form of the verb לחם—נִלְחָמוּ (*nilkhamu*; "they fought"; also twice in 5:19).

> The Lord came in the storm and caused a torrential downpour. The stars of the heavens, associated with the Lord's assembly elsewhere in the Old Testament and viewed as sources of rain in ancient cosmology, showered rain down upon the enemy. The ground grew muddy and the Kishon overflowed, making the Canaanite chariots useless. . . . To escape from the battle site at Taanach . . . [and to return] to their home in the north, the panic-stricken Canaanites had to cross the swelling Kishon, which swept many of them away along with their chariots and horses. The terrified survivors who happened to make their way northward were easy pickings for the pursuing Israelite forces.[25]

The storm and resulting torrent must have come as a surprise for Sisera and his troops; it is hard to imagine a seasoned commander taking his iron chariots into a terrain that could have been expected to become a quagmire of a floodplain. "Rather, what is surely envisioned here is a sudden and unexpected downpour following the close of the latter rains. Miraculously, the same God who turned water into dry land (Exod 14:21–22; Josh 3:14–17) now turns dry land into a sea of mud! As elsewhere, the Lord (not Baal!) controls the water (cf. Josh 10:11; 1 Sam 7:10; Job 38:1; Ps 18:9–15)."[26] Indeed, the entire universe had been enlisted to fight Israel's enemies (even if the entirety of Israel was not as enthused)! All this fighting is the consummation of the cosmic description of Yahweh and his activity that began the chapter (Jdg 5:4–5); even stars scrap and torrents terrorize (5:20–21). So much so, there is no mention of Barak and his army that waged an effective campaign in Judges 4: here, in Judges 5 (and one might say this is true also in Judges 4), they seem to be mere bystanders, if at all they are present on the scene!

At any rate, the cosmos comes out the winner, defeating the kings and leaving them empty-handed (5:19; also 5:30). The idea of a plurality of kings (5:3, 19) is probably rhetorical, there having been only one king, Jabin, in this battle (4:2, 17, 23, 24). "The way this is expressed in the poetry of the song is through the transformation of the battle between Barak and Sisera into a great final showdown between heaven and earth, between Yahweh

---

25. Chisholm, *Judges and Ruth*, 239–40. For stars as sources of precipitation in period literature, see Smith and Pitard, *The Ugaritic Baal Cycle*, 192. The biblical term "dew of heaven" (Gen 27:39; Deut 33:13) likely reflects this notion, too.

26. Brensinger, *Judges*, 65.

and *the kings of Canaan.*"²⁷ Notice that heavenly elements are involved in the actual battle in 5:20, with earthly elements participating in 5:21. In other words, the whole universe appears to be taking part in the campaign against Yahweh's enemies (earth and heaven were mentioned earlier in 5:4). All nature—cosmic (stars) and terrestrial (torrents)—joins the human participants of the battle to deliver a stunning defeat: the horses can be heard galloping away in retreat (5:22).²⁸

Yahweh's supremacy is unbounded, making it all the more incomprehensible that some of his people chose not to participate with him in his endeavors. While Yahweh is not specifically mentioned in 5:19–22, the reader is clearly being expected to fill the gap with the information provided in 5:4–5, where also cosmic ("heavens," "clouds") and terrestrial elements ("earth," "mountains"), along with water ("dripped"), announced the going forth of Yahweh into battle. While human participants are mentioned in 5:2, 8–9, 11d–15c, 18, the victory is ultimately Yahweh's. And if the entire universe took the side of Yahweh in this campaign, how unbecoming of some humans to have remained uninvolved, as non-participants! They were surely without excuse. The purpose of the author, then, is

> to highlight participation versus non-participation as the single most significant issue within this section. In fact, one can argue that even the focus on the involvement of both human and non-human participants at the centre of this section is fundamentally polemical in purpose. . . . if even nature participated together with humans to bring about a decisive victory against the enemy, then those who refused to participate and contribute to such a victory for YHWH's cause are indeed justifiably rebuked and curse.²⁹

The hymn in Judges 5 not only has a critique of non-participating tribes who "did not come to the help of Yahweh" (5:23), there are even curses that condemn those absentees. Right after this battle of the universe (against a puny Canaanite king), we are immediately returned to *terra firma* and the

---

27. Webb, *Judges*, 214. The "waters of Megiddo" (5:19) likely refers to the "torrent of Kishon" (5:21). There is also a play on the consonants between כְּנַעַן (*knaʿan*, "Canaan") and תַּעְנָךְ (*taʿnak*, "Taanach") in 5:19. The defeat of the Canaanites is bookended by "then" (אָז, *ʾaz*) + perfect masculine plural verb: "*then* they-fought" (i.e., the kings, 5:19) and "*then* they-beat" (i.e., the horses' hooves, 5:22a).

28. The retreat of Israel's foes is depicted (and sounded) with clever onomatopoeia in 5:22b: "galloping, galloping" is דַהֲרוֹת דַּהֲרוֹת (*daharoth daharoth*). Besides, the "beating" (הלם, *hlm*) of the cavalry's hooves in 5:22a is exactly replicated later in the "striking" (also הלם) of Sisera's head by Jael in 5:26.

29. Wong, "Song of Deborah," 15.

uneasy remembrance that all Israel did not participate in this battle (noted initially in 5:15d–17, but again in 5:23). Considering that reality, the angel of Yahweh (the first appearance of this being after 2:4) pronounces a curse on Meroz, a locale that perhaps epitomizes, *in toto*, the unwillingness of the non-participants to engage in war.[30] Meroz, we are told, "did not come" to battle (לֹא־בָאוּ, *lo'-ba'u*, 5:23) when the foreign kings "came" to battle (בָּאוּ, *ba'u*, 5:19). And so their "inhabitants" (from יָשׁב, *yshb*) are cursed. Interestingly enough, Reuben and Asher, too, "sat" (also יָשׁב) among sheepfolds and by the seashore, respectively, as they, like Meroz, "sat" out Israel's battle (5:16a, 17c).

5.3. Judges 5:24–31

THEOLOGICAL FOCUS 5.3

5.3 Participation in the endeavors of God with God keeps one in the realm of his blessing (5:24–31).

NOTES 5.3

5.3 *Participation in the endeavors of God with God keeps one in the realm of his blessing.*

All those delinquents of 5:15d–17, 23 are contrasted with a woman, a Gentile and related to an ally of the enemy king. But she is the one who takes the decisive action in the campaign against Canaan and for Israel. Indeed, so remarkable are Jael's accomplishments that she is placed on a par with Shamgar, the Philistine killer who wielded an ox goad (3:31); her era is labeled "the days of Jael" (5:6). Thus, the "cursing" and "utterly cursing" of the non-participating Meroz in 5:23 is juxtaposed to the "most blessedness" (×2) of Jael in 5:24: the verse commences and concludes with ברך (*brk*, "bless"). Jael is as fervently blessed (twice) as Meroz is intensely cursed (twice). Unlike the inhabitants of Meroz, Jael was neither an Israelite, nor a town-inhabitant: she was the wife of a Kenite and a tent-dweller (5:24)—all the more reason to consider this woman "most blessed," for she took the side of Yahweh when it was clearly unexpected for her to do so, as opposed to the expected participation of the Israelites. Just as Meroz is a synecdoche for the unwilling and non-participating Israelites, so Jael becomes the exemplar of the willing and participating entities, be they Israelite or Gentile, cosmic or

---

30. "Meroz" is found only here in the OT.

terrestrial, human or non-human. These participants (aka "the Jaelites") did exactly what the non-participants (aka "the Merozians") failed to do: help Yahweh! In sum, the thrust of the song of Judges 5 is on the action/inaction (i.e., participation/non-participation) of various individuals or groups.

Deborah's "motherhood" of Israel is extolled in the early part of the Song (5:7); Sisera's mother is excoriated in the later part (5:28–30). Indeed, one might see Jael, too, as a "mother," giving Sisera milk and curds (5:25).[31] That would make the main characters in the two sections, 5:24–27 and 5:28–30, women: Jael and Sisera's mother. One is a "mother" who kills Sisera; the other is a mother who gave birth to Sisera. Both Jael and Sisera's mother are described by their location and station: tent (5:24) and window (5:28), respectively. Jael puts a tent peg through her victim's "head" (5:26), while Sisera's mother's ladies-in-waiting speculate on the maidens each warrior would capture—"a maiden, two maidens, for every *head*" (i.e., for every person/warrior; 5:30). And so, Jael is exalted, while the other women, and especially Sisera's mother, are humiliated.[32]

Ultimately, then, Sisera's victory and his rape of Israelite women are thwarted by two women: under Deborah's leadership, Sisera's army is defeated; by Jael, Sisera himself is destroyed.[33] She, with finesse, elan, and panache, finishes off Sisera. But here, no thwarted Barak arrives to glimpse the corpse of his enemy (as in 4:27). Instead of the humiliation of Barak, who sees his honor evaporate (4:9), we are shown Sisera's mother and her ladies-in-waiting. It is this company that is now chastised: instead of returning home with rapacious spoil, Sisera is lying dead at the feet of a woman—the macabre joke is on them!

There are seven third person feminine singular verbs in 5:25–26: "she gave," "she brought," "she reached out,"[34] "she hammered," "she crushed," "she shattered," and "she pierced."[35] The feminine endings of the verbs (־ָה, *-ah*) and the nouns (*her* hand, *her* right hand) emphatically pronounce the

---

31. "Sisera, whose forces had been defeated because he had too much water (v. 21), now must beg a bit of water from a woman [5:25], an act which will shortly lead to his death" (Hauser, "Two Songs of Victory," 273).

32. O'Connell, *The Rhetoric of the Book of Judges*, 122–23.

33. In other words, the Canaanite worshipers of Baal and his female consort, Anat, were destroyed by the God of the storm (Yahweh) and by *his* female (human) allies!

34. תִּשְׁלַחְנָה (*tishlakhnah*, "*they* [feminine] reached out") is actually a plural verb.

35. The sequence of five verbs detailing Jael's violent action—מָחֲקָה, וְהָלְמָה, תִּשְׁלַחְנָה, וְחָלְפָה, וּמָחֲצָה, (*tishlakhnah, whalmah, makhaqah, umakhatsah, wkhalpah*; "and she reached out," "and she hammered," "she crushed," "and she shattered," "and she pierced," 5:26)—"is a model of cacophony—the sound of Jael's hammering virtually being driven into the ear of the reader" by the guttural and laminar sounds (ibid., 122).

gender of Jael.³⁶ This cascade of feminine verbs is balanced in 5:27 by an equivalent cadence of seven third person masculine singular verbs: "he sank," "he fell," "he lay," "he sank," "he fell," "he sank," and "he fell."³⁷ The descending cataract (both in phrase length and word count) looks almost as if the action is freeze-framed, literarily painted for the reader³⁸:

בֵּין רַגְלֶיהָ כָּרַע נָפַל שָׁכָב	Between her feet he sank, he fell, he lay,
ben ragleha kara' napal shakab	
בֵּין רַגְלֶיהָ כָּרַע נָפָל	between her feet he sank, he fell,
ben ragleha kara' napal	
בַּאֲשֶׁר כָּרַע	where he sank,
ba'asher kara'	
שָׁם נָפָל	there he fell,
sham napal	
שָׁדוּד	destroyed.
shadud	

---

36. It also helps that "tent peg" and "hammer" are also feminine! As in Judges 4, one may detect here a parody of the sexual act: the use of a tent peg, and Sisera's collapse between Jael's legs/feet (5:26–27). See Deut 28:57; Jdg 3:24; 1 Sam 24:3; Isa 7:20; Ezek 16:25, for "between legs/feet" as a euphemism for genitalia. Niditch also sees sexual imagery in Sisera's "sinking" (Job 31:10), "lying" (Gen 19:32, 34, 35; 34:2, 7; 2 Sam 11:4; 12:24; 13:11, 14; etc.), and his being "destroyed" (Jer 4:30): "ironically, it is a woman who is in the position of rapist, the enemy male general her victim" (*Judges*, 81). As was mentioned in Pericope 4 (Jdg 4:1–24), there is possibly a "juxtaposition of slaughter and sex" (Niditch, "Eroticism and Death," 51), as Alter also observes: "[T]he sharp focus of the poem is simply on the powerful figure of Jael the hammerer, standing over the body of Sisera, whose death throes between her legs, kneeling, then prostrate, may be, perhaps, an ironic glance at the time-honored martial custom of rape" (*The Art of Biblical Poetry*, 49). The expectation of Sisera's capture of sexual booty (5:28–29; see below) also raises the hint of eroticism in the interaction of Jael and Sisera. But Block is right: "The account is filled with irony, to be sure, but such sexual interpretations say more about the interpreter than the text" (*Judges, Ruth*, 240 n.441).

37. Reis notes how, in all, there are also seven instances of "hand" in Judges 4–5 (4:2, 7, 9, 14, 21, 24; 5:26): "that takes Sisera's death out of the hand of Jael and shows it to be the result of God's hidden hand in the affairs of men." The inclusion of "hand" in 4:21 where it might not have been necessary, and the deliberate substitution of "right" for "hand" in 5:26, so as not to disturb the sevenfold count, hints that Reis may be on to something here ("Uncovering Jael and Sisera," 45).

38. Modified from Younger, *Judges, Ruth*, 155.

And it all ends for Sisera: "destroyed." It describes Sisera's ruin with a finality that is stunning: "The place of conception ['between her feet'] has become the place of death."[39]

One "mother" (Deborah) sings (5:2); the other mother in the story (Sisera's) mourns (5:28–30). The latter, a noblewoman, is in an "aristocratic pose, looking out the lattice-work window . . . the conventionalized portrait of the queen mother or woman of status," accompanied by her ladies-in-waiting ("her wise princesses," 5:28).[40] The scene shift from 5:27 to 5:28 is jarring: from Jael's rustic tent, with a corpse on the floor (no doubt with blood and brains splattered all over[41]), to a genteel setting in the precincts of a palatial residence. Here is the "queen mother" lamenting the tarrying of her son's *chariots* (×2, 5:28)—the selfsame infamous conveyances of iron that had been the bane of the Israelites (1:19; 4:3, 13).

The focus of Sisera's women on "spoil" is considerable, repeated four times in 5:30. And it includes both humans and artifacts, the humans primarily women—רחם, *rakham*, literally meaning "womb" and in this context euphemistic for female genitalia, a crude synecdoche for "maiden."[42] The irony is pungent, for the statement reads: "A womb, two wombs for *the warrior's head* [i.e., 'each warrior']" (5:30b). Yes, Sisera's "head" did meet a "womb," one that killed him: "Instead of capturing a womb, a womb captured him. And thus the singers celebrate poetic justice."[43] In fact, even the use of "*two* maidens/wombs" in 5:30 is ironic, for it was, indeed, *two* women, Deborah and Jael, who brought about the destruction of Sisera.[44]

The poetic conclusion in 5:31a pronounces a death wish upon the non-participants, and a prosperity wish upon the participants—an appropriate summary for a hymn that has contrasted these two camps. The enemies of God are any and all who work against his plans and his purposes. The imprecation of 5:31a is deliberately ambiguous: it does not exclusively label non-Israelites, like Jabin, Sisera, et al., as Yahweh's enemies. That category

---

39. Fokkelman, "The Song of Deborah and Barak," 613. Or as Fewell and Gunn remark: "Destroyed by a woman whom he could have easily overpowered, he falls between her legs, stillborn" ("Controlling Perspectives," 404).

40. Niditch, *Judges*, 82.

41. Like spaghetti and meatballs with a lot of sauce decorating the inside of the tent, as I noted in a sermon on this story—yes, I did!

42. This obscene and derogatory term is in line with the "sex and slaughter" motif, the tragic sequel of many a battle from ancient times to the very present. Sisera's mother could certainly have used other terms referring directly to damsels, virgins, or young women, but her choice of this sexually charged term shows up the brutality of war.

43. Fewell and Gunn, "Controlling Perspectives," 408.

44. Chisholm, *Judges and Ruth*, 244 n.103.

could—and probably does—include even those *Israelites* who opposed the divine agenda, such as the non-participants in the battle against Sisera (5:15d–17, 23). Thus it remains an ongoing warning for those who call themselves the people of God but neglect to join in the endeavors of God, for God and his glory, with heart and soul and voice.

"Love" on the other hand (5:31a), characterizes those who are covenantally committed to God's plans and purposes. Loving God is enjoined throughout Scripture (Exod 20:6/Deut 5:10; Deut 6:5; Josh 22:5; 23:11), and its expressions include covenantal obedience (Deut 7:9; 11:1; 30:20; 1 Kgs 3:3; Isa 56:6) and covenantal faithfulness (Ps 31:23). The specifics of the blessing in Jdg 5:31 are interesting: the sun's "rising" (יצא, *yts'*) also described Yahweh's "going out" in 5:4 (and in 4:14). The only other uses of the verb in Judges 4–5 depict Jael "going out" to meet Sisera (4:18), and "going out" to meet Barak (4:22). Thus the ones who love Yahweh (including Jael, the "goer-outer") are clearly linked with Yahweh's own "going out"—in this case to do battle. These humans "go out" with deity! The martial use of the verb is underscored by the description, "like the sun in its *might*"—from גְּבוּרָה, *gburah*; the related word, גִּבּוֹר, *gibbor*, indicates "warriors" and is used as such in 5:13, 23. Thus, there is a close association between loving God and "going out" to fight his battles at his side as warriors, as did the participating Israelites and the one participating non-Israelite woman, the one "most blessed of women" (5:24 [×2]).

And so Pericope 5, as well as the story of Deborah and Barak, comes to an end, with the final line noting that the land had rest for forty years (5:31b), but without any mention of the death of the protagonists. Every other judge in the book is reported to have died (3:11; 4:1; 8:32, 33; 9:54–55; 10:2; 10:5; 11:39; 12:7; 12:10; 12:11; 12:15; 16:30–31), except in this narrative. Perhaps that goes with the ending: these two (the two women, Deborah and Jael) are "like the rising of the sun in its might." And so they continue to rise mightily and inspire the rest of God's people to follow their examples of faithfulness to Yahweh. In other words, those who "bless Yahweh" (and participate in his endeavors with him; 5:9) will themselves be "blessed" (like Jael; 5:24)—forever!.

SERMON FOCUS AND OUTLINES

THEOLOGICAL FOCUS OF PERICOPE 5 FOR PREACHING

5   Participation in the endeavors of God, as he fights for his people and empowers them, keeps one blessed (5:1–31).

Pericope 5: Judges 5:1–31   123

The notion of blessing for those who are aligned with God showed up also in Pericope 4 (Jdg 4:1–24): there the condition for blessing (honor) was faithful courage; here it is participation in the work of God.

Possible Preaching Outlines for Pericope 5[45]

I. Program of God
    God the Divine Warrior: no excuse for non-involvement (5:4–5)
    Dire state of Israel: no excuse for non-involvement (5:6b–7a)
    Dire consequences for enemies of God (5:28–30)
    Dire consequences for non-participants (5:31a)
    Move-to-relevance: God's program in our situation, our day

II. Passivity to God
    Participation of nature: no excuse for non-involvement (5:19–22)
    Tribes as non-participants with God (5:15b–17)
    Consequence: Cursed non-participants (5:23, 31a)
    Move-to-relevance: How we tend to be non-participants

III. Passion for God
    Leaders as participants with God, aligned to his program (5:7b–9)
    Tribes as participants with God (5:11–15a, 18)
    Non-Israelites as participants with God (5:6a)
    Irony: a non-Israelite, non-warrior, non-male joining God (5:24–27)
    Consequence: Blessed participant (5:24, 31b)
    Move-to-relevance: What the blessedness of participation looks like

IV. *Passionately participate with God!*
    Specifics on participating with God[46]

A simpler outline seeks to compare the two attitudes and their consequences:

I. CONDUCT
    Participation of nature: no excuse for non-involvement (5:19–22)
    Tribes as non-participants with God (5:15b–17)
    Leaders as participants with God, aligned with him (5:7b–9)
    Tribes as participants with God (5:11–15a, 18)
    Non-Israelites as participants with God (5:6a)
    Irony: a non-Israelite, non-warrior, non-male joining God (5:24–27)

---

45. This is a difficult pericope to outline in a manner that respects the textual order; after all, it is not narrative prose, but reflective poetry. Chunking the sermon into discrete ideas as shown below is probably the best way to proceed.

46. This sermon could conceivably be utilized to initiate major corporate undertakings of the church that manifest such participation with God in his program to reclaim his world: aid to refugees, evangelistic outreaches, inner city ministry, etc.

       Move-to-relevance: How we tend to be non-participants
II. CONSEQUENCES
       Cursed non-participants (5:23, 31a)
       Blessed participant (5:24, 31b)
       Move-to-relevance: What the blessedness of participation looks like
III. COOPERATION: *Participate with God in his work!*
       Specifics on participating with God

PERICOPE 6

Gideon: Panic and Pride

Judges 6:1–7:22

[Gideon's Call, Skepticism, and Panic;
God's Reassurances; Gideon's Pride]

REVIEW, SUMMARY, PREVIEW

Review of Pericope 5: In Jdg 5:1–31 the Song of Deborah extols God's victory over his enemies. As he, the Divine Warrior, proceeds into action, the call is for his people to participate in his works, with him—the key exhortation of the Song. Non-participants—tribes, individuals—are cursed. Participants—tribes, individuals, particularly the non-Israelite, non-male, non-warrior Jael, and even nature itself—are blessed.

Summary of Pericope 6: The sixth pericope of Judges (6:1—7:22) contains a number of episodes in the life of Gideon, mostly dealing with his fear, all stemming from a lack of trust in God: he pushes back against his commissioning, he is uncertain about his iconoclastic activities, his troop mustering manifests his doubt, as also does his testing of God with the fleece—all this despite God's reassurances regarding his promises, presence, and power. The ironic twist is that after

God enables Gideon to achieve victory over the enemy, this skeptic turns prideful and takes the credit for divine action.

Preview of Pericope 7: The next pericope (Jdg 7:23—8:32) continues and concludes the story of Gideon. His pride shows no containment: he denigrates God's victory over the Midianites, elevating the Ephraimites' capture of the Midianite leaders, and above that, his own capture of their kings. In his hubris, Gideon is completely ruthless, punishing all who dare stand in his way. Finally, his ambition for royal status and the perverse creation of an idol sucks Israel into the abyss of idolatry.

6. Judges 6:1–7:22

THEOLOGICAL FOCUS OF PERICOPE 6

6 Faithful trust in God, in his promises, presence, and power, marked by fearlessness and a refusal to take prideful credit for divine action, results in blessing (6:1—7:22).

  6.1 Reverence for God, including the remembrance of his blessings and the abandonment of ungodly values and practices, results in blessing (6:1–10).

  6.2 Faithful trust in God, his promises and presence, leads to fearlessness (6:11–27).

  6.3 Continuing faithfulness to God, with the humble acceptance of discipline, indicates devotion to God (6:28–32).

  6.4 Faithfulness and fearlessness of the people of God, in light of his incredible power, marks devotion to God (6:33—7:8).

  6.5 God's people refuse to take credit for divine action, eschewing foolish and faithless pride (7:9–22).

OVERVIEW

Gideon's story is made up of ninety-two verses distributed into three chapters; only Samson's with ninety-six verses in four chapters is longer.[1] And Gideon's is the only narrative where Yahweh speaks directly to a judge without a mediator. The Gideon-Abimelech complex (6:1—9:57) is a turning point in the Judges narrative; after this, Yahweh becomes increasingly

---

1. This commentary divides the four chapters of the Gideon story into two pericopes: Pericope 6 (6:1—7:22) and Pericope 7 (7:23—8:32).

harsh in his response to his people (10:13), and there is a notable decrease in divine activity.

As one looks at the story of Gideon, especially its earlier portions, one is struck by the similarities between this protagonist and the paradigmatic Israelite leader, Moses. Both Moses and Gideon are called to deliver Israel in the midst of foreign oppression (Exod 1:11–14; 3:10; Jdg 6:1–6, 14); in both cases, Israel responds by "crying" for help (Exod 2:23–24; Jdg 6:6, 7); when called, Moses and Gideon appear to be in hiding, working for a relative who maintains a cultic setup (Exod 3:1; 6:11, 25; Jdg 6:11); the angel of Yahweh, later designated as "Yahweh" and "God," appears to both (Exod 3:2–7, 11, 15; Jdg 6:11–17, 20); deity names himself in both call stories (Exod 3:14; Jdg 6:10); both Moses and Gideon are asked to "go," "sent" by Yahweh (Exod 3:10, 12; Jdg 6:14); both pushback against the call saying, בִּי אֲדֹנָי (*bi ʾadonay*, "O my Lord"), protesting their inadequacy (Exod 4:10, 13; Jdg 6:13, 15); both are assured of divine support—"Surely I will be with you" (Exod 3:12; Jdg 6:16); both are given a "sign" (Exod 3:12; Jdg 6:17; also "miracles" in Exod 3:20; Jdg 6:13); indeed, both receive two initial signs and still remain apprehensive (Exod 4:1–7, 10, 13; Jdg 6:17, 36, 39; 7:10); theophanies in both call accounts involve fire (Exod 3:2–3; Jdg 6:21); the only instances of locusts in Exodus and Judges are related to Moses and Gideon, respectively (Exod 10:4, 12, 13, 14, 19; Jdg 6:5; 7:12)[2]; the call of each is followed by further commands and the obedience of the one called (Exod 3:16–17 and 4:18–20, 29–30; Jdg 6:25–26 and 6:27–28).[3] However, the final outcome of the calls and of the subsequent deliverance Yahweh accomplishes through these representatives is strikingly different: Moses does not protest any more after the signs he is given, and ultimately Yahweh gets the credit for the salvation accomplished (Exod 14:30–31); but Gideon continues to fret and fear even after the signs and, after the battle, he arrogates to himself the honor of victory, culminating finally in an idol receiving the worship, not Yahweh (Jdg 8:22, 24–27).[4] While we may have anticipated a new Moses, unfortunately Gideon does not turn out to be one.

2. The locusts "go up ... against" (עָלָה ... עַל, *ʿalah ... ʿal*) and "settle" or "camp" in the land (Exod 10:14; Jdg 6:3–4): Yahweh's entomological punishment that was once directed against Israel's oppressors is now, in Gideon's day, directed against Israel, confirming the primacy of an internal opposition to God in Gideon's story, a problem from within (see Jdg 6:1, 9, and below).

3. There is also the commonality of "Midian": Moses's father-in-law, Jethro, was a priest of Midian (Exod 3:1; 18:1); and the Midianites afflict Israel in the Gideon narrative (Jdg 6:1–7, 11; etc.). See Bluedorn, *Yahweh versus Baalism*, 75–77; and especially Wong, "Gideon: A New Moses?" 529–45, for further details.

4. Later in the exodus story, however, the Israelites also fall into idol worship and, as in Gideon's story, jewelry is involved there (Exod 32:1–6; Jdg 8:21, 24–27).

Whereas the prior judges demonstrated relatively focused weaknesses, they were, on the whole, positive. Gideon, however, starts with serious deficiencies, and plunges downhill, even leading his nation astray, something his predecessors had not done. And so while there are positive aspects to Gideon's life story,[5] the negative aspects overwhelm his character as Pericopes 6 and 7 will show. In line with this negative assessment, after Gideon's dismal performance, no other major figure that follows him depicts any positive characteristic. After the heroics of Othniel, Ehud, and Barak (though, after Othniel, all had their weaknesses), here is Gideon who, at the start, tries to escape his commissioning; who, in the middle, is skeptical about Yahweh's assurances; and who, in the end, abandons Yahweh altogether. "[T]he enemy is no longer outside, but inside the people of Israel and inside each and every individual. The struggle is also not only a military one, but a moral and a profoundly religious one. The battle is, as it were, an internal struggle."[6] Israel was becoming Canaan!

6.1. Judges 6:1–10

THEOLOGICAL FOCUS 6.1

6.1 Reverence for God, including the remembrance of his blessings and the abandonment of ungodly values and practices, results in blessing (6:1–10).

NOTES 6.1

6.1 *Reverence for God, including the remembrance of his blessings and the abandonment of ungodly values and practices, results in blessing.*

After the lofty praises sung to Yahweh in Judges 5, from those atmospheric heights the reader is brought down to *terra firma* with an unmistakable thud: "Then the sons of Israel did what was evil in the sight of Yahweh" (6:1). Back to square one!

The structure of 6:1–10 is unusual. According to the paradigm of 2:11–19, one would have expected the raising of a deliverer right after the crying of the Israelites to Yahweh (6:6, 7).

---

5. See Jdg 9:16–17, 23–24, 56–57; Isa 9:4; 10:26; Heb 11:32.
6. Marais, *Representation in Old Testament Narrative Texts*, 108.

Paradigm	Gideon
2:11 Evildoing	6:1
2:14 (×2) To enemies for X years	6:1 Given 7 years
2:18 Groan	6:6, 7 Cry
2:16, 18 Judge raised	[6:14?]
2:18 Yahweh's support	6:16, 34 "with …" "Spirit"
2:16, 18 Fate of enemies	8:28 Subdued
2:19 Land's rest Judge	8:28, 32 40 years Dies

Instead we have a detour. With the introduction of a prophet in 6:8 (אִישׁ נָבִיא, *'ish nabi'*, the only [male] prophet in Judges)—almost exactly how Deborah was introduced (אִשָּׁה נְבִיאָה, *'isshah nabi'ah*, 4:4, the only prophetess in Judges)—one might have anticipated here that a Deborah-like figure would immediately raise up a deliverer on behalf of Yahweh. But no, we are treated to a round of deserved divine excoriation of the nation's behavior (6:8–10). Yahweh's accusation through the prophet has a number of first-person singular verbs that are bounded on either side with first person pronouns (אָנֹכִי, *'anoki*, in 6:8b; and אֲנִי, *'ani*, in 6:10a): "I brought up," "I brought out," "I rescued," "I drove way," "I gave," "I said." In spite of deity's emphatic presence and activity on behalf of his people, it is implied that Israel had chosen to fear not him, but the gods of the Amorites, and had opted to obey them, not Yahweh (6:10).

The wordplays in 6:1–10 are illuminating: Once Yahweh had delivered Israel from the "hand" of the Egyptians and from the "hand" of all their oppressors (6:9), but now he gives them into the "hand" of Midian (6:1). Once Yahweh "gave" his people the land (6:9); now he "gives" them over to the enemy (6:1). Once Yahweh had "brought up" Israel from Egypt (עלה, *'lh*, 6:8); now the Midianites *et al.* "come up" to attack them (also עלה, 6:3 [×2]). All because of Israel's disobedience (6:10). In fact, the narrator creates significant parallels between Yahweh's rebuke through his prophet, here in 6:8–10, and his rebuke through his angel, at Bokim (2:1–2).

Judges 6:8–10	Judges 2:1–2
Prophet:	Angel of Yahweh:
"Thus *says* Yahweh, the God of Israel,	And he *said*,
'It was I who *brought you up from Egypt* ...	"I *brought you up from Egypt*
and gave you their *land*,	and led you into the *land* ....
and *I said* to you,	and *I said*,
"I am Yahweh your God;	'I will never break My covenant with you
you shall not fear the gods of the Amorites	... you shall not make a covenant
in whose *land* you *live* [ישב, yshb].	with the inhabitants [from ישב] of this *land* ....
But you did not obey My voice."'"	*But you did not obey My voice.*'"

However, the results of these two divine rebukes are starkly different. In the earlier one, we are told that the Israelites "lifted up their voices and wept," and "they sacrificed to Yahweh" (2:5). Here nothing of the sort happens; there is absolutely no recorded response from the Israelites. A two-way relationship was rightly expected by deity who identified himself as Yahweh, their Deliverer. But to no avail!

The result was the oppression of the Israelites by the Midianites, depicted in 6:5 as locust-like.[7] The scope of the enemy's attacks was vast and predatory, and their intent was to drive off Israel from the land promised to them by God (6:4). This explains the fleeing of the Israelites into dens in the mountains and other caves and strongholds (6:2). Their predicament is depicted literarily:

```
A     Failed allegiance to Yahweh: "Sons of Israel did evil in Yahweh's sight" (6:1a)
   B     Historical details: present suffering (6:1b–5)
      C     Israel brought low "before Midian" (6:6a)
         D     "Sons of Israel cried to Yahweh" (6:6b)
         D'    "Sons of Israel cried to Yahweh" (6:7a)
      C'    "because of Midian" (6:7b)
   B'    Historical details: past deliverance (6:8–10a)
A'    Failed allegiance to Yahweh: "And you have not obeyed Me" (6:10b)
```

The sons of Israel crying out to Yahweh (*D, D'*) is textually hemmed in by "Midian" (*C, C'*), all because of their failed allegiance to Yahweh (*A–B, B'–A'*). Interestingly, the background data of oppression occupies two verses for

---

7. The Midianites, according to Gen 25:2–4, were the descendants of Abraham through his second wife Keturah. The label seems to be interchangeable with "Ishmaelites" (see Jdg 8:24 and Gen 37:25–36). Their allies, the Amalekites, had already been encountered in 3:13, where they were in cahoots with Eglon, king of Moab. Who the "sons of the east" were is not clear (6:3).

Othniel (3:7–8; eight years of oppression), three verses for Ehud (3:12–14; eighteen years of oppression), three verses for Barak (4:1–3; twenty years of oppression), three verses for Jephthah (10:6–8; eighteen years of oppression), and one verse for Samson (13:1; forty years of oppression). But here, in the Gideon story, it takes *ten* verses (6:1–10) to describe a period of oppression that is the shortest of them all: seven years (6:1). This is the first judge story in which significant detail is provided about the nature of the oppression and affliction (6:1–6), and this is the first narrative in which Israel's cry for help is answered by a rebuke (6:7–10). All in all, we see a decidedly negative characterization of the nation, more so than what has been portrayed thus far.[8] Truly, Israel was descending into the pits!

With the progressive Canaanization of Israel, God's people remain uncertain about Yahweh, his person and his purposes. The narrative expresses this uncertainty in the fluctuation of names for deity. While "Yahweh" (about twenty-five times in Judges 6–8), "angel of Yahweh" (6:11, 12, 21, 22 [×2]), "Yahweh the God of Israel" (6:8), and "Yahweh your/their God" (6:10, 26) are how God is characterized for the most part in the Gideon saga, there seems to be a precise pattern to the use of אֱלֹהִים, *'elohim*, "God." Almost every part of the narrative in Pericope 6 (Jdg 6:1–7:22) concerns a test of some sort, most of them with "if" and a conditional statement evoking the test, and with אֱלֹהִים somewhere in that section: Gideon wants a sign to test who is speaking to him (6:17: "if" in 6:17, and אֱלֹהִים in 6:20); Joash, Gideon's father, puts Baal to the test to defend his own honor (6:31–32: "if" in 6:31 [×2]; אֱלֹהִים = Baal in 6:24); Gideon tests Yahweh twice with the fleece and dew (6:36–40; "if" in 6:36, 37, and אֱלֹהִים in 6:36, 39, 40); Yahweh tests Gideon's troops with a water-lapping task and assuages Gideon's fear with a Midianite's dream (7:1–8, 9–15; "if" in 7:10, and אֱלֹהִים in 7:14). There is clearly a vacillation in Gideon's and Israel's understanding about who God really is.

6.2. Judges 6:11–27

THEOLOGICAL FOCUS 6.2

    6.2   Faithful trust in God, his promises and presence, leads to fearlessness (6:11–27).

---

8. O'Connell, *The Rhetoric of the Book of Judges*, 170.

NOTES 6.2

6.2 Faithful trust in God, his promises and presence, leads to fearlessness.

Unlike the other judges thus far, who were raised up by Yahweh without his explicit presence on stage, here deity has to show up personally to prod the recalcitrant Gideon into action. In 6:11 Gideon, like his fellow-Israelites, is in hiding, threshing wheat in a wine press to keep it from the hands of the Midianites. Yet, the angel of Yahweh addresses him as "O valiant warrior" (6:12)—a hint of cynicism directed towards a man engaged in his task under cover? Gideon is quite skeptical of this divine initiative as indicated by his first, and almost sarcastic, response to the angel in 6:13: "If . . . , why . . . ? And where . . . ?" He shows an abysmal ignorance of why Israel was suffering oppression, even though Yahweh, through his prophet, had just pointed out the reason: disobedience (6:10). Was Gideon oblivious to his nation's evil-doing, even as his father continued to maintain a Baal shrine (6:25)? Gideon appears not to have heard the prophet at all or, even if he did, it seems he did not believe him. In any case, the lengthy interactions between commissioner and commissioned (6:25, 36, 39; 7:2, 4, 7, 9) is unprecedented in the stories of the judges in this book: God is certainly patient.

And Gideon also seems not to have heard (or believed) the recent rehearsal of Yahweh's mighty acts by the prophet. Instead, Gideon recounts that "our fathers told us" that Yahweh had "brought us out of Egypt" (6:13)—a note of skepticism creeping in as he recounts hearsay testimony. This, when Yahweh had just declared unambiguously through his mouthpiece: "It was *I* who brought you out of Egypt" (6:8). Yahweh's assessment was that Israel had abandoned him (6:10). Gideon's assessment was that it was the other way around: Yahweh had abandoned his people and given them over to the Midianites—*God* was to blame for the current disaster. But was not Gideon's own commissioning proof that Yahweh had not abandoned his people?[9]

Even Gideon's second response to his call (6:15) seems misguided. That his family is "the least in Manasseh," seems fictitious. Joash, his father, we understand later, had considerable resources as an owner of bulls and a patron of altars, having at least ten servants, and a considerable reputation in the community—and all of this nobility and affluence during a seven-year period of intense Midianite oppression (6:1, 25–26, 31–32).

And then "the valiant warrior" proceeds, in his third response, to request a sign that would assure him that his interlocutor was Yahweh (6:17).

---

9. Webb, *Judges*, 230.

Altogether Gideon, the skeptic, does not come off looking good in this interaction.

Essentially, Yahweh's three utterances to Gideon dealt with his presence with the latter. The first two (6:12, 14) asserted Yahweh's presence with Gideon in the *present*; the third (in 6:16) promised Yahweh's presence with Gideon in the *future*, with an emphatic "Surely, I will be with you." That, for Gideon, should have been enough! But the irony is that Gideon, an Abiezrite ("Abiezer" = "[the divine] father is my aid"), is clueless about God's attempt to aid his people.[10]

But gradually realizing that his visitor is deserving of honor, Gideon prepares a magnificent meal for him (6:18–19). That Gideon is almost convinced of the divinity of his guest is further established as he goes about preparing an offering to "lay it before" the angel (6:18; the phrase always indicates a sacral context in the presence of Yahweh: Exod 16:33, 34; Num 17:7; Deut 26:4, 10; 1 Sam 10:25). Also, the verb "present" (Jdg 6:19, נגשׁ, *ngsh*, in the *hiphil*) has sacrificial connotations (Lev 2:8; Amos 5:25; Mal 2:12; 3:3). But the identity of his visitor is fully acknowledged by Gideon only after the miraculous consumption of his offering (Jdg 6:22), clear indication that the latter had found favor in Yahweh's eyes—exactly what Gideon had asked for as a test in 6:17. And so, after using "Lord" in 6:15, Gideon, recognizing the identity of his heavenly guest, addresses him in 6:22 as "Lord Yahweh" and, in 6:24, as "Yahweh."[11] In parallel, the narrator, too, shifts the label of the heavenly messenger from "angel of אֱלֹהִים" in 6:20 to "angel of *Yahweh*" in 6:21.

But this recognition of the divine messenger only makes the skeptical Gideon now fearful (6:22–23). All through, the man is shown to be deficient: at first he is disbelieving and sarcastic, unsure of both divine prophecy and divine presence (6:11–13). Then he tries to wiggle out of his responsibility with an excuse of weakness and insignificance, despite Yahweh's promise of strengthening and reassurance of presence (6:14–16). After that, Gideon, uncertain of the identity of his dialogue partner, wants proof in a tangible sign, which Yahweh graciously provides (6:17–21). Now, *seeing* deity, he is afraid (6:22). However, Yahweh bids him peace and exhorts him not to fear (6:23). But even that divine affirmation remains insufficient: see 6:27, his iconoclastic activities nervously undertaken at night; 6:36–40, his plea for more signs; and 7:10, his ongoing fear as acknowledged by Yahweh.

---

10. Block, *Judges, Ruth*, 260 n.519.

11. The earlier use of "Yahweh" by Gideon in 6:13 was tinged with considerable skepticism and sarcasm.

Gideon's surreptitious undertakings by night—obedience in destroying idols, but under cover of darkness: covert commitment[12]—hints at a compromised attitude to God, or at least one that is laced with apprehension, not exactly what ought to have characterized a "valiant warrior" who has just seen God, offered him an acceptable sacrifice, and won from him multiple assurances of divine presence (6:12, 14, 16, 21–24). One also wonders at Gideon's deployment of ten of his servants (6:27). Had not God specifically asked *him* to destroy the cultic items (6:25–26)? The text explicitly tells us that Gideon was afraid "of his father's household and of the men of the city" (6:27). While fear was a problem with Barak, too, here it stems out of a deep doubt about Yahweh, his promises, his purposes, and his presence.[13]

6.3. Judges 6:28–32

THEOLOGICAL FOCUS 6.3

6.3 Continuing faithfulness to God, with the humble acceptance of discipline, indicates devotion to God (6:28–32).

NOTES 6.3

6.3 *Continuing faithfulness to God, with the humble acceptance of discipline, indicates devotion to God.*

God holds the exclusive rights to the worship of his people, and so he instructs Gideon to tear the pagan altar down and build another Yahwistic altar on its ruins (6:25–26). "Pagan gods may tolerate the simultaneous worship of more than one deity, but Yahweh will brook no rivals."[14] Far more serious than Israel's subjugation to Midian was her submission to deities other than Yahweh—harlotry! Incidentally, when Joash refers to the altar of Baal, he calls it "his [Baal's] altar" (6:31–32 [×2]), but when Yahweh refers to it, it is the altar of Baal which is "of your father" (6:25). Clearly the Israelites were responsible for this apostasy and owned it!

One has to wonder about the whole Baal cult established in Gideon's father's household. Even as the Israelites have been crying to Yahweh about

---

12. The episode of idol-breaking is bookended by "night" (6:25, 27).

13. See Pericope 4 (Jdg 4:1–24). There the narrative does not speculate on a cause for Barak's fearfulness, only that his lack of boldness resulted in loss of honor/blessing.

14. Ibid., 265.

the oppression of the Midianites (for *seven years*, 6:1, 6, 7), it appears that Joash's Baal altar and the Asherah have been continuing to do good business on the side! Note that the bull that Gideon is commanded to sacrifice was *seven years* old (6:25). The usual idiom to express age is שְׁנִים [*n*]-בֶּן, *ben*-[n] *shanim* ("son of *n* years"), but here the phrasing is simply שֶׁבַע שָׁנִים, *sheba' shanim* ("seven years"), deliberately making it identical to the statement of the length of the Midianite oppression in 6:1: שֶׁבַע שָׁנִים.[15] Even as they were being disciplined for their disobedience (6:10), they were steeped in apostasy, reveling in bulls, altars, Baals, Asherahs, and all! So much so, when Gideon destroys the pagan cult by night (6:25-27; below), the men of the city want his life (6:28-30). Indeed, their investigation of this sacrilege literally demonstrates their zeal for Baal, in the three back-to-back imperfect verbs that describe it: וַיִּדְרְשׁוּ וַיְבַקְשׁוּ וַיֹּאמְרוּ, *wayyidrshu waybaqshu wayyo'mru* ("and they inquired, and they asked, and they said," 6:29). "Gideon had obeyed the Law of Moses . . . , but a whole Israelite town was ready to kill him for it" (Exod. 34:13; Deut. 7:5; Judg. 2:2).[16] In fact, that sentence of death ought to have been imposed on those idolaters, not on the iconoclast (Deut 13:1-18). This is the first time in Judges that the chosen judge-deliverer has to face opposition from his *own* people (Jdg 6:30), as he seeks to work for Yahweh. "[T]he Israelites of Ophrah have proven themselves to be perfect Canaanites, protecting Baal in the face of Yahweh's self-evident victory."[17] Yes, the Canaanization of Israel seems to be in full swing with no evidence of the people's humility or repentance in the face of divine punishment.

Gideon's act of "tearing down" (נתץ, *ntts*) the Baal altar is mentioned three times (6:28, 30, 32). No doubt this was a creditable act of obedience to divine command.[18] In Jdg 2:2, the command to "tear down" was accompanied by an injunction against "entering into" (כרת, *krt*) a covenant with the Canaanites. So when Gideon destroys the altars, "cuts down" (also כרת)

---

15. Nowhere in the Torah is the sacrifice of a seven-year-old bull commanded. Evidently there is a linkage being made between the sacrificial animal's age and the length of Israel's subjection to Midianite overlordship (Bluedorn, *Yahweh Versus Baalism*, 94-95). On the requirement of two bulls (6:25-26), the first was likely the animal used for the heavy work of demolition of a stone platform and the carrying of burdens, while the second, the seven year-old one, was being reserved for sacrifice as the burnt offering (Webb, *Judges*, 235). The other possibility is to read the text as saying: "Take the bull of your father, the second one, the one seven years old," giving Gideon only a single animal.

16. Chisholm, *Judges and Ruth*, 276.

17. Butler, *Judges*, 206. If this syncretism was going on in the small rural site of Ophrah, surely there must have been other duplicate "Ophrahs" throughout the land (Younger, *Judges, Ruth*, 177).

18. See Exod 34:13; Deut 7:5; 12:3, all employing נתץ.

the Asherah, and builds an altar to Yahweh atop its ruins (6:26, 28, 30), he is literally breaking the covenant with Baal and establishing a legitimate cult to Yahweh—singlehandedly.[19] And so he is renamed "Jerubbaal"—"Let Baal Contend" (a loose etymological label; 6:25).[20] Baal, Gideon's father Joash declared, could take care of his enemies himself, if he so desired (6:31–32).

6.4. Judges 6:33–7:8

THEOLOGICAL FOCUS 6.4

6.4 Faithfulness and fearlessness of the people of God, in light of his incredible power, marks devotion to God (6:33—7:8).

NOTES 6.4

6.4 *Faithfulness and fearlessness of the people of God, in light of his incredible power, marks devotion to God.*

For the first time since Othniel (3:10), the Spirit of Yahweh is involved with a deliverer: he "comes" upon Gideon (the verb, לבשׁ, *lbsh*, means to "clothe/envelop"). Then, like Ehud, Gideon "blows a trumpet" (3:27; 6:34) and, like Barak, Gideon "summons" his troops (4:10; 6:34, 35). Things look hopeful here, and Gideon seems to have gained some confidence. A trumpet summons his own clan, the Abiezrites (6:34), then messengers are sent to canvas Manasseh (6:35a), and later, they muster three more tribes (6:35b).[21] But actually things are not so rosy.

Strikingly, 6:35a and 35b begin identically with disjunctive clauses (with the sequence: subject-verb): "And-messengers he-sent . . . ." Both those unusual constructions deal with Gideon's sending messengers to various other tribes. This creates a gash in the narrative, separating 6:34ab from 6:35ab, and indicates that in the eye of the narrator, "Gideon's extended recruitment is not the *consequence* of his calling anymore but rather forms a *contrast* to his clothing with the spirit and his subsequent recruitment of his clan."[22] This suspicion is later verified: Yahweh's disagreement with Gideon's troop-mustering tactics is substantiated by the fact that, beyond

---

19. Bluedorn, *Yahweh versus Baalism*, 95.

20. On the other hand, "Gideon" (גִּדְעוֹן, *gid'on*, means "hacker, one who hews down" (from גדע, *gd'*, "to hew"; see Deut 7:5; 12:3; 2 Chr 14:3; 31:1; 34:4, 7, where the verb is used to describe the destruction of cultic images and stations).

21. Assis, *Self-Interest or Communal Interest*, 52–53.

22. Bluedorn, *Yahweh Versus Baalism*, 112 (emphases added).

Gideon's calling of his clansmen, the Abiezrites (6:34b), his *two* subsequent expansions of his army (6:35a, 35b) are later negated by *two* divine reductions (7:3, 4–8; below). His enthusiastic corralling of troops across Israel in 6:35 was not the result of his clothing by the Spirit. Unsure of Yahweh's power, the man thinks deity needs a little help, and so he engages in an extensive military draft.

In any case, one would have thought that with all these men eager to fight, Gideon would now be set for battle. Unfortunately that is not the case. Judges 6:36–40 and the following section, 7:1–8, are consumed by two monologues that are quite similar[23]:

"And Gideon said to God" (6:36–40)	"And Yahweh said to Gideon" (7:1–8)
Two turns to speak (6:36–37, 39)	Four turns to speak (7:2–3a, 4, 5b, 7)
"deliverance"; "hand" (6:36, 37)	"deliverance"; "hand" (7:2)
"test" (6:39)	"test" (7:4)
Test with fleece: twice (6:36–37, 39)	Test with troop reduction: twice (7:3, 5–6)
Natural: dew on fleece only	Natural: dismissal of fearful soldiers
Unnatural: dew on ground only	Unnatural: dismissal of drinkers

Gideon's focus is entirely on deliverance for Israel accomplished "by my hand" (×2 in 6:36, 37). That the narrator has only אֱלֹהִים throughout 6:36–40 (the fleece tests), not "Yahweh," suggests distance between this leader and God. Gideon is seemingly unable to distinguish between a generic deity and the specific covenant-keeping God of Israel. Neither is he fully convinced of the power of God and all that that divine power has already accomplished in 6:11–32. So a another series of diagnostic tests are ordered by Gideon.[24] This, despite the fact that Gideon acknowledges *twice* that God had said he would deliver Israel by Gideon: "as You have spoken" (6:36, 37; see 6:14, 16). In fact, Gideon has the gall to admit that he is "testing" God (6:39). The only other instances of the *piel* form of נסה, *nsh* ("test") in Judges is in 2:22 and 3:1, 4—dealing with Yahweh "testing" Israel for faithfulness. The tables have now been turned: now Gideon is "testing" *Yahweh*! That God complies with this man's impudent and imprudent testing is a testimony to God's grace. But, clearly, Gideon is still faithless and fearful.[25]

23. From ibid., 114–15.

24. The first set of exams were given to Yahweh in 6:17; deity passed with flying colors.

25. This episode of Gideon and the fleece and dew is also significant for reasons beyond the test of deity. Baal, the Canaanites believed, was the deity who provided rain and dew that made agriculture productive. See for example the ancient Canaanite myth of Aqhat, *Aqht C*, 42–46 (*ANET*, 153). In fact, one of Baal's daughters is named "Tallaya"

Surprisingly, there is no indication of what Gideon thought of the outcomes of these fleece tests in 6:36–40. Evidently, he (and his troops) continue to be fearful: 7:3 (the army's fear: "afraid and trembling") and 7:10 (the commander's fear). Thus, the location of the Israelite camp is, quite appropriately, at the Spring of *Harod* (חֲרֹד, *kharod*, is related to חָרַד, *kharad*, "to tremble," in 7:3—so, "Spring of Trembling," 7:1).²⁶ After all that has transpired thus far, Gideon is still doubtful, still unsure of Yahweh's deliverance, and still skeptical about Yahweh's power—even after he has just been "clothed"/empowered by the Spirit and has just seen incredible exhibitions of divine power over nature (6:34–40). This is man is surely "an unduly diffident deliverer."²⁷

The failure of Gideon to follow God fully parallels the disobedient and faithless response of the nation, Israel (6:3). When the consequences of their evildoing came to pass, the nation cried out in despair, but without any sign of repentance, and they continued to worship Baal. Nonetheless, God had mercy. In like manner, the individual, Gideon, is skeptical and doubtful time and again. Yet God continues to be gracious with him, repeatedly giving in to Gideon's presumptuous tests of deity. "Thus, Gideon . . . is a microcosm of Israel's reluctance to follow Yhwh wholeheartedly."²⁸

Anyhow, Yahweh is not going to proceed with the huge army Gideon has mustered (6:34–35). Therefore it is God's turn to conduct a "test" now (7:4)! "[F]or Yhwh it is not the deliverance that is in the foreground, but rather the demonstration of his power and his claim to be recognized and worshipped as god."²⁹ He demands that Gideon's forces be pruned, so that Israel may not become boastful (7:2). That Yahweh wants to reduce the

---

("Dew") (Chisholm, *Judges and Ruth,* 279). On the other hand, Scripture is clear that it is Yahweh who provides the dew and the rain: Deut 11:10–17; 1 Kgs 17:1; Hosea 14:5–8; Haggai 1:10–11. So we have here a contest: Yahweh vs. Baal, real power vs. false power. The interesting question, of course, is whose power Gideon will follow—Yahweh's or Baal's.

26. Later on, it will be Midianite army that is "panicked" (also חרד) by Gideon (8:12). There is some question as to the accuracy of "Mount Gilead" (הַר הַגִּלְעָד, *har hagil'ad*, in 7:3, for this location is *east* of the Jordan. Webb sees it as an "accidental miswriting" of הַר הַגִּלְבֹּעַ, *har hagilboa'* ("Mount Gilboa") which is situated close to the Spring of Harod (7:1) (*Judges,* 241–42).

27. O'Connell, *The Rhetoric of the Book of Judges,* 150. Schneider observes wryly that "when Gideon was first introduced he was threshing in a wine press, now he was fleecing on the threshing floor [6:37]. Gideon did nothing in the appropriate place [or way]" (*Judges,* 110).

28. O'Connell, *The Rhetoric of the Book of Judges,* 163.

29. Bluedorn, *Yahweh versus Baalism,* 126. The word used for "test," צרף, *tsrp*, is different from that used in 6:39 by Gideon, נסה. The former is a metallurgical term for the refinement of ore by removing impurity.

"number" (מִסְפָּר, *mispar*, 7:6) of the troops is remarkable, in light of the Midianites and their animals being "without number" (אֵין מִסְפָּר, *'en mispar*, 6:5; 7:12). It is not the fact of the *Midianites'* innumerability that is of concern, but *Israel's*—the number of their troops was far more than what God wanted! Later, Gideon hears the "recounting" of the Midianite soldier's dream (also מִסְפָּר, 7:15), assuring him of victory by the power of God, even with an attenuated army.

So Gideon performs a pruning of personnel: first the fearful ones are eliminated (7:3), then the kneeling drinkers—a rather arbitrary exclusion, apparently not based on any logic (7:4–7).[30] His army is whittled down to about one percent of the original number. Going with the numbers in 7:3, the reduction of troops is as follows: 32,000 → 10,000 → 300. This, in the face of 135,000 enemy troops (8:10)—Gideon ends up with one soldier for every 450 enemy combatants! Whatever confidence Gideon may have gained by his fleece-testing of Yahweh has now evaporated. Without God's power, he is reduced to nothing.

One must not forget that there is more than troop reduction going on here. Notice that the final 300 who remain pick up . . . *trumpets* (7:8; likely part of divine directions to the army)! There is no sign of any weaponry being distributed. Not only was the selection of troops quite idiosyncratic and unconventional, the actual battle promises to be so, too. But knowing what happened with trumpets in the hands of troops in another battle in the book of Joshua, this is certainly a promising, albeit odd, development.

6.5. Judges 7:9–22

THEOLOGICAL FOCUS 6.5

6.5 God's people refuse to take credit for divine action, eschewing foolish and faithless pride (7:9–22).

NOTES 6.5

6.5 *God's people refuse to take credit for divine action, eschewing foolish and faithless pride.*

---

30. The whole episode of lappers vs. kneelers (7:1–8), and that of the bizarre dream sequence later (7:9–15), not to mention the actual "battle" and the Midianites' defeat (7:16–22; see below), defeat reason. Strange things happen here: it is obviously not the work of Gideon and his men that achieves the victory over the enemy, but the power of God.

There was no way a 300-strong army was going to successfully take on 135,000 "Midianites and the Amalekites and all the sons of the east, ... as locusts abundant, and camels innumerable, like the sand on the seashore copious" (7:12). Anticipating that Gideon's fear would aggravate the situation, Yahweh takes the initiative and promises to give him yet another sign (7:9–11).

The introduction to Yahweh's earlier command to destroy the altar of Baal (6:25) is identical in wording to his current command to go against the Midianites (7:9): both begin with "And it came about, in that same night, Yahweh said to him . . . ." This was a confirmation that Yahweh would use Gideon successfully once more to demonstrate his superiority.[31] But Gideon is still fearful: the structure of 7:9–11, Yahweh's command to Gideon, emphasizes the latter's fear[32]:

7:9a	"*go down* against the CAMP"	
7:9b	"I have given it into **your hand**"	
7:10a		"afraid to *go down, go ... down* to the CAMP"
7:11a	"**your hand** will be strengthened"	
7:11b	"*go down* against the CAMP"	

Gideon's fear (7:10a) is bounded literarily on either side by Yahweh's encouragement to "go down" "against the camp" (7:9a, 11b), and on one side, by a promise that Midian had been given into Gideon's "hand" (7:9b) and on the other, an affirmation that Gideon's "hand" would be strengthened (7:11a). What will Gideon see and believe—the power of God or the power of man?

Following God's directions (7:9–11), Gideon and his servant arrive at the Midianite camp at the exact moment that an enemy soldier is recounting his dream to a friend who gives it an ominous interpretation (7:13–14). Just as Yahweh had promised to "defeat" Midian (נכה, *nkh*, 6:16), so also a miraculous loaf of barley bread comes tumbling into the camp of Midian and "strikes" the dreamer's tent (also נכה, 7:13): "and it fell, and it overturned, and it fell, the tent"—total destruction. The double use of the root נפל (*npl*, "fall," 7:13) reminds the reader that the same verb described the "fall" of Eglon (3:28) and that of Sisera (4:22; 5:27 [×3]); that fate would now befall (!) "Midian and all the camp" (7:14).[33] And it would all be a miraculous work of God, as the dream depicted and the Midianite interpreted (7:14).

---

31. Ibid., 129.
32. Modified from Fokkelman, *Reading Biblical Narrative*, 113.
33. Notice also that the innumerable hosts of Midian were "lying" (also from נפל)

It is strange that with the kind of numbers on the side of the Midianites they would be scared of a barley loaf of a man called Gideon. But this is supernaturally inspired fear and they are convinced that Gideon's God was against them. Their declaration that "God has given Midian and all the camp into his [Gideon's] hand" (7:13b) virtually echoes Yahweh's own promises (6:14, 16; 7:7, 9). The Midianites seem to have "a faith in God's power that seems to be sorely lacking among the Israelites," particularly in their divinely appointed leader, Gideon.[34] He had obtained the promise directly from Yahweh that he, Gideon, would be Yahweh's agent for defeating the Midianites (6:14, 16; and 7:7, 9); his request for a sign to verify the identity of this Promiser had been given (6:17–24); he had been granted success and safety in his destruction of a pagan altar (6:25–32); he had been clothed and empowered by Yahweh's Spirit (6:34b); he had mustered an army (6:34b–35; see 7:3); his request for more signs to test Yahweh had been affirmatively answered (6:36–40). Yet the man was still fearful (7:10) . . . until he heard it from the lips of a dreaming Midianite soldier. *Now* he's convinced, and he bows in worship (7:15)!

However, we are not told specifically whom or what Gideon worships. It might be a fair assumption that it is Yahweh, seeing that he utters the name immediately afterwards (7:15b). Yet we must pause. The verb, חוה, *khwh* ("to bow in worship") is used in the *hishtaphel* elsewhere in Judges only for the worship of gods *other* than Yahweh (2:12, 17, 19). So we are led by the narrator to suspect that Gideon's worship, "which outwardly is directed towards Yhwh, is not really focused on him."[35] Even Gideon's subsequent exhortation to his army that Yahweh had given Midian into "your hands" (7:15) seems flawed: Yahweh had never promised to give Midian into the *Israelites'* hand. The prior promises of Yahweh specifically noted "into *your* [Gideon's] hand" (7:7, 9, 11; so also the Midianite's interpretation in 7:14; and the individualized assurances to *Gideon*, not to the nation at large: 6:12, 14, 16 ["as *one man*"], 36). So there is ambiguity in both Gideon's actions and his words in 7:15. Ominously enough, this "bowing in worship" is the last interaction between Gideon and Yahweh. Later, this diminishing of deity becomes pronounced. There is no post-battle victory celebration that praises God, as was conducted by the Israelites after the exodus under Moses (Exodus 15). There is no triumphant paean, as was sung by Deborah after the defeat of the Canaanites (Judges 5). Instead, we will find a presumptuous Gideon who dares to usurp the glory of the conquest, an honor

---

in the valley (7:12).

34. Matthews, *Judges and Ruth*, 92.
35. Bluedorn, *Yahweh versus Baalism*, 136–37.

that belonged to God alone, by whose power alone the victory was won (see below).

Notice the differences between human activity and divine activity in the battle (7:20–21 and 7:22):

7:20–21	Human activity:	trumpets "blown"	Israelites stand	Midianites "flee"
7:22	Divine activity:	trumpets "blew"	Yahweh fights	Midianites "flee"

In 7:22, the subject of the "blowing" is, surprisingly, the 300 trumpets: it is as if the horns were going off on their own, as if to point out that absolutely no humans were involved at all![36] In fact, the text specifically states that "each man stood in his place" (7:20): they just *stood* there, while Yahweh went on a rampage! That creates a striking contrast between the Israelites' standing in place and the Midianites "running," "crying," "fleeing" (7:21). In any case, it is not the weapons of the Israelites, but their trumpets that are emphasized in the battle: "trumpet" appears eight times (7:8, 16, 17, 19, 20, 22) and "blow" six times (7:18, 19, 20, 22), clearly alluding to another miraculous victory that was won by Yahweh, when also the humans did nothing but "blow trumpets" (Josh 6:4, 8, 9, 13, 16, 20). So much so, one wonders where the "sword" in the battle cry of the soldiers came from (Jdg 7:20); Gideon's instructions had never called for a slogan with "sword" (7:18). Indeed, the absence of swords is pungently ironic, for all Gideon's army had were trumpets, pitchers, and torches (7:16). And there is no indication that these 300 Israelites did anything but blow trumpets, break pitchers, and expose torches (and scream). Very specifically, we are told that both their right and their left hands were occupied holding trumpets and torches, respectively (7:20).[37] Indeed, the only "sword" employed in the battle is the weapon of "one [Midianite] against another even throughout the whole army"— a "sword" that was "set" by Yahweh (7:22), ironically slaying 120,000 "*swords*-men" (lit., "*sword*-drawing men") (8:10).[38] In other words, no swords were wielded here by Gideon and his men! The victory was all of God's doing.

In retrospect, the earlier war cry, "For Yahweh *and for Gideon*" (7:18), also looks odd. Ehud, in his battle, aroused his troops with "Yahweh has given your enemies the Moabites into your hand" (3:28). And Deborah similarly: "This is the day in which Yahweh has given Sisera into your hand" (4:14).

---

36. Assis, *Self-Interest or Communal Interest*, 80.

37. That Gideon's strategy was probably authorized by Yahweh seems evident in its humanly obvious inutility and ridiculousness, as well by the allusion to the battle of Jericho.

38. Block, *Judges, Ruth*, 291.

In fact, Gideon, too, had exhorted his troops in like fashion: "Yahweh has given the camp of Midian into your hand" (7:15). So why the sudden urge for Gideon to personalize this assault on the Midianites (7:18), especially when Yahweh's expressly stated goal was to *not* share the glory of victory with humans (7:2)? It looks as if Gideon was doing exactly that—seeking to share the honors with Yahweh for the anticipated triumph.[39] Even his subsequent instructions to his troops seem a bit self-centered, as he asks them to mimic him (7:17–18). This man wants a piece of the limelight. In sum, Yahweh's suspicions about Israel and Gideon (7:2) turn out to be true: the humans had equated deity's power with their own puny (non-)efforts and had become boastful (7:18, 20).[40] The strife between Yahweh and Baal had now become a contention between Yahweh and Israel who dared to steal Yahweh's glory.

Perhaps the misconstrual began with the interpretation of the Midianite's dream that juxtaposed sword, Gideon, and God: "This is nothing but the *sword* of *Gideon*" (7:14b). But even here, man and God were *not* equated; God was acknowledged to be the prime mover: "*God* has given Midian and all the camp into his [Gideon's] hand" (7:14c). But in its translation by Gideon (7:18) and by his army (7:20), something got lost: individual responsibilities got adjusted, and no distinction was made between the one who waged the war and the One whose power gave the victory. This is especially striking since in every other victory of every other judge until now, Yahweh's actions are given priority: 3:10, 28; 4:14 (and even in this account, 7:15). But for Gideon, this noble sentiment is quickly corrupted and he sees himself as partially responsible for what was entirely a work of God, an equal partner in Gideon-Yahweh, Inc. Woefully, there is no sign of Yahweh in this scene (7:15–18). "The most significant irony of the narrative is that Yahweh does convince Gideon of a power beyond reason—belief—and that Gideon ascribes that power to himself, to Gideon, rather than to Yahweh."[41] Skepticism, sadly, had turned into swagger.

---

39. A dedicatory cultic description dated to 604 BCE discovered in Ekron reads לבעל ולפדי, *lb'l wlpdi* ("for Ba'al and for Padi"): Ba'al-zebub was the "god of Ekron" (2 Kgs 2:1–3); Padi, the king of Ekron, is named in other inscriptions (see *ANET*, 287–88). Such a combination of deity + monarch in a single dedication may be what is envisaged here in Jdg 7:18, 20 (also see 2 Sam 15:21 for a similar use in an oath formula) (Gitin and Cogan, "A New Type of Dedicatory Inscription," 193–202). All of this gives one the sense that Gideon has become the *de facto* ruler of Israel, a suspicion that becomes verified in the next pericope, Pericope 7 (Jdg 7:23—8:32).

40. Contrary to Deut 8:17–18; 32:26–27.

41. Klein, *The Triumph of Irony*, 67.

SERMON FOCUS AND OUTLINES

> **THEOLOGICAL FOCUS OF PERICOPE 6 FOR PREACHING**
> 6 Faithful trust in God, without pridefully taking credit for divine action, leads to blessing (6:1—7:22).

Since there are several themes here that show up in other pericopes, some distinctions must be made. Pericope 4 (Jdg 4:1–24) dealt with Barak's faithless fear that lost him honor and blessing. The theological thrust of this current pericope, though also it deals with Gideon's fear, is best focused on his foolish arrogation of credit for what God had done. This is the story of a fearful and skeptical man who, ironically, when God has helped him accomplish a miraculous victory in battle, takes prideful credit for divine action—a danger faced by all children of God. Pericope 7 (Jdg 7:23—8:32) will show a Gideon whose hubristic ambition knows no limits, as he engages in personal vendettas and self-promotion. The theological thrust there is his uncontrolled thirst for power.

Possible Preaching Outlines for Pericope 6

For this first outline, I've tried to include as much of the story as possible (it probably ought to be condensed further), in an attempt to show the progressive deterioration of Gideon's character, with the counterpoint of all the assurances given him. A single move-to-relevance in the fourth move (serving the first four moves together) should be sufficient.[42]

    I. Gideon's Reservation
        Background: Israel's evildoing, divine punishment and rebuke (6:1–10)
        Gideon's three skeptical responses (6:11–18)
        God's reassurances (6:19–24)
    II. Gideon's Uncertainty
        Gideon's uncertainty: his nocturnal activity; Israel's idolatry (6:25–32)
        God's support through his Spirit (6:34)
    III. Gideon's Doubt
        Gideon's mustering of troops, twice testing God (6:35–40)
    IV. Gideon's Panic
        God's pruning of the army (7:1–11)
        Gideon's fear (7:3, 9–10)
        God's confirmation through a dream (7:12–15)

---

42. Or the first four moves/points could be consolidated into a single move, without as much detail—"Gideon's Panic."

  Move-to-relevance: How we are skeptical and fearful, not trusting God
V. Gideon's Pride
  God's defeat of Midian; Gideon and his passive "war" (7:16–22)
  Gideon's arrogation of honor (7:18)
  Move-to-relevance: Our taking prideful credit for divine action
VI. *Trust God, abandon pride!*
  Specifics on overcoming the delusion of our own abilities

Another option worth considering is to lump all of Gideon's skeptical attitudes and actions into one move and follow that up with all of God's reassurances in the second.

I. Gideon's Alarm
  Background: Israel's evildoing, divine punishment and rebuke (6:1–10)
  Gideon's three skeptical responses (6:11–24)
  Gideon's doubt: twice testing God (6:35–40)
  Gideon's fear following a divine pruning of his army (7:1–15)
  Move-to-relevance: How we are skeptical and fearful, not trusting God
I. God's Assurance
  God's reassurance of his presence and Gideon's success (6:11–24)
  God's responses to Gideon's tests (6:35–40)
  God's confirmation of Gideon's victory through a dream (7:1–15)
  Move-to-relevance: God's promises that we can trust
III. Gideon's Arrogance
  God's defeat of Midian; Gideon and his passive "war" (7:16–22)
  Gideon's arrogation of honor (7:18)
  Move-to-relevance: Our taking prideful credit for divine action
III. *Trust God, abandon pride!*
  Specifics on overcoming the prideful delusion of our own abilities

PERICOPE 7

Gideon: Power and Perversion

Judges 7:23–8:32

[Gideon's Vendettas; His Claim to Royalty;
His Promotion of Idolatry]

REVIEW, SUMMARY, PREVIEW

Review of Pericope 6: In Jdg 6:1—7:22, Gideon's fear is foregrounded, stemming from his lack of trust in God, manifest in his reluctant commissioning, nocturnal iconoclasm, unsanctioned troop mustering, and presumptuous testing of God. All this, despite God's assurances regarding his promises, presence, and power. The irony of the account is that once God enables Gideon to achieve victory over the enemy, this skeptic turns prideful and takes the credit for divine action.

Summary of Pericope 7: The seventh pericope of Judges (7:23—8:32) continues and concludes the story of Gideon. His pride shows no containment: he engages in an illicit mustering of troops, he denigrates God's victory over the Midianites, elevating the Ephraimites' capture of the Midianite leaders, and above that, his own capture of their kings. In his hubris, he is completely ruthless, punishing any and all who dare stand in his way. Gideon's ambition leads him to seek royal status, its paraphernalia and its power. Ultimately, his perverse creation of an idol sucks Israel into the abyss of idolatry—the disastrous consequence of uncontrolled ambition.

Preview of Pericope 8: The next pericope, Jdg 8:33—10:5, has the story of Abimelech, the continuation—and natural consequence—of Gideon's story. This ruler was unsanctioned by God and appointed by humans, paid from Baal's temple. A totally unmerciful despot, ruthless and brutal, this ungodly leader wantonly kills his own siblings and many fellow Israelites. He meets his just deserts in appropriate divine retribution exacted upon him.

7. Judges 7:23–8:32

THEOLOGICAL FOCUS OF PERICOPE 7

7 Godliness is expressed in the rejection of self-glorifying vendettas and pursuits of power (7:23—8:32).

   7.1 The godly person eschews the pursuit of personal glory (7:23—8:3).

   7.2 The godly person rejects self-glorifying, personal vendettas against one's own (8:4–17).

   7.3 The godly person rejects self-glorifying personal vendettas even against one's foes (8:18–21a).

   7.4 The godly person demonstrates no misdirected ambition to attain power (8:21b–32).

OVERVIEW

After Jdg 7:22, with Israel's victory over the Midianites accomplished, one would have expected the narrative to conclude with the notice of the Midianites being subdued and the land obtaining rest, followed by an announcement of Gideon's death and its aftermath. But a statement to that effect shows up only in 8:28: so 7:23—8:27 intervenes between 7:22 and 8:28, the bulk of this pericope.[1] This "interpolation" adds some unsavory dimensions

---

1. In most of the preceding judge stories, the defeat of the enemy coincides with the report of the land's rest and the death of the judge (3:10–11, 29–30). With the Deborah-Barak story, the interpolation of the song in Judges 5 puts off the notice of the land's rest *after* the victory celebrations (4:3–24 with 5:31b); there is no death of judge in that story.

to Gideon's life—his battle with his own people and his adoption of idolatry, the national significance of which concludes the Gideon saga[2]:

A	Gideon fights idolatry (6:1–32; "Ophrah," 6:11, 24)	Pericope 6
B	Gideon fights Israel's enemies (6:33–7:22)	
B'	Gideon fights Israel (7:22–8:21)	Pericope 7
A'	Gideon adopts idolatry (8:22–32; "Ophrah," 8:27, 32)	

Appropriately enough, Yahweh almost disappears from this disconcerting pericope! Pericope 6 (Jdg 6:1—7:22) focused considerably on Yahweh (he or his agents made thirteen discrete utterances: 6:8–10, 12, 14, 16, 18, 20, 23, 25; 7:2–3, 4, 5, 7, 9–11). But there is no mention of Yahweh here in Pericope 7, with the exception of Gideon's invocation of his name as part of a threat (8:7) and in an oath (8:19). In other words, here the text turns its spotlight exclusively on Gideon and his self-promoting enterprises. But there is אֱלֹהִים (*ʾelohim*, "God") in 8:3, Yahweh converted to "God" in the hearts and minds of his people—and sadly, even in the heart and mind of his leader. So it comes as no surprise that, later in the narrative, the reader sees "Israel's transition from partial to total worship of Baal-Berith after Gideon's death (8:33)."[3] Canaanization has set in!

7.1. Judges 7:23–8:3

THEOLOGICAL FOCUS 7.1

7.1   The godly person eschews the pursuit of personal glory (7:23—8:3).

NOTES 7.1

7.1   The godly person eschews the pursuit of personal glory.

The summoning of troops in 7:23–25 harks back to an earlier mustering in 6:35, where also Manasseh, Asher, and Naphtali were involved (Zebulun, though present in that account, is missing here). That first assemblage in Judges 6, it was noted in Pericope 6 (Jdg 6:1—7:22), was not in accordance with divine plan, necessitating a significant reduction of troops at Yahweh's

---

2. Table adapted from Gooding, "The Composition of the Book of Judges," 74. What began as localized idolatry (6:25–32; note references to "Ophrah") ends with statewide idolatry (8:24–27, 33; note, again, references to "Ophrah").

3. Polzin, *Moses and the Deuteronomist*, 171.

instigation. Here, Gideon repeats that mistake, completely negating the shrinkage of his army Yahweh had ordered.[4] He had forgotten the whole purpose of Yahweh's pruning of Israel's forces—to keep him and the nation from boasting (7:2). The focus is now back on Gideon, who has virtually countered the grandness of Yahweh's plans and performance in this battle.

The Midianite's dream in 7:13 suggested that the victory of Gideon would be achieved in one dramatic finale (by one falling loaf!). But Gideon's transaction of this war involves a multiplicity of campaigns and stratagems including a re-mustering of those troops Yahweh had seen fit to eliminate. But unlike before, deity does not intervene here to set Gideon straight. Indeed, one wonders why Gideon would need extra troops after Yahweh had "set the sword of one against another, even throughout the *whole* army," and when that enemy army had fled far and wide (7:22). This was probably an attempt by Gideon to steal some of the glory of victory for himself, his showing off before fellow-Israelites. One remembers that in 7:21, a mere 300 people were involved in *doing nothing* (except blow trumpets, break pitchers, expose torches, and yell and scream). That probably was humbling for Gideon. After all, what honor is there in standing still while someone else (Yahweh) does all the glamorous work?

And whence this sudden urge of Gideon to fight, particularly seeing the multitude of his hesitations in the past (6:13, 15, 17–22, 27, 36–40; 7:1–8, 9)? Now that the bulk of the enemy has been defeated, Gideon is all valorous and venturesome. The coward has become confident, so much so the scope of his actions takes Gideon and his army east of the Dead Sea, to Karkor (8:4, 10). The Midianites that Gideon was pursuing had clearly left Israelite territory and the threat to Israel had thereby been eliminated, raising the question of whether another grand mustering of troops by Gideon was necessary (7:23–24).[5] And besides, Yahweh is not at all involved in Judges 8. All of this raises suspicions about Gideon's undertakings.

In fact, this is more than an attempt to finish off the enemy leaders and kings and wipe out the remnant of the enemy forces. A strange alternation

---

4. Both in 7:8 and in 7:23, the recruits (sent home in one case, summoned in the other) are "men of Israel." So this current human expansion is a counteraction of the earlier divine reduction.

5. The subsequent execution of the leaders of Midian—Oreb on a "rock" and Zeeb on a "winepress" (7:25)—remind us of the settings of Gideon's call in 6:11–24 ("rock," 6:21; "winepress," 6:11, though a different Hebrew word is used for the latter). With these allusions to Gideon's commissioning, one may assume that this killing of enemy leaders was appropriate; thus far the slaughtering of enemy leaders has been mentioned in all judge stories: 3:10 (implied), 21–22; 4:21–22 (also see 1:7). But Gideon's mobilization of troops for this purpose—and, indeed, whether he needed to chase the Midianite leaders and kings in territories not allotted to Israel in the first place—is questionable.

is created thrice in 7:23—8:17: pursuit of Midianite foes vs. clashes with Israelite fellows[6]:

7:23–25	Midianite leaders
8:1–3	Ephraimites
8:4–5	Midianite kings
8:6–9	Succothites/Penuelites
8:10–12	Midianite kings and army
8:13–17	Succothites/Penuelites
8:18–21	Midianite kings

The clashes with Israelites are literally interspersed with Gideon's pursuit of the leaders of Midian, Oreb and Zeeb, and the kings of Midian, Zebah and Zalmunna. The narrator seems to be emphasizing a dangerous equivalence in Gideon's eyes between foes and fellows, Midianites and Israelites. And so the man called by Yahweh to defeat his enemies is now, equally zealously, fighting his own countrymen.

In any case, the leaders of Midian, Oreb and Zeeb are the ones captured initially (7:25). The first instance of "killed" in Judges occurs in 7:25 (הרג, *hrg* [×2]), a verb that gets much currency later in this pericope and in the next (8:17, 18, 19, 20, 21; 9:5, 18, 24 [×2], 45, 54, 56). These instances form fourteen of the sixteen uses of the root in Judges (the other two occur in 16:2; 20:5). Since Abimelech's story is uniformly negative in outlook and scope (see Pericope 8: Jdg 8:33—10:5), the use in Gideon's story of a verb, הרג, that is extensively employed in the former is surely pejorative. Gideon has become the enemy-killer—but what is worse is that he has transformed into an *Israelite*-killer, too (8:17; see below)!

It all began with the contention of the Ephraimites (8:1) that they had not been invited with the other tribes earlier on to participate in the anti-Midian campaign (6:35; 7:24). Their call had come only when it appeared that the fleeing remnant of Midian would traverse their territory. Irrespective of whether this offence was real or merely perceived, Gideon responds diplomatically to the stinging questioning of the Ephraimites—an emphatic contrast to how he responds to the Succothites and Penuelites later (8:4–9, 13–17). His self-deprecation (twice: "What did I do . . . ?" and "What was I able to do . . . ?" [8:2a, 3b]) seems commendable. Yet, one notes that in 8:3, Gideon refers to deity as אֱלֹהִים ("God"), not as "Yahweh," and this when speaking to fellow-Israelites. But, more ominously, Gideon's apparently tactful answer to the Ephraimites—using motifs from his winepress provenance

---

6. From Assis, *Self-Interest or Communal Interest*, 81.

(6:11): "gleanings" and "vintage" (8:2)—actually reveal his own glory-seeking obsession. He soothes the contenders with the declaration that the "gleanings" gathered after the harvest (i.e., the killing of the enemy leaders by the Ephraimites [7:25]), was of greater honor and glory than the "vintage," the harvest itself (i.e., the routing of the army by Gideon's forces, symbolized by "Abiezer" [8:2]). In other words, Gideon thinks that the military victory over the army—actually accomplished solely by Yahweh (7:22)—is of *less value* than the capture of Midian's leaders by the Ephraimites. And so if the battle were merely the "vintage," and the killing of the *leaders* of Midian the "gleanings," how much more important would be the killing of the *kings* of Midian, that he, Gideon, aspired to accomplish (see below)? This was pure and unalloyed hubris. Gideon was seeking the highest honor and greatest glory in the battle. God got the "vintage" (the bronze medal); the Ephramites get the "gleanings," of greater value (the silver medal); but Gideon was planning to skim off the *crème de la crème*, of greatest value (the gold medal)! Thus this account of the episode with the Ephraimites serves the purpose of portraying Gideon's hierarchy of values: Yahweh's triumph in battle at the bottom, Ephraimites' capture of leaders in the middle, and his own capture of kings uppermost.[7] Or in other words, God's work deserved the lowest grade, the Ephraimites' work merited a middling grade, but Gideon's own work would win the highest grade. In one fell swoop, he both denigrates God's help and exalts his own powers and achievements.

This was a man laboring under the misconception that what he was doing was worthy of greater glory than what Yahweh had done. Perhaps he was trying to compensate for his own inaction and insignificance in the actual battle, where he and his army simply "stood," blowing trumpets, breaking pitchers, exposing torches, and making noise (7:20–22). Now he needed to do *something* to salvage his honor, all of which Yahweh had corralled for himself. One remembers, from Pericope 6, that Yahweh's explicit intention in taking the initiative in the battle was to prevent the Israelites (and their leader, Gideon) from boasting (7:2)—but this was exactly what Gideon was doing now.

---

7. This might also explain the considerable text-space devoted to the capture, taunting, and execution of those kings at the hand of Gideon himself—a personal, singlehanded dispatching of those rulers and the obtaining of mementoes of that medal-winning accomplishment.

7.2. Judges 8:4–17

THEOLOGICAL FOCUS 7.2

7.2 The godly person rejects self-glorifying personal vendettas against one's own (8:4–17).

NOTES 7.2

7.2 The godly person rejects self-glorifying, personal vendettas against one's own.

The "pursuit" in 8:4 is interesting on its own: of all the instances of the verb רדף, *rdp*, in Judges (1:6; 3:28; 4:16; 4:22; 7:23, 25; 8:4, 5, 12; 9:40; 20:43), this is the only time when the object of pursuit is not mentioned. This chase, the narrator seems to imply, is pursuit for the sake of pursuit. The whole affair has devolved into a personal vendetta, a moral fiasco that emphasizes Gideon's flawed character.[8]

Rather glibly, Gideon asserts to the Succothites: "When Yahweh has given Zebah and Zalmunna into my hands . . . " (8:7). But there had been no promise from Yahweh to Gideon to that effect. And there is no celebratory reference to Yahweh later, when Gideon finally captures those kings of Midian, making his pious declaration in 8:7 quite empty. Either Gideon was merely using "Yahweh" to scare his listeners, or he had become quite presumptuous, assuming that Yahweh was sanctioning all of his violent post-battle excesses. In any case, his employment of "Yahweh" in connection with the punishment he would wreak on the Succothites is clearly out of line. And in Gideon's dealings with the Penuelites, Yahweh does not show up at all (8:8–9). Later, another loose employment of "Yahweh" rolls off Gideon's tongue in 8:19, as part of an oath. The truth is that there is really no participation by Yahweh in Judges 8, except in Gideon's own unfocused mind (8:7, 19).[9] He is really in this for himself and he is really in it alone.

And notice how Gideon phrases his request to the Succothites: "Please give loaves of bread to the people who are following me, because *they* are weary, and[10] *I* am pursuing Zebah and Zalmunna, the kings of Midian"

---

8. Bluedorn, *Yahweh versus Baalism*, 152. One must also note that Gideon's search for support and provisioning fails *twice* (8:5–6, 8), a discomfiture that becomes the cause of his contention with the Succothites and Penuelites. The reader is forced to ask whether Yahweh was in this undertaking at all.

9. This, as opposed to Yahweh's definitive involvement in 7:22.

10. Bluedorn reads the conjunction as adversative: "*but* I . . . " (ibid., 154).

(8:5). Not only does he draw a contrast between himself (using the pronoun אָנֹכִי, 'anoki, "I") and his troops (using the pronoun הֵם, hem, "they"), he also asserts that *they* are weary, but that *he*—ostensibly not weary—is pursuing (all on his own?) those enemy kings. Again, one gets the feeling that this man, Gideon, with seemingly undiluted vigor and energy is pursuing a personal agenda, and that he will do it all on his own, even if his followers are left behind, the poor fatigued saps!

What is equally abhorrent is that after he has accomplished his objective of capturing the Midianite kings (8:12), his first action is not the execution of these captives, but the reprehensible and unduly malevolent punishment of his own fellow-Israelites, the Succothites and the Penuelites (8:13–17). Only after he is done with these shameless acts against his own countrymen does he proceed to deal with the foreign kings (8:18–21). It appears as if Gideon is enjoying himself in psychopathic fashion, paying people back for offending him. That Gideon took the objections of the Succothites (8:5), and presumably that of the Penuelites, too (8:8), as a personal affront is made clear in 8:15, where he labels the response of the leaders of Succoth as a "taunt."

Gideon's capture of a youth, who provided a list of the leaders of Succoth (8:14), was fortunate for the Succothites, "for given what happened next at Penuel, Gidoeon might have simply butchered the whole town had he not worked from a list" of culpable individuals.[11] Incidentally, the hit list has the names of "seventy-seven" elders. The only two other instances of "seventy-seven" in the OT is in connection with Lamech: in Gen 5:31 he lives to be a hundred and "seventy-seven." But the other reference in relation to the same individual is more significant: in 4:24 Lamech crows about being avenged "seventy-seven"-fold. Now another avenger is on the scene unleashing his wrath on "seventy-seven" (Jdg 8:14).

Gideon's promise to the Penuelites is ironic: he will tear down their tower "when I return *in peace*" (8:9). The man returns, but not in peace—he has war on his mind: he not only tears down the tower at Penuel, but also kills the men of the city (8:17). The reuse of הרג, "to slay," in 8:17—of the killing of the Penuelites—recalls the killing of the Midianite leaders in 7:25 (the first use of the same verb in Judges). "This is not the killing that happens in the heat of battle, but the cold-blooded payback killing that happens after it, when the man who now has unchallengeable power uses it to settle old scores."[12] It appears, then, that Gideon has done to random fellow-Israelites what was reserved for enemy rulers (also see 8:18, 19, 20, 21, for other uses

11. Sasson, *Judges 1–12*, 362.
12. Webb, *Judges*, 257.

of הרג in this pericope). "Gideon, so to speak, replaces the oppression by the Midianites and becomes Israel's new oppressor."[13] Gideon's destruction of Succoth and Penuel follows (8:16–17)—a war being executed by an Israelite leader/army upon other Israelites.

Strangely, after 7:14, the next time Gideon is referred to as the "son of Joash" is here in 8:13, after he has captured Zebah and Zalmunna, the pair of Midianite kings. Perhaps this is to remind us of how far the "son of Joash" had come since his call in Judges 6. Notice the employment of agricultural metaphors: once he "threshed" wheat in fear (חבט, *khbt*, 6:11), now he "threshes" humans with ferocity (דוש, *dush*, 8:7). Earlier he "tore down" the altar of Baal and the Asherah (נתץ, *ntts*, in 6:28, 30, 31, 32); now he "tears down" the tower of the Penuelites (נתץ, 8:9, 17). But the former action was an expression of Yahwistic zeal, for the glory of God; the latter, a manifestation of vengeful frenzy, for his own glory. He has certainly come far, this "son of Joash," now wreaking destruction "with chilling ruthlessness and apparent relish" upon his own kind.[14] Gideon's impetuosity and impatience in this pericope is a dramatic contrast to Yahweh's grace and patience with Gideon's own doubt, hesitation, and skepticism (see Pericope 6, especially 6:12–24, 36–40; 7:9–14), time and again providing signs and proofs when Gideon demanded them (and doing so even when unasked, 7:9–11), without any hint of ire towards this faithless man. "This judge seems to have no compunction about torturing or killing those Israelites who have doubts in *him*, which is a sharp contrast to the treatment he received from Yahweh when Gideon was in doubt."[15] From the skeptical and dubious hesitation he displayed in Pericope 6, Gideon goes on to demonstrate domineering and tyrannical hubris in Pericope 7. Quite a contrast; quite a change.

7.3. Judges 8:18–21a

THEOLOGICAL FOCUS 7.3

7.3 The godly person rejects self-glorifying personal vendettas even against one's foes (8:18–21a).

---

13. Bluedorn, *Yahweh versus Baalism*, 160.
14. Webb, *Judges*, 256.
15. Klein, *The Triumph of Irony*, 62.

NOTES 7.3

7.3 The godly person rejects self-glorifying personal vendettas even against one's foes.

With the mention of the 120,000 "*sword*-drawing men" who had perished (8:10), the reader is reminded of Yahweh setting the *sword* of one against the other (7:22). That had been followed by the enemies "fleeing," the victors "pursuing," and the leaders being "captured" (7:22, 23, 25). So with this new mention of "sword" in 8:10 we wonder if Yahweh is going to be involved again. But alas, he is not. There is "fleeing," "pursuing," and "capturing" (8:12), but no sign of Yahweh. Not only is Yahweh absent from this undertaking, it is as if the entire Israelite army is invisible: it is all Gideon—*he* goes up, *he* attacks, *he* pursues, *he* captures, *he* routs, and *he* returns the victor—all third person masculine singular verbs (8:11–13). This is quite unlike the earlier battle where the role of Gideon's men was equally prominent, albeit in an utterly passive and non-militaristic way (employing trumpets, pitchers, torches, and voices), while Yahweh did all the fighting (7:19–22). Here, then, is a unilateral enterprise, literally depicted as being conducted exclusively by and for Gideon. God can keep his vintage and the Ephraimites their gleanings. Gideon was going for bigger and better stuff. No bronze or silver for Gideon; he wants the gold! And in pursuit of this ultimate medal, Gideon "routs" (חרד, *khrd*) the "whole army" of the Midianite kings (8:12).[16] The only other use of this verb in Judges is in 7:3: there it was Gideon's men all a-"tremble" (also from חרד) at the Spring of "Trembling" ("Harod," again from חרד, 7:1). Gideon and his gang had overcome their terror of their enemies, only to terrorize their enemies.

An indication of Gideon's obsession with getting the glory of capturing Zebah and Zalmunna is the fact that this duo is mentioned ten times in eight verses (8:5, 6, 7, 10, 12 [×2], 15, 18, 21 [×2]). But it is only in 8:18–19 that we discover Gideon's true motivation for his pursuit of the Midianite kings: *revenge* for the killing of his siblings. But that is exactly how Gideon has been operating for most of this pericope. This commander, transformed into a violent despot, seeks reprisals against those who have crossed him: the Succothites, the Penuelites, and now the Midianite kings. In fact, Gideon makes a shocking confession to these kings (with an oath naming Yahweh!): he might have saved their lives had they not murdered his siblings. That

---

16. It is unclear whether Gideon had more than 300 men with him in this conflict (8:4, 12) to defeat the 15,000 remaining Midianites (8:10). It seems more likely that a larger contingent had (re)joined Gideon: even though they came upon the Midianites unawares (8:11), there is no indication of any miraculous defeat here as had happened earlier (7:19–22).

would have been an unprecedented sparing of foreign rulers that contravened established patterns of holy war. Elimination of enemy rulers was *de rigueur* in the conduct of such battles (1:7; 3:10, 21–22; 4:21; 5:26–27; and even in the Gideon story in 7:25).[17] But about Yahweh's desires, Gideon could not care less. He does finally execute Zebah and Zalmunna (8:21), not because that was how enemy leaders had to be dealt with, but rather because they had killed his brothers!

Gideon's oath in 8:19, employing "Yahweh," sounds reverent, but it is nevertheless suspicious, for nothing he has done in this pericope has evidenced any thought for what Yahweh would want or would have him do. This is nothing but "an empty exploitation of the divine name in violation of the Third Commandment (Exod 20:7; Deut 5:11)," and "a glib reference to Yahweh to sanctify his personal vendetta."[18] Particularly since this oath and the kings' execution follows Gideon's wanton violence against Penuel and Succoth, it is hard to believe the vindictive, vengeful Gideon has suddenly turned virtuous and Yahwistic. To some extent, this relationship between Gideon and the ones slain by the Midianite regents explains the vigor of Gideon's pursuit of his siblings' killers. But his thirst for revenge, explosive enough to damage anyone who stands in his way, be they Israelite or otherwise, is inexcusable. And that is the dynamo that drives this entire pericope, taking the focus away from national interests, and more importantly, Yahwistic concerns, relegating them all to the inconsequential.[19]

The introduction of Jether, Gideon's firstborn, in 8:20–21 forms an interesting cameo, reminding us of the Gideon of two chapters ago. Jether is a chip off the old block: he was "afraid" (ירא, *yr'*, 8:20), just as Gideon was (ירא, 6:23, 27; 7:10); and he was but a "youth" (8:20), equivalent to Gideon's protestation that he was of the "youngest" in his family (6:15). The diffidence of Jether, a reflection of Gideon-past in 6:11—7:14, brings about quite a contrast with Gideon-present in 7:24—8:21, who, in turn, is reflected in another equally vindictive and brutal son, Abimelech (Pericope 9: Jdg 8:33—10:5). In other words, the reluctant and fearful Jether resembles

---

17. Also see Josh 8:23, 29; 10:16–18, 22–28, 36, 39; 11:10, 12, 17; etc. Saul's sparing of Agag, the Amalekite king, brought about divine wrath (1 Sam 15:8–9, 23; also see the case of Ahab sparing Ben-hadad, 1 Kgs 20:29–43). Indeed, as Wong notes, "not a single case can be found in the conquest narratives where a captured enemy king is spared" (*Compositional Strategy*, 167). Though whether Gideon's pursuit of the Midianite leaders and kings beyond the boundaries of Israel (8:4, 10) was called for is disputable.

18. Block, *Judges, Ruth*, 294–95.

19. While the Torah does speak to avenging shed blood (Num 35:12–28; Deut 19:4–6, 11–13; Josh 20:4), such instances do not pertain to killing in times of war, as was likely the context of the slaughter of Gideon's siblings (Webb, *Judges*, 261).

Gideon-as-he-*was*; the vengeful and self-seeking Abimelech resembles Gideon-as-he-*became*.

7.4. Judges 8:21b–32

THEOLOGICAL FOCUS 7.4

7.4   The godly person demonstrates no misdirected ambition to attain power (8:21b–32).

NOTES 7.4

7.4   *The godly person demonstrates no misdirected ambition to attain power.*[20]

For the first time, we are given a hint of Gideon's antecedents as royalty, or as thought to be royalty: the captured kings, Zebah and Zalmunna, indicated that they thought of Gideon's siblings as "sons of a king" (8:18). This royal connection "indirectly raises the issue of how king-like Gideon himself has become in his own eyes, and in the eyes of his followers."[21] Immediately after this quasi-royalty allusion in 8:18, we are introduced to Jether, Gideon's firstborn, to whom is delegated the gruesome task of killing the captured enemy kings by the sword (8:20). All of this looks very suggestive: a king and his firstborn, with a princely responsibility given to the latter. With what we know of Jael's triumph (and Barak's *loss* of honor) from Judges 4–5 (Pericopes 4 and 5), this opportunity to finish off enemy rulers is a bestowal of honor, from a regent to the next in line to the throne.

The story of the killing of the Midianite kings has a strange appendix: Gideon appropriates the "crescent ornaments on their camels' necks" (8:21b). Had he now become interested in accumulating possessions and property? One would have thought that the capture and execution of the Midianite kings was the gold medal Gideon had sought, belittling the silver medal won by the Ephraimites (the Midianite leaders, Zebah and Zalmunna), and depreciating the bronze won by Yahweh (a large chunk of Midianite army—120,000 swordsmen). Now he wants more than a gold medal?[22]

20. The Theological Foci in this Pericope (and often elsewhere) are stated in the positive, though the example set by the protagonist is obviously negative.

21. Ibid., 258.

22. I'm reminded of the immortal lines uttered by Irving "Irv" Blitzer (played by John Candy) in the 1993 movie *Cool Runnings*: "[A] gold medal is a wonderful thing. But if you're not enough without one, you'll never be enough with one." From the

"[T]hese baubles represent Gideon's fascination with royalty, and form the first indication that he will be mesmerized by their material glamour. . . . [T]hey represent the field of vision of the grasping Gideon and are the objects of his obsession."[23] Interestingly, Gideon's desires appear to parallel those of Sisera's mother. Both are interested in the spoils of war, especially embroidery or jewelry that adorn the "neck" (5:30; 8:21, 26).[24] That the Israelite is acting like a Canaanite is a sure deprecation of Gideon's continuing ungodly practices; but they only get worse.

The Israelites' attribution to Gideon of "deliverance" from the hand of Midian (8:22) is not entirely wrong (see 6:14, 15), but even Gideon recognized that the deliverance of Israel was the work of Yahweh, though through him, Gideon ("You will deliver Israel *by my hand*, as You have spoken," twice, in 6:36–37). Indeed, Yahweh himself wanted to preclude any attempt on the part of the Israelites to take the honor of deliverance for themselves (7:2), stating in no uncertain terms: "I will deliver you" (7:7). Even a Midianite soldier had understood that it was God who had given Midian into Gideon's hand (7:14).[25] Then there was that small matter of three hundred weaponless Israelites standing still—but blowing trumpets, breaking pitchers, exposing torches, and making noise—and just watching Yahweh slay 120,000 Midianite swordsmen! The long and short of it is that this attribution of deliverance to Gideon, made by the men of Israel in 8:22, is preposterous and sacrilegious, particularly when they make no mention of Yahweh's hand in this deliverance. In fact, they ought to have crowned the real Deliverer, Yahweh, their king.[26]

It seems obvious that this offer of kingship was not expressly prompted by Gideon. But prior events, in retrospect, indicate that Gideon had been making "a calculated move to raise his own profile, thereby making himself a natural candidate should the people ever consider having a king"—the

---

Internet Movie Database, "Cool Runnings (1993) Quotes," n.p. Gideon certainly wasn't "enough."

23. Fokkelman, *Reading Biblical Narrative*, 148.

24. The total weight of the earrings collected, 1,700 shekels of gold (8:26), comes to over 40 lbs of the metal! The very fact that all this loot was counted and weighed indicates a mercenary avarice on the part of Gideon. Besides earrings, Gideon's collection included crescents, pendants, robes, and neck bands (8:21, 26). See Isa 3:18–19, for divine disapproval of Israel's "crescents" and "pendants."

25. Earlier, both Gideon and his army had equated human and divine efforts to rid themselves of the Midianites; their battle cry was "For Yahweh and for Gideon" (7:18), and "A sword for Yahweh and for Gideon" (7:20). But here it is entirely one-sided: the Israelites think that Gideon—and he alone—is their deliverer.

26. Indeed, we are told in 8:34 that the sons of Israel "did not remember Yahweh their God who had delivered them."

inclusion of his name alongside Yahweh's in the battle cry, for instance (7:18, 20).[27] There is no question that Gideon's peremptory, regal, and forceful actions thus far contributed to this call from his "subjects" that simply sought "to formalize *de jure* what is already *de facto*."[28] The syntax of the Israelites' affirmation of Gideon is emphatic: "Rule over us, even you, even your son, even your son's son" (8:22)—a dynastic succession for the future. Unfortunately for the "men of Israel," sixty-nine of Gideon's sons perish at the hand of an illegitimate son, Abimelech, who inherits every trait that the latter Gideon displayed—hubris, ferocity, and all. All of this only makes Gideon's rejection of the people's offer of kingship hollow and insincere (8:23), as subsequent events prove.

Gideon's manufacture of an ephod from the earrings and other jewelry that was booty from his capture of the Midianite kings (8:26–27) is eerily similar to Aaron's creating a golden calf from earrings taken from the Egyptians (Exod 12:35–36; 32:1–8), further adding to the deplorable nature of this episode, both "makings" (עשׂה, *'sh*, Exod 32:1, 4, 20; Jdg 8:27) occurring after a miraculous deliverance of Israel by Yahweh.[29] Essentially then, these activities were slaps in face of deity. By the way, "gold earrings" occurs in the OT only in these two incidents of cultic transgression: Exod 32:2–3 and Jdg 8:24, 26. The presence of an ephod is in itself a sign of disorder and decay, for "[t]he only unambiguously positive allusions to the ephod occur in the commands and performance in Exodus for setting up the ritual objects for the sanctuary and for garbing all the priests in linen ephods. All other references, however, including the one here in Judges 8, are in contexts that suggest a deviation in some way from the will of God" (see especially 1 Sam 2:28; Hos 3:4—"harlotry" also occurs there, as here in Jdg 8:27). Indeed, the only other instance in the OT of anyone "*making* [עשׂה] an ephod" is in Jdg 17:5, the story of another major cultic faux pas.[30]

27. Wong, *Compositional Strategy*, 168.

28. Block, *Judges, Ruth*, 299.

29. An "ephod" was a priestly garment (Exod 28:4–31; 39:2–22; etc.), but in this case, in light of all the gold involved, it was probably a replica of a garment, and not intended to be worn. Or perhaps the term is metonymous for an idol upon which the ephod was draped.

30. Sharon, "Echoes of Gideon's Ephod," 93. She notes that the *purple* of the robes (Jdg 8:26) is elsewhere the color of idolatrous accouterments: see Jer 10:9 (purple garments on idols); and Ezek 27:7, 16 (purple awnings of Tyre's ships and purple fabric of their sunken maritime cargo), not to mention the link between purple and royalty (Esth 1:6; 8:15). "Taken all together, the intertexts associated with the finery of spoils gathered by Gideon for the making of his ephod—rings of gold, crescents, pendants, and garments of purple—bode ill for Gideon's enterprise in constructing an ephod" (ibid., 95).

And so the "harlotry" that was part of the paradigm of 2:11–19 (see 2:17), now, for the first time in Judges, comes to pass as "all Israel" engages in "harlotry" (8:27). Thus Israel has commenced evildoing in preparation for the next round of oppression *even before* the current cycle is completed, with the instigator of this harlotry being a judge-deliverer, one of Israel's own leaders![31] In fact, Gideon literally engages in harlotry, having sexual relations with a Canaanite (8:31).

The only other time "snare" occurs in Judges is in 2:3, in the warning/indictment of the angel of Yahweh at Bokim. But there it is used of the gods of the Canaanites being a "snare" to the Israelites. Here in 8:27, with the gold ephod, the Israelites had successfully "snared" themselves by creating their *own* gods, with no help at all from the pagans. The impact of Gideon's actions affects not only himself and his household, but "all Israel," who "played harlot with it" in Ophrah, Gideon's hometown (8:27).[32] And thus an anti-Yahwist cult is created by Gideon in the very spot where another anti-Yahwist cult had been destroyed by him (6:25–32).[33] This closing state of the saga of Gideon is grotesque and grievous. The rest of Gideon's story—or rather, the continuation of Gideon's story in the life of his son, Abimelech (8:33—9:57)—is hardly unexpected: the disastrous consequence of what Gideon initiated "looks like a leaf from a Canaanite history notebook."[34] Gideon was a microcosm of Israel's disobedience and harlotry: the nation and its leader had become Canaan.

Judges 8:28 returns to the subject of the now-subdued Midianites,[35] and the story of Gideon begins to wind down to a close—or so we expect,

---

31. Bluedorn, *Yahweh versus Baalism*, 177. First Chronicles 5:25 and Ps 106:39 employ the same metaphor of "harlotry" to refer to the period of the judges. In Jdg 8:33, soon after the death of Gideon, the Israelites are again shown to be dabbling in "harlotry," this time with the Baals, making "Baal-Berith" ("Baal of the Covenant") their god. Gone was any concern for Yahweh and *his* covenant (2:1, 20); the Israelites were more interested in covenants with false gods.

32. The syntax יַצֵּג + אֹת[וֹ] + בְּ + בְּ in Jdg 8:27 (*ytsg* + *'oto* + *b* + *b*, "he set + it + in [his city] + in [Ophrah]") is exactly repeated in 2 Sam 6:17, for the relocation of the ark: "they set + it + in [its place] + in [the middle of the tent]" (ibid., 174). This contrast with a later act of Yahwistic devotion does not bode well for Gideon's profane performance.

33. One wonders if the same shrine that Gideon had destroyed in Ophrah in Judges 6 was now being reconstructed by its very "Hacker."

34. Block, *Judges, Ruth*, 250. See Pericope 8 (Jdg 8:33—10:5) for Abimelech's sordid story.

35. The Midianites, we are told, "did not lift up their *heads* anymore" (8:28)—"indeed no Midianite agency is subsequently involved in any injury to Israel in the Bible" (Assis, *Self-Interest or Communal Interest*, 111). The reference to "heads" is a bit of grim gallows humor: the "heads" of the two Midianite leaders, Oreb and Zeeb, had just been separated from their bodies (7:25).

knowing how the Othniel, Ehud, and Barak accounts concluded with their enemies' defeats (3:9, 30; 4:23–24 with 5:31b). But, wait, there is more: in 8:29, Gideon is ominously called "Jerubbaal" ("Let Baal Contend"—and yes, Baal had contended, and Baal had won; see 6:32; 8:33; and 9:4, 46),[36] and in his retirement the man remains quite busy, accumulating a haremfull of wives and concubines (violating Deut 17:17; also see Jdg 3:6),[37] and producing a full/perfect complement of royal progeny—seventy (8:30). He even had an illegitimate son, through a Shechemite concubine, whom he proceeds to name, with regal hauteur, "Abimelech" ("My Father is King," 8:31).[38] One way or another, Gideon would be king!

To summarize, Gideon seems to have made the right answer in declining kingship, but his rejection rings hollow (8:22–23) for a number of reasons: in his execution of summary justice to all and sundry, he has been acting like a tyrannous ruler; his brothers look like him and they all appear to be royalty (8:18); Gideon is offered kingship right after he has killed enemy *kings* (8:22); in 8:23, Gideon employs the word משׁל (*mshl*, "to rule"), and later Abimelech, the one appointed to "rule" (משׁל, 9:2), becomes *king* (9:6), making Gideon's aspirations clear, even though the word "king" was not used in the offer to Gideon; Gideon demands a share of the spoils of war, a treasure fit for a king (8:24–26), retaining the emblems of royalty; he manufactures an ephod and sponsors a cult that snares him, his household, and his nation (8:27, 33); Gideon establishes his hometown, Ophrah, as his capital where he "sat" (ישׁב, *yshb*, 8:29; see Pss 2:4; 9:7; 29:10; 55:19; 61:7; 102:12; Lam 5:19; Mal 3:3, for the verb ישׁב indicating enthronement); he keeps a large harem (Jdg 8:30); he fathers seventy sons (8:30, a royal household); he has the audacity to name an illegitimate son "Abimelech" ("My Father is King," 8:31); he is buried in a dynastic tomb (8:32; the only judge with such a privilege that is usually granted to kings: 1 Kgs 2:10; 11:43; 14:31; 15:8, 24; etc.); and Jotham's fable in Pericope 8 is consistent with Gideon's appropriation of kingship (Jdg 9:8–17).[39] Of course, there is no

---

36. The only time Gideon is called in full "Jerubbaal, the son of Joash," is here in 8:29, wrapping up all the negative influences in Gideon's life detailed in Pericope 6 (Jdg 6:1—7:22) and Pericope 7.

37. Concubines are distinct from wives, though they may have had a "secondary wife" status (Jdg 19:3–5; 20:4). However, such unions were forbidden and were in violation of Exod 34:15–16; Deut 7:3–4, though Jdg 3:6 warned that unions between Israelites and Canaanites would happen.

38. "Abimelech" can also mean "The (Divine) King is My Father," but in light of the nuances of the story that point to Gideon's self-focus and hubris, this is unlikely. Perhaps the ambiguity of the name itself tells the story of a Yahwist who ended up being anti-Yahwist (Klein, *The Triumph of Irony*, 71).

39. From Block, ""Will the Real Gideon Please Stand Up?" 359–63.

indication anywhere that Yahweh had chosen Gideon for kingship (as per Deut 17:14–20); in fact, Yahweh is nowhere around in Judges 8. So when all is said and done, Gideon was exceeding his commission and beginning to appropriate a portfolio that had not been assigned to him by God, "an aberrant and illicit kingship."[40] And the consequences of his illegitimate and ruthless ambition was that the nation lapsed into florid idolatry!

Gideon's death "at a good old age" puts him in the exalted company of only two others who had that privilege in the OT: Abraham and David (Gen 15:15; 25:8; 1 Chr 29:28). This is a gracious assessment of Gideon's good deeds and his faith in Yahweh, depicted at least in the initial stages of his Midianite campaign (also see Heb 11:32; and perhaps 1 Sam 12:11, though he is labeled "Jerubbaal" there).

But even with the death of Gideon reported in Jdg 8:32, the narrator is not done; the complications that have arisen in this judge's life continue to outlive him and create even more chaos: Gideon's anti-Yahwist cult, his concubinage with a Canaanite woman, his nefarious, vengeful actions inflicted on his own people, all have ramifications for individual, tribe, and nation. The cultic syncretism inaugurated by Gideon (8:24–27a) escalates into national apostasy (8:27b, 33) and brings about judgment from Yahweh (9:23–24, 56–57).[41] One wonders if it would not have been better for Israel in the first place *not* to have been delivered by Gideon! And this slippage of Israel into paganism happens even before the death of the current judge, a declension aided and abetted by that very individual who sets the framework for an even greater fall after his days (8:27, 33). "The spiral has begun to plummet."[42]

The narratives of the first three major figures in Judges (Othniel, Ehud, and Barak) concerned their faithful attitudes to God and dealt with external enemies, resulting in "rest for the land"—but a downward slide had already commenced during their days. The story of the middle figure in the array of prominent characters in Judges, Gideon, concerned his furthering of self, dealt with both external *and* internal enemies, and ended in "rest for the land," but with ongoing apostasy. The accounts of the last three figures (Abimelech, Jephthah, Samson) concern only the furthering of self, and deals only with internal enemies, concluding without any "rest for the land" being attained.[43]

---

40. Idem, *Judges, Ruth*, 301.
41. O'Connell, *The Rhetoric of the Book of Judges*, 152–53.
42. Schneider, *Judges*, 130.
43. Assis, *Self-Interest or Communal Interest*, 127–29.

Three striking developments in the Gideon narrative are noted by Webb. Firstly, for the first time Israel's cry to Yahweh in the face of opposition meets with stern rebuke from him; with Jephthah, it will be a refusal to act; with Samson, there is no cry for help at all. Secondly, the apostasy of the nation is well advanced even before the passing of the protagonist, with his own actions making a major contribution to the recidivism; Jephthah is far more flawed and self-focused; Samson is almost unrecognizable as a deliverer-judge figure. Thirdly, internal conflicts become prominent for the first time, with Gideon attacking his fellow-Israelites; Abimelech is far worse; and all of this culminates in the civil wars of Epilogue II (19:1—21:25; Pericopes 13 and 14)—the land never has "rest" again in Judges after 8:28.[44] The man may have been named "Let Baal Contend" ("Jerubbaal"), but all he has done thus far is contend with *Yahweh*. And this judge goes from fainthearted (6:11—7:14,) to fearless (7:15–23), to feckless (7:24—8:21), to faithless (8:22–32). From idolatry in Ophrah (6:25) to idolatry in Ophrah (8:27)—that is the précis of the Gideon story. And the vile state of the nation becomes a nursery for the next tyrant, Abimelech, who has no redeeming feature at all.

SERMON FOCUS AND OUTLINES

THEOLOGICAL FOCUS OF PERICOPE 7 FOR PREACHING

7   Godliness involves abandonment of self-glorifying vendettas and of power (7:23—8:32).

While Pericope 6 (Jdg 6:1—7:22) dealt with Gideon's prideful and delusional taking of credit for divine action, this pericope focuses on Gideon's self-glorifying vendettas and his craze for power (as well as the dire consequences thereof for himself, his tribe, and his nation—florid idolatry). Whereas in Pericope 6, the faithless skeptic ends up stealing God's glory, here in Pericope 7, the stealer of God's glory ends up playing God, usurping his priorities and prerogatives.

Clearly, Gideon's hubris is center staged here, as it was in the previous pericope. The focus of the earlier pericope is best seen as godless pride in one's own ability. This one is best tackled as pride that promotes one's power-hunger, at all costs, and that results in disaster.

Possible Preaching Outlines for Pericope 7

I.   Gideon's Payback

---

44. Webb, *Judges*, 295–96.

　　　　Absence of deity (except for 8:7, 19—"Yahweh"; and 8:3—"God")
　　　　Gideon's illegitimate summoning of troops (7:23–25)
　　　　Gideon's pursuit of kings and glory (7:23–25; 8:4–5, 10–12, 18–21)
　　　　Gideon's violence against Israelites; his hierarchy of values (8:1–9, 13–17)
　　　　Gideon's intent to spare the kings (vs. killing his fellowmen) (8:18–19)
　　　　Move-to-relevance: Our pride that seeks self-promotion at all costs
　II.　Gideon's Power
　　　　Gideon's claim to royalty (8:18, 22, 24–26, 31, 32)
　　　　Gideon's pursuit of power and its paraphernalia (8:18, 21, 24–26)
　　　　Move-to-relevance: Our pride that seeks power and prestige
　III.　Gideon's Perversion
　　　　Gideon's idolatry and its promotion (8:24–27)
　　　　Consequences of Gideon's misplaced ambition (8:27–33)
　　　　Move-to-relevance: Disaster that comes with pride and ambition
　IV.　*Aspire to humility!*
　　　　Specifics on cultivating humility and curbing ambition

A simpler structure puts Gideon's misbehavior into the first move and its consequences in the second: a Problem-*Consequences*-Application outline.

　I.　PROBLEM: Gideon's Pride
　　　　Gideon's misplaced values (army/leaders/kings, in that order; 7:23—8:3)
　　　　Gideon's intolerance of anyone standing in his way (8:4–17)
　　　　Gideon's craze for power (8:18–26)
　　　　Move-to-relevance: Our pride that seeks self-promotion and power
　II.　CONSEQUENCES: Gideon's Perversion
　　　　Gideon's idolatry and its promotion (8:24–27)
　　　　Consequences of Gideon's misplaced ambition (8:27–33)
　　　　Move-to-relevance: Disaster that comes with ungodly pride and ambition
　III.　APPLICATION: *Aspire to humility!*
　　　　Specifics on cultivating humility and curbing ambition

PERICOPE 8

Abimelech

Judges 8:33–10:5

[Abimelech's Appointment, Ungodliness, and Retribution]

REVIEW, SUMMARY, PREVIEW

Review of Pericope 7: In Jdg 7:23—8:32, Gideon's pride shows no containment: he denigrates God's victory over the Midianites, elevating the Ephraimites' capture of the Midianite leaders, and above that, his own capture of their kings. In the pursuit of his hubristic goals, he is completely ruthless, punishing all who stand in his way. Finally his ambition for royal status, and his perverse creation of an idol draws Israel into the abyss of idolatry.

Summary of Pericope 8: The eighth pericope of Judges (8:33—10:5) has the story of Abimelech, a continuation—and natural consequence—of Gideon's story. The narrative is marked by the absence of both Yahweh and of an external enemy. Instead, the Israelite protagonist, Abimelech, is Israel's enemy. Unsanctioned by God and appointed by humans, and paid from Baal's temple, this ungodly ruler turns out to be an unmerciful despot, ruthless and brutal, wantonly killing his own siblings and many fellow Israelites. He meets his just deserts in appropriate divine retribution.

Preview of Pericope 9: The next pericope, Jdg 10:6—12:5, is the story of Jephthah. The idolatrous Israelites are excoriated by God who refuses to deliver them from their enemies. So the Israelites take matters into their own hands and appoint Jephthah. He attempts to force God into action with a recital of Israel's history and by vowing a sacrifice in return for victory in battle. His tragic vow forces him to sacrifice his only child, a daughter. Thoroughly paganized, he then goes forth and slaughters fellow-Israelites over a personal taunt.

8. Judges 8:33–10:5

THEOLOGICAL FOCUS OF PERICOPE 8

8 The illicit thirst for power, destructive in its ramifications, brings about the fitting retribution of God (8:33—10:5).

    8.1   God's people living like unbelievers has dire consequences, even for generations that follow (8:33–35).

    8.2   The illicit thirst for power is ultimately destructive to self and to others around (9:1–21).

    8.3   God visits evildoers with retribution befitting the evildoing (9:22–57).

    8.4   Divine punishment does not mean the absence of divine grace (10:1–5).

OVERVIEW

Though Abimelech is not included in the roster of judges, his narrative appears to follow the paradigm of the judge stories set in Jdg 2:11-19. We see Israel's evildoing (8:33-35; as in 3:7, 12; 4:2; 6:1), a personal detail of the protagonist (8:31; as in 3:9, 15; 4:4, 6; 6:11), the action he initiates (9:1-5; as in 3:10, 16; 4:10; 6:34; 7:15-16), and his death (9:53-54; as in 3:11; 4:1; 8:32-33). Absent, though, are other major elements such as: Israel being given or sold into the hands of enemies, their cry under oppression, the raising of a judge, the support of Yahweh, a victory won by the Israelites, and rest attained by the land.

Of all the narratives in the book of Judges, Yahweh's presence is felt the least in this account of Gideon's son, Abimelech. Deity is present, but almost always as אֱלֹהִים (*'elohim*, "God"), not "Yahweh" (8:34; 9:7, 9, 13, 23, 56, 57). And in every instance, this occurs as part of a pejorative statement by the narrator or by Jotham (see below). There is no direct link between Abimelech and God at all! "The recognition of Yahweh that was intermittently forced from Gideon [6:13, 22 (24); 7:15, 17; 8:7, 19, 23] has completely disappeared. Israel is now so much like the remaining nations that surround them that the names of any one of these nations could be substituted in the story wherever Israel is mentioned, and the story would remain entirely intelligible."[1] Canaanization is almost complete! Besides, though deity is present, he participates in a most unusual way—by sending an *evil* spirit (9:23).[2]

The absence of any external enemy is striking. While there is an assertion that the Israelites abandoned God and worshipped Baal (8:33–34), there is no notice of divine punishment in the form of an outside oppressor subjugating Israel. Instead, *Abimelech* is the enemy, convulsing the hill country with violence, instability, and insecurity. Even his death report—the first murder of an Israelite protagonist in Judges—is silent about any deliverance he effected, the years he served, or the honor of an interment, only stating grimly that his killing was divine retribution for his wickedness (9:54–55).

In a narrative that focuses mostly on Shechemites, the framing of Pericope 8 with references to Israelites at crucial points (8:34–35; 9:22; 9:55) indicates that the storyteller "sets the Shechemites as an example for Israel, and their Baal worship as an example of general Israelite idolatry."[3] Besides, Abimelech's influence appears to have been spread out through the land: "Israel" is mentioned in 9:22, 51; also see 9:25, 41, 50.[4] In any case, Shechem was a symbolic location: Abram's first altar upon entering Canaan was located there (Gen 12:6); Jacob's sons conquered Shechem (Genesis 34); Joshua's covenant renewal at the conclusion of his campaigns was held there (Josh 24:1); Joseph's bones were buried in Shechem (24:32); and it was located in the valley between Mt. Gerizim and Mt. Ebal, the mountains of blessing and cursing (Deut 11:29). "A town that was traditionally associated with

---

1. Polzin, *Moses and the Deuteronomist*, 174.

2. Judges 8:34 also mentions Yahweh, but only to remind the reader that he had been forgotten by the sons of Israel.

3. Bluedorn, *Yahweh versus Baalism*, 198. For Israel's idolatry in the Body of Judges, see 3:7, 8, 9, 12, 14, 15; 4:1, 3, 23, 24; 6:1, 2, 6; 10:6, 8, 10; 13:1.

4. Yet there is no mention of any particular Israelite tribe in action; instead, Abimelech maintains a private force of mercenaries (9:4), a king in an era of "no king" (Jdg 17:6; 18:1; 19:1; 21:25). It is noted explicitly that Abimelech "went" to Shechem (9:1); it seems he was dwelling elsewhere before his ambitious program brought him here. In fact, even in this narrative, there is no indication that he lived in Shechem at all (9:31, 34–37, 41, 44, 50). He was simply using his family antecedents to realize his obsession with power; he has no personal connection to the place.

renewed loyalty to the Lord had now become the site of an enthronement that represented a blatant rejection of God's authority."[5]

Joshua 24 implies that Shechem was fully Israelite. But it is a fair assumption that the population was mixed, for Gaal's appeal to the Shechemites in Jdg 9:28 refers to the non-Israelite Hamor as the sponsor/founder of that city (see Genesis 34), implying a strong Canaanite presence there, as well.[6] No doubt they were all existing together in harmony, sharing Baal (Jdg 8:33 and 9:4, 46) and, in light of 3:5–6, sharing genes as well, like Abimelech himself, of mixed parentage: 8:31. In Jotham's fable, he addresses the *ba'als* of Shechem (9:7; i.e., their leaders; see below), accusing them of unfaithfulness to Jerubbaal who had fought "for *you*" and "delivered *you*" (9:17): evidently, his audience was Israelite. Later we are told that Abimelech's followers were "men of Israel" (9:55). Altogether, it is best to consider the story of the Shechemites and their *ba'als* as a commentary on Israel and her defection from Yahweh.

8.1. Judges 8:33–35

THEOLOGICAL FOCUS 8.1

8.1   God's people living like unbelievers has dire consequences, even for generations that follow (8:33–35).

NOTES 8.1

8.1   God's people living like unbelievers has dire consequences, even for generations that follow.

It does not take very long after Gideon's passing for the Israelites to commit "harlotry," this time with the Baals, and particularly with Baal-berith (= "Baal of the Covenant," 8:33; 9:4; also see 9:46). Rather than being faithful to Yahweh and his covenant (2:1–2), the Israelites swear their allegiance to a false god and *his* covenant. Baal had usurped Yahweh's place!

Not only were the Israelites unfaithful to Yahweh, "not remembering" him (8:34; see Deut 8:18), they had also failed to "show lovingkindness [חֶסֶד, *khesed*]" to the household of Gideon, God's ordained leader of Israel (Jdg 8:35). To "show lovingkindness" was to maintain covenantal faithfulness,

---

5. Chisholm, *Judges and Ruth*, 313.

6. Canaanite and Israelite coexistence was bad enough in itself (see Pericope 1: Jdg 1:1—2:5).

often predicated of the relationship between God and his people (see Exod 15:13; 20:6; 34:6, 7; Num 14:18, 19; etc.). Thus the Israelites were unfaithful both to God and to his appointed leader (Jdg 8:34–35). Indeed, the notation of the Israelites' disloyalty to the house of Jerubbaal brackets this Pericope (see 8:35 and 9:56–57, as well as 9:16–19). And so they get the leader they deserve: Abimelech.

The person of Abimelech is unique in the stories of the various protagonists in Judges. Neither a king nor a judge called or raised by Yahweh, he insinuates himself into rulership by popular acclaim (9:1–3), by employing mercenaries (9:4), and by killing potential rivals (9:5). There are similarities between Abimelech and Adoni-bezek, the Canaanite king (1:4–7). Both are rulers, and both kill those within their own ethnic group, Canaanite kings in one, Israelite siblings in the other (seventy in each case: 1:7; 9:5). For their brutality, both Adoni-bezek and Abimelech meet their just deserts, and retribution seems to be the theme of both accounts (1:7; and 9:24, 56–57). Their punishments fit the crimes (1:6; and 9:53, a "stone" is involved in both Abimelech's diabolism and his destruction). Indeed, even Bezek and Shechem, the haunts of Adoni-bezek and Abimelech, respectively, are geographically proximal.[7] With Abimelech looking like—indeed, looking worse than—the Canaanite king, Israel has become her own worst enemy. And Yahweh responds, but punitively, unlike in the previous accounts. Israel had become more and more like Canaan.

There is much in this story that appears to be part of the Yahweh vs. Baal narrative that began in Gideon's story. For one, Gideon shows up in Judges 9 only as "Jerub*baal*": 9:1, 2, 5 (×2), 16, 19, 24, 28, 57. Though Abimelech is the son of Jerub*baal* (9:1), he allies himself with the Shechemites: "I am your bone and flesh" (9:2), to which the "*ba'als*" of Shechem (בַּעֲלֵי, *ba'alim*, "leaders," 9:2, 3, 6, 7, 18, 20 [×2], 23 [×2], 24, 25, 26, 39, 46, 47, 51[8]) acknowledge Abimelech: "He is our brother" (9:3). The son of Jerub*baal* has now become the brother of the *baals* of Shechem.[9] Together, Jerub*baal* and

---

7. Wong, *Compositional Strategy*, 204–6.

8. An inordinate emphasis on this word, even when not referring to the god, Baal, underscores the apostasy of the land (Baal himself shows up in 9:4). These *ba'als* of Shechem were likely to have been the elite of the city of Shechem. Notice that even *after* Abimelech had slaughtered the "people" (9:45), the *ba'als* survived to take refuge in the temple of El-berith (9:46). See, as well, the distinction between "men and women and all the *ba'als* of the city" in 9:51.

9. In Gen 14:13, the word בעלי is translated "allies," those who were associated with the patriarch Abraham, perhaps as treaty partners, for they shared the spoils of war. The term "may very well be an idiom, or perhaps a technical term, designating one who enters into a covenant relationship," making these *ba'als* in Judges 9 human subscribers to a formal treaty with the "divine" Baal (Lewis, "The Identity and Function of El/Baal Berith," 413).

the *baal*s of Shechem echo בַּעַל, *ba'al*, for a total of twenty-five instances in fifty-seven verses—in almost every other verse of Judges 9.

> The strong emphasis on this element [בעל] either directly or paronomastically identifies the Abimelech narrative as dominated by Baalism as represented by Abimelech and the Shechemites, and the concurrent absence of the name יהוה [*yhwh*, "Yahweh"] at the same time lets Yhwh appear silent, though not absent, as the narrator's explanation (9:23–24) and concluding remarks (9:56–57) reveal. With the near absence of Yhwh and the full presence of Baalism, however, the Abimelech narrative will attempt to demonstrate Baalism's power.... [But] Yhwh remains the only god who acts anywhere in the entire Gideon-Abimelech narrative.[10]

These naming idiosyncrasies in Judges 9 utilizing the charged word *ba'al* also reflect the progressive Canaanization of Israel, with Baal seemingly having prevailed against Yahweh. So much so, Abimelech is paid by his employers, the *ba'als* of Shechem, with money from the house of *Ba'al*-berith ("Baal of the Covenant," 9:4, later also labeled El-berith, "God of the Covenant," 9:46). Clearly, we are being informed as to which side Abimelech belongs in the Yahweh vs. Baal contest. Further substantiating this (dis)loyalty, Abimelech kills his "brothers" "on one stone" (9:5)—sacrificial victims to Baal perhaps, reminiscent of Jerub*baal*'s sacrifices to Yahweh (6:20–21, 25–26).[11] One must remember that Abimelech's atrocities took place at "his father's house at Ophrah" (9:5): ironically, it was in Ophrah that there once was a Baal altar that was destroyed by Gideon/Jerub*baal* (6:25–27), and where later, under the auspices of Gideon himself, the aforementioned shrine to Baal—"Baal-berith"—was established (8:33). Abimelech, no Yahwist, was clearly a Baalist. This story is therefore "the clashing of the two deities, *mano a mano,* in the form of their respective human agents."[12] It appears that Baal had contended (= "Jerubbaal," or "Let Baal Contend," 6:32), and Baal had won![13]

One remembers that Gideon had "set" (8:31) his son's name as Abimelech, avoiding the usual "*call* his name ..." (see 1:26; 2:5; 6:24, 32; 13:24;

---

10. Bluedorn, *Yahweh versus Baalism*, 202.

11. "[A]ll of Gideon's sons could have been killed 'on one stone' only by murdering them serially, one after the other. This was a calculated, brutal act of murder, not a quick slaughter of unsuspecting victims" (Block, *Judges, Ruth*, 312).

12. Endris, "Yahweh versus Baal," 179–80. Abimelech who slaughtered his brothers is a representative of Baal; thus the woman who killed Abimelech is a fitting representative of Yahweh (9:53–57).

13. So while Pericope 8 begins with a mention of the "all the good which he [Gideon] had done for Israel" (8:35)—and he *had* done some good—it ends with a stark statement of "the evil of Abimelech which he had done to his father" (9:56).

15:17, 19). So not only did Gideon produce a half-Israelite/half-enemy child, he *set* this boy's fate as the son of a king ("Abimelech" = "My Father is King"), one who would seek to be king himself.[14] Thoroughly depraved, Abimelech shows no evidence of having done anything good. With his name echoing thirty-seven times in Judges 9, this is the distressing story of an anti-hero.

There are quite a few similarities between the Gideon and Abimelech stories[15]:

GIDEON Story	ABIMELECH Story
Evildoing of Israel (6:1)	Evildoing of Israel (8:33–35)
"Then it came about …" (6:7)	"Then it came about …" (8:33)
Called near an oak (6:11, 19)	Crowned near an oak (9:6)
Abandonment of "Yahweh God of Israel" (6:8–10): who "delivered" Israel from the "hand of all your oppressors"	Forgetting of "Yahweh, their God" (8:34–35): who "delivered" them from the "hand of all their enemies"
Gideon avenges his siblings' murder (8:19)	Abimelech murders his siblings (9:5)
Gideon is appointed by Yahweh (6:12–16) and works for Yahweh (6:25–27)	Abimelech is appointed by Baalists (9:4–6) and works for Baal (9:4–5)
Opposition: Ophrathites (6:28–32)	Opposition: Jotham (9:7–21)
Yahweh's "Spirit" (6:34–35)	God sends an evil "spirit" (9:23)
Gideon's royal ambitions (8:22–32)	Abimelech's royal ambitions (9:1–57)
Gideon "divides" troops into "three companies" and they "capture" and "slay" (7:16, 24, 25) involving fire (7:20)	Abimelech "divides" troops into "three companies" and they "capture" and "slay" (9:43, 45) involving fire (9:48)
Followers to mimic Gideon (7:17)	Followers to mimic Abimelech (9:43)
Violent deeds of Gideon (7:24–8:32) after a decisive victory (7:22) with no involvement of Yahweh against his own people using נתץ, ntts, "raze/destroy" (8:17) involving a tower (8:17)	Violent deeds of Abimelech (9:1–55) after a decisive victory (8:10–13) with no involvement of Yahweh against his own people using נתץ (9:45) involving towers (9:46, 49, 51–52)
Two cities suffer: Succoth and Penuel (8:14–16, 17)	Two cities suffer: Shechem and Thebes (9:46–49, 50–54)

---

14. Klein, *The Triumph of Irony*, 70.

15. From Bluedorn, *Yahweh versus Baalism*, 183–85; and Klein, *The Triumph of Irony*, 76–77.

But there are significant differences as well. Despite its negative outcome, the Gideon story was Yahweh-centered; the Abimelech story, on the other hand, is Baal-centered (see the numerous occurrences of *baʿal*; and Gideon is referred to only as "Jerub*baal*"). Yahweh played a positive role, pro-Gideon, in the latter's narrative, but he takes on a negative role, anti-Abimelech, in his. External enemies were prominent in Gideon's story, while it is the internal enemy that is the problem in Abimelech's. Gideon had the Spirit of God, Abimelech an evil spirit from God. The father fought to deliver Israel (at least initially); the son fights purely for personal glory. Gideon's judgeship gave the land rest, but Abimelech's rulership achieves nothing of the sort. And, at the end of their respective bloody campaigns, Gideon survived, but Abimelech does not. The consequences of Gideon's actions, though damaging to his person, family, and nation, are overall assessed as positive (8:34–35; 9:16–17; 1 Sam 12:11; Heb 11:32); the consequences of Abimelech's actions are thoroughly negative in the narrator's eyes (Jdg 9:22–23, 56–57). The Abimelech story was the natural consequence of a father's deviant behavior, and brings about the divine consequence of retribution upon an unchaste father, an unvirtuous son, an unfortunate household, and an ungodly nation.

8.2. Judges 9:1–21

THEOLOGICAL FOCUS 8.2

8.2 The illicit thirst for power is ultimately destructive to self and to others around (9:1–21).

NOTES 8.2

8.2 The illicit thirst for power is ultimately destructive to self and to others around.

While it was the people who had asked Gideon to "rule" (מְשֹׁל, *mshl*, 8:22–23 [×4]), Abimelech seizes the initiative to "rule" (מְשֹׁל, 9:2 [×2]) all by himself. He challenges his relatives to do that "which is good [טוֹב, *tob*] for you," as he offers them the choice of himself or the seventy sons of Jerubbaal as their ruler(s) (9:2). It turns out that in response to the "good" (טוֹבָה, *tobah*) that Gideon had done to Israel (8:35; also see 9:16), the reciprocation by Abimelech was considered "good" by those in Shechem—the murder of Gideon's seventy sons (9:3–4), a grim undertaking that Abimelech accomplished after the *baʿals* of the city financed his operation from the temple of Baal-berith (9:3). So the takeover by Abimelech, son of Jerub*baal* is supported both by *Baal* and his *baʿals*—a Canaanite undertaking, through and through, and thus, Abimelech becomes the official representative of Baalism, just as Gideon in 6:25–27 became the official representative of Yahwism. One, supported by Baal's temple, kills his siblings (the sons of the Baal-fighter, Jerubbaal, 9:4–5); the other, supported by Yahweh, destroyed a Baal altar (6:27–32).

Abimelech speaks only thrice in the entirety of his narrative: in 9:2, 48, 54, at the boundaries of the story. All his utterances are self-focused and egoistic: he wants to rule (9:2), he wants to be followed in his ferocity (9:48), and he wants to escape the ignominy of dying at the hand of a woman (9:54). Forget deity, Abimelech has no concern even for household, clan, or state. Right at the start, he displays his craving for status, honor, and position, for which he is willing to do *anything*, even perpetrate a horrific series of homicides. "The scene is inconceivable—one victim after another after another on the same single stone. Body upon body upon body dispatched with unspeakable horror, in a kind of slaughter reserved for animals (1 Sam 15:33–34). Again and again and again until all seventy (save one) have been eliminated from possible usurpation of 'his throne.'"[16] And thus Abimelech becomes king (9:6).[17] The threefold recurrence of the root מלך in 9:6 (וַיַּמְלִיכוּ אֶת־אֲבִימֶלֶךְ לְמֶלֶךְ) (*wayyamliku ʾet-ʾabimelek lmelek*, "and they *kinged* My-Father-is-*King* as *king*")—emphasizes Abimelech's infatuation with kingship. So Abimelech becomes an "anti-judge" prompted only by self-interest and designs on the monarchy. He is not called or appointed by God, and deity is marked in this narrative by his near-total absence.

The section, 9:7–21, following the establishment of Abimelech as ruler, deals with the speech of Jotham (the only one of Gideon's seventy sons who escaped the slaughter) and is bracketed by Jotham's movements: "he went and stood" (9:7); and "Jotham escaped and fled and went . . . " (9:21). As well, there is reference in the opening and closing comments to the "*baʿals* of Shechem" (9:7, 20 [×2]). In Jotham's parable, the trees' intent to anoint a king—"they went forth" (from הלך, *hlk*) to do so (9:8)—is highly unorthodox, and resembles the Shechemites who also "went" (הלך) to anoint a king (9:6). This was a usurpation of Yahweh's responsibility to set up a ruler for his people. But unlike Abimelech, the plants that were approached declined the offer of kingship, unwilling as each was to relinquish fruitfulness and

---

16. Younger, *Judges, Ruth*, 220.

17. The "Beth-millo" is likely to be "a sacred spot, a raised hill where a temple may be built"; the coronation takes place in the presence of the *baʿals* of the city at this location, by a sacred tree (9:6, 20) (Niditch, *Judges*, 115).

public service simply to "wave/hold sway" over the rest of the trees (9:9, 11, 13), implying that sovereign rule was an unproductive enterprise. This is clearly a denunciation of Abimelech's claim and ascendancy to power.

The "shade" offered by the bramble in 9:15—symbolic of a ruler's sovereign patronage and protection (Isa 30:2; Ezek 31:6, 12, 17)—is laughable: thornbushes do not provide shade, making this story a theater of the absurd![18] Yet the madness of the bramble is an appropriate reflection of the mania of Abimelech; both plant and human crave power and dominion. Not only is Abimelech's hubris highlighted in the bramble's utterances and demands—as well as its/his lack of qualification—so also is the folly of those who would make it/him king. "The implication is that the people who designate the ruler have as much responsibility as the ruler," an appropriate focus in a book that is all about errant leadership.[19]

The "cedars of Lebanon" in Jdg 9:15 likely stood for the prideful *baʿals* of Shechem addressed by Jotham (see Isa 2:12–13). Surprisingly, the bramble did not merely accept the invitation to rule, but actually threatened those who made the offer (Jdg 9:15), promising fire and a blistering destruction of those "cedars of Lebanon." The parable does not bode well for the Shechemites, those who appointed Abimelech king.

Jotham's parable focuses on "truth," occurring at the end of the fable (9:15) and at the beginning of its interpretation (9:16, and carried over in 9:19, after a parenthetical comment in 9:17–18). Also note that "integrity" figures in 9:16, 19, as also does "good" (טוֹבָה, 9:16). Thus, Jotham's speech critically introduces into an utterly immoral situation these moral criteria—integrity, truth, and goodness, all measured ultimately by a divine standard.[20] In sum, Gideon had done "good" (טובה, 8:35) and deserved to be treated "well" (טובה, 9:16). Instead, Abimelech (and his sponsors) had introduced a human standard of "goodness" (see the related root, טוב, 9:2), by elevating himself, a renegade and a fratricide, to rulership. If the Shechemites demonstrated "truth and integrity" in their actions, and if they had done "good" to Jerubbaal and his house as he deserved, there would be rejoicing (9:16, 19). If not, the Shechemites and Abimelech would destroy one another (9:20)—a judgment that turns out to be a "curse" (9:57).

Yet for all its moral indignation, Jotham's curse is issued merely in defense of Gideon (9:16–19). The rightful riposte to the rapacity of Abimelech ought to have been a defense of *Yahweh*, who alone was King and

---

18. Fire from the bramble (9:15) is equally ridiculous!

19. Schneider, *Judges*, 140.

20. "Integrity" is תָּמִים, *tamim*, from which יוֹתָם (*yotam*, "Jotham" = "Yah[weh] is Integrity/Perfect") is derived. It is an astute parry by "Yah[weh] is Integrity/Perfect" to the devious plot of "My Father is King."

king-Maker. *He* was the one Israel had forgotten (8:34) and whom Israel had failed to deal with in "truth and integrity" and with "good," not Gideon (9:16–19). In the end, divine justice prevails, as this neglect of truth, integrity, and goodness is justly recompensed by Yahweh sending an "evil" spirit (9:23–24).

8.3. Judges 9:22–57

THEOLOGICAL FOCUS 8.3

8.3   God visits evildoers with retribution befitting the evildoing (9:22–57).

NOTES 8.3

8.3   God visits evildoers with retribution befitting the evildoing.

The subsequent narrative of 9:22–57 is quite dense and obscure. It may be intentional: "A study of the verses describing the confrontation shows that their main object is to leave the reader in uncertainty, even though he receives a great deal of information."[21] Things are messy for the evildoers, reflected in the opacity and befuddlement of the account itself.

That Abimelech "ruled" (שָׂרַר, *sarar*) over Israel for three years is noted in 9:22.[22] He does not "judge" as did Othniel (3:10); he is not a deliverer as was Othniel and Ehud (3:10, 15); and he is not a prophet as was Deborah (4:4). Though this is the only instance of the verb "rule" in Judges, its cognate noun, שַׂר, *sar*, "ruler/commander," occurs in 4:2, 7; 5:15; 7:25; 8:3, 6, 14; 9:30; 10:18, but always in situations of conflict and violence. "Abimelech had been made a king by the Shechemites, but he ruled more like a warlord, and probably brought the rest of Israel to heel by threatened or actual violence."[23] And so, in a clear break from the standard paradigm of 2:11–19, no rest for the land is adduced at the end of his story—this, after a uniform forty years (or a multiple thereof) of rest for the land in every preceding case (3:11, 30; 5:31b; 8:28). Besides, Abimelech's reign, given here in the middle (9:22) rather than at the end of the pericope, is uniquely short—three years. The patience of God has its limits, and divine payback for the evildoing of Abimelech and the Shechemites is the swiftest in Judges.

---

21. Assis, *Self-Interest or Communal Interest*, 156–57.

22. The usual verb for "rule" in Judges is either מָשַׁל (*mshl*, 8:22, 23; 9:2; 14:4; 15:11) or מָלַךְ (*mlk*, 9:8, 10, 12, 14; etc.). A drastically different kind of regency is being envisaged for Abimelech.

23. Webb, *Judges*, 279–80.

Yahweh's retribution commences with the very unusual situation of 9:23. Whereas the Spirit of God comes upon Othniel (3:10), Gideon (6:34), Jephthah (10:29), and Samson (13:25; 14:6, 9; 15:14), now God sends an *evil* spirit to operate in the murky relationship between Abimelech and the *ba'als* of Shechem.[24] This sending initiates a sequence of events that turns the king against his sponsors, and converts sponsors to antagonists, resulting in the downfall of all those doers of evil. The juxtaposition of God's sending the evil spirit (9:23a) and the *ba'als* of Shechem "dealing treacherously" with Abimelech (9:23b) suggests a cause and effect relationship, at least to the narrator. Out of nowhere, without any prior hint of disharmony between Abimelech and the *ba'als*, one fine day the latter begin to "deal treacherously" against the former (9:23b), setting ambushes and taking to highway robbery (9:25), creating a perilous situation that devours everyone.[25] This was a complete reversal of the Shechemites' alliance with Abimelech, the only detectable and immediate cause being the sending by God of that "evil spirit." There is another ominous note in 9:24: the seventy sons of Jerubbaal are said to have been killed by Abimelech, their "brother." But this man of violence had just called the Shechemites his "brothers" (9:2), a label they had reciprocated to Abimelech (9:3). One wonders what will happen to these latest brothers of the crazed Abimelech, in his already bloodied hands.

At the conclusion of the pericope, the narrator makes another declaration about poetic retributive justice (9:56–57; also see 9:22–24). "God causes the evil that Abimelech and the men of Shechem do to rebound on their own heads. The details of the narrative show this process being worked out with almost mathematical precision," with parallel structures depicting Abimelech's rise and fall[26]:

---

24. Other instances of God using evil-/ill-bearing spirits: 1 Sam 16:14; 18:10; 19:9; 1 Kgs 22:22 (= 2 Chr 18:21); 2 Kgs 19:7; Isa 19:14; 29:10. Also see 2 Sam 24:1 with 1 Chr 21:1. Though רָעָה, *ra'ah*, can refer to evil in the non-moral sense of calamity or ill, here the contrast with the other sendings of the Spirit of God in Judges certainly implies that this רוּחַ רָעָה, *ruakh ra'ah*, was of a very different species—an evil spirit, dark and foreboding.

25. The "ambush" set by the *ba'als* of Shechem (9:25) finds its counter in a later "ambush" set by Abimelech (9:32, 34, 43).

26. Ibid., 268. Table modified from Younger, *Judges, Ruth*, 217.

Abimelech's Rise (9:1–24)
- **A** Abimelech's treachery (9:1–6)
  - He goes to Shechem, to deal with "brothers" (9:1–2)
  - **B** Jotham's fable related (9:7–21)
    - **C** Narrator on retribution (9:22–24)

Abimelech's Fall (9:25–57)
- **A'** Shechem's treachery (9:25–41)
  - Gaal comes to Shechem, accompanied by "brothers" (9:26)
  - **B'** Jotham's fable fulfilled (9:42–55)
    - **C'** Narrator on retribution (9:56–57)

Tit for tat: evil gets repaid by evil.

Taking advantage of the instability in Abimelech's days, another opportunist, Gaal, makes his way to Shechem, and wins the trust of the *baʿals*, turning them against Abimelech. Why and how Gaal managed to gain their confidence is unclear. "This uncertainty is intentional and is designed to show the ease with which the citizens of Shechem commission a man as king and then reject him and take another in his stead."[27] Gaal is the son of "Ebed," which means slave—a patronymic repeated five times in this story (9:26, 28, 30, 31, 35).[28] Along with Abimelech, the son of a concubine (8:31) or a maidservant (9:18), it shows how the choices of the *baʿals* of Shechem are suspect. There is clearly a sense of repeated history in this account with parallels between 9:1–6, the entrance of Abimelech, and 9:25–41, the entrance of Gaal.[29]

Narrative Element	Judges 9:1–6	Judges 9:25–41
Arrival of a man in Shechem	9:1	9:26
Man accompanied by his "brothers"	9:1–3	9:26, 31, 41
Denunciation of current/potential rulers	9:2	9:28
Questions re: ruling in Shechem	9:2–3	9:28–29
Genealogical tie to Shechem asserted	9:3	9:28
Shechemites trust conspirator	9:3	9:26
Conspirator confronts (potential) ruler(s)	9:5	9:30–41

---

27. Assis, *Self-Interest or Communal Interest*, 159.

28. Four times in 9:28 the root עבד, *ʿbd*, shows up: thrice as the verb "to serve," and once with Gaal's suffix, "Ebed." His name, Gaal, means "loathsome," making "Gaal" likely a nickname. He is, thus, "Loathsome, the son of a Slave." And not much better in name, character, and deed than "My Father is King," the son of a concubine/maidservant turned tyrant.

29. Boogaart, "Stone for Stone," 50–51.

Gaal brings his own supporters with him, his "brothers" (9:26). Under Gaal's patronage, "they" (the *ba'als* of Shechem and possibly Gaal's junta) perform a series of acts described with seven *wayyiqtol* verb forms in 9:27, and ending in a final and eighth verb, this time an intensive *piel waw* consecutive verb: "and they went out . . . , and they gathered . . . , and they trod . . . , and they held . . . , and they entered . . . , and they ate, and they drank, *and they cursed* . . . ." In a quasi-religious setting, they celebrate their god[30] with the fermented liquor that they produce and, perhaps under its influence, they imprecate against Abimelech. This is the bedlam of a mob of ruffians and rowdies under the influence of both kinds of "spirit," alcoholic and demonic. At any rate, the fact they "cursed" (קלל, *qll*) is remarkable: God was already bringing about the fulfillment of Jotham's "curse" (קללה, *qllh*, 9:57).

All of this hyperactive display of machismo leads Gaal to throw down the gauntlet to Abimelech (9:28–29). Gaal's argument is that he is the true Shechemite, a descendant of Hamor, not Abimelech, merely the son of a concubine (9:28). Literally, his question reads: "Why should-we-serve-him—we?" The overall conflict, no doubt stirred by the evil spirit sent by God, is almost a doublet: 9:26–41 parallels 9:42–45. Both commence with Shechemites "going out into the field: (9:27, 42); both events are "told" to Abimelech (9:25, 42); in response to both, Abimelech divides his troops into "companies" and sets up an "ambush" (9:34, 43); when the Shechemites "come out" in both instances, Abimelech "arises" and attacks (9:35, 43); on both occasions the opponents "fight" one another (9:39, 45).[31]

During Abimelech's ambush, Gaal appears to see Abimelech's companies coming in to attack "from the tops of the mountains" (9:36) and "from the highest parts of the land" (9:37a); perhaps Jotham's own verbal attack from the "top of Mt. Gerizim" (9:7) is being fulfilled. Gaal saw yet another company coming "by the way of the diviner's oak [אלון, *'elon*]" (9:37b); it was also by an "oak" that Abimelech was crowned king (אלון, 9:6), not to mention the occurrence of a number of trees in Jotham's fable (9:8–15). Conflict ensues, and Abimelech acts against the rebellious Gaal, resulting in the latter's defeat (9:39–41).[32]

---

30. I.e., "they made praise [הלולים, *hillulim*]" (Lev 19:24 has the only other instance in the OT of the word). The "temple of Baal-berith" (9:4), Beth-millo (9:6, 20), "the temple of their god" (9:27), and "the temple of El-berith" (9:46), are all likely related, if not identical, structures. In a Canaanite myth, *Aqht A*, 34–35 (*ANET*, 150), "temple of Baal" and "temple of El" occur in parallel.

31. Bluedorn, *Yahweh versus Baalism*, 235.

32. One is struck by all the news that is "told" to Abimeleceh: 9:25, 42, 47. Each such "telling" unleashes a ferocious response from the chieftain, first upon Shechem itself, then upon those who went out into the field the next day, and finally upon those who sought refuge in its tower.

But Abimelech is not content with driving out Gaal; he, like his father in his latter years, has to overreact (in paranoia?): he captures the city, kills all its people (including his relatives?), razes it, and "sows it with salt" (9:42–45).[33] He then proceeds to burn alive all who had taken refuge in the temple of El-berith, about a thousand people, including the *ba'als* of Shechem, his erstwhile patrons (9:46–49).[34] Abimelech had made Gideon's family barren; now he makes Shechem barren. The wanton ruthlessness exhibited on the mere whim of revenge is horrific. Gaal and his gang had celebrated in the temple of their god (9:27); now the Shechemite *ba'als* and a thousand others were burnt alive in it (9:46–49).[35] Yes, indeed, fire had come out of the bramble to consume the cedars of Lebanon (9:15, 20).[36] All his rivals, all his siblings (from both sides), and all his patrons (the *ba'als*), indeed the very city he sought to rule, Shechem, had finally been destroyed. What the man had done to his "brothers," his father's sons (9:5), is now also done to his "brothers," his mother's relatives (9:1). Anyone that went against Abimelech was in danger of being consumed by this man's demented extermination of real and perceived enemies.

After Shechem, one would have thought Abimelech would have had enough carnage for a season. But, no, he decides to go against Thebez, too, and destroy *its* tower and people with the same means he used for the tower of Shechem: fire (9:50–52). We are given no reason for this insatiable appetite for violence or for the choice of that town. "[G]iven the paranoia he has already exhibited in his total destruction of Shechem, it is probably unnecessary to seek any rational explanation (however thin or perverse) for his attack on Thebez, for it is the nature of paranoia to subvert rationality, and of leaders who suffer from it to commit excesses that eventually bring about their own destruction. So it was with Abimelech."[37] But here he is undone with a woman dropping a millstone on his head (9:53).[38]

33. It is unclear what the significance of the salting is; perhaps it was a ritual of Baalism to invoke a curse on the land and to render it infertile, barren, and ruined (Deut 29:23; Ps 107:34; Jer 17:6; Zeph 2:9) (Block, *Judges, Ruth,* 330).

34. These were the Shechemite *ba'als,* governors whose "best-laid schemes gang agley, An' lea'e nought but grief an' pain" (modified from Rabbie Burns, the Bard of Ayrshire, and his "Tae a Moose," 1785).

35. There is an ironic wordplay in Abimelech's preparations for the conflagration: Abimelech lifts a branch and lays it "against his *shoulder*" (9:49); "shoulder" is שְׁכֶם, *shkem,* which is identical to "Shechem," שְׁכֶם.

36. Jotham's parable comes to pass: "trees" and "fire" are found in this pericope in 9:8, 9, 10, 11, 12, 13, 14, 15, 20; and 9:48, 49, 52.

37. Webb, *Judges,* 292.

38. The "upper millstone," a grinder used in conjunction with a lower stone was probably between 4–9 lbs in weight, sufficiently light for a woman to have heaved it

If one probes the precision of Jotham's fable, one would expect fire to consume Abimelech in turn, as well (9:20). Fokkelman shows that this is a pun on אֵשׁ, *'esh,* "fire." In 9:49 one has אֵשׁ ("fire"), אִישׁ (*'ish,* "men"), and אִשָּׁה (*'isshah,* "women"); in 9:51, again we have אִישׁ ("men"), and אִשָּׁה ("women"). In 9:52, we hear of Abimelech's plan to destroy the tower of Thebes also with אֵשׁ ("fire"). Then, all of a sudden, an אִשָּׁה ("woman") comes on the scene, Abimelech's plot to use אֵשׁ to destroy the Thebezites backfires (pun intended!), and he is destroyed (9:53).[39] The irony is pungent: "Abimelech uses his mother and her relatives to gain power, apparently kills them in the slaughter of Shechem, and then succumbs to the 'certain [literally, "one"] woman' of Thebez in an unnecessary battle."[40] The "one" (אֶחָד, *'ekhad*) woman is a notable adjective for the killer of Abimelech—the man who killed his siblings on "one" (אֶחָד) stone (9:5, 18), when he, the "one" (אֶחָד) man (9:2), sought to rule Shechem.

Despite his every effort to ensure that the final stroke of death was administered by a man (9:54), Abimelech is remembered as one who underwent the ultimate ignominy of being killed by a woman (2 Sam 11:21). "In the warrior culture of the times, to die at the hands of a worthy adversary of equal or superior rank or strength might have been counted honorable. But to be killed by an inferior enemy, a woman no less, and not even a woman of note, but just a *certain* [one] *woman,* a nobody, was to be completely undone; and Abimelech knows it."[41] That Abimelech tells his armor bearer to kill him lest it be said of him, "A woman *slew* [הרג, *hrg*] him" (9:54), is significant. Abimelech was the one who had "slain" (הרג) his brothers (9:5, 24 [×2]), and "slain" (הרג) the people in Shechem (9:45). He now acknowledges that what the "one" woman did to him was payback for his own slaughter of many: What you sow, you reap!

This is the second instance in Judges of a woman dispatching a malignant opponent: Jael's killing of Sisera, too, was accomplished by a head injury inflicted by an unconventional weapon; she, too, was a woman who entered late in the narrative, and was used by Yahweh to accomplish his purpose, be it military victory in one case, or poetic justice in the other (see Pericope 4: Jdg 4:1–24). But in the earlier incident it was a foreigner who was slain by the woman. Here it is an Israelite who is. "Things have seriously

---

over a low parapet (Chisholm, *Judges and Ruth,* 322 n.59).

39. Fokkelman, "Structural Remarks," 39.
40. Butler, *Judges,* 249.
41. Webb, *Judges,* 293. The wound inflicted by the millstone was fatal (the verb used by Abimelech in 9:54 to describe the woman's action is הרג, *hrg,* "to slay"), but the immediate cause of death was the stab wound: the verb used for the armor bearer's action is the *polel* of מות, *mot,* "to die."

deteriorated when the bondage from which Israel has to be delivered in this fashion is no longer bondage to some foreign power but a bondage to one of Israel's own number who, instead of being a deliverer of Israel, has installed himself as a tyrant, and is maintaining his tyranny by ruthless destruction."[42]

Surprisingly, almost at the instant Abimelech dies, the "men of Israel" decide enough is enough, quit the battle, and each departs "to his place/home" (9:55). "This evil spirit is not exorcised until the chief instigator of the evil is struck down, whereupon his followers, as if waking from a bad dream, put down their weapons and go home without completing their assault on Thebez."[43] It is as if they return home resignedly, but not to any rest, for no such respite is noted in the text. In fact, never again in Judges will the people of Israel have rest; the enemy that is internal, and the foes they have become to themselves, will preclude any rest for the nation.

That this was a fulfillment of Jotham's curse is evident in the parallels between 9:23–24 and 9:56–57[44]: both delineate the reaction of God to evil-doing by Abimelech and the Shechemites, and the ultimate consequences thereof.

JUDGES 9:23–24
And God sent an evil spirit
A   between Abimelech,
    B   and between the *ba'als* of Shechem,
    B'   and the *ba'als* of Shechem dealt treacherously
A'   with Abimelech

so that the violence done to the seventy *sons of Jerubbaal might come* ... on Abimelech ... and on the *ba'als* of Shechem.

JUDGES 9:56–57
A   God returned
    B   the evil of Abimelech
        C   which he had done to his father, in killing his seventy brothers
    B'   and all the evil of the men of Shechem
A'   God returned on their heads

and the curse of Jotham the *son of Jerubbaal came* upon them.

The only one who wins in this narrative is God, whose retribution is justly distributed to the involved parties, Abimelech, Shechemites, *ba'als*,

---

42. Gooding, "The Composition of the Book of Judges," 74.

43. Webb, *Judges*, 281. Thankfully, Abimelech does not seem to have left any descendants, unlike his father Gideon (8:30–31).

44. Modified from O'Connell, *The Rhetoric of the Book of Judges*, 167 n.214, 169 n.220.

and all: disaster, destruction, and death (9:56–57). And thus the nightmare ends—at least the current one![45]

8.4. Judges 10:1–5

> **THEOLOGICAL FOCUS 8.4**
>
> 8.4 Divine punishment does not mean the absence of divine grace (10:1–5).

NOTES 8.4

8.4 Divine punishment does not mean the absence of divine grace.

After the grit and gore in Judges 1–9, readers are allowed a breath or two of fresh air with the accounts of the minor judges in 10:1–5. A semblance of stability and security seems to have been established in the land, despite the absence of any rest after the reign of the nefarious Abimelech. "It may be that these 'peaceful interludes' did not provide the stories of grand adventure occasioned by times of war, but still, the details preserved in these minor judge narratives provide insight into the values of this transitional time," between the major judges of the book. The accounts of these minor judges make no mention of Yahweh's intervention into human affairs of their times, and these leaders seemingly arise on their own cognizance—usually wealth, reputation, influence, and family. Nor is there any notation of the spirituality of the nation in their days. But at least there is no bloodshed, only "the trappings of a peaceful and prosperous life: asses and cities, children and weddings and even grandchildren. And there is continuity and stability. The judge works and lives and dies and is buried. And another judge arises and works and lives and dies and is buried. In three cases, a reference to sons suggests an additional measure of continuity."[46] Perhaps it is precisely because of the inadequate performances of the major leaders—moving the nation towards instability and civil war—that these minor leaders are introduced as foils.

That Tola is specifically noted to have arisen "after Abimelech" (10:1) links the former's story to that of his bloodthirsty predecessor. "It is 'after Abimelech' that Tola arises. Need the narrator say more? Israel does not need deliverance from foreign powers; it needs to be restored to order after

---

45. Butler, *Judges*, 250.

46. Beem, "The Minor Judges," 165. Nelson suggests a separate paradigm for the minor judges that includes a transitional introduction, family/clan/tribe information, years of service, and death and burial details ("Ideology, Geography," 352).

the rampage of Abimelech."[47] And so Tola "arose," "saved," "lived," "judged," "died," and "was buried" (10:1–2)—nothing spectacular, nothing flashy, just the crucial elements to conduct a peaceful life, to create an orderly environment, and to govern a stable nation under the solid leadership that he provides for twenty-three years. Besides, Tola is the only judge, major or minor, for whom antecedents are provided back to a third generation, often indicative in the OT of respectable standing.[48]

While we know Shamgar saved Israel from the Philistines (3:31), we have no indication as to whom Tola saved Israel from (10:1)—no external enemy is mentioned. Perhaps that is deliberate, for we have just seen a vicious *internal* enemy, Abimelech, in action (and indeed for the remaining major judges, Jephthah and Samson, their internal demons are a greater problem than any external oppression). It may well have been Abimelech's chaos that Tola saved the nation from.

Jair is the Gileadite who precedes the Gileadite major judge, Jephthah (10:3–5). Tola likely had to face the aftereffects of Abimelech's rampages, and his focus was on the *present* of his day. But Jair's tenure is marked by peace and prosperity, and so his sons, donkeys, and cities, including one named after him (Havoth-jair), mark his judgeship as stable, keeping the focus on the *future*. Unlike the days of Shamgar (5:6) and of Abimelech (9:25), when travel was risky and unsafe, in Jair's time his sons go about on their donkeys, and establish their cities in peace.[49] One must not miss the assonance: יָאִיר (*ya'ir*, "Jair"), עַיִר (*'ayir*, "donkey"), and עָיר (*'ayir*, "city"). Though the pericope ends on a relatively peaceful note, all is not well in Israel. The downward slippage has become more severe, Canaanization has all but become established in Israel, and her remaining major judges will push the nation over the precipice.

SERMON FOCUS AND OUTLINES

THEOLOGICAL FOCUS OF PERICOPE 8 FOR PREACHING

8 The illicit thirst for power, destructive in its ramifications, brings about fitting retribution from God (8:33–10:5).

Pericope 6 (Jdg 6:1—7:22) dealt with Gideon's prideful and delusional taking of credit for divine action; Pericope 7 (Jdg 7:23—8:32) was concerned with Gideon's self-glorifying vendettas and his craze for power (and the

---

47. Beem, "The Minor Judges," 149.

48. But he, an Issacharite, lived and died in Ephraim (10:1) for reasons unknown.

49. For donkeys as a means of royal transportation, see Gen 49:11; Jdg 5:10; 2 Sam 13:29; 18:9; 1 Kgs 1:33; Zech 9:9; Matt 21:5; Luke 19:30.

consequences thereof)—the sermon on Pericope 7 heralded a call for humility. Here, Pericope 8 (Jdg 8:33—10:5) takes the Gideon story a baneful step further, with the narrative of a vicious tyrant, Abimelech. He intensifies the faults of Gideon by several notches, and suffers the consequences. The focus thus is best placed on the appropriate divine justice that he suffers as recompense. Ungodly and aggressive pursuit of power, merciless and ruinous, will get its just deserts from God. The minor judges at the end of this pericope may be mentioned briefly here or with the next set of them in Pericope 9: Jdg 10:6—12:15.

Possible Preaching Outlines for Pericope 8

I. Ungodly Behavior
   Yahweh's absence in the story
   Absence of an external enemy
   Evildoing of the Israelites (8:33–35)
II. Unsanctioned Leader
   Human appointment of Abimelech as ruler (9:1–4)
   Payment from Baal's temple (9:4); *ba'al*-centering of the narrative
III. Unmerciful Despot
   Abimelech's cruelty and his thirst for power (9:5–6, 25–49)
IV. Unerring Justice
   Abimelech's condemnation in Jotham's parable (9:7–21)
   Appropriate divine retribution for evildoing (9:22–24, 50–57)
V. *Ungodliness may provoke divine retribution!*[50]
   Specifics on how to relinquish ungodliness and avoid punishment

As in the prior pericope—where Gideon, like Abimelech, was a negatively portrayed character through and through—a Problem-Consequences-Application outline works here:

I. PROBLEM: Abimelech's Rottenness
   Yahweh's absence in the story
   Absence of an external enemy
   Evildoing of the Israelites (8:33–35)
   Human appointment of Abimelech as ruler (9:1–4)
   Payment from Baal's temple (9:4); *ba'al*-centering of the narrative

---

50. Obviously, this is not an imperative. There is nothing magical about putting applications in the imperative, though that may be the clearest way to propose them. But preachers may use their discretion and be more implicit about imperatives. "Ungodliness" is fairly broad; one might narrow it down to unconcern for God's interests or bellicosity, both of which are prominent in the Abimelech story.

Abimelech's despotic cruelty and his thirst for power (9:5–6, 25–49)
II. CONSEQUENCE: God's Retribution
Abimelech's condemnation in Jotham's parable (9:7–21)
Appropriate divine retribution for evildoing (9:22–24, 50–57)
III. APPLICATION: Our Response: *Ungodliness may provoke divine retribution!*
Specifics on how to relinquish ungodliness and avoid punishment

PERICOPE 9

Jephthah

Judges 10:6–12:15

[God's Displeasure; Human Installation of Ruler;
Jephthah's Vow and His Violence]

REVIEW, SUMMARY, PREVIEW

Review of Pericope 8: In Jdg 8:33—10:5, we have the story of Abimelech, the continuation—and natural consequence—of Gideon's story. His narrative is marked by the absence of both Yahweh and an external enemy: the Israelite protagonist, Abimelech, was Israel's enemy. Unsanctioned by God and appointed by humans, paid from Baal's temple, this ungodly ruler turned out to be an unmerciful despot, ruthless and brutal, wantonly killing his own siblings and his fellow Israelites. He meets his just deserts in appropriate divine retribution.

Summary of Pericope 9: The ninth pericope of Judges (10:6—12:15) contains the story of Jephthah. The idolatrous Israelites are excoriated by God who refuses to deliver them from their enemies into whose hand they have been given. So the Israelites take matters into their own hands and appoint Jephthah. He attempts to force God into action with a recital of Israel's history and with a vow of sacrifice if he is victorious in battle. He is, but his tragic vow leads him to sacrifice his only child, a daughter. This disaster does not seem to have taught him much, for he then goes forth and slaughters fellow Israelites over a personal taunt.

> **Preview of Pericope 10:** The next pericope, Jdg 13:1—14:20, forms the first half of Samson's story. God's grace is evident from the start: Samson is divinely conceived and dedicated for a divine destiny, blessed and endowed with the Spirit. For all that, nation, parents, and chosen deliverer are imperceptive and indifferent to God and his work. Samson does what is right in his own eyes and neglects his Nazirite regulations, resulting in a life of conflict marked by loss, as this dissolute judge gives in to his sensual passions.

9. *Judges 10:6–12:15*

THEOLOGICAL FOCUS OF PERICOPE 9

9 Failure to live holy lives serving God, manipulation of God for selfish purposes, and adopting the practices of unbelievers can lead to tragic loss of blessing (10:6—12:5).

9.1 Failure to live holy lives serving God has serious consequences for God's people (10:6–16).

9.2 Attempts to accomplish one's goals unilaterally, without wholeheartedly seeking the initiative and aid of God, are futile (10:17—11:11).

9.3 God cannot be manipulated to meet the selfish needs of his people (11:12–33).

9.4 Attempts to manipulate God can lead to tragic loss of blessing (11:34–40).

9.5 Adopting the practices of unbelievers accelerates a downward spiral of wickedness that is destructive (12:1–15).

OVERVIEW

With the assassination of Abimelech, the house of Gideon is wiped out, except for Jotham who decamps from the scene and is not heard of any more (Jdg 9:21). Jephthah is the next major protagonist in Judges, who also brings an end to his generation by sacrificing his only child, a daughter. After him, Samson, likewise, as far as we know, leaves no progeny, and gets himself killed at the end of his narrative. None of these leaders achieve any rest in the land. In other words, after Gideon, there is nothing but calamity and disaster, with no sign of any good anywhere or in anyone, and the nation rapidly plunges into anarchy.

Minor judges cluster around the Jephthah narrative, two before (10:1–5) and three after (12:8–15).[1] The reason for this collocation is unclear, though the fact that Jephthah had only one child (11:34), who was killed, stands out amidst the prolific minor judges on either side of his story who have between them hundred sons, thirty daughters, thirty daughters-in-law, thirty grandsons, and even a hundred donkeys (10:4; 12:9, 14)! That makes Jephthah, in the middle, a pathetic figure.

This pericope, too, is marked by minimal presence of and action by Yahweh. After the rebuke of 10:10–16, Yahweh's only actions in the story of Jephthah are the endowment of his Spirit upon the judge-deliverer (11:29), and his defeat of the Ammonites (11:32–33).[2]

Paradigm	Jephthah
2:11 *Evildoing*	10:6 Continues
2:14 (×2) *To enemies for X years*	10:7 Sold 18 years (10:8)
2:18 *Groan*	10:10 Cry
2:16, 18 *Judge raised*	[—]
2:18 *Yahweh's support*	11:29 "Spirit"
2:16, 18 *Fate of enemies*	11:32, 33 Given Subdued
2:19 *Land's rest Judge*	12:7 [—] Dies

---

1. The former set has Tola and Jair. Jair is explicitly "the Gileadite" (10:2), and Tola, too, came from the Transjordan, in the region of Gilead (10:1), linking them both with the next major judge figure, Jephthah, a Gileadite (11:1).

2. However, deity is referred to several times: by Jephthah in his speech to the king of Ammon (11:21, 23, 24, 27); by the narrator in the context of Jephthah's vow (11:30); and by Jephthah and his daughter in their dialogue (11:35, 36 [×2]).

Another negative: Jephthah's reign is also the shortest of the judges: six years. So, in sum, Jephthah's rulership was brief, his progeny was abolished, and his burial was unmarked (unlike that of the minor judges arrayed around him).[3]

There are five episodes in the Jephthah narrative, each of the central three marked by the motif of the spoken word, דָּבָר, *dabar*, that is part of a dialogue[4]:

Episode	Dialogue
Episode 1	**Yahweh and Israel (10:6–16)** Israel (10:10, 15); Yahweh (10:11–14)
Episode 2	**Gilead and Jephthah (10:17–11:11)** Gilead ([10:18;] 11:6, 8, 10); Jephthah (11:7, 9) דבר, *dabar* (11:10, 11 [×2], "to speak"/"word")
Episode 3	**Jephthah and Ammon (11:12–28)** Jephthah (11:12, 15–27); Ammon (11:13) דבר (11:28, "message")
Episode 4	**Jephthah and his daughter (11:29–40)** Jephthah (11:35, 38); his daughter (11:36–37) דבר (11:37, "thing")
Episode 5	**Ephraim and Jephthah (12:1–6)** Ephraim (12:1, 4, 5b, 6b); Jephthah (2–3, 5a, 6a)

The opening of one's mouth also recurs as a motif in 11:35–36, all warning against the folly of impulsive and thoughtless utterances. Even the name "Jephthah" (יִפְתָּח, *yiptakh*) is derived from the root, פתח, *ptkh*, "to open."[5]

---

3. Even his military successes are underwhelming. Yahweh had sold the Israelites into the hands of the Philistines and into the hands of the Ammonites (10:6), but Jephthah accomplishes a deliverance of Israel only from the latter; the saga of the Philistine oppression continues into the narrative of the next judge, Samson. Biblical literature treats longevity, posterity, and prominent interment as rewards for righteousness. For long life, see Deut 5:33; Ps 91:16; Prov 3:1–2; etc.; for progeny, see Gen 22:17; 33:5; Ps 127:3–5; etc.; for burial, see Gen 35:29; 49:33; 50:12–13; Isa 14:18–20; Jer 16:4; etc.

4. From Block, *Judges, Ruth*, 342.

5. Claassens notes that the bulk of the narrative space in this pericope is spent on Jephthah's speech (360 words) and not on his deeds (129 words) ("Notes on the Characterisation," 111).

9.1. Judges 10:6–16

> **THEOLOGICAL FOCUS 9.1**
>
> 9.1 Failure to live holy lives serving God has serious consequences for God's people (10:6–16).

NOTES 9.1

9.1 Failure to live holy lives serving God has serious consequences for God's people.

Judges 10:6–18, the longest of all the condemnatory introductions to the judge stories, details the comprehensive unfaithfulness of Israel to Yahweh. Yahweh's rebuke begins with a statement of his delivery of the Israelites from *seven* nations/people groups: Egyptians, Amorites, Ammonites, Philistines, Sidonians, Amalekites, and Maonites (10:11–12). This corresponds in number to the sets of gods Israel was serving (10:6)—*seven*: Baals, Ashtaroth, gods of Aram, gods of Sidon, gods of Moab, gods of Ammon, and gods of Philistia (10:6). Even as the seven defeated enemies point to the completeness of Yahweh's deliverances, the seven worshiped groups of deities indicate the totality of the Israelites apostasy. They serve every god occupying every pantheon in every nation around them. The only deity they fail to serve is the true God, Yahweh.[6] Yahweh's people, whom *he* had "chosen" (Deut 7:6; 14:2), had now "chosen" their own deities (Jdg 10:14)!

Thus far, there have also been exactly *seven* major and minor judges: Othniel, Ehud, Shamgar, Barak, Gideon, Tola, and Jair. In parallel, those seven sets of gods the Israelites served form a chronological/literary parade of deities as they are encountered in the judge stories: the Baals and Asherahs (see 3:7), the gods of Aram (likely related to Cushan-rishathaim, king of "Mesopotamia" [אֲרַם נַהֲרַיִם, *'aram naharayim*], 3:8), the gods of Sidon (nowhere else in the book), the gods of Moab (related to Eglon, king of Moab, 3:12), the gods of Ammon (related to the Ammonites in the Jephthah story, 10:9), and the gods of the Philistines (related to the Philistines in the Samson story, 13:1; also see 3:31).[7] Israel, in each of those accounts, had

---

6. See Deut 12:1–4, 29–31.

7. Assis, *Self-Interest or Communal Interest*, 175–76. The absence of Canaanite gods in the list (related to Jabin, king of Canaan, 4:2) is perhaps because Baal and Ashtaroth were their primary deities or because they shared the gods of Sidon. The gods of the Midianites (related to the enemy in the Gideon story, 6:1) are also not mentioned: this nomadic group likely did not have an institutionalized cult (ibid., 176 n.4). At the same time, 10:11–12 also lists oppression from the Egyptians, Amorites, and Maonites,

been afflicted and oppressed by the pagan devotees of these gods, making their current loyalty to these deities incomprehensible. Another way of conceptualizing the listing of these gods is by a geographic layout: Aram (Syria) and Sidon to the north; Moab and Ammon to the east; the Philistines to the south and west. Thus all throughout their movements in both time and space, the Israelites had been adding one god after another to their own menagerie, their circle of apostasy widening outward and spiraling downward, all the while rejecting the one true God, Yahweh (10:6).

Yahweh's accusation is followed by foreigners' affliction of Israel, and finally by the Israelites' acknowledgement of their culpability.

A	Served Baals (10:6)		
	B	Forsook Yahweh (10:6)	**Accusation**
		C Did not serve Him (10:6)	
			D Consequence (10:7–9)	**Affliction**
		C' Sinned against Thee (10:10)	
	B'	Forsaken our God (10:10)	**Acknowledgement**
A'	Served Baals (10:10)		

But one notices that in 10:10 the Israelites confess only their Baalistic tendencies, not their servitude to the rest of the gods. So this insincere cry to Yahweh meets with a unique response from deity: he refuses to help (10:11–14)! God was not going to listen to those who would not listen to him. Only then do the Israelites agree to put away the foreign gods (10:15–16), suggesting the hypocrisy of their earlier appeals—this was certainly not repentance.

In the first two judge-cycles (Othniel and Ehud), Yahweh responded instantly to the cries of his people. In the third (Barak), a prophetess mediated his intention to raise a leader, and a deliverer, albeit a fearful one, was immediately on the scene. In the fourth (Gideon), a prophet came on stage to confront Israel with their sin, and the deliverer's arrival was delayed by some necessary ritual cleansing (and the elimination of his own doubts). In this, the fifth (Jephthah), there is an outright refusal from Yahweh to succumb to the manipulations of his people (10:11–13). In fact, he is expressly sarcastic, asking them to find help from all the gods they had chosen to serve (10:14). One can sense the distance between Yahweh and his people increasing dangerously as the book advances. The consequences go beyond

---

groups that are not encountered in Judges, emphasizing that what is written is a selective history for a specific purpose—authors *do* things with what they say.

the spiritual. In the physical realm, we find that the oppression of the Israelites has also progressively intensified: from one enemy at a time (3:8; 3:12–13 [albeit with foreign aid]; 4:2; 6:1) to, now, *two* enemies together, the Philistines and the Ammonites, and on a larger geographic canvas on either side of the Jordan River (10:7–8).

God's rejection of the Israelites' appeal here seems to have knocked some sense into them, albeit temporarily (see 13:1): they put away the foreign gods they were worshiping and "served" Yahweh (10:15–16)—the counter of what was described in 10:6. However, even then, the only response from God is one of ire: "And His soul/person was short [impatient] because of the exertions/labor [quasi-repentance] of Israel" (10:16b).⁸ No help is forthcoming from the aggrieved deity. The Israelites will have to fend for themselves, and they, in fact, attempt to do so: the Gileadites decide to find themselves a deliverer (10:17–18), even as the Ammonites are mustering in Gilead, dangerously close.

9.2. Judges 10:17–11:11

> **THEOLOGICAL FOCUS 9.2**
>
> 9.2 Attempts to accomplish one's goals unilaterally, without wholeheartedly seeking the initiative and aid of God, are futile (10:17—11:11).

NOTES 9.2

9.2 *Attempts to accomplish one's goals unilaterally, without wholeheartedly seeking the initiative and aid of God, are futile.*

Note the parallels in 10:17:

10:17a	Sons of Ammon	were *summoned*	and they camped …
10:17b	Sons of Israel	were *gathered*	and they camped …

---

8. The idiom, "soul was short," indicates frustration and exasperation: Num 21:4; Jdg 16:16; Job 21:4; Zech 11:8. It was the false "exertions/labor" (עמל, *'ml*) to win his favor that drove Yahweh to this limit. In light of Prov 24:2 (where עמל parallels "violence"), Isa 10:1 (where it parallels "iniquity"), and Hab 1:13 (where it parallels "evil"), these "exertions/labor" of the people in Judges 10 are clearly negative. The word עמל can also mean "suffering" (Deut 26:7; Pss 25:18; 90:10; Jer 20:18; etc.), but it does not seem likely that Yahweh would be exasperated with his people's suffering.

One was "summoned"—the *niphal* of צעק (*tsʿq*, "to summon") always implies a "summoner," i.e., a leader (6:34, 35; 7:23, 24; 12:1; 18:22, 23)—and the other was "gathered," hinting at the problem the Israelites were facing: the lack of a leader, explicitly noted in 10:18.[9] God was not going to provide one, and so the princes of Gilead ask the same question (10:18) that the people of Israel had asked at the beginning of the book of Judges (1:1):

Judges 1:1	Judges 10:18
"*Who* shall go up for us against the Canaanites in the *beginning* *to fight* *with* them?"	"*Who* is the man who will begin *to fight* *with* the sons of Ammon?"

But in the earlier case, the Israelites were united and on the offensive, inquiring of *Yahweh* about commencing the campaign. Here, in 10:18, Israel is on the defensive, and asking *themselves* the question, and offering a reward for the successful volunteer. Jephthah is the only major judge-deliverer to have been chosen entirely by men, and not by God. Not a good sign.

Similarities with the prior account of Abimelech abound: one is the son of a concubine and an outsider, while the other is the son of a harlot, an outsider and an outcast (8:31; 11:1–2); both their stories deal with relatives/clansmen (9:1–6; 11:1–11) who, after negotiation, appoint them ruler and chief, respectively, in the precincts of a religious shrine (9:6; 11:11); both protagonists associate with "worthless men" (9:4; 11:3); both slaughter their fellow-Israelites (9:26–57; 12:1–6); and both come to a tragic end, leaving no future after them (9:50–57; 11:34–35). The reader hopes for the best, but the signs lead one to expect the worst.

Ironically, the "valiant warrior" chosen is the "son of a harlot" (11:1). So while his military capacity is notable, his community standing is not.[10] So here is Jephthah, an outcast, likely without any legal rights (11:3), a refugee in the land of "Tob" (טוב, *tob*, "good," 11:3, 5). The Israelites had recently pled in desperation with Yahweh to "do to us whatever seems *good* [טוב] in Your eyes" (10:15), and Yahweh had done exactly that: he sent them Jephthah

---

9. What seems to have been Gilead's fight is actually *all* Israel's: it is the "sons of Israel" who are gathered and who camp in Mizpah (10:17), though the campaign may have been spearheaded by the Gileadites.

10. As opposed to a concubine, who was considered a secondary wife, a harlot had no status. But Jephthah's father, Gilead, is immediately named (11:1), perhaps giving Jephthah an adopted rank. Besides, it is implied that he lived in his father's house, at least until his step-siblings drove him out, cheating him of his inheritance (11:2).

from "Tob"/"Good"! At any rate, this man loses no time surrounding himself with "worthless fellows" (11:3), all likely sustaining themselves by banditry. "[T]he mother's profession, the father's actions [in having relations with a harlot], the character of Jephthah's half-brothers, and Jephthah's own lifestyle all point to a thoroughly Canaanized environment."[11]

The account of a brewing war in 10:17–18 is interrupted with a flashback, signaled by a circumstantial clause in 11:1 and the introduction of Jephthah in 11:1–3, before matters of war are resumed in 11:4. All the Gileadites want is freedom from the Ammonite yoke, and they attempt to obtain this liberty by hook or by crook, underbidding and renegotiating, by human contrivance, design, and manipulation.[12] On the other hand, all Jephthah wants is recognition and restoration of status: one suspects that even Jephthah's "If you take me back to fight . . . " (11:9) hints at the legal restitution of a status that had been stripped from him.[13] For Jephthah, all this warring against an enemy is merely a means to an egoistic end, evidenced in his use of personal pronouns in his dialogue with the Gileadites: אֹתִי . . . אַתֶּם (ʾattem . . . ʾoti), "you [hate] me" (11:7) and אֹתִי . . . אַתֶּם, "you [take back] me" (11:9). Though Yahweh is not at all active in this scene, both Jephthah and the Gileadites continue to use him. First, Jephthah piously invokes Yahweh in his stipulation (11:9), thus elevating military victory to the status of a divine endorsement of his endeavors, to enhance his status and authority with the Gileadites. Then, the Gileadites employ "Yahweh" in an oath (11:10), and, finally, both Jephthah and the Gileadites formalize their agreement before Yahweh in Mizpah (11:11), reducing Yahweh to a mere listener: "Yahweh will be the one who *listens* between us" (i.e., as a witness, 11:10).[14] What

---

11. Block, *Judges, Ruth*, 352.

12. In their own cogitations, the Gileadites had decided they need a "head" (10:18; perhaps indicating a non-specific and general leadership/rulership). But to Jephthah they only offer the post of "chief" (11:6; perhaps restricted to military leadership, as in Josh 10:24; Isa 22:3; Dan 11:18). They were, thus, bidding low, but Jephthah rebuffs that offer, questioning their past treatment of him and implicitly raising the ante (Jdg 11:7). So the Gileadites then sweeten the deal: they will make him "head" (11:8). Jephthah restates the contract to confirm matters (11:9), and the Gileadites reaffirm their intent (11:10). So Jephthah signs on the dotted line and they make him both "head" *and* "chief" on the spot (11:11). It all seems rather devious.

13. While 11:2 mentions the half-brothers of Jephthah driving him away, in 11:7 Jephthah accuses the elders of Gilead of having done so. Perhaps there was some collusion between the brothers of Jephthah and the Gileadites, with the elders legally ratifying the relatives' ejection of the concubine's son.

14. Even this procedure before Yahweh in Mizpah is suspect: thus far there has been no indication that Mizpah was ever a legitimate cultic site. All of this looks like "a glib and calculated effort to manipulate Yahweh" (Block, *Judges, Ruth*, 356). We find out in 11:29–31 that Jephthah's wild vow was also made in Mizpah.

Yahweh wants or what his will might be in the whole matter is, apparently, unimportant. "So Yahweh reenters the story obliquely, neither speaking nor being addressed, but on the lips of Jephthah as a trump card in his negotiations with the elders, and on the lips of the elders themselves . . . as a silent witness of all that takes place."[15] They are all going through the motions of a ritual.

9.3. Judges 11:12–33

THEOLOGICAL FOCUS 9.3

9.3   God cannot be manipulated to meet the selfish needs of his people (11:12–33).

NOTES 8.1

9.3   *God cannot be manipulated to meet the selfish needs of his people.*

The next section, 11:12–28, takes more than a third of the Jephthah story by word count (345 out of 1,000 words in the Hebrew text), and consumes seventeen verses.[16] The actual battle, on the other hand, is confined to a mere two verses (11:32–33). We see Jephthah here acting monarchical, placing himself on a par with the king of Ammon, sending envoys (11:12–14) and undertaking diplomatic initiatives. In fact, Jephthah makes the battle with Ammon quite personal: "What is between *you* and *me*?" he challenges the foreign king (11:12), referring also to Israel's land as "*my* land" (11:12)—the land east of the Jordan. Of course, the Ammonite king calls it "my land," too (11:13). Later, the war is again noted explicitly to be between Jephthah and the Ammonite king, as the former declares: "And *I* have not sinned against *you*, but *you* are doing evil to *me* by fighting with *me*" (11:27). This is turning out to be a personal battle, with Jephthah's acceptance into society hinging on his victory; he desperately wants to win and no longer be a "nobody."

It also appears that this outsider/outcast, the son of a harlot, is quite well versed in the three-century-old history of the conflict between Israel and its neighbors (11:26).[17] And, at least in his recounting, he is an ardent

---

15. Webb, *Judges*, 312.
16. Block, *Judges, Ruth*, 357 n.57.
17. See Exodus 13–14; Numbers 20–23; Deuteronomy 2–3. This section of the

Yahwist (11:21, 23, 24, 27). But his invocation of Yahweh seems to be more an expression of one-upmanship than any real zeal for deity. His introduction of Israel's God into the powwow is to make Israel's claim more secure and to contrast her with Ammon, whose gods did not help the Ammonites take possession of any land. Ergo, Israel gets to keep the land that *their* God (Yahweh) gave them, just as the Ammonites keep the land their god gave them.[18]

While this back and forth between Jephthah and the king of Ammon appears to be a good-faith negotiation, in reality it is hardly so. The warring sides had already mustered and arrayed (10:17) when Jephthah sent messengers to the Ammonite ruler (notice "to fight," in 11:4, 5, 12, 27). This parley, then, is not an attempt at peace, especially since Jephthah had been hired expressly to "fight" (11:6, 8, 9). Therefore, all of Jephthah's verbosity, from the very start of the "negotiations," comprises a declaration of war.[19] Hardly negotiations, these were preludes to battle.

But there is an ulterior motive, too, in Jephthah's discourse here. "With an appeal to divine justice at its core, Jephthah's challenge is effectively pushing God into entering the fray on Israel's behalf, that is, also on Jephthah's. The argument is . . . that Ammon is threatening to annul results achieved in Moses' days. If there is any validity to Moses' conquests, God had better take Jephthah's side."[20] And, of course, the resulting success, if it panned out, would improve Jephthah's standing amongst his people, something the man had been yearning for all along. So, in 11:27, the litigant, Jephthah, brings his case before the divine Judge, Yahweh: Jephthah claims he has not

---

pericope also proves that Israel's memory regarding past events was selective and skewed. Each time, after a judge had died, the nation had returned to evil, *not remembering* the past (Jdg 2:7, 10, 12, 17, 19, 20; 3:7)—they had even *forgotten* Yahweh (3:12; 4:1; 6:1; 10:6–8). But the truth is that they had *not* forgotten; when they needed to, they (or at least Jephthah, representing Israel) were able to salvage details quite efficiently. This makes their paradigmatic evildoing in this book reprehensible.

18. The Israelites had first captured that territory from the Amorites (Numbers 21), who had taken it over from the Moabites. But now, in Jephthah's day, the Ammonites were making a claim on that land (Jdg 11:13). Jephthah's reference to Chemosh as "your [i.e., the Ammonites'] god" (11:24) is problematic, for the god of the Ammonites was not Chemosh, who was the god of the Moabites (Num 21:29; 1 Kgs 11:7, 33; as well as the Mesha inscription and Moabite seals), but Milcom/Molech (1 Kgs 11:5, 7, 33; 2 Kgs 23:13). Perhaps Chemosh had been taken over into the Ammonite pantheon.

19. Sasson, *Judges 1–12*, 434, provides a contemporary parallel in a letter from the Mari archive: "[U]nlike an ultimatum, it makes no demands for change but uses the lesson of history as a backdrop for announcing hostility. Gods are not invited to judge between causes when there is yet room for bridging differences; to the contrary, they enter the fray to give victory to the just."

20. Ibid., 435.

sinned, but that the king of Ammon has done evil to him. In any case, the discussions conclude without result (11:28) and battle lines are drawn.

The effect of the Spirit of Yahweh coming upon Jephthah is expressed in three uses of "passing through [עבר, *'br*]" in 11:29: "he [Jephthah] *passed through* Gilead and Manasseh; and he *passed through* Mizpah of Gilead, and from Mizpah of Gilead he *passed through* to the sons of Ammon"—likely a troop mobilization, as Gideon also undertook when Yahweh's Spirit came upon him (6:34–35). Jephthah's story should have continued from 11:29 to 11:32, with the commencement of the battle, but no, there is an ungodly detour—Jephthah's vow (11:30–31). Another עבר occurs in 11:32, making the vow of 11:30–31 an interruption between all these "passings through." The sequence of events, therefore, goes like this: coming of the Spirit and mustering of troops ("passing through" [×3], 11:29) → *vow/bargaining with Yahweh (11:30–31)* → battle ("passing through," 11:32–33).

In return for battlefield success orchestrated by Yahweh, Jephthah would offer up as a burnt sacrifice whatever came to meet him upon his successful return home (11:30–31). This is nothing but a tragic disruption of the work of the Spirit with a horrific vow completely unbecoming of a Yahwist, an attempt to prod God into action for selfish purposes. Given the Israelites' syncretism (10:6), it is quite conceivable that Jephthah imagined that Yahweh functioned like those other gods, easily manipulated, influenced, and directed.[21] But with Yahweh's Spirit, Jephthah would have been triumphant anyway, as had been the judge-deliverers before him. His vow was entirely unnecessary.

Jephthah's were careless words, imprudent, and thoughtless; his mind seemed to have been solely on winning the battle and gaining recognition for his victory. Notice the first person pronoun suffixes: "the one coming out, who comes out from the doors of *my*-house to meet-*me* when *I*-return in peace from the sons of Ammon" (11:31).[22] It might have been a national war, and a just one, but Jephthah was engaging in it solely for personal benefit. And to this end, he attempts to manipulate Yahweh with his vow

---

21. Pardee reproduces a Ugaritic prayer in which several lines indicate a similar pre-battle vow to Ba'al: "O *Ba'lu*, [if[you drive the strong one from our gate / The warrior from our walls / A bull, (O) *Ba'lu*, we shall sanctify / A vow, (O) *Ba'lu*, we shall fulfill" ("Ugaritic Science," 232).

22. In Jephthah's oath, "the one coming out [הַיֹּצֵא, *hayyotse'*]" (11:31) is a masculine singular participle that could indicate an inanimate object ("wilderness," in Num 21:13), a word (Num 32:24), or a person (Jer 5:6). An animal may well have been intended, but would it "greet [קרא, *qr'*]" a victorious warrior on his homecoming (Jdg 11:31 and 1 Sam 18:6; but see Jdg 14:5 and Job 39:21)? In a similar example in Josh 2:19 of someone going out the doors of a house, it unambiguously refers to a human being.

(11:30).²³ So, "[i]ronically, after resting his case confidently with Yahweh the judge (11:27), Jephthah now slips a bribe under the table," violating Deuteronomic prohibitions of attempts to influence judges' decisions (Deut 16:19; 27:25; and especially 10:17 that declares that Yahweh does not take bribes). Jephthah's private interests belie his public declarations.²⁴ He had to win this battle to maintain his newly found status in Gilead, and he was willing to go to any length to do so.

Janzen argues that the thrust of Jephthah's case against the king of Ammon was that Ammon had no claim on Gilead (Jdg 11:24). God had appointed certain parcels of land to Israel, forbidding them from taking any other (Deut 2:3–9, 19–23; 3:12–17); what Israel took in the Transjordan was land gifted directly to them by Yahweh (Deut 2:24–36; 3:12–17; Jdg 11:21–23). But one notices that later, in Jdg 12:1–6, Ephraimites attempt to take over Gilead (12:4)—land allotted to another—culminating in a massive slaughter of these aggressors who spoke with a foreign accent (12:5–7; see below). Thus, these "foreign" Ephraimites, like the Ammonite foreigners, are portrayed as those who did not have rights in land not given to them by God. In between these two land-related aggressions, by foreigners and by Israelites acting like foreigners, we have the story of Jephthah's *foreign* child sacrifice. Thus we have the sequence: foreigners attempting to take Israelite land (11:12–29) → *Israel worshiping like foreigners (11:30–40)* → an Israelite tribe acting like foreigners attempting to take over other tribes' land (12:1–7).²⁵ Thus, the vow and the sacrifice performed by Jephthah was a critical hinge in the process of Israel's deplorable Canaanization.

Yet, the victory of Jephthah is remarkable: "He struck/slaughtered them with a very great striking/slaughter,"²⁶ and he "subdued" the sons of Ammon before the sons of Israel, with twenty of their towns taken (11:33). In 3:10, the enemies were "given" into Othniel's hand; in 3:30; 4:23; and 8:28, they were "subdued" under Israel in the accounts of Ehud, Barak, and Gideon, respectively. Here, however, the Ammonites are both "given" into Jephthah's hand (11:32) *and* "subdued" by Israel (11:33). But unlike the other accounts where victory was followed by the land's rest (3:20; 5:31; 8:28), there is no mention of such rest after Jephthah's triumph. How could there be, after a victory negotiated with a child sacrifice? What should have

---

23. Incidentally, it is in this vow that Jephthah speaks to God for the first and only time in the book.

24. Webb, "The Theme of the Jephthah Story," 39–40.

25. Janzen, "Why the Deuteronomist Told about the Sacrifice," 351–53.

26. While the antecedent of "he struck" in 11:33 is somewhat ambiguous, it appears that it is Yahweh who is still the subject (and the prime actor in the battle, as in 4:15; 8:22).

been a magnificent triumph over Israel's enemies bringing glory to Yahweh and honor to Jephthah becomes a horrific catastrophe for the nation, commemorated annually (11:39–40).

9.4. Judges 11:34–40

THEOLOGICAL FOCUS 9.4

9.4   Attempts to manipulate God can lead to tragic loss of blessing (11:34–40).

NOTES 9.4

9.4   Attempts to manipulate God can lead to tragic loss of blessing.

The rest of the chapter details the gruesome aftermath of the battle. "Behold" in 11:34 expresses the unexpected nature of the greeting Jephthah received—from his daughter: "only she, an only [child]; besides her, he had neither son nor daughter" (11:34). Her description adds to the pathos of what will soon ensue.

The father's reaction (11:35) is understandably one of agony, but his words (or lack thereof) undercut his expressions of grief. He offers to his only child—the sacrificial victim—no iota of compassion and no shred of comfort. She is essentially left to fend on her own. Jephthah seems to be smitten with grief more for himself than for his daughter. In his mind, *she* has driven him to his knees as one who troubles him (11:35), when in fact, it was his own egocentricity and manipulative tendencies that had brought about this tragedy. In what is almost a rebuke of his daughter, he accuses her of having brought "trouble" (עָכַר, ʿkr) upon him, catastrophe and disaster.[27] Jephthah's daughter's reply to the outburst is pointed, centering on her father and his (rash) mouth (11:36)[28]:

---

27. As a proper noun, עכר refers to the Valley of Achor, where Joshua punished Achan and his household, accusing them of having brought "trouble" (עכר) upon Israel and upon whom, in turn, God would bring "trouble" (עכר, Josh 7:24–26). Jephthah's daughter was her father's "Achor," his undoing! There is also the wordplay of כרע (krʿ, "to bring to one's knees") and עכר, in הַכְרֵעַ הִכְרַעְתִּנִי וְאַתְּ הָיִיתְ בְּעֹכְרָי (hakreaʿ hikraʿttini waʾtt hayit bʿokray, "you have surely brought me to my knees and you have become one who troubles me," 11:35).

28. "Jephthah" is יִפְתָּח, yiptakh, "He [God] has opened" (from פתח, ptkh, "to open"), and he proceeds to create a play on his name in 11:35–36: "I have *opened* my mouth," though he uses פצה, ptsh (a verb used synonymously with פתח: Num 16:30 and 16:32; Ezek 2:8 and 3:2). This verb is echoed by Jephthah's daughter in Jdg 11:36.

A	"My father, you have opened your mouth
B	to *Yahweh*;
C	*do* to me
D	that *which*
E	came out of your mouth,
D'	because of that *which*
C'	He *did* for you—
B'	*Yahweh*:
A'	revenge on your enemies, the sons of Ammon."

The structure of the direct discourse in 11:35b–38a shows Jephthah literarily confining his daughter between his utterances[29]:

A	And he said …. (11:35b)
B	And she said to him …. (11:36)
B'	And she said to her father …. (11:37)
A'	And he said …. (11:38a)

There seems to have been a pause in Jephthah's daughter's speeches, between 11:36 and 11:37: each of those verses begins with "And she said to him/her father . . . ." Perhaps she hoped to hear from her parent between 11:36 and 11:37, but he has nothing to say: no word of sympathy, assurance, or even recognition of her pain. And there is no attempt to back out of the vow or to seek means of redeeming the sacrifice. Jephthah is still thinking only of himself, and his indifference magnifies his egocentric behavior. He produces only one word after his daughter has spoken her piece(s): "Go" (11:38).

The pathos of Jephthah's vow is its seeming irrevocability. Jephthah "returns" (שוב, *shub*) with the Gileadites as "head" (11:9); he "returns" (שוב) triumphant in battle (11:31); but his words—they cannot be "returned" (שוב, 11:35). How could a man who seemed thoroughly cognizant of Israelite history have been so ignorant about child sacrifices in Israel (Deut 12:31; 18:10; also see Jer 7:31; Ezek 16:20–21; 23:39[30]), or about the redemption of its victims as provided for in the Mosaic Law (Exod 13:2, 13; Lev 27:1–8; Num 18:15)? In any case, Yahweh's silence in all this is deafening.[31]

---

29. From Trible, *Texts of Terror*, 98–99.

30. Rulers of Israel engaging in these horrific acts were strongly rebuked: 2 Kgs 16:3; 17:17; 21:6.

31. Perhaps it is the obvious nature of divine abhorrence of human sacrifice that renders any comment in Jephthah's story superfluous for an original audience familiar with scriptural proscriptions of that ritual.

The purpose of Jephthah's daughter requesting two months away (Jdg 11:37–38) is unclear. Whatever her intent, her companions went with her and wept with her, in solidarity with her tragedy. Unfortunately, it was not her father who mourned with her, but her companions. Perhaps that is why, even though the woman's first words in Scripture are "My father" (11:36), her last words are "my companions" (11:37). One must also consider that during the two whole months of his daughter's lamentation on the mountains with her companions (11:38–39), Jephthah, as far as we know, made no attempt to do something about his rash vow. To the end (her end!), he remains recalcitrant, non-compliant, and self-centered. And so his only child is condemned to die.

All along Israel as a nation had refused to obey God or keep their word/covenant with him, a fact emphasized in 10:6–16. If that was the national practice, why was Jephthah obliged to keep his word to God now? Why did he not break his vow to deity as blithely as his national compatriots had been doing all along? The reason must have been that Jephthah was convinced God had granted him victory *because of his vow*. And now if he kept his part of the bargain, he figured, he would have even more success down the line. In other words, to his Canaanized mind, benefits for the future (obtained by manipulating deity) outweighed his grief for the present (caused by sacrificing his daughter)! And so in five Hebrew words the nightmarish act is accomplished: "And-he-did to-her his-vow which he-had-vowed" (11:39).[32] She dies anonymous and virginal (emphasized thrice: 11:37–39), and Jephthah's line is wiped out (11:34).

The "commemoration" (11:40) is actually a "recounting" or "recitation." Ironically, it is an unnamed girl who is remembered, not her father, a major judge-deliverer of Israel. And most distressingly, it is not a victory accomplished by Yahweh over his people's enemies that ends up being celebrated; it is the disastrous outcome of a father's pagan attitudes that is lamented, year after year, by the nation. One would think that after the tragic end of his daughter and the establishment of a national, annual, four-day commemorative custom (11:39–40), this would be the end of the Jephthah story, but it is not. The man has already made a horrific vow and killed his own daughter, but now he wreaks havoc on a major tribe in Israel. Personal ambition knows no bounds, especially when it stems from a sense of insecurity!

---

32. The multiple mentions of Jephthah "doing" something to his daughter ("to me/her," 11:36, 37, 39) is further evidence that an actual sacrifice was carried out. Plus, it seems highly unlikely that an annual custom would arise in Israel simply to remember one who was given to celibacy all her life and who "worshipped G-d in purity!" Ramban (Nachmanides), *Commentary*, 482.

9.5. Judges 12:1–15

> **THEOLOGICAL FOCUS 9.5**
>
> 9.5 Adopting the practices of unbelievers accelerates a downward spiral of wickedness that is destructive (12:1–15).

NOTES 9.5

9.5 Adopting the practices of unbelievers accelerates a downward spiral of wickedness that is destructive.

As they did in Gideon's war against the Midianites (7:24—8:3), the Ephraimites take offence at the fact that they had not been invited to fight the Ammonites. So they threaten to burn Jephthah and his house (12:1). The Ephraimites' action of crossing over to accost the Gileadites is tantamount to annexation, not unlike the action of the Ammonites: both "muster [צעק, *tsʿq*]" troops and move into Gilead's territory (10:17; 12:1). That this taking of umbrage by the tribe happens at least two months *after* the Ammonite war (11:32–33, 37–38) raises the specter of a smoldering offense that could erupt into flames.

The Ephraimites' threat to burn Jephthah's house down with him is ironic: Jephthah has just incinerated his own daughter! Perhaps it was the nature of the threat that inflamed (!) Jephthah, but in any case, he does not attempt to defuse the situation as Gideon did (8:1–4). In the same way that he dropped the name of Yahweh in his negotiations with the Gileadites (11:9, 10, 11) and with the Ammonite king (11:21, 23, 24, 27), Jephthah mentions Yahweh in 12:3 as the source of his triumph. The Ephraimites, therefore, should shut up and quit complaining, he implies. This is a case of Yahweh trucked in again, like a totem, to bolster Jephthah's case before his contenders. It seems that Jephthah's rejoinder, as in 11:12–28, was not really meant to mollify or appease, but was actually a statement of intent to fight: in both instances, he questions the aggressors about their justifications for coming to "fight" (11:12, 20, 25, 27; and 12:1, 3, 4). In any case, as before, Jephthah's rebuttal of the Ephraimites is marked by its egocentricity: "*I* and *my* people"; "*I* called you"; "you would not deliver *me*"; "*I* took *my* life in *my* hand"; "Yahweh gave them into *my* hand"; "Why, then, have you come up to *me* this day, to fight against *me*?" (12:3–4; quite similar to 11:12).[33] Likely Jephthah is exaggerating his distress for effect and for personal gain. Again,

---

33. In a pericope that has a lot to do with openings of mouths, the word "said" occurs eight times in the six verses of 12:1–6 (12:1, 2, 4, 5 [×2], 6 [×3]).

one sees concern not for deity, nation, or tribe, but for *one* individual—"I, me, mine."[34]

In return, the Ephraimites denounce the Gileadites as "fugitives of Ephraim" (12:4). Just as the Gileadites had considered Jephthah an outcast (11:1–3, 7), so also the Ephraimites now consider Jephthah illegitimate, a "fugitive" (12:4). Soon it will be the Ephraimites who become "fugitives" themselves (12:5). Their slur only generates a firestorm of fury, and the self-glorifying (and insecurity-engendered) rage of Jephthah explodes. War commences. There is no Yahweh involved in this battle either: this is an intertribal conflict without any divine warrant. In 12:4, we are told that the Gileadites defeated Ephraim, but that is not the end of the story. With cunning and cruelty, on the basis of the (mis)pronunciation of a word, the Ephraimite escapees are tagged and slaughtered by Jephthah and the Gileadites—42,000 of them (12:4–6)! Once again we have the entirely avoidable and totally unnecessary horror of bloodshed. Jephthah's battle began with a foreign enemy; he has now become the internal enemy battling his own people. A leader of Israel who had sacrificed his daughter had now slaughtered his brothers! A horrific demonstration of leadership, indeed!

The ending is pitiful (12:7): there is no notice that the Ammonite threat has been averted (as in 3:30; 4:23; 8:28, of other foreign enemies) or that rest has come upon the land (as in 3:11, 30; 5:31; 8:28, after the reigns of previous judges). And Jephthah has the shortest reign of all the judges in the book—six years. It will be chaos from here on.

It is quite remarkable that outside of Jephthah, no one else is named in this pericope—not the elders of Gilead, not the king of Ammon, not even Jephthah's daughter. This is quite unlike the narratives of his predecessors: Ehud had Eglon; Barak had Deborah, Jael, and Sisera; Gideon had Joash, Purah, Oreb, Zeeb, Zebah, Zalmunna, and Jether; even Abimelech had Jotham, Gaal, and Zebul.[35] But here, Jephthah and Jephthah alone, and Israel and Israel alone, are the sources of error and terror: they are their own enemies . . . and the enemies of Yahweh!

After the disasters of a heartless filicide of an only daughter and a wanton fratricide of fellow Israelites, once again we are suddenly dropped into a very different world, that of the "minor" judges, with their daughters, and daughters-in-law, and sons, and grandsons, and donkeys, and eponymous cities. These prolific households give hope for long-term stability across the land: Ibzan from Bethlehem—the south (12:8–10), Elon from

---

34. George Harrison's song by that title—supposedly based on the *Bhagavad Gita* 2:71–72 that mentions "the ego-cage of 'I,' 'me,' and 'mine'"—was sung by the Beatles and released in their 1970 album *Let It Be*, their last new track before the band broke up.

35. And even Samson, the last and worst of the judges, has Manoah and Delilah.

Zebulun—the north (12:11–12), and Abdon from Pirathon in Ephraim—the center (12:13–15). As in the cluster of minor judges encountered earlier (10:1–5), the concerns of the individuals herein do not seem to be military deliverance or matters of national interest or cultic significance. This may be evidence of the relative normalcy of the era of their judgeship after the halcyon days that preceded it. Yet the eras of the three minor judges in 12:8–15 (after Jephthah), a total of twenty-five years, is far shorter than the reigns of the two minor judges in 10:1–5 (before Jephthah), fifty-five years. While relatively in equilibrium, the land is quickly lurching towards a catastrophic end.

Ibzan is the first of these minor judges after Jephthah (12:8–10). He is quite similar to Jair, the one who immediately preceded Jephthah (10:3–5). Both had thirty sons, but Ibzan also has thirty *daughters*. And it is specifically noted that Ibzan also brought in another thirty *daughters*(-in-law) for his sons. This gives Ibzan sixty female children—a stark contrast to his predecessor who murdered his only female child who, in her last days, bemoaned her virginity. Ibzan, we are also told, gave his daughters in marriage "outside the family" and brought in daughters "from outside" for his sons—alliances that generally solidify and stabilize society, and extend political influence.

One notices that the details of Gideon and of those minor judges whose children are mentioned are deliberately structured around the story of Jephthah, who kills his only child[36]:

A   **70**, the children of Gideon (8:30)
     [*3 generations*: Gideon, his father, and his sons]
   B   **30/30/30**, the sons, donkeys, and cities of Jair (10:4)
       [*2 generations*: Jair and his sons]
     C   **1**, the daughter of Jephthah (11:34)
         [*3 generations*: Jephthah, his father and mother, his daughter]
   B'   **30/30/30**, the sons, daughters, and daughters-in-law of Ibzan (12:9)
       [*2 generations*: Ibzan and his children]
A'   **70/70**, the (grand)children and donkeys of Abdon (12:14)
     [*3 generations*: Abdon, his children, and grandchildren]

Of Elon, only his days as judge and his death and burial details are noted (12:11–12). Of interest is that he was interred in "Aijalon" (אַיָּלוֹן, *'ayyalon*): its consonants make it identical to "Elon" (אֵילוֹן, *'elon*)—perhaps the judge had given his name to the city (12:12). In any case, while Elon's

---

36. Modified from Smith, "The Failure of the Family," 289. One minor judge in each of the surrounding clusters, Tola in the first and Elon in the second, is not recorded as having children.

is the skimpiest of the minor judge accounts, his is the longest rulership among them: ten years.

Abdon's cameo is notable for its mention of "son(s)": he is, himself, the *son* of Hillel; he has forty *sons* and thirty grand*sons* (12:13–14). Incidentally, the donkeys they rode on were also male.[37]

At the beginning, we saw this pericope describe Israel's instability and turmoil on at least three fronts: religious (10:6–16), political (10:17–18; 11:12–2), and familial/societal (11:1–11). Those initial problems are now compounded at the end. Religiously, it was bad enough to worship foreign gods, but it is worse to worship them by adopting the practices of their pagan devotees—human sacrifice. Politically, it was bad enough to be afflicted by an external, foreign enemy, but it is worse to be brutalizing one's fellow-Israelites as an internal enemy (the conflict with and slaughter of the Ephraimites, 12:1–6). Familially/societally, it was bad enough to be driven out by one's own family, but it is worse to subject your own child to the horror of a sacrifice. On every front things have significantly deteriorated under Jephthah.

SERMON FOCUS AND OUTLINES

THEOLOGICAL FOCUS OF PERICOPE 9 FOR PREACHING

9 Manipulation of God and the adoption of the world's practices can lead to tragic loss of blessing (10:6—12:15).

Jephthah's story reminds us of the danger of adopting ungodly attitudes and practices: the result can be disaster. Here, the focus is on his attempt to manipulate God (a pagan practice) and its consequence—child sacrifice (another pagan practice). The story ends in his brutal killing of fellow-Israelites (even more pagan-like conduct).

---

37. The mention of Hillel in 12:13, is simply part of the name of the judge—"Abdon ben Hillel": it does not indicate another generation contemporaneous with Abdon and his descendants. Whether the mode of transportation of Abdon's progeny (donkeys—a royal privilege?) signifies a dynastic tendency is unclear (12:14). One also wonders whether the plethora of children that Ibzan and Abdon had also points to the existence of a harem necessitating a level of resources available only to monarchs. Another suspicious note in these accounts of the minor judges may be the in-laws sought from "outside," by Ibzan (×2; 12:9): exogamy and intermarriage *outside* Israel? Abdon, in this regard, is said to have been buried "in the hill country of the *Amalekites*," another note of dubious distinction, perhaps to remind the reader of the incomplete nature of Israel's conquest. All in all, even the age of minor judges has become shaky.

Possible Preaching Outlines for Pericope 9

I. Israel's Position
   Minimal presence of Yahweh
   Evildoing of Israel, suspect repentance, consequence (10:6–16)
   Leaderlessness in Israel (10:17–18)
   Unilateral installation of a leader; Yahweh not involved (11:1–11)
II. Jephthah's Prelude
   Jephthah's egoistic battle to force God's involvement (11:12–28)
   Jephthah's vow—manipulation of God (Canaanization) (11:30–31)
   Move-to-relevance: How we attempt to manipulate God
III. Daughter's Predicament
   Spirit of God, troop mustering and victory (11:29, 32–33)
   Jephthah's lack of sympathy (11:34–38)
   Sacrifice (11:39–40)
IV. Jephthah's Perversion
   Jephthah's vicious and pagan acts of violence against Israelites (12:1–6)
V. Jephthah's Postlude
   Jephthah: rulership brief, progeny destroyed, burial site unmarked
   Jephthah, a tragic figure in the midst of prolific judges (12:7–15)
   Move-to-relevance: Potential consequences of manipulating God
VI. *Live under God, not over God!*
   Specifics on submitting to God, rather than manipulating him

A Problem–Consequence–Application outline can again be created from Jephthah's story. Here I include his daughter's predicament and his subsequent brutality against the Ephraimites as consequences of his own sense of insignificance and his tragic attempt to manipulate God and overcome his inferiority.

I. PROBLEM: Jephthah's Inferiority; Manipulation of God
   Evildoing of Israel, suspect repentance, consequence (10:6–18)
   Unilateral installation of a leader; Yahweh not involved (11:1–11)
   Jephthah's egoistic battle to force God's involvement (11:12–28)
   Jephthah's vow—manipulation of God (Canaanization) (11:30–31)
   Move-to-relevance: How we attempt to manipulate God
II. CONSEQUENCE: Disastrous Loss; Continuing Canaanization
   Spirit of God, troop mustering and victory (11:29, 32–33)
   Jephthah's lack of sympathy and his sacrifice (11:34–40)
   Jephthah's vicious and pagan acts of violence against Israelites (12:1–6)
   Jephthah: rulership brief, progeny destroyed, burial site unmarked
   Jephthah, a tragic figure in the midst of prolific judges (12:7–15)
   Move-to-relevance: Potential consequences of manipulating God
III. APPLICATION: *Live under God, not over God!*
   Specifics on submitting to God, rather than manipulating him

PERICOPE 10

Samson: Favored but Feckless

Judges 13:1–14:20

[Samson's Dedication, Destiny, and Blessing;
His Succumbing to His Passions]

REVIEW, SUMMARY, PREVIEW

Review of Pericope 9: In Jdg 10:6—12:5, the story of Jephthah commences with the idolatrous Israelites excoriated by God who refuses to deliver them from their enemies. The Israelites take matters into their own hands and appoint Jephthah as ruler. He attempts to force God into action with a recital of Israel's history, and with a vow to sacrifice if he is victorious in battle. He is, and he sacrifices his only child, a daughter, following which, thoroughly paganized, Jephthah goes forth and slaughters fellow-Israelites.

Summary of Pericope 10: The tenth pericope of Judges (13:1—14:20) forms the first half of the narrative of Samson. God's grace is evident from the start: Samson is divinely conceived, divinely dedicated for a divine destiny, divinely blessed, and divinely endowed with the Spirit. For all that, nation, parents, and chosen deliverer are imperceptive and indifferent to God and his work. Samson insists on doing what is right in his own eyes and neglects his Nazirite regulations, all resulting in conflict and loss for this devotionless man who gives in to his sensual passions.

Preview of Pericope 11: The next pericope, Jdg 15:1—16:31, concludes the Samson story. The vengeful and self-serving attitude of the judge is on full display as he and the Philistines go at each other with increasing brutality. After a dalliance with a prostitute, Samson ends up with Delilah, the fourth woman in his life, who makes four attempts to learn the secret of his strength. Finally Samson caves in, repudiating his call from God. Not even aware that deity has left him, he finally dies in a suicidal-homicidal disaster.

10. Judges 13:1–14:20

THEOLOGICAL FOCUS OF PERICOPE 10

10 Lack of devotion to God and rejection of Yahweh's interests in favor of selfish passions leads only to trouble, though God's initiatives of grace continue (13:1—14:20).

    10.1 Lack of devotion to God and lack of responsiveness to divine initiatives have serious consequences (13:1–25).

        10.1.1 *God's grace and sovereign initiative are visible even in dire circumstances.*

        10.1.2 *Lack of devotion to God and spiritual obtuseness leads to lack of responsiveness to divine initiatives.*

        10.1.3 *Rejection of one's divinely initiated call has serious consequences for self and community.*

    10.2 Disregard for Yahweh's interests, parental concerns, and personal calling, in favor of selfish passions, leads only to trouble (14:1–20).

OVERVIEW

Samson is the last judge in the book, and his story gets the most space—four whole chapters and ninety-six verses, comprising the usual life account and, in addition, a unique birth narrative that announces his divine destiny (13:1–25). The story moves from his birth (conception and delivery by a barren woman) to his death (destruction and suicide by a disabled man). Names help create *inclusios*:

Judges 13:2	Judges 13:25	Judges 16:31a
"Dan"	"Dan"	
	"Zorah and Eshtaol"	"Zorah and Eshtaol"
"Manoah"; "Zorah"		"Manoah"; "Zorah"

"Dan" is referred to only in 13:2 and 13:25a (setting off the story of Samson's birth); "Zorah and Eshtaol" is found only in 13:25b and 16:31a (setting off the stories of Samson's adulthood); and "Manoah" and "Zorah," are together located only in 13:2 and 16:31a (setting off the entirety of Samson's life).[1]

The paradigm of 2:11–19 is almost completely broken down when it comes to the Samson saga, except for the grievous report that the Israelites continued to do evil and that God punished them with forty years of subjugation (the longest on record in Judges, and twice as long as the nearest in length [4:3]), and for the recurring activity of Yahweh's supporting Spirit in the life of this judge. Besides these elements, the paradigm is almost non-existent: the nation does not cry out to Yahweh—Israel seems to be content with the inimical situation they have found themselves in; their enemies are not brought under their control and, in fact, the nation fights no wars against their oppressors, and it is the judge who, all by himself, periodically wages a misdirected and wrongly motivated campaign against them; the nation hands over the judge to the enemy; the judge gets himself killed; and there is no rest for the land. It all comes to a dreadful end that prepares one for the even greater darkness of those ruinous events in the Epilogues of the book.

---

1. Other such bracketing elements at the beginning and end of the Samson saga include ברך, *brk*: "bless" (13:24) and "knee" (16:19); פעם, *pʿm*: "stir" (13:25) and "times" (16:20); the arrival of Yahweh's Spirit (13:25) and the departure of Yahweh (16:20).

Paradigm	Samson
2:11 Evildoing	13:1 Continues
2:14 (×2) To enemies for X years	13:1 Given 40 years (13:1)
2:18 Groan	[—]
2:16, 18 Judge raised	[13:2–25?]
2:18 Yahweh's support	13:25; 14:6, 19; 15:14 "Spirit"
2:16, 18 Fate of enemies	[—]
2:19 Land's rest Judge	16:30 [—] [Dies]

Samson's story, unlike the preceding ones, is almost completely preoccupied with the judge's personal antics. And so this last judge, Samson, turns out to be diametrically opposite the first judge, Othniel. The latter had a model marriage, he conducted a war against the enemy without fussing, hesitating, or prevaricating, and he successfully delivered Israel, to give the land rest for forty years. On the other hand, here we have a judge who has a weakness for women, who is willing to violate his calling, who executes his personal vendettas unilaterally, and who gets himself killed in the end, with no defeat of the enemy accomplished, no rest for the land attained.

There are some recurring patterns in the stories of Samson. After the birth narrative, there are two major movements for the Samson story: the first with Samson going to Timnah to get married (14:1), culminating in a slaughter of Philistines (15:14–20; 15:20 has a note of Samson's judgeship for twenty years); the second with Samson going to Gaza (16:1) to engage a prostitute, again culminating in a massacre of the Philistines and this time his own death as well (16:30; 16:31 also has a note of Samson's judgeship for twenty years).[2] These two parts of the Samson saga, 14:1—15:20 and 16:1–31, resemble each other in several ways: both have women involved

---

2. For ease of handling in the pulpit in a way that yields two distinct and sufficiently discrete theological thrusts, this commentary will divide the Samson account into two pericopes, 13:1—14:20 (Pericope 10) and 15:1—16:31 (Pericope 11).

with Samson (the Timnite; and the harlot and Delilah), and deal with a matter not known to others (a riddle; and the secret of Samson's strength); in both, Samson is bound and given to the Philistines (by the Judahites; and by Delilah), and in both stories he is empowered by Yahweh to conduct operations against the enemy (14:19; and 15:14; 16:28–30). One also notices that all the events of Samson's life appear to be precipitated by his yearning for sexual contact: 14:1–2 (with the Timnite); 15:1 (with the Timnite again); 16:1 (with a harlot in Gaza); 16:4 (with Delilah). He does have a problem!

10.1. Judges 13:1–25

> **THEOLOGICAL FOCUS 10.1**
>
> 10.1 Lack of devotion to God and lack of responsiveness to divine initiatives have serious consequences (13:1–25).
>
> 10.1.1 *God's grace and sovereign initiative are visible even in dire circumstances.*
>
> 10.1.2 *Lack of devotion to God and spiritual obtuseness leads to lack of responsiveness to divine initiatives.*
>
> 10.1.3 *Rejection of one's divinely initiated call has serious consequences for self and community.*

NOTES 10.1

10.1.1 God's grace and sovereign initiative are visible even in dire circumstances.

The birth of a child to an Israelite couple in Judges 13 and the raising of a deliverer for his people are unilateral acts of grace on the part of God. This divine initiative is quite surprising, after the progressively worsening failures of all the judges in the past, and especially after Yahweh's outright refusal to heed the Israelites' cry for help during the days of the preceding judge, Jephthah (10:11–14). Besides, despite the exceedingly long period of oppression in this pericope (forty years, 13:1), there seems to have been no concern expressed by the Israelites—no plea for help, no attempt to catch the ear of deity. But God graciously tries again, even without his people seeking him, this time attempting to steer things from the womb.

Throughout, the workings of the divine are prominent: Yahweh sends a messenger, the angel of Yahweh, whose name is "Wonderful," an authoritative envoy declaring matters, directing behavior, delineating sacrifices, and doing miracles (13:1–3, 9–21); a barren woman miraculously conceives a child who is destined to become a deliverer of Israel (13:3–5), this despite the Israelites not even seeking rescue from oppression (13:1); the child so born is to be dedicated lifelong to Yahweh as a Nazirite, so much so even his mother is to abstain from strong drink and unclean foods (13:3–5); Manoah's progressive recognition of the numinous—from "man of God" (13:6, 8) to "angel of Yahweh" (13:21) to "God/Yahweh" (13:22, 23)—causes fear and awe; divine prophecy comes to pass in the birth of Samson (13:24); and divine destiny is being fulfilled in Yahweh's blessing of the child and his stirring by God's Spirit (13:24–25).

That the angel who appeared to Manoah's wife began with "You will conceive" (perfect tense in 13:3), which changes to "You have conceived" (or "You are pregnant," a predicate adjective in 13:5) has fueled speculation of some sort of sexual union between the angel of Yahweh and Manoah's wife.[3] But the context should inhibit such conjectures: 13:8 has Manoah requesting that the angel of Yahweh "come to us *again*," and 13:9 has "came *again* to the woman," clearly not a second sexual union. As for explaining the change in the gravid status of Manoah's wife, the predicate adjective might simply be a prophetic guarantee.[4] In any case, the absence of any initiative from Manoah in this undertaking and the fact that, unlike in other stories where barren women become pregnant, there is no explicit reference to Manoah's wife conceiving (see Gen 21:2; 25:21; 30:23; etc.), emphasize divine involvement in this conception—it is certainly miraculous.

At his birth, it is striking that Samson was blessed by Yahweh—to no other judge was such a blessing explicitly given and noted (Jdg 13:24). Indeed, no other person in Judges is blessed by Yahweh.[5] And soon—it is unclear how long after his birth—Yahweh's Spirit works on Samson (13:25). The word "stir" is not used of the relationship between Spirit and any other judge. Upon Othniel and Jephthah, the Spirit merely "came" (3:10; 11:29); by the Spirit, Gideon was "clothed" (6:34); and between Abimelech and the Shechemite *ba'als*, an *evil* spirit was "sent" (9:23). Samson, though, receives the Spirit of Yahweh on *four* discrete occasions: he "stirred" Samson in 13:25; and he "came mightily" upon him in 14:6, 19; 15:14—evincing a great deal

---

3. The idiom בוא אל, *bo' 'el*, "came to" (13:6), can have that connotation: Gen 38:16; 39:14, 17; Jdg 15:1; 16:1; etc.

4. It is, of course, physiologically possible that fertilization occurred between the two instances of the angel's utterance about conception, even with intercourse between the couple having possibly occurred *before* the angel appeared on the scene. See Chisholm, *Judges and Ruth*, 391.

5. There are optative statements of desire that certain individuals be blessed (5:24; 17:2), and Yahweh is blessed by his people (5:2, 9), but deity never blesses another human in Judges but Samson.

of verve and vigor and vitality in the arrival of Yahweh's Spirit.[6] But, sadly, never once does Samson acknowledge the Spirit's work. Later he would not even be aware that Yahweh had left him (16:20).

Every one of the preceding judges, except for the paradigmatic Othniel, appeared on the narrative scene with a disadvantage of some sort: Ehud, the devious, was left-handed (3:15), Barak, the timid, needed a woman at his side (4:8), Gideon, the skeptic, was the youngest of a minor family (6:15), and Jephthah, the pagan, was the outcast son of a concubine (11:2). Samson, on the other hand, seems to have been blessed with every advantage right off the block: a divine conception-annunciation story, his dedication as a Nazirite by Yahweh himself, a divine foretelling of his commission as one who will "begin to deliver Israel from the hands of the Philistines" (13:5), and multiple endowments of the Spirit. If there ever were a judge who might deliver Israel, it would be Samson. That he would only "*begin* to deliver Israel" from the Philistines is itself ominous: it was not going to be completed in Samson's lifetime. So this was going to be a judge whose work would remain unfinished; indeed, his story is one of a reversal of readerly expectations. All those blessings, but unfortunately Samson would lose it all (16:20), and accomplish less than any of his predecessors did.

For all the vigorous activity of Yahweh in Samson's story (Judges 13:1—16:31), deity is never shown to be speaking to his chosen deliverer (though Samson does cry out to him: 15:18; 16:28), quite a contrast to the patient and persevering interactions of God with Gideon in Pericope 6 (Jdg 6:1—7:22). "Yahweh is underway in the world to free his people from Philistine tyranny, though not a soul in the story knows it and his chosen instrument looks very like an oversexed buffoon."[7]

Sovereign working is inscrutable. In this pericope, Samson falls for a Philistine woman—"it was of Yahweh" (14:4). On his way to Timnah to arrange his marriage, Samson is confronted by a lion that he kills, empowered by the Spirit of Yahweh (14:5-6). These divinely ordained events ultimately "begin" the delivery of Israel from the Philistines, as the angel of Yahweh foresaw (13:5). So Samson becomes "Yahweh's unwitting agent provocateur," deity's tool to inaugurate the deliverance of his people.[8] Will Samson live up to his calling and responsibility, and will he respond to all the gracious divine initiatives in his life?

---

6. And no other judge is endowed with Yahweh's Spirit more than once.
7. Wharton, "The Secret of Yahweh," 58.
8. Webb, *Judges*, 366.

10.1.2 Lack of devotion to God and spiritual obtuseness leads to lack of responsiveness to divine initiatives.

The barrenness of Manoah's wife corresponds with the oppression of the Israelites—profitless, fruitless. But, unlike the case of the infertility of the matriarchs, Sarah, Rebekah, and Rachel, there is no concern on part of husband or wife about infertility (as in Gen 15:2–3; 16:1–2; 25:21; 30:1–2), no complaint about childlessness (as in Gen 30:1), no notation of parental age (as in Gen 25:19, 26), no indication of other means employed to obtain a child (as in Gen 16:1–4), no experimenting with aphrodisiacs (as in Gen 30:14–15), and no engagement in prayer (as in Gen 25:21).

Even the woman's name is withheld from the reader, despite her central role and her favorable depiction in this pericope, compared to that of her husband whose name and antecedents are provided (Jdg 13:2).[9] So we expect him to be the protagonist in this pericope, but Manoah, despite his pedigree, is quite dense, and it is the woman who is spiritually more perceptive. It is to her that the angel of Yahweh appears—twice (13:3, 6 and 13:9–10). After the angel's first appearance to his wife, Manoah attempts to summon the messenger himself (13:8–9), but the man overall seems quite the cynic and perhaps a tad jealous: his appeal to have the angel "come to *us* that he may teach *us*" sounds petulant (13:8). Dissatisfied with and doubtful of the experience of his wife, Manoah wants to find out firsthand "what to do for the boy," even though his wife had just told him that she was to abstain from alcohol and unclean things (13:7–8). Despite the husband's request, the angel again "comes to the woman" only (13:9), and so it is Manoah who finally has to "come to the man" (13:10).

Manoah's wife had earlier told him of "the man of God" who had "appeared" to her (13:6–7). But when the angel comes the second time to Manoah's wife and she informs her husband (13:9–10), Manoah approaches and asks the visitor if he was indeed the "man" who had spoken to her (13:11), again voicing incredulity, and exhibiting no suspicion as to who this person might be. The angel gives him the benefit of a one-word answer: "I [am]" (13:11). Rather skeptically, Manoah proceeds to seek clarification on "the boy's mode/rule of life and his vocation"—how he was to accomplish his Nazirite status (13:12). Perhaps that is why the angel of Yahweh constantly keeps the focus on the wife, detailing how *she* should act (13:4–5, 7, 13–14). In any case, the angel provides no further information than what was given to Manoah's wife earlier, merely repeating (now for the third time in the chapter, but with less detail) the restrictions on consuming alcohol

---

9. There are four women in Samson's life and, deliberately, only the fourth, Delilah, is named (see Pericope 11: Jdg 15:1—16:31).

and contacting things unclean (see 13:4, 7, 14). In this second visit, the angel begins and ends with exhortations to the woman: "To all which I spoke, let the woman attend" (13:13); and "To all that I commanded, let her attend" (13:14; see below).[10] All this to say, Samson's dedication to Yahweh was one that deity was taking very seriously. Unfortunately, the humans appear to be out to lunch.

After all this, Manoah wants to feed the angel, and later attempts to discover his name (13:17, 19). The mystery of the angel's "Wonderful" name (13:18) may have had more to do with his intimate identity with Yahweh, rather than with the name itself—Yahweh's name had already been self-disclosed through Moses to Israel (Exod 3:13–15). It was this numinous identity that would be beyond Manoah's comprehension, hence "Wonderful" (Jdg 13:18). Besides, Manoah seeks to "honor" his guest "*after/when your words come to pass*"—he is still the skeptical soul (13:17). And so the angel rebukes Manoah (13:18). While the woman did not quiz her heavenly visitor, guessing the "man of God" was actually an "angel of God," "very awesome" (13:6), Manoah did not seem to have the necessary deference (13:17).[11] And why should he, considering that he saw his guest only as a "man of God" (13:8, 11)?

In any case, as if in answer to Manoah's doubts, the angel of Yahweh with the "Wonderful" (פֶּלִאי, *peli'y*) name proceeds to perform "wonders" (פלא, *pl'*) with the grain offering of the couple (13:19–20). The cognate noun, "wonder," is used frequently in connection with the acts of God in the OT, thus further amalgamating the identities of the angel of Yahweh and

---

10. Perhaps now the angel is rebuking the woman, too, for leaving out the critical element of the boy's national destiny (13:5) in her report to Manoah (13:6–7). Another omission on her part was the Nazirite requirement that the child's hair not be shorn (13:5). But the woman adds the datum that their son would be a Nazirite from the womb "to the day of his *death*" (13:7), something that the angel of Yahweh had *not* mentioned in the announcement of 13:3–5. "It is surely a little unsettling that the promise which ended with the liberation—though, pointedly, only the *beginning* of liberation—of Israel from its Philistine oppressors now concludes with no mention of 'salvation' but instead with the word 'death'" (the last word in the woman's report to her husband, 13:7) (Alter, *The Art of Biblical Narrative*, 101). Strikingly enough, it is when this deliverer violates the stipulation for growing hair that *death* claims him (16:19–21, 30–31). A less significant omission in the wife's recounting of the annunciation to her husband is that of the phrase "and be careful/guard yourself" (13:4). Manoah's wife also utilizes "unclean" in its feminine form (in the prohibition of eating unclean food; 13:7), rather than the masculine used by the angel of Yahweh (13:4).

11. Of the sixteen uses of נוֹרָא in the OT (*nora'*, "awesome/fearsome": niphal participle masculine singular from ירא, *yr'*, "to fear"), fourteen times it is employed in connection with deity: the woman was on the right track.

Yahweh.[12] Only at the end of the scene does Manoah's ignorance in 13:16 ("Manoah did not know") finally become recognition ("he knew," in 13:21). Then he acknowledges the "angel of Yahweh" but exclaims that they have seen אֱלֹהִים (ʾĕlōhîm, "God"; 13:22). His wife, on the other hand, perceives "Yahweh" (13:23)—she of the keener spiritual insight: she alone employs "Yahweh" in speech in this chapter.

There are a number of similarities between Gideon's sacrifice (6:17–24) and Manoah's (13:15–23): both are in the context of Yahweh's deliverance (6:14; 13:5); both sacrifices have a kid (6:19; 13:19); both offerings are placed on a rock (6:20; 13:19), and both are consumed by the heavenly messenger with fire (6:21; 13:20); the sacrificant in both cases fears that he has seen the angel of Yahweh or God (6:22–23; 13:22), and both times he is reassured that he will not die (6:23; 13:23). We know that in Gideon's case his activities were shrouded with doubt: the sacrifice was, in fact, a test of the divine messenger's authenticity. In light of these similarities and Manoah's continuing incomprehension of the identity of his visitor, no doubt he, too, was being as skeptical as Gideon. That it was Manoah, not so much his wife, who was ignorant is underscored in the later statement that, after Manoah and his wife saw the wonders performed by the angel, it is *Manoah* who is said to have then realized the identity of their visitor. His wife, as noted earlier, had already guessed correctly (13:21; see 13:6, 23).

The cameo dealing with Manoah's fear of dying after seeing God is a comic interlude in an otherwise "awesome" and "wonderful" incident (13:22–23; see 13:6, 18). Manoah was right, for no one could see God and live (Exod 33:20) but, as his wife explained to him, Yahweh had already accepted their offering, besides permitting them to experience this "awesome" and "wonderful" phenomenon/person/oracle ("all these things," Jdg 13:23). Surely he would not let them die now, certainly not when the woman is pregnant with the promised child (13:5). In sum, Manoah is as clueless about the things of God as his son will be. The father's blindness parallels the son's: like father, like son, though in the latter's case, it is carried to extreme levels of negligence, foolhardiness, and danger (and ends in literal blindness, 16:21).

Overall, Manoah is the benighted one, while his wife fares better, but not by much. This appears to reflect the state of the nation in those days: leaders unenlightened, ignorant, diffident, and disinterested in matters of godliness and morality and in following after Yahweh, and the people not any better. Nor is there any expectation on their part that Yahweh may

---

12. Exod 15:11; Pss 77:11, 14; 78:12; 88:10, 12; 89:5; 119:129; Isa 9:6; 25:1; 29:14; Lam 1:9; Dan 12:6.

intervene in the affairs of the nation. This lack of devotion renders all the characters here oblivious to the workings of God and his initiatives.

The naming of the child is curious—his mother calls him "Samson," שִׁמְשׁוֹן (shimshon, from שֶׁמֶשׁ, shemesh, "sun")—so, "Sun-Like," or "Solar," or just plain "Sunny." One wonders if this is a nod to the pagan ambience surrounding Israel at this time, as they coexisted with the Canaanites. In fact, the sun god was a popular Canaanite deity, and there was a city a few miles south of Zorah and Eshtaol, Samson's base of operations (13:25), called "Beth-Shemesh," "House/Temple of the Sun." So this was obviously not a name to be given to a child destined to be a Nazarite and a deliverer of Israel, especially after a heavenly annunciation, two theophanies, and the performance of wonders before a barren couple. Naming Samson after the sun, we have a dangerous dabbling in paganism. Not a good sign.

10.1.3 Rejection of one's divinely initiated call has serious consequences for self and community.

"Nazirite of God" commences the phrase in 13:5, emphasizing the special status of Samson: "a Nazirite to God he will be, the young man, from the womb." "Nazirite" comes from the verb נזר, *nzr*, "to abstain," and describes a dedicatory separation to Yahweh, usually voluntary and for a limited time (Num 6:1–21). Such a separation included at least these elements: restriction of alcohol consumption, proscription of unclean foods, prohibition of hair trimming, and avoidance of contact with the "unclean," particularly corpses. As in Samson's case, it appears that in some circumstances it was permissible for others (parents) to take such a Nazirite vow on behalf of a child (and see 1 Sam 1:11, 24–28). In any case, not only was Samson's separation involuntary, it was also lifelong, from conception to demise (Jdg 13:5, 7). And in this case, even the mother had to follow dietary proscriptions, including the avoidance of "unclean" food (13:4, 14).[13] All of this was intended to emphasize Samson's total dedication to Yahweh and his work. Notice the structure of 13:13b–14, the reiteration of the angelic command to the woman, as uttered to Manoah:

---

13. *All* Israelites were to abide by the rule against eating anything unclean, but it is likely that the nation in that day was insensible to these niceties of the law.

A	"*all* that I said"; "she shall observe [*niphal*]"	**(13:13b)**
B	"*all*" from the vine; "not eat"	**(13:14a)**
C	"wine or strong drink"	**(13:14b)**
B'	"*all*" uncleanness; "not eat"	**(13:14c)**
A'	"*all* that I commanded"; "she shall observe [*qal*]"	**(13:14d)**

The careful structuring with multiple repeats of "all," again emphasizes the importance of following directions carefully, yet only the consumption of alcohol and unclean things is noted—and that for the third time (13:4, 7, 14). This more common Nazirite restriction may have been "part for the whole," synecdoche for the totality of the Nazirite stipulations.

In the rest of the Samson saga we find that every one of these Nazirite requirements are violated. Samson does not avoid alcohol ("vineyard" in 14:5; "feast" in 14:10; "Sorek" = "Choicest Vine" in 16:4); he consumes unclean food (14:9); he comes into contact with corpses (14:8–9, 19; 15:8, 13, 15; 16:7–12, 30); and he gets his hair cut (16:15–22).[14] Besides, his close and intimate contacts with "the inhabitants of this land" (2:2) keep him from ever being clean.[15] Samson's calling is violated left and right in his story.

Samson's dedication, special calling, and destiny, Yahweh, of course, knows. So do Samson's parents, as well as the narrator and readers. But all along, Samson acts as if he was (blissfully) ignorant. However, he reveals his comprehension of his unique status in his actions (keeping his contact with a corpse secret, 14:9, for instance) and later in his confession to Delilah (16:17). That makes the negligence to his divine dedication deliberate and all the more reprehensible.

10.2. Judges 14:1–20

THEOLOGICAL FOCUS 10.2

10.2 Disregard for Yahweh's interests, parental concerns, and personal calling, in favor of selfish passions, leads only to trouble (14:1–20).

---

14. See below and the next pericope for details.

15. Even if the resulting uncleanness with all these violations was temporary, we have no indication that Samson recognized this or made attempts to cleanse himself ritually. One wonders how he could have conducted his divinely ordained career of "beginning" to deliver Israel without killing Philistines and breaking at least this Nazirite requirement of Numbers 6. But that is to dive into the unclear depths between divine sovereignty and human responsibility.

Pericope 10: Judges 13:1–14:20   219

NOTES 10.2

10.2 Disregard for Yahweh's interests, parental concerns, and personal calling, in favor of selfish passions, leads only to trouble.

The first section of Samson's adult life (14:1–20) is a sequence of remarkable events in which Yahweh, though invisible to the actants, plays a crucial role in orchestrating events—an interweaving of sovereign divine action with free human choice. Yahweh is active (13:25; 14: 4, 6, 19), yet Samson seems to be exercising his own initiative, controlled by his own passions.

When the Spirit was involved with a judge prior to Samson, invariably the very next scene was a successful battle waged against the enemy with that particular judge at the helm of an army (3:10; 6:34; 11:29). So, after 13:25, we expect Judges 14 to detail a war, a campaign, or a skirmish of sorts. Our expectations are met, in a roundabout way, when thirty Philistines are killed, by Samson alone (no army here, no tribe involved), and for his own purposes (not for Yahweh's), the result of the judge's uncontrolled sexual drive and fury.

Right at the start, we are told that Samson went down to Philistine country, Timnah: in fact there are five instances of "going down" (ירד, *yrd*) in this pericope: 14:1, 5, 7, 10, 19b—all of them breaking boundaries as Samson and/or his kin pass from Israelite territory to Philistine land: *going down*hill in more ways than one. One wonders if it was that easy to go from Israel to Philistia. These movements signal that the coexistence between Israelites and Philistines had become a matter of course, a *fait accompli*, an unsurprising reality, a routine detail of daily life.

Nonetheless, all this "going down" is countercultural, and we suspect something is afoot and it is: Samson has "seen" someone—a Philistine woman (רָאָה, *ra'ah*, 14:1, 2).[16] And in another countercultural move, Samson demands that his parents arrange a marriage with her—exogamy: twice we are told that this woman was one of the "daughters of the Philistines" (14:1, 2).[17] Samson refuses to listen to any pleading from his parents, thus evidencing a rejection of authority in his life (14:3a).[18] He issues a peremp-

---

16. This is the second woman in Samson's life introduced with רָאָה; the first was Samson's mother (13:3, where also the verb showed up in the *niphal*, "appeared").

17. See Exod 34:16; Deut 7:1–3; Jdg 2:2; 3:6 for divine displeasure with such unions. God's people were to maintain the integrity and devotion of Yahwism, unadulterated by the paganism of non-Israelites, a very present danger with exogamy.

18. Later we are told that his parents traveled with him to Timnah (14:5), but they are completely ignored as far as Samson's alliance with the Timnite is concerned: he goes down, talks to her, and still thinks she looks "right" (14:7). The parents' concerns are not an issue for him.

tory diktat: "*Now* get/take her for me as wife" (14:2; repeated slightly differently in 14:3).[19] Seemingly, he cannot even wait; he wants her *now*. Of course, one may also wonder why Samson's parents only raise the problem of exogamy and not other moral issues equally concerning to Yahweh with such marital alliances: like Samson's Nazirite status, his divine destiny as deliverer from the Philistines, and the Yahwistic implications of intimate relationships with pagans. The parents fail to put forth any spiritual reasons advocating endogamy.[20] The recurring emphasis in this section on "mother" or "father" (14:3 [×3], 4 [×2], 5 [×2], 6 [×2], 9 [×2], 10, 19; there is also "your brothers" and "our people" in 14:3) "reveals this to be a tale about kin and nonkin, endogamy versus exogamy," and thus about respecting God's interests and parental concerns.[21] Samson was grossly violating established moral guidelines here.

A	"I saw a woman …		
	B Now, therefore, *get her for me* as wife."		Samson
		C "Is there not, among … all our people,	
		D a *woman*,	
		E that you go to *get*	Parents
		D' a *woman*	
		C' from the uncircumcised Philistines?"	
	B' "Get her for me,		
A'	for she is right in my eyes."		Samson

In 14:3, the emphatic placement of the feminine pronoun is enlightening: "Her—get for me." Notice also that "get/take" occurs thrice, in 14:2, 3, 8. He sees, he wants, he *takes*! And all because "she is right [ישר, *yshr*] in my eyes" (14:3b), a fact that the narrator chooses to repeat in 14:7, emphasizing Samson's misplaced gaze, misaligned pleasure, and mistaken assessment. The theme of doing "right" is a frequent one in the Torah, particularly the doing of what is "right in the eyes of Yahweh" (Exod 15:26; Num 23:27; Deut 6:18; 12:25, 28; 13:19; 21:9; etc.; Deut 12:8 deprecates the doing of what is "right

19. Parentally arranged marriages were the norm in early biblical history (Gen 21:21; 24), reflected in the legal phrasing "giving one's sons and daughters in marriage" (Deut 7:3). This happens even in Judges: Othniel, the model judge in the paradigm, marries Achsah with the permission of her father (Jdg 1:12–15).

20. If *any* circumcised peoples would have been acceptable to Samson's parents (uncircumcision seems to have been their main objection to Samson's alliance with the Philistines, 14:3), perhaps one of the other Canaanite groups that were non-Philistine would have sufficed for marital alliances: circumcision was also practiced by non-Israelite peoples in the ancient Near East.

21. Niditch, *Judges*, 151.

in one's own eyes"—the way of the fool, as Prov 12:15 has it). Invariably, there is a moral component to this "rightness," something that was lacking in Samson's appraisal of the Timnite (Jdg 14:3, 7). This is an ominous foreshadowing of what would happen in the Epilogues of Judges and the indictment there of the Israelites who were also doing what was "right in their own eyes" (17:6; 21:25). "Samson's going down to Timnah is the beginning of a movement toward moral chaos, not just for himself but for Israel."[22]

Samson's sense of separateness as an ordinary Israelite (circumcised vs. uncircumcised) is being seriously compromised in his marital affiliation with a Philistine. One wonders how his even greater separation to God as a dedicated Nazirite can be sustained. This is not exactly the sort of behavior one expects from a deliverer of Israel, divinely destined in a heavenly annunciation, consecrated as a Nazirite, blessed by deity, and moved by his Spirit.

The observation that Samson was hanging around a vineyard is puzzling (14:5): a Nazirite was forbidden to consume any product from grapes, neither the juice, nor the fruit (Num 6:3), as Samson's parents were explicitly told thrice (Jdg 13:4, 7, 14). That he subsequently puts on a feast for the Philistines (14:10), likely involving alcohol, is also telling: the word "feast," מִשְׁתֶּה, *mishteh*, is derived from the verb "to drink," שָׁתָה, *shatah*.[23] So here we have a man supposed to be a teetotaler organizing what was likely a frat party! We are told this was customary for Philistine young men (14:9); apparently, Samson is becoming more and more Philistine-like in his actions.

Then there is the confrontation with the lion (14:6). The beast comes out of nowhere and the whole thing appears to be rather peripheral to the story. But as we read along we recognize the cascade of events that this clash between man and animal sets off: the incidental finding of honey in the carcass, the resulting riddle and the betrayal by his wife as she provides the Philistines with its answer, Samson's debt to them culminating in the killing of thirty Philistines, his crass and crabby abandonment of his wife and later, his return to her (14:5–20). That sparks another conflict, when he realizes his father-in-law has given her away to another, and Samson destroys a great deal of Philistine property, in retaliation for which the Philistines kill his wife and father-in-law, and Samson, ever the avenger, gets back at them with "a great slaughter" (15:1–8), etc.

---

22. Webb, *Judges*, 366.

23. Incidentally, the most common type of pottery discovered in Philistine settlements is the "strainer-spout 'beer jug.'" See Block, *Judges, Ruth*, 431 n.319. Such "feasts" were frequently associated with "wine" (Esth 1:5–10; 5:5–14; 6:14; 7:2–8; Isa 5:12; Dan 1:16) and "strong drink" (1 Sam 25:36; Jer 51:39; also see Gen 26:30; Job 1:4; Isa 25:6; Jer 16:8).

But there major issues in this pericope with the lion cameo itself. Samson overcomes the lion in the power of the Spirit, and later he comes into contact with its carcass (14:8). Death and Nazirities, we already know, are a *verboten* combination. The prohibition in Num 6:6 is against contact with dead human bodies, but נפש, *npsh*, can also refer to an animal carcass (Gen 1:20, 24, 30; 2:7; 9:12, 15–16; etc.). Besides, honey from the remains of an animal is obviously unclean food, for *all* Israelites (Lev 11:24–25, 39–40).[24] And to make things worse, Samson fails to tell his parents the source of his food as he shares it with them (Jdg 14:9), most likely because he was aware it was taboo: his Nazirite status was known to both his parents (13:4–5, 7, 13–14) and to himself (16:17). This then was a deliberate scheme to trick his parents into breaking Yahweh's covenanted laws with his people, a serious case of dishonoring one's forbears.[25] There was an utter lack of concern on Samson's part not only for his own ritually unclean state, but for that of others as well. His callous act is expressed dynamically in the Hebrew that reads: "And he walked, walking and eating, and he walked to his father and to his mother, and he gave to them and they ate" (14:9). Earlier, regarding the Timnite woman, he "sees" (ראה, *r'h*, 14:1, 2), he wants, and he takes (14:2, 3, 8). Now in 14:8, regarding honey, he "sees" (ראה), he takes, and he eats. Everything he does is geared for the satiation of his fleshly appetites, be it for sex or for food. In the process, he cares not a whit for covenant, for propriety, for parents, or even for Yahweh. All that matters is what is "right" in his eyes (14:3, 7).

The cultural background of all that goes on in 14:10–18, with riddles, bets, and such, extended over the days of feasting, is obscure. The riddle itself is enigmatic from our vantage point: the eater produces something to eat, and a strong man produces something sweet (14:14). At any rate, we have Samson making a bet that his Philistine companions would not solve the riddle (14:10–14). The payment to the winner from the loser involved thirty sets of linen undergarments and sets of outer garments—one for each of Samson's thirty companions if he lost, and an identical number of garments for him if they were the losers (14:12).

Understandably, the Philistines have no answer to Samson's impervious riddle and so they approach Samson's wife. They threaten her not only

---

24. We do not know how many days intervened between Samson's killing of the animal and his discovery of honey in its carcass, but a miraculously rapid decomposition seems to have set in, followed by an immediate occupation by honeybees, and an equally precipitate production of the sweet stuff by these insects.

25. It is a puzzle as to where Samson's parents were when the lion attack occurred. It appears they were with him (14:5), but we are told in 14:6, 9 that they were unaware of what had happened. Perhaps Samson's "turning aside" later in 14:8 implies that a similar detour had occurred earlier.

with personal danger, but also with death for her entire household (14:15).²⁶ Samson's wife here is clearly is not a foreign seductress entangling Samson in her web; rather she is acting out of pure expedience and under duress, to save her life and that of her family. But her constant "nagging" of Samson for a whole week to inveigle the riddle's answer out of him should have raised his suspicions then and there (14:17–18).²⁷ In any case, she betrays the man who put his trust in her. The Timnite woman had referred to the Philistine intimidators as "the sons of *my* people," identifying herself with them (14:16)—a hint of trouble that Samson should have caught. Samson, too, implies that his loyalties lie with his parents—if he had not told *them* the riddle, he asks, why would he tell *her* (14:16). Quite an incompatible couple! But Samson finally caves, sacrificing his loyalty to his people! Unfortunately his interest all along has only been the satisfaction of his passions. In the end, he succumbs to the woman, and the Philistines obtain the answer to the riddle and win the bet. Samson accuses them of "plowing with his heifer"—using illegitimate tactics (14:18) and, with murder and larceny on his mind, Samson kills thirty Philistines in Ashkelon (twenty miles southwest of Timnah), strips off their clothing, and pays his debt to the Philistines. The matter of the riddle is over, Samson has paid up, and we hope that that's the end of that. Now for the honeymoon!

Hardly! Humiliated and betrayed, he turns wrathful—"his anger burned" (14:19)—and he abandons his wife without consummating their marriage, and returns to his father's house (14:19–20). His ire has left in its wake a deprived woman, just a piece of discarded property to be handed over to another (14:20). Again, Samson has no thought for anyone but himself. Indeed, not even for Yahweh, for in killing those Philistines, he has once again come into contact with corpses, another violation of his Nazirite status.

But the silver lining in all this is that, despite the mayhem, Yahweh's Spirit was at work, and for the first time, the Philistines are actually attacked by the judge-deliverer, Samson (14:19). The cause-and-effect relationship is clear: the movement of the Spirit leads to a mini-war against the Philistines

26. That the Philistines ask the Timnite woman if she had invited them to "despoil" (ירש, *yrsh*, also "drive out") them is significant (14:15). The word was used extensively in Judges 1 to indicate the Israelites' "driving out" (or not doing so) the inhabitants of Canaan, as God had intended for them to do (1:19, 20, 21, 27, 28, 29, 30, 31, 32, 33; also 2:6, 21, 23). Thus there is a subtle hint here that, indeed, the Philistines *were* being "despoiled"/"driven out"—the beginning of Samson's deliverance of Israel, perhaps (13:5).

27. Later another woman's "nagging" will be Samson's downfall (16:16)—the only two instances of the verb in the whole book. The timing of all these riddle-related events in this pericope (14:14, 15, 17, 18) is a bit confusing. In 14:15, the MT has "on the seventh day," but it is best to follow the LXX here and read "on the *fourth* day," to fit with the failure of the Philistines to answer the riddle in three days (14:14).

at Ashkelon (as with other movements of the Spirit in Judges culminating in war: 3:10; 6:34; 11:29). That this is war, indeed, albeit with the loss of only thirty enemy lives, is hinted at in the term "spoil" (חֲלִיצָה, *khalitsah*)—what Samson took off the persons of his victims (14:19). A military term, it is used only one other time in the OT, in 2 Sam 2:21 for armaments taken off a slain soldier. Samson's personal vendetta had thereby been escalated to a war. What began with thirty companions (Jdg 14:11) and grew to involve his wife's people/relatives (14:16), had now expanded to "the men of the city" (14:18). He *had* begun to deliver the Israelites from the Philistines (13:5)!

In sum, God works in mysterious ways, even when his agenda is completely obscured in the protagonist's mind—Samson was as imperceptive, indifferent, and devotionless as his parents were (and as all Israel was in those days). Entirely self-centered, he has no concern for parents or propriety, tribe or nation, man or God, and does not see exogamy and consorting with the Philistines as problematic. He brazenly violates his Nazirite calling, lurking in vineyards (14:5), handling corpses (14:6, 8, 19), consuming unclean food (14:9), and organizing drinking feasts (14:10).[28] Indeed, he even implicates his parents in his consumption of unclean food (14:6, 9). Subsequently, the oblivious Samson engages in frivolous pursuits with Philistines. He is dense and senseless, undiscerning and unmindful of the dangers of confiding in a foreign spouse who nags him for his secrets. At his betrayal, he can keep neither his passions nor his anger in check, and he slaughters thirty Philistines to strip them of their clothing to pay off his debt—another Nazirite requirement broken. All this was a frittering away of Samson's magnificent calling, his supernatural endowment, and his heavenly destiny.

SERMON FOCUS AND OUTLINES

THEOLOGICAL FOCUS OF PERICOPE 10 FOR PREACHING

10 Though God remains gracious, a devotionless rejection of divine interests in favor of selfish passions leads only to trouble (13:1—14:20).

In this sermon, it may be best to go with the control of one's sensual and selfish passions as depicted in this pericope—Samson's insistence on doing what was "right" in his eyes. Though his fleshly passions will resurface in Pericope 11 (Jdg 15:1—16:31), there the focus is best kept on Samson's repudiation of his dedication and call, less prominent in this pericope. Here the spotlight on preventing one's passions from running amok will suffice.

---

28. And for more violations, see Pericope 11 (Jdg 15:1—16:31).

Possible Preaching Outlines for Pericope 10

I. Godlessness and Grace
    Israelites' continued evildoing (13:1)
    Imperceptive parents; naming of "Samson" (13:6–23)
    Graciousness of God (13:1, 3, 19, 24, 25)

II. Favored and Feckless
    Divine conception, dedication, and destiny (13:2–5)
    Divinely blessed and endowed (13:24–25)
    Samson's insistence on doing what is right in his eyes (14:1–4, 7)
    Samson's neglect of the Nazirite regulations (14:4–5, 8–9, 10, 19)
    Consequence of Samson's uncontrolled passions (14:12–20)

IV. *Control your passions!*[29]
    Specifics on how to control your passions[30]

A rearrangement that distinguishes God's work and man's responses (i.e., that of the Israelites, Samson's parents, and of Samson, himself) yields:

I. God's Action
    Graciousness of God (13:1, 3, 19, 24, 25)
    Samson's divine conception, dedication, and destiny (13:2–5)
    Samson: divinely blessed and endowed (13:24–25)

II. Man's Reaction
    Israelites' continued evildoing (13:1)
    Imperceptive parents; naming of "Samson" (13:6–23)
    Samson's insistence on doing what is right in his eyes (14:1–4, 7)
    Samson's neglect of the Nazirite regulations (14:4–5, 8–9, 10, 19)
    Consequence of Samson's uncontrolled passions (14:12–20)

III. Our Counteraction[31]: *Control your passions!*
    Specifics on how to control your passions

---

29. In a hypersexed western society, this is a very appropriate call; application may go in a number of specific directions, based on preacher, audience, and the Holy Spirit. Conceivably, one might even take a break for a couple of weeks from the Judges series after this sermon to deliver a few topical addresses on contemporary issues relating to sexual propriety.

30. Perhaps the application could also be related to being more perceptive and devoted to God and his interests.

31. I.e., to prevent/counter the negative consequences such as happened to Samson.

PERICOPE 11

Samson: Spirited but Slack

Judges 15:1–16:31

[Samson's Revenge; His Sensual Passion; His Defection; His Death]

REVIEW, SUMMARY, PREVIEW

Review of Pericope 10: In Jdg 13:1—14:20, the first part of Samson's story, God's grace is evident: Samson is divinely conceived and dedicated for a divine destiny; and he is divinely blessed and endowed with the Spirit. For all that, nation, parents, and chosen deliverer are quite imperceptive and indifferent to God and his work. Samson does what is right in his own eyes and neglects his Nazirite regulations, resulting in conflict and loss for this devotionless man who gives in to his sensual passions.

Summary of Pericope 11: The eleventh pericope of Judges (15:1—16:31) concludes the grievous story of Samson. The vengeful attitude of the judge is on full display as he and the Philistines go at each other with increasing viciousness. After an especially miraculous victory, Samson engages in some self-serving celebration. Then, his sensual passions still uncontrolled, he consorts with a Philistine prostitute. Finally, he ends up with Delilah, the fourth woman in his life, who makes four attempts to learn the secret of his strength. Samson caves in, and repudiates his call from God. Not even aware that deity has left him, he finally dies in a suicidal/homicidal disaster.

Preview of Pericope 12: The next pericope, Jdg 17:1—18:31, deals with the misdemeanors of Micah, his mother, the Levite, and the Danites. Stealing, idolatry, cursing, syncretism, and brutality abound. There is not a single positive note sounded or a single positive character pictured: the result of godless leadership is a godless society. And in the end, all culpable parties get their just deserts.

11. Judges 15:1–16:31

THEOLOGICAL FOCUS OF PERICOPE 11

11 A rebellious and narcissistic spirit that disdains one's divine calling, manifesting in unbridled fleshly passion and vengeful actions, leads to destruction (15:1—16:31).

    11.1 Acts of revenge manifest a false self-righteousness and only make situations worse (15:1–8).

    11.2 Disdain for one's divine calling coincides with a vainglorious narcissism that drives one's own ambitions (15:9–20).

    11.3 Unbridled fleshly passions that prompt one to abandon the call of God in one's life lead to destruction (16:1–22).

    11.4 A rebellious spirit persists in displaying self-glorifying attitudes and engaging in vengeful actions (16:23–31).

OVERVIEW

Samson's life is chaotic, but the inspired account of his life is far from disorderly. The parallels between Judges 14 and 15 evidence a careful construction of the stories, with every section of each chapter beginning with a verb of movement (except for 15:1: "visit" here only implies movement)[1]:

---

1. Adapted from Kim, *The Structure of the Samson Cycle*, 103–4; and Sodon, "Samson," 77. There is a פתוחה, *petukhah*, before 14:20, shown by a פ, *p*, in the mt, signifying a literary break between 14:19 and 14:20. There are also several verbal links between 14:20 and what follows closely after it: "companion," in 14:20 and 15:2, 6; "wife," in 14:20 and 15:1, 6; תהי (*thi*, the *qal* imperfect third-person feminine singular of היה, *hyh*,

JUDGES 14	JUDGES 15
14:1–4	**15:1–3**
Samson went down/woman (14:1)	Samson visited/wife (15:1)
Speech: Samson/parents (14:2)	Speech: Samson/father-in-law (15:1)
Parental objection (14:3)	Parental objection (15:1)
Samson's rejection of other women (14:4)	Samson's rejection of another woman (15:2–3)
14:5–6	**15:4–6a**
Samson went down (14:5)	Samson went (15:4)
Animal involved/Samson's power (14:5–6)	Animals involved/Samson's ingenuity (15:4–5)
14:7–9	**15:6b–8**
Samson went down (14:7)	Philistines came up (15:6)
14:10–20	**15:9–20**
Father went down (14:10)	Philistines came up (15:9)
Speech: Samson/Philistines/Timnite (14:12–18)	Speech: Judahites/Philistines/Samson (15:6–13)
Philistines threaten a third party (14:15)	Philistines threaten a third party (15:11)
Accusation of disloyalty (14:16–18)	Accusation of disloyalty (15:11–13)
Yahweh's Spirit/Samson's victory (14:19)	Yahweh's Spirit/Samson's victory (15:14–17)

Indeed, "going up" and "going down" (עלה, *'lh*, and ירד, *yrd*, respectively) occur sixteen times in the Samson saga (14:1, 2, 5, 7, 10, 19a, 19b; 15:6, 8, 9, 11, 13; 16:5, 21, 31a, 31b): there is movement across the boundaries of Dan and Philistia, between circumcised and foreskinned, between rural and urban areas, from wife to harlot, ...[2] This is a man who breaks every boundary known to him.

Yet, as was also found in Pericope 10 (Jdg 13:1—14:20), it is evident that God was working sovereignly amidst the bizarre transactions of Samson's life. Yahweh's Spirit had "stirred" Samson as he began his relationship with the Timnite (13:25; 14:4); he "came mightily" upon him and empowered him to kill a lion and thirty Philistines (14:6; 15:19); and he "came mightily" upon Samson again, giving him supernatural strength to break his bonds and slay a thousand Philistines with a donkey's jawbone (15:14). Even after Yahweh had departed from Samson (16:20), deity empowered this flawed man with bloody hands and a brutal mind (and a shorn head) to topple a temple, killing three thousand Philistines (and himself) in the process (16:27–30).

"be") in 14:20 and 15:2; and the wordplay of רעה, *r'h*, in 14:20 ("to be a friend") and 15:3 ("evil"). See Kim, *The Structure of the Samson Cycle*, 267. But the gap in time between 14:20 and 15:1 suggests that Pericope 11 begins at 15:1.

2. Modified from Butler, *Judges*, 332.

11.1. Judges 15:1–8

THEOLOGICAL FOCUS 11.1

11.1 Acts of revenge manifest a false self-righteousness and only make situations worse (15:1–8).

NOTES 11.1

11.1 Acts of revenge manifest a false self-righteousness and only make situations worse.

At some unspecified time in the recent past, Samson, in a rage, had abandoned his wife (see 14:20; Pericope 10: Jdg 13:1—14:20). Now he wants sex—"I will *go in* to my wife"[3]—and so he decides to make amends. Bearing a goat's kid, "the ancient counterpart of the box of chocolates,"[4] Samson proceeds to his wife's house (15:2) where he is told that she has been given away to one of his companions (14:20; 15:2, 6). So his father-in-law does not permit him to "go in" (14:15). Unrequited desire now becomes inflammatory fury.

Even though the Timnite's father offers Samson a substitute, a sister ostensibly younger and prettier ("good," 15:2) than his wife, Samson is dissatisfied. He had decided what was "right" in *his* eyes and he wanted what *he* had seen (14:3, 7). "Good" was not enough; it had to be "right." Nothing else would do; no one else would do. And nobody was going to tell Samson how to pick his women! He who had once insisted that this woman be gotten for him (14:2–3) was not going to let her now be taken from him. That he had left the wedding ceremonies seething with rage and abandoning his wife is apparently of no concern to him, though his father-in-law saw it effectively as a divorce—the two infinitive absolutes are emphatic: "I *certainly* thought you *absolutely* hated her" (15:2).[5]

In response, Samson turns violent, and wreaks havoc on the Philistines' agroeconomy and their inventory of staples: grain, grapes, and olives (15:4–5). He prefaces it by saying, "*This time* I am blameless towards the Philistines when I do them harm" (15:3), clearly implying that his first furious assault on thirty Philistines (14:19) was not a justified attack even by his

---

3. For the idiom, see Gen 16:2; 29:21; 30:3; 38:8; etc.
4. Boling, *Judges*, 234.
5. Earlier, Samson's wife had accused him of "hating" her (14:16); it is therefore quite likely that she, rightly or wrongly, had continued to assume his hatred of her when he abandoned her, and conveyed this sentiment to her father.

own savage standards. One wonders why he blames the Philistines en masse for a perceived offence against himself perpetrated by his father-in-law. Samson's logic is skewed and inscrutable, answering only to his passions, whether sexual desire or violent rage. A lack of control in everything he does characterizes Samson, the divinely appointed deliverer, and counters the teaching of the Torah that Yahweh owns vengeance (Deut 32:35).

The fusillade of *waw* consecutive verbs that describe Samson's aggression against Philistine property gives one a sense of his wrath (Jdg 15:4–5): "And he went . . . , and he caught . . . , and he took . . . , and he turned . . . , and he put . . . , and he set fire . . . , and he sent . . . , and he burned . . . ." This is a well planned and well conducted undertaking intended to desolate the Philistines: capturing three hundred foxes, preparing a hundred and fifty torches, uniting the feisty animals tail to tail with appropriately placed torches, then transporting this live set up of tail-paired animals, lighting the torches, and releasing the foxes (truly weapons of mass destruction!)—and all of this without any help whatsoever. Samson is a one-man powerhouse![6] This is a remarkable (albeit unwitting) "beginning" of the deliverance of Israel from the hands of the Philistines foreshadowed in 13:5.

After 14:3, the next instance of "Philistines" is in 15:3. In the intervening portion (see Pericope 10: Jdg 13:1—14:20), the people Samson was dealing with, though Philistine, were not labeled as such, probably because the incidents were localized to Timnah. Even Samson's attack in Ashkelon is directed to "thirty of *them*" (14:19). But with this current assault on property, the scope has broadened. It is no longer an insular affair in Timnah. The larger populace of the Philistines is now involved—notice how they label Samson's father-in-law "the Timnite," suggesting that "Philistines" now encompasses more than just Timnites. The ripples of Samson's violence are spreading and the arenas of his conflicts are growing.

The collateral damage of Samson's blitzkrieg is that the Philistines blame his wife and father-in-law for the fiasco and burn both of them alive (15:6); ironically, this is what the Philistines had threatened the woman with in the first place (14:15).

Of course, Samson is not going to let *that* go by without reacting. His intent to avenge himself (15:7) tells the reader about his total lack of understanding of the consequences of tit-for-tat operations. Such reciprocated viciousness on the part of both parties only escalates in both intensity and extent with each turn, every action provoking an equal and opposite reaction, ending only when one or both parties are destroyed (and both are:

---

6. The pairing up of foxes was a stroke of genius. Leaving each fox to its own devices would probably not have caused as much havoc: each animal scampering away hastily to escape its own flaming tail would have limited the mayhem.

16:28–30). In any case, "he struck them, calf against thigh [i.e., ruthlessly]—a great slaughter" (15:8), and then decamped to a cleft in the rock of Etam. Perhaps it was an attempt to keep his promise to quit after this most recent vengeful outburst (15:7), uncontrollable man that he was. That the scope and extent of Samson's aggression are widening is again indicated in the Philistines "camping" in Judah and "spreading out" in Lehi—both verbs likely indicating military activity (15:9).[7] A personal vendetta waged over a woman has now exploded into an international conflagration.

These incessant rounds of revenge are depicted clearly in 15:10–11 in the dialogues of the Judahites, first with the Philistines (15:10 and then with Samson (15:11).

A	"… to **do** to him (15:10dα)	Philistines
B	*as* he **did** to us" (15:10dβ)	
C	"What then is this you have **done** to us?" (15:11c)	Judahites
B'	"*As* they **did** to me (15:11eα)	
A'	so I **did** to them" (15:11eβ)	Samson

Samson see, Samson "do"—"As they *did* to me so I *did* to them" (15:11).[8] And so the vicious cycle continues to spiral out of control.

In summary, these acts of revenge—which have nothing at all to do with Samson's dedication to his God, and which show no concern for the welfare of his nation—are both self-perpetuating and snowballing. The seemingly never-ending chain reaction of back-and-forth events detailed in Judges 15, culminates in Samson killing himself, along with three thousand Philistines, in the temple of Dagon (16:25–30); but he had done this because they had captured him, blinded him, and enslaved him (16:5–24); but they had done this because he had escaped from them with the gates of Gaza (16:3); but he had done this because they sought to kill him (16:1–2); but they had done this because he had slaughtered a thousand Philistines with a donkey's jawbone (15:14–20); but he had done this because they had caught and bound him (15:9–13); but the Philistines had done this because Samson had slaughtered many of them (15:7–8); but he had done this because they had burned alive his wife and her father (15:6); but they had done this because he had burned their fields and grain (15:3–5); but he had done this

---

7. For "camping," see Josh 8:11; 10:5, 34; 11:5; Jdg 6:4, 33; 7:1; 10:17; 11:20; 20:19; etc. For "spreading," see 2 Sam 5:18, 22.

8. Note the numerous echoes of "do" in Judges 15 (15:3, 6, 7, 10 [×2], 11 [×3]), mostly "doings" of vengeance and retaliation. "To smite" occurs thrice, as well, 15:8, 15, 16.

because his Philistine father-in-law had given away his wife (14:20—15:2); but his father-in-law had done this because Samson had abandoned her in a rage (14:19); but he had done this because his Philistine wife had betrayed him (14:16–18); but she had done because the Philistines threatened her household with death (14:15); but they had done this because Samson was out to make them look foolish with an enigmatic riddle (14:12–14) . . . .[9] The escalation of violent acts, one upon another, is unimaginable—all for revenge, and that is the thrust of this pericope.

11.2. Judges 15:9–20

> **THEOLOGICAL FOCUS 11.2**
>
> 11.2 Disdain for one's divine calling coincides with a vainglorious narcissism that drives one's own ambitions (15:9–20).

NOTES 11.2

11.2 *Disdain for one's divine calling coincides with a vainglorious narcissism that drives one's own ambitions.*

What is striking in the cameo of 15:9–13 is the response of the Judahites (Israelites, of course) to this "war"— Philistines vs. Samson. Three thousand Judahites assemble, not to fight the Philistines, but to subdue one of their own, Samson—who was singlehandedly engaging the enemy—and to turn him over to his (their!) foes.[10] It is perhaps not surprising then that Samson did not trust his fellow Israelites: he asks for a promise that they not kill him (15:12). In turn, the Judahites, unable to trust this violent man, bind him before handing him to the Philistines (15:13). The Israelites' contentment with their own subordination to the Philistines and their desire not to rock the boat is striking—in fact, they prefer things to be this way and are willing to go to any length to maintain status quo, even if it means betraying God's ordained deliverer to the Philistines. They would rather do that than fulfill God's calling for Israel to take over the land and to defeat their enemies. And so they acknowledge that "the Philistines are rulers over us" (15:11). Should it not have been Yahweh who ruled over them?

---

9. Adapted from Polzin, *Moses and the Deuteronomist*, 188.

10. Later Samson would singlehandedly kill *three thousand* Philistines—or at least that many (16:27).

Notice the similarity of the utterances of the Philistines and the Judahites:

15:10d	[*Philistines:*]	"to bind	Samson	we have come up	to do to him ...."
15:12b	[*Judahites:*]	"to bind	you	we have come down	to give you ...."

When the Judahites begin to emulate the enemy, one wonders who Samson's real enemies are. Yahweh plans to deliver Israel "from the hand of the Philistines" (13:5), but the Israelites plan to give Yahweh's deliverer "into the hand of the Philistines" (15:12)! The irony continues: Just as the Philistines had killed their own because they had aggravated Samson (15:6), so also the Israelites betray one of their own (to sure death) because he had aggravated the Philistines. The Israelites are now no different from the peoples surrounding them: Canaanization is complete! And Judah, once the leader of the nation in 1:1–2, has now degenerated into being a lackey of the enemy.

In any case, the Judahites hand him over to the Philistines who, seeing their prey, surge to attack, in a manner reminiscent of the lion's assault in the previous pericope: one roars, the other shouts, as they rush "to meet him" (קרא, *qr'*, 14:5; 15:14). In both incidents, we have Yahweh's Spirit also "rushing mightily" upon Samson (14:6; 15:14). Here the Spirit undoes what the Judahites had done to Samson: his bonds drop off his hands. And a most unlikely weapon is located: the jawbone of a donkey. The narrator takes pains to inform us that it was "fresh" (15:15); with that, Samson's Nazirite status is compromised yet once more with his handling of another unclean object, the *fresh* jawbone of a donkey, likely the remains of a recent kill, probably still bloodied and sinewed. But a thousand Philistines fall victim to Samson and his jawbone—more contact with unclean corpses!—and the victor celebrates with a ditty (15:16).[11]

But one notices that the triumphant song makes no mention of deity, unlike the hymn of Deborah (Judges 5), or even that of the Philistines, later (16:23–24), that extols their god, Dagon. Even with an obviously God-empowered victory, Samson has nothing to say about anyone but himself. He seems to be oblivious of the workings of Yahweh in his life. The memorialization of the place as Ramath-lehi (רָמַת לֶחִי, *ramat lekhi*, "Jawbone Heights") reflects his implement of war, the "jawbone," לְחִי, *lkhi* (15:17). Always self-focused!

---

11. The verse that Samson composes is clever: the Hebrew words for "donkey" and "heap" are homonyms, חֲמוֹר, *khamor*.

The slaughter of a thousand Philistines with a donkey's jawbone was evidently a laborious task and Samson became "very thirsty" compelling him to call on Yahweh (15:18). For the first time in Samson's saga, he seems to be aware of Yahweh's presence, though addressing deity only as "You" (15:18). And, for the first time, he acknowledges Yahweh's having given deliverance in the recent battle—but into *his*, Samson's, hand.[12] The construction Samson employs in 15:18—"give deliverance *by the hand of X*"—is suspiciously self-focused; Block notes that such a syntax occurs nowhere else in the OT.[13]

Samson is self-serving again, with the reference to Yahweh almost a secondary issue; rather it is his thirst and his fear that he will fall into the hand of the Philistines that is primary for him.[14] His is a rather petulant cry that almost challenges God: "It will look bad for you, if I die of thirst and fall into the hand of the uncircumcised." He seems overly concerned about issues of defilement, especially as he labels the Philistines "the uncircumcised." Whence this sudden concern, when all along thus far Samson has only demonstrated disdain for the cleanness demanded by his Nazirite status. He has no fear of uncleanness as he cohabits with Philistines, contacts corpses, cavorts in vineyards, celebrates with feasts, counterattacks with animal body-parts . . . .

Samson's logic is odd: If he died of thirst first, how could he fall into the hand of the Philistines (15:18)?[15] In any case, God graciously obliges and miraculously produces water that revives the strongman. Ironically, Samson names the place "En-hakkore" (עֵין הַקּוֹרֵא, *'en haqqore'*, "Spring of the Crier"), relating it to his own crying out (קרא, *qr'*) and not to Yahweh's provision of water (15:19). Ever the narcissist.

Perhaps it was Samson's remarkable victory, the killing of a thousand Philistines with nothing but a donkey's jawbone, that finally gave him enough credibility among his people to be established as judge over them for two decades (15:20). Usually such a notice of judgeship concludes with a reference to the death of judge (3:10–11; 8:28, 32; 10:2, 5; 12:7, 9–10, 11–12, 14–15). The break from such a pattern is notable. Indeed, one might see all of Judges 16, the rest of this pericope, as an expanded and detailed death

---

12. "Deliverance" here may simply mean Samson's personal victory over the Philistines, not necessarily any awareness of the "beginning of the deliverance" foreseen in 13:5. Even his self-designation, "Your servant," need only be a polite reference to himself as a supplicant of deity. See Chisholm, *Judges and Ruth*, 414 n.21.

13. *Judges, Ruth*, 447 n.382.

14. Thus far, Samson has shown no reluctance to fall into their female arms.

15. And the man who will soon carry a heavy gate for forty odd miles, and that mostly uphill (16:3), cannot survive a bit longer without water?

report that concludes once again with a notice of Samson's rule for twenty years (16:31). Thus there is a bookending of this elongated death notice by the period of Samson's judgeship. But, again unlike prior notations that conclude the stories of the judges, there is no mention of rest for the land.

11.3. Judges 15:9–20

> **THEOLOGICAL FOCUS 11.3**
>
> 11.3 Unbridled fleshly passions that prompt one to abandon the call of God in one's life lead to destruction (16:1–22).

NOTES 11.3

11.3 Unbridled fleshly passions that prompt one to abandon the call of God in one's life lead to destruction.

"Samson passes through a series of three women who mark the spectrum of female sexual partners—wife, whore, and mistress . . . ." There are, thus, "two protracted involvements ['wife': 14:1—15:20 and 'mistress': 16:4–31] sandwiching a one-night stand ['whore': 16:1–3]."[16] The first woman Samson went after, he wanted to marry. The third, he loved. If these were the only dalliances included in the text, one might give Samson a pass for fairly decent behavior. But with the inclusion of the second tryst, with a harlot, we see that Samson's compulsions have a darker side: his yearning for sex, and that with foreign women.

All of Samson's earlier conflicts began with his "going down" and his "seeing" a Philistine woman in Timnah (14:1); so also this fling commences with his "going down," this time to "see" a Philistine harlot in Gaza (16:1).[17] He is repeating the same profligate act that had brought him into contact with the Philistines for the first time. "Other judges in the book had many women/wives, but references to these women were always noted in connection to children and inheritance or power, never in the context of a character's sexual appetite. In this story the role of women and their

---

16. Alter, "Samson Without Folklore," 48. Though of course non-sexual, the fourth woman involved in Samson's life story, as given to us, was his mother (see Pericope 10: Jdg 13:1—14:20).

17. And here is the third woman in his life introduced with "see" (רְאֵה, *ra'ah*); the others, thus far, were his mother (13:2 has רְאֵה) and his wife, the Timnite (14:1 has רְאֵה): see Pericope 10 (Jdg 13:1—14:20). It is the fourth in this series that will be Samson's undoing.

sexuality is a major governing characteristic of the Judge which leads to his death."[18]

Gaza was about forty-five miles south of Zorah/Eshtaol (Samson's hometown), the southernmost one of the Philistine cities, making Samson's journey deliberate and not accidental. "He went . . . and he saw . . . and he went in to her" (16:1), as if it was the most obvious thing to do. It was foolish enough to visit a prostitute, but to do so in enemy territory was not only unconscionable, it was downright stupid. So unfettered are his passions that good sense escapes him. One also wonders how the Gazites heard about Samson's nocturnal antics (16:2). It is a fair guess that it was the harlot who leaked the information to her townsfolk. All his trysts with women have only brought Samson peril thus far (the next one will see him perish). Had he not recently learned that he was weak without Yahweh's help and strength (15:18–19), and had he not perceived that his thirsts could only be quenched by trusting Yahweh, not by haunting brothels? Like Israel, hardhearted and stubborn, Samson, too, had forgotten his calling, and had lapsed into an anti-Yahwistic pattern of life.

At any rate, upon being surrounded in the harlot's house/brothel, Samson is not particularly perturbed: he "lies" till midnight—the verb שכב, *shkb*, can also indicate sexual intercourse (Gen 19:32, 34; Lev 18:22; etc.)—and then decides to decamp, but not before causing some havoc (Jdg 16:2). He does not just pass through the gate of the city, he takes it with him (16:3). "It would have been a formidable barrier, especially when fully manned. But Samson has spent all his life breaching barriers: between the permissible and the forbidden, holy and profane, man and animal, Israelite and Philistine, Naziriteship and normality. Barriers have never been able to contain him. They appear to him only as challenges which rouse him to a renewed frenzy of breaking through. So it is here again."[19] More *waw* consecutives give us the details with economy of effort and elegance of style: "and he lay . . . and he rose . . . and he seized . . . and he uprooted . . . and he placed . . . and he carried . . . ." (16:3). How he got past the ambush that had been lying in wait for him "all night at the gate of the city" (16:2) is inexplicable. Then, gates and all, he makes his way to a mountaintop near Hebron (16:3).[20] There

---

18. Schneider, *Judges*, 218.
19. Webb, *Judges*, 395.
20. Hebron was the prominent city of Judah in those days. So, in effect, Samson brought the purloined gates to the Judahites who had earlier turned him over to the Philistines. The detailed description of the gate with its doors, two posts, and bars (16:3) make it substantial. Chisholm notes that the gate likely weighed between 5,000 and 10,000 pounds. He speculates that to move a 5,000-pound structure about 40 miles, up 3,000 feet, in an estimated 18 hours, would require 28.5 horsepower! A Herculean task,

is certainly more to this than meets the eye, suggesting that even though Yahweh is not mentioned in this cryptic and peculiar vignette, and certainly not acknowledged by our protagonist, deity seems to have been shepherding Samson to safety.

Without its gates, Gaza was rendered vulnerable. This would have been an opportune moment for Samson to muster the Judahites and mount an attack on the Philistines. But the man appears to have been perfectly content with mounting an exhibition of strength that had no real purpose or utility apart from boosting his own ego and giving him possession of a sizable trophy. In short, there seems to be no interest on the part of Israel or its appointed deliverer, Samson, to accomplish the agenda of Yahweh.

Experience had taught Samson nothing! Samson's discovery of the Philistines' "setting up an ambush" (16:2; from ארב, 'rb, "to lie in wait") ought to have prepared him for the future, but it does not. They do it again in the last episode of the pericope (16:4–31): he is "ambushed" (16:9, 12; also using ארב). Not to mention that he ought to have learned from the betrayal by his Philistine wife.[21] "It is in the nature of a fatal character flaw that it exposes the person who has it to danger again and again, until it finally destroys him."[22]

It all begins as he lands in the Sorek Valley and falls in love with Delilah (16:4).[23] But what was he doing in the *Sorek* Valley (= "Valley of the Choicest Vine," see Isa 5:2; Jer 2:21)? His presence here is suspicious, as ominous as his presence in a vineyard (Jdg 14:5) and his facilitation of a feast (14:10)—all associated with alcohol, prohibited for a man of Samson's dedication. It is "déjà vu all over again."[24]

---

indeed, but entirely unnecessary and exclusively self-serving! See Chisholm, *Judges and Ruth*, 416n126.

21. There are a number of parallels between the Timnite ferreting out the answer to Samson's riddle and Delilah inveigling the secret of Samson's strength: both are initiated by the Philistines (14:15 and 16:5); both women "entice"/"press" Samson (14:15 and 16:5); both attempts take several days (14:17; 16:16); and both women get Samson to "tell" (14:15, 16, 17 and 16:6, 10, 13, 15, 16, 18).

22. Webb, *Judges*, 396.

23. The fact that the Sorek Valley (16:4) borders Danite territory, and because Delilah is a Semitic name, it may well be that the woman was an Israelite and not a Philistine. However that is unlikely; if she were an *Israelite* traitor, that would have been a "tellable" fact that the narrator would certainly not have omitted. Younger notes that Philistine inscriptions point to a number of their own individuals bearing Semitic names (*Judges, Ruth*, 316). "Delilah" is linked to "night," לַיְלָה, *laylah*, an appropriate name for the lover of one named after the sun, "Samson" (from שֶׁמֶשׁ, *shemesh*, "sun"). But it is a cinch that when Sunny Boy meets Night Woman, things are not going to go well!

24. Berra, *The Yogi Book*, 9.

Delilah's remuneration for betraying Samson is 1,100 pieces of silver "each"—likely from each of the five lords of the Philistine pentapolis (five-city metroplex). If 10 pieces of silver a year was the average annual wage (17:10), this bribe of 5,500 pieces of silver turns out to be an astronomical sum: about 550 times the annual wage! "[Delilah] is every bit as mercenary as the prostitute of Gaza, but far more upmarket—and lethal."[25] He may love her, but to her, this "oversexed buffoon" is simply a good source of income![26]

Ironically, while a woman, Jael, once lured a foreign warrior chieftain, Sisera, to his death, now it is a foreign woman, Delilah, who is luring Israel's foremost warrior-judge, Samson, to his. Delilah "fastened" (תקע, *tqʿ*) Samson's hair with a "pin" (יתד, *ytd*, 16:14), recalling Jael's "striking" (תקע) a "tent peg" (יתד) into Sisera's head (4:21). Both actions are performed by women in private quarters upon sleeping victims. "[W]hat has happened that the Israelite judge endowed with the greatest physical strength ends up being portrayed as Sisera, the Canaanite abuser of God's people?"[27] The tables have been turned: that is how far Israel had fallen.

This commentary has kept track of the women in Samson's life, thus far three of them—all unnamed—introduced in juxtaposition to the verb (רָאָה, *raʾah*): his mother (13:2 has רָאָה), his wife (14:1 has רָאָה), and his harlot (16:1 has רָאָה). But not the fourth named woman, Delilah. This one, Samson *loved*. The *fourth* woman is different—the fourth time is a charm! And this fourth charmed woman tries four times to get Samson to reveal his secret and he succumbs . . . at the *fourth* try.

The first three times, Samson bluffs her (16:6–9, 10–12, and 13–14). The *fourth* time (16:15–21), when she plays the "love" card, accusing him that his "heart" was not with her (16:15), Samson tells her all that was in his "heart" (16:17; and see 16:18 [×2]). Indeed, for Delilah's three exhortations to "tell" (16:6, 10b, 13b), and her three accusations that Samson was not "telling" (16:10a, 13a, 15), three times it is stated that Samson "told" her all in his heart (16:17, 18a, 18b).[28]

Each of the first three attempts of Delilah was successfully countered by deceptions from Samson. But he slips closer and closer to the truth each time: while his first two replies dealt with cords and ropes,[29] and the third

---

25. Webb, *Judges*, 400.
26. Wharton, "The Secret of Yahweh," 58.
27. Younger, *Judges, Ruth*, 319.

28. Not surprisingly, the result of all this opening of "heart" on the part of Samson is that the Philistines finally end up with "a good heart" (16:25; i.e., "high spirits").

29. Though Samson is bluffing Delilah, the fact that he is inviting contact with fresh and undried "cords," likely made of tendons or sinews (16:7, 8), also shows how little he thinks of his Nazirite status. One also has to wonder what Samson was doing

braiding his hair, the *fourth* time he comes out with the truth about shaving his hair.³⁰ There is also a movement towards himself that is implied in the pronominal suffixes of the verbs he employs in his answers to Delilah: from "if *they* bind me . . ." (16:7, 11), and "if *you* weave . . ." (16:13), to the *fourth* reply: "if *I* am shaved . . ." (16:17). His resolve is breaking!

There is more going on with Samson's *fourth* response to Delilah. For one, the narrator introduces Samson's final response differently. The first three times it was "And he/Samson said to her . . ." (16:7, 11, 13). But the *fourth* time it is: "*And he told her all in his heart* and he said to her . . ." (16:17). Fourth time is a charm!

Then there is the matter of verb tenses. The verbs in the protasis of the first three responses of Samson are imperfects: 16:7, 11, 13 have "if they bind . . . ,"³¹ and "if you weave . . . ." But in the *fourth* response, the verb in the protasis changes to a perfect: 16:17 has "if I am shaved . . . ." Even the tenses weep for the man's fall!

But what gives away Samson's motivation is his "confession" in the apodosis of his *fourth* reply. The first three times he tells Delilah he will become weak and be "like *any one* [*any other*] man" (כְּאַחַד הָאָדָם, *k'ekhad ha'adam*, 16:7, 11, 13). But the *fourth* time, he acknowledges he will be come weak and be "like *every* man" (כְּכָל־הָאָדָם, *kkal-ha'adam*, 16:17).³² He wanted to be like *every* man! This was a renunciation of his calling, a repudiation of his dedication, a resignation from his Naziriteship. This was defection. He had thrust God out. He had slapped God's face. He was washing his hands of this whole God-business. He just wanted to be like *every* man: enjoying his women, doing whatever was "right in his eyes" (14:3, 7), throwing family, tribe, nation, and God to the winds!³³

---

when all this binding (×2) and braiding and shaving was going on. How was he not aware of what was being done to him, each of those four times? Was he in a drunken stupor?

30. In the hair-braiding attempt, Delilah takes "the seven locks of his hair" to weave them into the fabric on a loom (16:13, 14). This is the only physical description of Samson that we have: his never-cut hair was braided in seven locks (16:13, 14, 17). If Samson were shaped like Superman, it would have been obvious that his strength was exclusively muscular; it is therefore quite likely that he was an ordinary-looking guy, except for his odd hair length and style. And so the Philistines are convinced, rightly, that Samson's power was supernatural or magical. So much so, they accept as truth all of his (misleading) suggestions for depleting his strength (16:7, 11, 13, 17), even though it is not at all obvious what any of them may have to do with the man's might.

31. Samson's response in 16:11 has an imperfect + infinitive: "if they tightly bind . . . ." The apodosis is missing in 16:13 MT; the missing section is reconstructed from the LXX in English translations.

32. He also adds, this fourth time, that his strength would leave him (16:17).

33. And that was what the Israelites wanted to do, too, become like Canaanites, to

Another striking element in the final scene involving Samson and Delilah is the revelation that Samson was aware all along of his Nazirite status (16:17). Unfortunately, he had never taken it seriously, and even now was willing to violate his dedication to Yahweh for the love of a woman and get shorn (16:4, 15). Samson's statement to Delilah reflects the words of Yahweh's angel to Samson's mother in 13:5 almost verbatim, clearly indicating that the man was aware of the prophecy to his pregnant mother.

Judges 13:5	Judges 16:17
"And no razor shall come upon his head, for the boy will be a Nazirite to God from the womb."	"No razor has come upon my head, for I [have been] a Nazirite to God from the womb of my mother."

He must have heard it from her; now he passes on the information to another woman.

Delilah also recognizes that finally Samson was being truthful ("he had told her all in his heart," 16:18), so she summons the Philistines even before she begins to work on Samson, telling them "he has told me all in his heart" (16:18). The Philistines, equally confident, arrive with cash in hand (16:18). She cuts Samson's hair and the end draws nigh (16:19–20).[34]

There seems to be a contradiction between Samson's confession in 16:17 (that he would become weak after a haircut) and his confidence in 16:20 (that he would escape as he had done before). While he did tell Delilah (16:17) the truth about his Nazirite status and its link with his hair and his strength, 16:20 implies that Samson was still assuming that he could escape on his own merits, with his own might, Yahweh's absence and Nazirite renunciation notwithstanding. His strength, Samson surmises, is his own possession to do with as he pleases, when he pleases. Perhaps in Judges 16, he has started to believe the strength he has exhibited against lions, foxes, and Philistines is his own. Besides he had already violated other Nazirite constraints with impunity, so why not get a haircut as well? Hubris, to the very end, in assuming he did not need deity anymore.

---

get rid of the Yahwistic constraints on their lives as they reveled in sex, sacrilege, and selfishness!

34. The verb וַתְּגַלַּח, *wattgallakh*, is a feminine singular, "and she shaved" (16:19). Thus it is likely that her calling "to the man" (לָאִישׁ, *la'ish*) was directed toward Samson, to check whether he was asleep (Sasson, "Who Cut Samson's Hair?" 338).

But Samson was wrong. The repudiation of his call had decimated his strength. In 16:17, 19, we see strength "leaving [סור, *sur*]" Samson. But in 16:20, it is *Yahweh* who "leaves [סור]" Samson: *God* was his strength.[35] At first it was the Delilah and the Philistines who "did not know" Samson's strength, or the source thereof (16:9); in the end it is Samson who "did not know" that Yahweh had left him (16:20). Sadly, the man is unaware of his dangerous plight. He thinks nothing has changed and expects to escape "as at other times" (16:20). But the one chosen by Yahweh to commence the deliverance of Israel (13:5) has now been abandoned by that same deity. "In the end his vitality is drained away, and he is left without strength, without sight, without freedom, without dignity, and without God!"[36] It is all over now, except for a last hurrah. Judges 16 began with a foolish visit to a harlot in Gaza (16:1), and ends with the result of his follies leading him bound and captive to Gaza again—this time to die (16:21).[37]

11.4. Judges 16:23–31

THEOLOGICAL FOCUS 11.4

11.4 A rebellious spirit persists in displaying self-glorifying attitudes and engaging in vengeful actions (16:23–31).

NOTES 11.4

11.4 A rebellious spirit persists in displaying self-glorifying attitudes and engaging in vengeful actions.

---

35. The subsequent sequence of events is illuminating: his hair is gone (16:19a), and his strength is gone (16:19b) *because* Yahweh is gone (16:20b). Later his hair regrows (16:22), and his strength returns (16:29–30) *because* Yahweh enables him (16:28). Notice that even with the regrowth of his hair, Samson needs a young man to "strengthen" his hands (חזק, *khzq*, 16:26); it is only after his prayer to Yahweh for "strengthening" (also חזק, 16:28), that his own might returns, albeit temporarily, for the final *coup de grâce* (16:29–30). Samson's hair, in sum, "is not the source of Samson's strength: Its function rather is purely symbolic. It serves as a token of faithful allegiance" (Kim, *The Structure of the Samson Cycle*, 354).

36. Block, *Judges, Ruth*, 463.

37. The foolishness of Samson's actions is literarily depicted in the numerous words in this pericope dealing with binding and bonds: 15:10, 12, 13a, 13b, 14; 16:5, 6, 7, 8, 10, 11, 12, 13, 21bb, 21bg, 25 (the last two have "house of binding" = prison). See O'Connell, *The Rhetoric of the Book of Judges*, 222.

The possessive pronoun "our" echoes eight times in the sixteen words of the two utterances of the Philistines (16:23–24): "our god" (×2), "our enemies/enemy" (×2), "our hands" (×2), "our land," "our slain" (all first-person plural suffixes). The verb "to praise," the action they perform before their god, Dagon, is וַיְהַלְלוּ (*wayhalᵉlu*, "and they praised"). It is striking that after *his* victory over the Philistines, Samson never bothered to praise God (15:16); but here, the Philistines do, after *their* victory over Samson (16:23–24).

Samson's relegation to a prisoner's lowly task of grain grinding (16:21) has a touch of poetic justice to it: he who destroyed much of the Philistines' grain (15:4–5) is now producing grain for them (16:25). And if Dagon (דָּגוֹן, *dagon*) is the god of "grain" (דָּגָן, *dagan*), then Samson here is serving Dagon himself (not that he has been serving Yahweh in the past). With his eyes gouged out by the Philistines, "Sunny Boy" was now in darkness (16:21). Of course, his *real* darkness had begun when Yahweh departed from him (16:20). The one who did whatever he decided was "right" in his eyes (14:3, 7; also 16:1, "saw"), is now rendered eyeless and sightless. Samson literally becomes a laughing-stock: thrice we are told that the Philistines "made sport" of him (צחק/שחק, *skhq/tskhq*, "to laugh," 16:25, 27).

It is curious that the narrator describes Samson's hair as "beginning" to grow back (16:22). Samson was the one who was divinely destined to "begin" delivering Israel from the Philistines (13:5)—hope born. After his birth, Yahweh's Spirit "began" to stir Samson (13:25)—hope intensified. Unfortunately, what "began" with Delilah's betrayal (16:19) was his demise—hope lost. Now, for the final time, something is "beginning" again, the regrowth of Samson's hair (16:22)—hope regained.[38] This will be a pyrrhic victory, but the "beginning" of something hopeful, nonetheless.

Note the recurrences of "time(s)" (פעם, *p'm*) in this pericope: "three *times*" the Philistines were unsuccessful (16:15); but the fourth "time," Delilah was sure of success (16:18). On the other hand, Samson thought this last capture was "as other *times*" and that he could successfully escape (16:20)—he was wrong. He had played with fire one "time" too many. With Delilah, the *fourth* woman and pattern-breaker, in her last attempt, the fourth "time," he loses his heart, his secret, and his life. But now, in the final scene, Samson begs God, "one last *time*," to give him deliverance (16:28), and he is successful. He brings down the building (16:25–30), killing at least three thousand men and women, possibly more (the "lords" of the Philistines do not seem to be part of the count, 16:27).[39]

---

38. A dermatological note: Hair grows at the rate of about 0.4 mm a month. Following his shaving, it would have taken a month for the regeneration of a centimeter of scalp hair.

39. The "roof" of the building that Samson managed to collapse (16:27) was

Samson's appeal to God for "remembrance" stands in the tradition of making entreaty to Yahweh on the basis of his special relationship to his people (Pss 25:6; 74:18; 89:50; 106:4; 132:1; 137:7). But thus far, despite his dedication to Yahweh from the womb, Samson has shown no sign of recognition of any such special relationship. Only twice does Samson ever "cry out" to Yahweh (as far as we are told: Jdg 15:18; 16:28), or even acknowledge his presence in his life: both times he perceived his condition terminal, and both times Yahweh answered his prayer—once for deliverance *from* death, now for deliverance *to* death. And, here in 16:28, Samson's address of deity is still a bit dodgy: he calls him "lord" (אֲדֹנָי, *'adonay*), "Yahweh," and "God" (אֱלֹהִים, *'elohim*—what the Philistines called Dagon in 16:23–24). Unsure till the very end, the man seems to be hedging his bets, hitting deity with every divine name he knows.

Also, the man's attitude to life has seemingly not changed at all: in this his last stand, he wants "revenge" for the loss of his eyes—self-focus is his obsession and personal vendettas are his pursuit, all the way to the bitter end![40] Besides, Samson's prayer is not very different from the song the Philistines just performed in 16:23–24: both are dominated by first-person pronominal suffixes. Samson has six in his utterances in 16:28, 30: "*my*-lord," "remember-*me*," "strengthen-*me*," "*I*-may-be-avenged," "*my*-eyes," and "*my*-soul."[41] There is no concern at all for Yahweh, his reputation, or his plans for his people. And ironically, the man seeks revenge for the loss of his eyes which organs, of course, were the primary cause of all his woes (14:1, 3, 7; 16:1, 21, 28). Yet, God answers his prayer, because in the entire life of Samson, particularly at its gruesome end, it is *Yahweh* who had to be vindicated and avenged of all the dishonor and shame brought upon his name by his so-called deliverer, his ne'er-do-well Nazirite. And deity vindicates himself!

Three thousand Judahites once turned him over to the Philistines (15:11–12); now at least three thousand Philistines perish (16:27). That Samson killed more while dying than he did while living (16:30) signals that though this was not his finest hour, it certainly was his greatest accomplishment: people, lords, and god—all perish. In the *end*—with a fivefold echo of the root מות, *mwt*, "death," in 16:30—the deliverance of Israel from the Philistines had *begun* (13:5), but not without a dark note of tragedy struck in these final lines of the Samson saga, that of a life wasted.

---

probably more like a balcony overlooking a central courtyard.

40. Samson's plea is literally "that I may take revenge with one revengeful act." One remembers that revenge is forbidden in the Torah, for it is Yahweh who is the avenger, not man: Lev 19:18; Deut 32:35; 1 Sam 24:12; Jer 15:15.

41. The Philistines had eight (16:23–24; see above).

And so the last judge of Israel (at least in this book) dies—the only one to do so in an encounter with the enemy. "His life has been inextricably bound with the Philistines from the beginning."[42] In fact, the only interactions Samson had with Israelites were with his parents, whom he disobeyed, disagreed with, and deceived, and the Judahites, who turned him over to the enemy. He never sought to fulfill God's agenda for his life, instead he attempted to fulfill his own agenda of lust and egomania, all in relation to the Philistines.[43] And with his final plea, "Let me die with the Philistines!" (16:28), Samson asserts his total identification with them. He who lived with the Philistines, dies with the Philistines!

SERMON FOCUS AND OUTLINES

THEOLOGICAL FOCUS OF PERICOPE 11 FOR PREACHING

11 Rebellious disdain of one's divine calling, expressed in uncontrolled lusts and vengeful actions, can lead to destruction (15:1—16:31).

The theological thrust of the text is Samson's defection, so the sermon should move towards that end, as shown in both outlines below. All the vengeful and self-serving actions of Samson reflect the renunciation of his dedication and the repudiation of his divine call.[44]

Possible Preaching Outlines for Pericope 11

   I. Spiraling Revenge
      Samson's fury (15:1–5)
      Philistines' homicidal retaliation (15:6)
      Samson's recompense (15:7–8)
      Revenge and escalating violence (15:9–11; 16:21–31)
      Move-to-relevance: How we engage in tit for tat
   II. Selfish Reactions
      Samson's solo performances; the Judahites' treachery (15:10–13)

---

42. Webb, *Judges*, 414.

43. It is indeed strange that even with his abnormal sexual drive, the man leaves no descendants. Every major judge (and most of the minor ones), with the exception of the first three—Othniel, Ehud, and Barak—are said to have left descendants; even Deborah is called a "mother" (5:7).

44. By "call," I do not necessarily mean some supernatural revelation, dream, or voice. It is a combination of one's "head" (who one is, the fingerprints God has left on one's life, one's personality), one's "heart" (one's passion), and one's "hand" (the fruit one has borne) that usually brings one to the realization of what one is supposed to do with life, an acknowledgement of God's gifting for certain ministries—i.e., one's "call."

         Samson's contact with more corpses (15:8, 14–15)
         Samson's self-serving celebrations and appeals (15:16–20)
         Samson and his sensual passions (16:1–3)
         Move-to-relevance: Our succumbing to selfish passions
    III. Shunning Response
         The fourth woman, the fourth attempt (16:4–20)
         Samson's fourth reply: renunciation of his call (16:7, 11, 13, 17)
         Destruction of the ignorant delinquent (16:20, 28–31)
         Move-to-relevance: Our temptation to give up on our call
    IV. *Be faithful to the call!*
         Specifics on being faithful to the divine call[45]

This story also lends itself to a "single-move" sermon, so long as the preacher is careful to add implicit or explicit moves-to-relevance, all focusing on Samson's defection:

    I. Samson's Defection
         Revenge and escalating violence (15:1–11)
         Samson's contact with more corpses (15:8, 14–15)
         Samson's self-serving celebrations and appeals (15:16–20)
         Samson and his sensual passions (16:1–3)
         The fourth woman, the fourth attempt (16:4–20)
         Samson's fourth reply: renunciation of his call (16:7, 11, 13, 17)
         Destruction of the ignorant delinquent (16:20, 28–31)
         Move-to-relevance: Our temptation to give up on our call
    II. Our Devotion: *Be faithful to the call!*
         Specifics on being faithful to the divine call

---

45. Since this is the last judge story, application may be a sort of recap of what prior sermons have advocated: integrity (Ehud), courage (Barak), faith and humility (Gideon), submission (Jephthah), etc. To be such a person as called by these texts is to be faithful to God's call.

PERICOPE 12

Micah, Levite, Danites

Judges 17:1–18:31

[Idolatry, Theft, Cursing, Syncretism, Brutality]

REVIEW, SUMMARY, PREVIEW

Review of Pericope 11: In Jdg 15:1—16:31, we have the conclusion of the Samson story. The vengeful and self-serving attitude of the judge is on full display as he and the Philistines go at each other with increasing viciousness, and as he consorts with a Philistine prostitute. Finally, Samson ends up with Delilah, the fourth woman in his life, who makes four attempts to learn the secret of his strength. Samson caves in, repudiating his call from God. Not even aware that deity has left him, he finally dies in a suicidal/homicidal attempt.

Summary of Pericope 12: The twelfth pericope (Jdg 17:1—18:31), comprising Epilogue I, deals with the misdemeanors of Micah, his mother, a Levite, and the Danites. Stealing, idolatry, cursing, syncretism, and brutality abound, without there being a single positive note sounded or a single positive character pictured. The result of godless leadership is a godless society. And the ultimate consequence is loss: all culpable parties get their just deserts.

Preview of Pericope 13: The next pericope, Jdg 19:1–30, is the first part of Epilogue II (Jdg 19:1—21:25). The near-total breakdown of law and order and the lack of any concern for the weak and defenseless in society is evidenced by the culpability of the raped and murdered woman's husband, her father, her host, and the Gibeahites whose horrific brutality rivals that of Sodom and Gomorrah. This is what happens in a leaderless and godless society.

12. Judges 17:1–18:31

THEOLOGICAL FOCUS OF PERICOPE 12

12 The consequence of godless leadership is utter godlessness in society that invites the discipline of God (17:1—18:31).

12.1 The consequence of godless leadership is utter godlessness in society (17:1–13).

12.2 Ungodly attitudes and activities invite the discipline of God (18:1–31).

OVERVIEW

Othniel is the perfect model of a judge; Ehud is deceptive; Barak is fearful; Gideon is skeptical and hubristic (and Abimelech is a bloodthirsty butcher—not a judge figure); Jephthah is a manipulator and child-sacrificer; Samson cannot control his fleshly passions and defects from his calling. It is no wonder, then, that at the end the book of Judges, in the Epilogues (17:1—21:25), the nation collapses into gross idolatry and civil war—the consequences of the deterioration that had begun in the days of the judges (depicted in the Body: Jdg 3:7—16:31): the Canaanization of Israel. As go the leaders, so go the people![1]

Epilogue I (Pericope 12: Jdg 17:1–18:31) and Epilogue II (19:1—21:25—Pericope 13: Jdg 19:1–30 and Pericope 14: Jdg 20:1—21:25) parallel the Prologues in structure and themes.

---

1. In every one of the bizarre episodes that comprise the Epilogues, there is an echo of a specific event that occurred in the life of a major judge in 3:7—16:31 (see Introduction).

Judges 1	Socio-political decline	**Prologue I**
Judges 2	Religious decline	**Prologue II**
Judges 3–16	Major and minor judges	**Body**
Judges 17–18	Religious collapse	**Epilogue I**
Judges 19–21	Socio-political collapse	**Epilogue II**

Both Prologue II and Epilogue I deal with religious issues. The former shows how successive generations of Israelites went deeper into idolatry; the latter shows how things get even worse, with even Levites—only *two* generations after Moses—conniving in and furthering the development of idolatry, both private and public.[2] Prologue I and Epilogue II, on the other hand deal with socio-political issues (see Pericopes 13 and 14).

Epilogue I and Epilogue II are related in a number of ways. The former (Pericope 12) deals with the Danites, and the latter (Pericopes 13 and 14) with the Benjaminites. These two tribes would, respectively, lead the Northern and Southern Kingdoms later, emphasizing that the decay in morality here affected the entire nation. In both Epilogues, the particular crisis is precipitated by an anonymous Levite. In 17:1–18:31, we see a Levite in Bethlehem (Judah; 17:7–8) moving to Ephraim (and thence to Dan; 17:1; 18:27–29), and the pericope ends with a reference to Shiloh (18:31). In 19:1—21:25, we have a Levite in Ephraim (19:1) searching for his concubine in Judah (Bethlehem; 19:1–2); this pericope also concludes with references to Shiloh (21:12, 19–23). Both Epilogues have priestly characters making inquiries of God regarding proposed actions (18:5–6; 20:27–28); and both have troops of six hundred men playing important roles (18:11, 16–27; 20:47; 21:7). Each Epilogue has an initial crisis that involves individuals; this is soon resolved, but the events in both cases result in far greater complications for the nation at large—"the alternation between the individual and the tribal levels is meant to suggest a sickness in Israel which permeates all levels of society, personal, familial, and national."[3]

That both Epilogues deal with Levites—the custodians of the Law (Deut 17:9, 18; 24:8; 27:9, 14)—reminds the reader of the unfortunate role Israel's leadership played in the moral downfall of the nation (portrayed in the Body: Jdg 3:7—16:31). Not to mention the fourfold lament, twice in

---

2. Major issues of multi-generational idolatry are addressed in Prologue II (2:6—3:6) and in the corresponding Epilogue I (17:1—18:31): see 2:10–19; 3:6; and 17:1–6. Also in both are the abandonment of covenant and cultic loyalty to Yahweh (2:10—3:6; and 17:7–13; 18:2–6, 14–26, 30–31).

3. Satterthwaite, "'No King in Israel,'" 77.

each part of the Epilogue, for a rudderless nation, adrift and capsizing (17:6; 18:1; 19:1; 21:25).

17:6	"no king in Israel"; "every man did what was right in his eyes"
18:1	"no king in Israel"
19:1	"no king in Israel"
21:25	"no king in Israel"; "every man did what was right in his eyes"

In the Epilogues, there is no judge, no king, and no leader, only people doing what is right in their eyes, and an abundance of horrifying violence, culminating in a civil war that almost eradicates an entire Israelite tribe. Such a statement of leaderlessness might well have be an expression of the Israelites' rejection of Yahweh as their true ruler (see Exod 15:13–18; 19:6; Num 23:21; Deut 33:5; Jdg 8:23; and 1 Sam 12:12). God is, of course, *always* King, but these notices declare that, for all practical purposes, God's people went about their lives *as if* there were no king![4] The contrary, "doing what is right/good in the eyes of Yahweh" recurs in the Mosaic Law: Exod 15:26; Lev 10:19; Deut 6:18; 12:25, 28; 13:18.[5] This lends credence to the notion that the "king" referred to here is the divine regent, Yahweh. Such an idea does not militate against "king" also indicating a godly leader (unlike the ones in this book) acting under the aegis of the true King, Yahweh. Indeed, it was the increasing *ungodliness* of the judge-leaders depicted in

---

4. Wong notes that 2 Chr 15:3–6 points to the time of the judges as a period when Israel was "without the true God, and without a teaching priest, and without the law," resulting in "distress" (צרר, *tsrr*, shows up in 15:4 and Jdg 2:15; 10:9; a synonym, צרה, *tsrh*, is found in 2 Chr 15:5 and Jdg 10:14). Of course, Yahweh was known to the people of Israel, and the priesthood and law were well established; besides 2 Chr 15:4 mentions that God could be sought and found by those who wanted to seek and find him. So the absence of God, priest, and law noted by the Chronicler therefore must have been referring to "the non-honouring of YHWH and instructing priest and the law in Israel during the period of the Judges. . . . [T]he only way YHWH and the law could meaningfully be absent from Israelite society would be for them to be absent from the perspective of a society that has chosen to ignore them." Likewise, the Epilogues in Judges are quite bereft of any initiative taken by Yahweh or of any inclination of the Israelites to seek him wholeheartedly (the perfunctory approaches to deity in Judges 20–21 do not count). See Wong, *Compositional Strategy*, 220, 223. Besides, the only Israelite in Judges labeled "king," Abimelech, was utterly Canaanized (see Pericope 8: Jdg 8:33—10:5), just as the Israelites are now depicted in the Epilogues. "[G]iven that the only Israelite king found in the book is one whose embrace of Canaanised values and behaviour is exactly the problem that gave rise to the kind of depravity found in Gibeah, it is hard to see how the refrain [of 17:6; 18:1; 19:1; 21:25] can possibly be viewed as a recommendation of human kingship in Israel" (ibid., 209).

5. Frequently found as approbation of Israelite kings: 1 Kgs 11:33, 38; 14:8; 15:5, 11; 22:43; 2 Kgs 10:30; 12:2; 14:3; 15:3, 34; 16:2; 18:3; 22:2.

Jdg 3:7—16:31 that had led to such an anarchic and *un*godly situation in Jdg 17:1—21:25. Leaderlessness and godlessness go together. The leaderless people behaved as if there were no God, and did what was right in *their* eyes, not what was right in *God's* eyes. Indeed, Deut 12:8 expressly prohibited such attitudes and actions, for doing what was right in one's own eyes was equivalent to "doing what was *evil* in God's eyes"—another recurrent phrase in the Mosaic Law: Deut 4:25; 9:18; 17:2; 31:29.[6] What earlier was stated as "evil in the eyes of Yahweh (Jdg 2:11; 3:7, 12; 4:1; 6:1; 10:6; 13:1) had now become "Everyman" doing "what was right in his eyes" (17:6; 21:25).[7] The enemy was no longer external, but internal: Israel, itself, was its own enemy.

Nearly all of the Ten Commandments are broken in Jdg 17:1—21:25 (Epilogues I and II): other gods and idols are worshiped (17:3–5); Yahweh's name is taken in vain (17:13); parents are dishonored (17:1-2); innocent victims are slain (18:27; 19:26-29; 21:10); adultery and rape are committed (19:22-25); others' property is stolen (17:2; 18:21-27); false witness is borne (20:1-7); and what belongs to a neighbor is coveted (18:27-31; 21:8-24).[8] Idolatry is particularly prominent in this pericope (Pericope 12: 17:1—18:31). It had now gotten so bad that people did not think twice before engaging in that evil, considering it a form of Yahwism (17:1-5; 18:6, 31): syncretism! Besides, this pericope, in particular, shares several themes with Deuteronomy 12—what was prohibited there is practiced with abandon here[9]:

Themes	Deuteronomy 12:1–32	Judges 17:1–18:31
Cultic sites/idols	Destroyed (12:2–3)	Constructed (17:3–4)
Central shrine	Endorsed (12:4–18, 26–27)	Ignored (17:2–5, 13; 18:31)
What is right in one's eyes	Prohibited (12:8)	Practiced (17:6)
Levites supported	At central shrine (12:12, 18, 19)	At private shrines (17:7–13; 18:19–20, 30)

---

6. Also frequently found, but as disapprobation of Israelite kings: 1 Kgs 15:26, 34; 16:25, 30; 2 Kgs 3:2; 8:18, 27; 13:2, 11; 14:24; 15:9, 18, 24, 28; 17:2; 21:2, 20; 23:32, 37; 24:9, 19.

7. That both these expressions include at least idolatry is clear from Jdg 2:11-13; 3:7, 12; 4:1; 6:1; 13:1 (and see Deut 12:8).

8. Olson, "The Book of Judges," 864–65.

9. From O'Connell, *The Rhetoric of the Book of Judges*, 240.

Only two people are named in Pericope 12: Micah (17:1—18:27) and Jonathan (18:30). Pericope 13 (Jdg 19:1–30) does not contain a single named individual. Pericope 14 (Jdg 20:1—21:25) has only Phinehas (20:28). This general absence of named characters reflects the depersonalization and chaos of society that is the consequence of inadequate leadership (depicted in Judges 3–16). "It is only ethical and moral values that give a person a name, a place in time and in space, and a world."[10] But only in the Epilogues, in all of Judges, does one find priests and Levites, and the cultic sites, Bethel and Shiloh. "Thus the most immoral chapters in the book are at the same time those employing the most religious language."[11] The irony is pungent! The nation, including its revered and sacred institutions, is in serious decline.

12.1. Judges 17:1–13

THEOLOGICAL FOCUS 12.1

12.1 The consequence of godless leadership is utter godlessness in society (17:1–13).

NOTES 12.1

12.1 The consequence of godless leadership is utter godlessness in society.

Pericope 12 (17:1—18:31) tells three stories, dealing with Micah (17:1–5), Micah and the Levite (17:6–13), and Micah, the Levite, and the Danites (18:1–31). The narrator's sparse non-narratival comments are placed neatly at the seams: 17:6 and 18:1.[12] But scattered throughout this pericope are terms with unambiguously negative connotations: "idol" (17:3, 4; 18:14, 17, 18, 20, 30, 31), "molten image" (17:3, 4; 18:14, 17, 18), "ephod" (17:5; 18:14, 17, 18, 20), "teraphim" (17:5; 18:14, 17, 18, 20), "my gods which I made" (18:24), and "what Micah had made" (18:27).[13] All this with deity being

---

10. Klein, *A Triumph of Irony*, 143.

11. Butler, *Judges*, 373.

12. Appropriately enough, the first verse of the episode dealing with Micah (17:1–5) begins with "man" (17:1), and the last verse of the episode dealing with Micah and the Levite who becomes a priest (17:6–13) ends with "priest." The transitional verse, 17:5, begins with "man" and ends with "priest."

13. "Priest" (the illegitimate species thereof, of course) shows up in 17:5, 10, 12, 13; 18:4, 6, 17, 18, 19, 20, 24, 27, 30). For the proscription of "idols," see Exod 20:4–5; Lev 26:1; Deut 4:16, 23, 25; 5:8–9; 27:15; etc.; for that of "molten images," see Exod 32:4,

blithely referred to as "Yahweh" by these idolaters (17:2, 3, 13; 18:6; but as אֱלֹהִים, 'elohim, "God," by the Danite apostates in 18:5, 10). Confusion not only reigns, it pours!

That the story of Micah and his money comes right after the Samson-Delilah episode (16:4–20) is striking because in both stories, 1,100 pieces of silver are featured (16:5; 17:2), and in both there is a betrayal (one of a lover by his paramour, the other of a mother by her son). What an ostensibly foreign woman, Delilah, did is surpassed by an Israelite. "The commandment of Exod 20:15 ["You shall not steal"] is broken among *Israelites,* and it is broken within the most intimate sphere, the family."[14] Israel is in a bad way!

Indeed, Micah violates two of the commands in the Decalogue right away: he steals, and he dishonors his parent (Exod 20:12, 15; Deut 5:16, 19). His seeming repentance is only a fear of his mother's curse (Jdg 17:2), not an act of remorse: he states explicitly that he is confessing because he heard the curse (17:2). If he had been following the Torah and were truly repentant, Micah would have confessed his sin at the tabernacle, made restitution for his crime, and sacrificed a guilt offering as atonement (Lev 6:1–6). He does nothing of the sort.

Micah's mother is no better: she curses one day and she blesses the next (Jdg 17:2).[15] She is thankful enough that she dedicates the silver to Yahweh, but she does so in a totally reprehensible and sacrilegious manner, making an idol and a molten image out of the metal (17:3).[16] Besides, after her declaration that she would "solemnly/wholly dedicate" the silver for this

---

8; 34:17; Lev 19:4; Deut 9:12, 16; 27:15; etc. Ephods were part of the accouterments of priests in the cult of Yahweh, but outside of the Yahwistic cult, they were forbidden: Exod 28:6–14; 1 Sam 22:18; 23:6–12; as well as Jdg 8:27 (the only other occurrence of "ephod" in Judges). "Teraphim" were vestiges of pagan rituals and never a part of Yahwism: Gen 31:19–35; 1 Sam 15:23; 19:13, 16; 2 Kgs 23:24; Ezek 21:26; Hos 3:4; Zech 10:2.

14. Klein, *The Triumph of Irony,* 144. Other parallels between this pericope and the preceding Samson saga include: mention of Zorah and Eshtaol (13:2, 25; 16:31; and 18:2, 8, 11), and Mahaneh-dan (13:25 and 18:12); and the fact that the saga of Samson, a Danite, is followed by a story of the Danites (18:1–31). Based on the similarity of silver pieces involved, Schneider even suspects that Micah's mother may have been Delilah herself (*Judges,* 231–32).

15. The verb אלה, *'lh,* "to curse/swear," is infrequent in the Pentateuch, and used only of very solemn undertakings (Gen 24:41; 26:28; Deut 29:12, 14; etc.). "Micah's mother apparently uses Yahweh's name much as Micah seeks to use Yahweh, for her own convenience: she assumes the right to make oaths and invoke blessings, and to do these on behalf of a worldly tangible—silver" (Klein, *A Triumph of Irony,* 149).

16. That she went to a silversmith to accomplish her purposes is significant (Jdg 17:4); 1 Sam 13:19 notes the absence of blacksmiths in Israel, which means she would have had to approach a Philistine workman.

purpose, she seems to have kept back the bulk of the money and used only two hundred pieces for her idolatrous fancies.[17] Her son, a chip off the old weird block, continues his mother's anti-Yahwistic endeavors by building a shrine ("house of God," 17:5; see Deut 12:4–27[18]) to house an ephod and teraphim, and by consecrating one of his sons as a priest—an illegitimate appointment.[19] So we have a houseful of gods, an illegitimate and forbidden assortment of deities in a DIY sanctuary. Thus a mother's cultic aberration (17:3–4) leads to her son's heretical actions (17:5), and later to the apostasy of a tribe (18:1–30), and that of a whole nation (18:31).

The ironies are plentiful in this pericope. Micah's name itself belies his actions: מִיכָיְהוּ, *mikayhu*, means "Who is like Yahweh?" (17:1, 4).[20] The man, a thief who betrayed his mother (albeit now repentant, 17:1–2), who has a theophoric name exalting Yahweh's uniqueness, acts as if every other god is better than Yahweh. He goes on a despicable binge of anti-Yahwism, creating an ephod and teraphim and installing his son as a priest for his household shrine (17:4–5). Later, "Who-Is-Like-Yahweh" expands his aberrant cultic endeavors as he corrals a stray Levite (17:7–9), and sponsors him as his own priest in his household shrine, for a monthly wage (17:10; 18:4). As he had done his son (17:5), Micah then consecrates the Levite (17:8–12).

---

17. It is unclear what is happening with Micah's mother promising to "return them to you" (17:3); perhaps this line is misplaced and belongs in 17:2, in the mouth of Micah.

18. "Shrine" in Jdg 17:5 is literally בֵּית אֱלֹהִים (*bet 'elohim*) raising the question: Is אֱלֹהִים referring to Yahweh, or does it simply indicate "gods" in light of all the paganism being depicted in the account? Perhaps the ambiguity is deliberate: Micah thinks it will be a Yahwistic shrine, even while populating it with pagan gods! Towards the end of the pericope, the legitimate shrine is labeled again as בֵּית אֱלֹהִים, this time clearly pointing to the genuine cultic center of Yahweh at Shiloh (18:31). Amit considers Micah's "house of God" in 17:5 as Bethel (also see Gen 28:17, 22) for the following reasons: the location of Micah's shrine is not identified (Jdg 18:1, 8; 18:2, 13, especially when other sites are specifically noted: 17:7, 8, 9; 18:12); the cultic sites of Bethel and Dan were linked to each other (1 Kgs 12:26–33; 2 Kgs 10:29), and golden calves were placed there, one in each (in our story, too, the cultic items placed in Micah's shrine and in that of the Danites are identical); Bethel also had a non-Levitical, illegitimate, priesthood (1 Kgs 12:31–32; 13:33); and midrashic tradition connected Micah with Bethel (*b. Sanh.* 101a) (*Hidden Polemics*, 110–17).

19. Micah is never said to be a Levite. Therefore the "consecration" of his son as priest is entirely out of order, as irregular and heterodox as everything else he (and his mother) has done. "Consecration" is literally "filling the hand" (Jdg 17:5, 12; see Exod 28:41; 29:9, 29, 33, 35). It probably refers to the ceremonial filling of the appointee's hand with some token of his office. But in Jdg 18:4, the Levite tells the Danite spies that he had been "hired" suggesting that "it is the filling of the hand in quite another sense that occupies the Levite's mind!" (Webb, *Judges*, 433).

20. Micah, מִיכָיְהוּ (*mikayhu*, 17:1, 4), becomes מִיכָה (*mikah*) for the rest of the story.

The oddities involving the Levite are equally unwholesome: his inexplicable wanderings (17:7–9),[21] and his being hired for a pittance (17:10)[22] to be a private priest to a private man in a private shrine.[23] Micah's request that the Levite, described as "a young man" (17:7) become "a father" to Micah (17:10),[24] and the Levite's treatment by Micah as one of his, Micah's, sons (17:11) is also odd—a topsy-turvy relationship. Once the Levites had been the guardians of God's honor and reputation, executing those who worshiped idols (specifically, מסכה, *mskh*, "molten image" in Exod 32:4, 8, 25–29). Now, this Levite was the patron of an illegitimate shrine with idols and ephod and all (including a מסכה; Jdg 17:3, 4; 18:14, 17, 18). "He has lent his support to the perversion of his countryman, failed to keep Yahweh's ways, and demonstrated partiality to this man with money.... The religious establishment in Israel has been thoroughly infected with the Canaanite disease."[25] Apostasy!

Above all, there is the ambitious certitude of Micah that Yahweh will prosper him, now that he had a Levite as a priest (17:13), as if all that was needed was a combination of mechanically performed acts, however improper, that would automatically trigger blessings from deity like a good-luck charm. "[H]e is totally oblivious to the fact that his approach, specifically his capitalization on the presence of a Levite to manipulate the

---

21. The Levite's antecedents, that he was "from the family of Judah," are puzzling, for Judahites are not Levites. He "sojourned" in Bethlehem, suggesting again that he was not a Judahite, for the root גור, *gwr*, "to sojourn," is applied to one who "lives among people who are not his blood relatives" (Kellerman, "גור *gûr*," 443). The best explanation for his Judahite connection is that he was born to parents already living among the people of Judah; so "from the family of Judah" simply delineates his birthplace. But later we find out that the Levite was Jonathan, the son of Gershom, the son of Moses (Jdg 18:30), making him a Kohathite (Exod 6:18–20; 1 Chr 23:12–15). The Kohathites were assigned Ephraim, Dan, or western Manasseh (Josh 21:4–5, 20–26), not Bethlehem. In any case, the Levite left Bethlehem "to stay wherever he might find a place" (17:8, 9)—just a vagabond without any attachment to person, place, or deity, apparently. Interestingly, "sojourning there [Bethlehem]" (17:7) is גָּר־שָׁם (*gar-sham*); those same consonants form גֵּרְשֹׁם (*gershom*), Gershom, the name of the Levite's father (18:30). Incidentally, Deut 17:18 and 21:5 see Levites and priests as equivalent, the perspective of our pericope as well, though only descendants of Aaron (not of Moses, as was the Levite here, 18:30) could assume the priesthood (Num 3:10; 18:1–7).

22. And not for the remuneration demanded by Deut 18:1–5. Later, in Jdg 18:19–20, the Levite will accept a more lucrative offer with perks—this self-made priest delivers God-in-a-box to the highest bidder!

23. As opposed to serving in a community of priests for the community of God's people in the community's central shrine.

24. A title of honor, as an oracular advisor discerning divine will (see Gen 45:8; 2 Kgs 6:21; 8:9; 13:14).

25. Block, *Judges, Ruth*, 490.

deity, is fundamentally pagan."²⁶ Needless to say, Yahweh does not deign to prosper Micah and his foolish enterprises (as the latter had expected, 17:13). In the next section of this pericope, Micah's gods and his priest are appropriated by the marauding Danites, leaving Micah bereft of his rabbit's foot, his four-leaved clover, and his horseshoes.

In sum, between the two of them, "Micah and his mother have broken at least half of the Ten Commandments in only five verses . . . . They have created another god besides God; they have made an idol; they have used God's name wrongly; and Micah has stolen, thereby failing to honor his mother (and he may also have coveted along the way)."²⁷ And neither mother nor son (or even the grandson) seems to recognize the incongruities and ironies of their actions. This is a stark depiction of the sort of evil that had permeated generations of Israelite society under the judges. At the beginning of the book, the nation struggled with the temptation to consort with foreign gods (2:6—3:6). There is no such struggle now, at the end of the book: Israelites are cheerfully manufacturing their own gods and blurring the lines of division between false deities and the true God, Yahweh. The deterioration of moral values is worsening and is being passed on to every new generation. That the narrator comments on "Everyman" doing what was right in his own eyes (17:6), right after the events of 17:1-5, shows his disparagement of the indiscretions of Micah and Co.²⁸ Micah and his mother were not the exceptions, but the rule—the entire nation was corrupt. And all this is occurring in the Ephraimite hill country, the very place where the legitimate shrine of Yahweh was located—at Shiloh (18:31; 21:19).

One recalls the syncretism that had already brought trouble upon Israel: the ephod of Gideon (8:27) and the human sacrifice of Jephthah (11:30-31, 39). These events of Epilogue I are simply the consequences of what had been initiated earlier. The very multiplication of cultic items—idols, molten images, ephods, teraphim, shrines—are a dangerous indication of how low the nation had sunk. But it would get even worse.

---

26. Ibid., 489. And In 18:14 we see another detail of the cultic set up of Micah: he has an entire campus of religious paraphernalia: "in these *houses*"!

27. McCann, *Judges*, 120.

28. Likewise, the narrator's comment in 18:1a, following immediately upon the heels of Micah's actions in 17:6-13, is also a literary censure of what has just happened in that leaderless and godless society.

12.2. Judges 18:1–31

THEOLOGICAL FOCUS 12.2

12.2　Ungodly attitudes and activities invite the discipline of God (18:1–31).

NOTES 12.2

12.2　Ungodly attitudes and activities invite the discipline of God.

The Danites were searching for land because "until that day it [i.e., the land] had not fallen to them in the midst of the tribes of Israel as a possession" (18:1), despite the fact that they had already been allotted territory (Josh 19:40–48).[29] In other words, the parceled-out land had not yet been taken into possession at the time of the judges: Jdg 1:34–36 had already informed us that the Danites had been stymied in the conquest of their territory, confined by the Amorites into the hill country. So now they seek better vistas. "The Danites' response to the crisis is natural but humanistic. Instead of confessing their sin of unbelief and appealing to Yahweh for aid, they do what is right in their own eyes."[30] If we had seen a wayward Israelite or two (or three) in Judges 17, now we are shown a whole wayward *tribe* in Judges 18.

In 18:2, the Danites undertake a "sending" of spies, but without the benefit of divine initiative, sanction, or Spirit. There are a number of analogies between the account of the sending of spies in Numbers 12–14 and that in Judges 18 (albeit with only few verbal parallels); there are also significant contrasts as shown[31]:

---

29. See Num 34:2; Ezek 47:14, 18, 22 for analogous "falling" of the land, i.e., possession by the Israelites.

30. Block, *Judges, Ruth*, 494–95.

31. See O'Connell, *The Rhetoric of the Book of Judges*, 236. The similarities indicate a deliberate attempt to link the present even to the one in the past.

Element	Numbers 12–14	Judges 18
Analogies		
Spies sent	13:2–17	18:2
Arrival in hill country	13:7	18:2
Northern extent	13:21	18:28
רחב, rkhb	13:21 (= "Rehob")	18:10 (= "spacious")
Positive report: land	13:27; 14:7–8 ("very good")	18:7–10 ("very good")
Positive report: people	13:30; 14:9	18:7, 27–28
Contrasts		
Divine initiative	13:1–2	
Negative report	13:2–33; 14:36–37	
Negative response	14:1–4, 10, 36	
Weeping	14:39	
Conquest	14:40–45 (failure)	18:27–29 (success)
Aftermath	14:24, 30–31, 38 (success)	18:30 (failure)

While the entire enterprise of the Israelite spies in Numbers 12–14 commenced as a result of a divine initiate, the Danite endeavors were entirely of human origin (Jdg 18:1–3). Their attempt to hear from God through Micah's Levitical oracle (18:5–6) was utterly pagan. These spies, later, provide no negative reports about the people or the land. In fact, with repetitions of the land's accessibility and defenselessness (18:7, 27–28), the Danites are shown to be bereft of scruples. As cowardly opportunists and plunderers they steal Micah's idols and bribe his Levite/priest to accompany them (18:17–26). Unlike the Israelites in an earlier day, the tribespeople of Dan responded enthusiastically and promptly to their spies' rosy reports (18:11–13). The aftermath is failure, as their sanctuary ultimately is destroyed (18:30–31).[32]

Likewise, with the spy-story in Joshua 2 that is transformed into a parody in Judges 18, there are both similarities and contrasts[33]:

---

32. Ibid., 236–37.
33. See Block, *Judges, Ruth*, 496.

Joshua 2:1	Judges 18:2
And Joshua the *son of Nun* sent *two men*	And the *sons of Dan* sent *five men* from their family out of their whole number noblemen,
from Shittim, *as scouts* secretly,	*from Zorah and Eshtaol* *to scout* the land and search it,
saying, "Go, see *the land* especially Jericho." And they went, *and they came*	and they *said* to them, "Go, search *the land.*" And they came to the hill country of Ephraim,
to the house of a prostitute whose name was Rahab, *and they* lay *there.*	*to the house* of Micah, *and they* lodged *there.*

The differences between the accounts in Joshua 2 and Judges 19 are: the character of the host (Rahab, Josh 2:9–13; Micah, Jdg 18:6–7)—one becomes a Yahwist, the other is an idolater; the actions of the host—Rahab helps the nation, but Micah ensnares the entire nation in idolatry; and the character of the spies—they show חֶסֶד, *khesed*, ("lovingkindness"), to the host in Josh 2:13, but rob the host in Jdg 18:18–20. All this reflects how low the nation had sunk by the end of Judges.

The story continues with the Danite spies arriving at Micah's house and "recognizing" the voice of the Levite (18:3). Perhaps it was the latter's accent that gave him away; maybe they knew him from before. In any case, the Levite acquiesces to the request of the spies to "inquire of God," a typically pagan oracular inquiry (18:5; see Exod 18:15; 1 Sam 9:9; 22:15). They wanted an answer from *God* (אֱלֹהִים, *'elohim*), not Yahweh. Yet the Levite/priest replies in the name of Yahweh (Jdg 18:6), the only time the name occurs in Judges 18. But his answer is quite ambiguous: "In front of [נֹכַח, *nokakh*] Yahweh is your way in which you are going" (18:6). The semantic range of נֹכַח also includes "opposite of" (see Exod 26:35; 40:24; Josh 15:7; 18:17; as well as the only other uses of the word in Judges: 19:10; 20:43), thus making the outcome inscrutable: Yahweh might be for or against the Danites' undertaking. "Since the Levite has been and will be further depicted in the story as an arch-opportunist, his response, or better yet the narrator's report of his response, rivals a Delphic oracle in ambiguity."[34] But to the Danites, these seemingly auspicious words of the Levite legitimate the subsequent slaughter of harmless people (Jdg 18:10, 27). The "multi-layered irony" here is stunning: the Danites (abandoning their God-allotted territory) ask a Levite (who has left his allotted residence and is far from the central shrine) to inquire of idols and images made of pilfered silver to determine if their endeavor will prosper in God's will.[35] This story is as morally repugnant and grotesque as the one that preceded it in Judges 17!

When they return, the spies report that *God* (אֱלֹהִים) had "*given*" Laish into the Danites' hand (18:10), and that they should "*go*," "*take*," "*enter*," and "*possess*" the land (18:9). The combination of "go" and "possess" with deity's "giving" is particularly evocative of the Israelite conquest of the Promised Land (see Deut 1:8; 6:18; 8:1; 9:23; 10:11; 11:8; 11:31; Josh 1:11; almost always quoting God himself, and employing the same verbs). All of these hot-button terms, along with the invocation of deity, injects pious but insincere notes into an entirely human production.

Laish (or Leshem, Josh 19:47), was outside Israelite territory, about thirty miles north of the Sea of Galilee. These were a peoples dwelling "in quiet" and "in security" (Jdg 18:7). That "there was no one humiliating anything in the land, one taking possession forcibly," likely means that they were untroubled by any potential external takeover by hostile elements. The extended, and somewhat unclear clauses composed of participles and nominal phrases indicate the stable and secure situation of Laish and its inhabitants. So much so, in 18:9, the Danite spies report that what they scouted out was "very good," "spacious," and with "no lack of anything on the earth," occupied by "quiet" and "secure" people (18:9–10). Ironically, "quiet" (שָׁקַט, *shqt*, "rest") is the very attribute of peace that Yahweh had promised the Israelites (Josh 11:23; 14:15), and it was the very "rest" that had, until Gideon, been accomplished in the land by the judges (Jdg 3:11, 30; 5:31; 8:28). But now the restless Israelites (Danites) have to engage in wanton slaughter of a defenseless and peaceful people, disturbing the Laishites' "rest" to obtain "rest" for themselves. And this in a land *not* allotted to them, and without the borders of Israelite land. There is no indication that Laish was one of the cities Yahweh had intended the Israelites take over. Moreover, the helpless people of Laish are never the subject of an active verb, instead they get five participles: "living," "being quiet," "being secure," "not being humiliated," and "[not] being taken possession of" (18:7 and, later, a sixth tragic one,

---

34. Polzin, *Moses and the Deuteronomist*, 198.
35. Klein, *The Triumph of Irony*, 155.

"no one delivering," 18:28). In contrast, the report of the Danite spies have a number of active verbs: "arise," "go up," "we have seen," "be still," "go," "take," "enter," and "possess" (18:9).[36]

Besides, Ezek 38:10–11 has Yahweh explicitly condemning an attack on innocent people living "quietly" and "in security"; he calls it an "evil plan."[37] This was a clear violation of Deuteronomic war policies. In fact, Deut 20:10–15 stipulated that for non-Israelite cities at "a great distance" from Israelite settlements, an offer of peace had to be made first. Even if such an offer was rejected and a battle ensued, only the men were to be "struck with the sword," and everyone else and everything else spared (20:12–14; but see what happened in Jdg 18:27).[38] The wanton destruction of Laish by the Danites completely disregarded divine law. The conquering of Laish would not be very different in kind from their overpowering of Micah and appropriating his goods.

The account of the take over of Laish begins with a "setting out" (וַיִּסְעוּ, *wayyisʿu*, 18:11) and ends with a "setting up" (וַיָּשִׂימוּ, *wayyasimu*, 18:31; different verbs, but obviously alliterated).[39] The narrative could have moved directly from 18:11–13a to 18:27b–29 if the interest was only in the Danites acquisition of land. Instead, there is the apparent side story in 18:13b–18:27a that details the stealing of Micah's idols and his Levite, ensuring that the focus is maintained upon aberrant cultic practices and the resulting divine retribution.[40]

Wishing Micah "peace" (18:15), the Danites, armed and ready, steal his cultic accouterments and his patron, the Levite-priest (18:16–20). "Six hundred men armed with weapons of war" occurs thrice, redundant but threatening (18:11, 16, 17), demonstrating the cowardly action of the Danites as they intimidate Micah. The "taking" of the religious items is mentioned by the narrator four times (18:17, 18, 20, 27, each time with "took," לקח, *lqkh*); to this, one could add Micah's own woeful lament: "You have *taken* the gods which I made" (18:24). One remembers that לקח was used of Micah's own robbing in 17:2 (×2), and of his mother's "taking" the silver to have idols and images made (17:4). What was stolen, now gets stolen again, and will, one day, be stolen once more into captivity (18:30). In divine providence,

---

36. Marais, *Representation in Old Testament Narrative Texts*, 137.

37. Wong, *Compositional Strategy*, 39 n.35.

38. Chisholm, *Judges and Ruth*, 460. Native Canaanite populations, in contrast to more distant peoples, were condemned to חֵרֶם (*kherem*, the "ban" of holy war, Deut 20:16–18).

39. Six hundred armed men make the trip; including women and children, that number may be closer to 2,500, plus chattel (18:11, 21).

40. Block, *Judges, Ruth*, 503.

what Micah had done was being visited on his own head, with poetic justice: the stealer is stolen from, and false idols from a false private shrine now populate a false tribal shrine.[41]

Element	Judges 17	Judges 18
"Came" to Micah's house	17:8	18:2
Stealing: "take"	17:2 [×2]	18:17, 18, 20, 24, 27
Loot for "house of God"	17:3–4	18:31
Enticement of Levite	17:9–12	18:15, 18–20
Destruction of shrine	[Implied in Jdg 18]	18:30

All the culpable parties get their comeuppance, the consequence of moral promiscuity.

Interestingly, after the arrival of the Danites at Micah's house, the Levite who acted as Micah's priest is only referred to as the "priest"—no longer is he called a Levite. His changing sides has, apparently, been a mark of upward mobility, a promotion. Indeed, the offer to become the father and priest to an entire tribe (rather than remaining as the cult official for the house of one man) was what tempted the Levite to switch his allegiance, which he did with "gladness of heart" (18:19–20). Thereupon, he grabs Micah's idol, ephod, teraphim, and image from the five men who had taken them from Micah's shrine (18:17), thus effectively being reconsecrated in his new office,[42] and "went among the people," joining the migrating crowd as an honorary Danite (18:20).[43] This is nothing but an act of betrayal, but not at all surprising given the rest of the preposterous events of this pericope. Everyone is merely doing what was right in his eyes!

There cannot be a more disparaging label for the idolatrous items created by Micah than what comes out of his own mouth: "my gods that I made," not to mention the wretchedness of his utter dependence on them: "What do I have left?" (18:24). The theme of Micah's handcrafted gods is taken up by the narrator again in 18:27 and 18:31, always in a pejorative manner and as a pointed refusal to dignify these manmade relics by the term "gods."[44] Making a god for oneself was explicitly prohibited in the Decalogue (Exod 20:4). The plundering Danites belligerently point out to

---

41. See Amit, *Hidden Polemics*, 108.

42. By that action, the priest's "hand is filled" (= "consecrated," 17:5, 12) by the five men with these cultic paraphernalia.

43. Chisholm, *Judges and Ruth*, 458.

44. Davis, "Comic Literature," 159.

the protesting Micah that he still has his life and that of his household left . . . if he behaves (Jdg 18:25)!

With the same ruthlessness and inclemency they had exhibited toward Micah, the Danites move north and slaughter the peaceful but powerless denizens of Laish (18:27-28). Bauer notes that a "Yahweh war" (holy war) story has a number of elements: mustering of troops with trumpets, army labeled as Yahweh's people, men being consecrated, sacrifices being offered, deity being consulted, confirmation that Yahweh has "given . . . into your hand," Yahweh proceeding before the army, enemies identified as Yahweh's enemies, fear of God falling upon the enemy, the "ban" (חֵרֶם) being carried out, spoils consigned to Yahweh, etc. Of these, we see only a dubious consultation with "God" (אֱלֹהִים, 18:5-6), an equally groundless assertion that אֱלֹהִים has "given it into your hand" (18:10), and the partial חֵרֶם that fails to give Yahweh the spoils of war (18:27). Besides, this is the action of a single tribe and not one undertaken by the nation, as such wars were to have been. The Danites are simply engaging in "their own 'unholy' war of conquest, which has nothing to do with Yhwh."[45] One cannot but notice the difference between the description of Laish in 18:7 and in 18:27-28—the pathos is palpable:

Judges 18:7	Judges 18:27–28
secure/quiet and secure	quiet and secure
no oppressor humiliating	
	no one to deliver them
far from Sidon	far from Sidon
no dealings with anyone	no dealings with anyone

By 18:27-28, they *did* have an external oppressor humiliating—nay, slaughtering—them, and at that time they had no one to deliver them: another literary indictment of the Danites' cold-bloodedness and ungodliness.

After finishing up with Laish, the Danites promptly "set up *for themselves*" the idols they had stolen from Micah (18:30)—another entirely unsanctioned and unilateral transaction to serve the needs of these cultists, with no regard for, or input from, deity. And now, in 18:30, we suddenly learn that the Levite's name was Jonathan (יְהוֹנָתָן, *yhonatan* = "Yahweh has given"), a grandson of Moses—the height of irony![46] "Here is the crowning

---

45. Bauer, "Judges 18," 40-41. See Deut 13:12-18; 20:1-20 for the terms of a holy war.

46. The MT has "Manasseh" as the father of Gershom, but it is written with a suspended or superscripted נ, *n* (מְנַשֶּׁה, *mⁿshh*). Some medieval Hebrew manuscripts retain

scandal of the Danites' idolatrous shrine: it brought dishonor even on the revered name of Moses!"[47] Religious syncretism and wanton morals had infected the very agency designed to immunize the nation against these afflictions—the Levitical priesthood—and even the family of the one most esteemed in Israel. In sum, "Dan has not contributed to Israel's conquest of Canaan at all, but to Canaan's conquest of Israel. For it will not be Yahweh who is worshiped there, but Micah's idol."[48]

The Torah had explicitly commanded that Yahweh be worshiped "at the place which Yahweh your God will choose" (Deut 12:5, 11, 18; 31:11; etc.). Willfully negligent of such responsibilities and obligations, the Danite cult created a "renegade worship center," to rival the legitimate cultic site of Shiloh (Jdg 18:30–31)—an illegitimate station that persisted till the beginning of the Assyrian captivity of the Northern Kingdom in 734 BCE (2 Kgs 15:29).[49] The mention of Shiloh underscores the horrific nature of what the Danites had done. This would be a perennial symbol of Israel's apostasy: "Dan" becomes a byword for rank impiety in the prophets (2 Kgs 10:29; Jer 4:15; Amos 8:14; etc.).

Not surprisingly, the next verse (that commences Pericope 13) repeats the refrain of the absence of a king in Israel (19:1a).

> The story of Micah and the Levite thus represents the apostasy and the degeneration of Israelite society as it influences family life and cultic institutions. It is a world where everything is free for the taking by either those who can afford it or those who have the most power. With no eyes to behold and to measure, other than their own, chaos reigns in the world of the judges. Yahweh is absent except for the thwarted visions the characters might have had of Him. He did not act, nor did He speak. He was a mere memory within a curse or a blessing.[50]

משה, *mshh*, "Moses" (substantiated by LXX: Μωυσῆ, *Mōusē*). The change was likely made to protect Moses's reputation and to align this story, somewhat anachronously, with one who would sponsor and patronize the worst apostasy witnessed in Israel (2 Kgs 21:1–18). See Rashi (Yitzhaki), *Judges*, 150 and *b. B. Bat.* 109b. That Jonathan was the "son" of Gershom could also mean that he was simply a "descendant" of Gershom; 1 Chr 23:16 mentions the "sons" of Gershom, but names only one, Shebuel (also in 1 Chr 26:24). But the fact that Phinehas, the son of Eleazar, the son of Aaron, was the priest at Bethel in those days (Jdg 20:26–28) points to the proximity of these events to the exodus (see Exod 6:25; Num 25:7, 11; 31:6; Josh 22:30–32; etc.).

47. Webb, *Judges*, 448. "Our writer may appear to be dispassionate but there seem to be traces of acid in his ink" (Davis, "Comic Literature," 159).

48. Webb, *Judges*, 447.

49. Chisholm, *Judges and Ruth*, 54, 462.

50. Marais, *Representation in Old Testament Narrative Texts*, 138.

264　JUDGES

Israel's Canaanization is pretty much complete. Now all that remains is for the nation to fall apart, and fall apart it does, in the next two pericopes that close the book of Judges.

SERMON FOCUS AND OUTLINES

THEOLOGICAL FOCUS OF PERICOPE 12 FOR PREACHING
12 Godless leadership leads to godlessness in society that invites the discipline of God (17:1—18:31).

The godlessness depicted in this pericope by the various protagonists (Micah, his mother, the Levite, and the Danites) may be taken in several different directions in a sermon. Idolatry seems to be the common linkage between Judges 17 and 18, so perhaps that could be addressed. Thus, one of the marks of good leadership is proper worship (it is the negative, though, that is depicted in this pericope: no leadership, false worship).

Possible Preaching Outlines for Pericope 11

I. Godlessness: Micah, his mother, the Levite
　Namelessness of characters (except Micah and Jonathan)
　People doing what was right in their eyes (17:6; 18:1)
　Stealing, idolatry, cursing, and syncretism (17:1–6)
　Levite's support of an illegal shrine (17:7–13)
　Consequence: Micah's loss (18:21–27a)

II. Godlessness: Danites
　Parody of Numbers 12–14 and Joshua 2 (Jdg 18:2–13, 27–30)
　Danites' paganism (18:5–6, 14–20, 30)
　Danites' theft (18:21–27a)
　Danites' brutality (18:7–10, 27b–29)
　Consequence: Danites' loss (18:30–31)

IV. *Worship God alone!*[51]
　How specifically to worship God alone

Keeping the causes separate from the consequences yields another possibility:

I. CAUSE: Godlessness of Micah, his mother, the Levite, and the Danites
　Namelessness of characters (except Micah and Jonathan)
　People doing what was right in their eyes (17:6; 18:1)

---

51. If a break is needed in the series, a couple of weeks for topical sermons on true/biblical worship may be undertaken.

Stealing, idolatry, cursing, and syncretism (17:1–6)
   Levite's support of an illegal shrine (17:7–13)
   Parody of Numbers 12–14 and Joshua 2 (Jdg 18:2–13, 27–30)
   Danites' paganism (18:5–6, 14–20, 30)
   Danites' theft (18:21–27a)
   Danites' brutality (18:7–10, 27b–29)
II. CONSEQUENCE: Loss
   Consequence: Micah's loss (18:21–27a)
   Consequence: Danites' loss (18:30–31)
III. CONDUCT: *Worship God alone!*
   How specifically to worship God alone

PERICOPE 13

The Powerful and the Powerless

Judges 19:1–30

[Culpability of Husband, Father, Host, and Society in the Rape-Murder of a Woman]

REVIEW, SUMMARY, PREVIEW

Review of Pericope 12: In Jdg 17:1—18:31, Epilogue I, the misdemeanors of Micah, his mother, the Levite, and the Danites are depicted. Stealing, idolatry, cursing, syncretism, and brutality abound, without a single positive note sounded or a single positive character pictured. The result of godless leadership is a godless society. And the ultimate consequence is loss for all culpable parties.

Summary of Pericope 13: The thirteenth pericope of Judges (19:1–30) is the first part of Epilogue II (Jdg 19:1—21:25). Here there is complete anonymity of characters and a universal absence of deity. The near-total breakdown of law and order and the utter lack of any concern for the weak and defenseless in society is evidenced by the culpability of the raped and murdered woman's husband, her father, her host, and the Gibeahites—the horrific brutality of the latter rivaling those of Sodom and Gomorrah. This is what happens in a leaderless and godless society.

Preview of Pericope 14: The next pericope, Jdg 20:1—21:25, is the last in the book. Here an illicit holy war is undertaken by Israelites against Israelites, with such unity as was never visible in initiatives against foreigners anywhere in this book. To the end, the Israelites are rebellious and recalcitrant, even blaming God for what transpired: 65,000 killed with a tribe almost decimated. Then, more evildoing occurs—kidnappings and rapes. Everyone was, indeed, doing what was right in his own eyes.

13. Judges 19:1–30

> **THEOLOGICAL FOCUS OF PERICOPE 13**
>
> 13 Lack of concern and care for the weak and defenseless, combined with immorality, marks a godless and leaderless community (19:1–30).
>
> 13.1 A lack of concern and care for the weak and defenseless marks a godless and leaderless community (19:1–10).
>
> 13.2 A lack of morality marks a godless and leaderless community (19:10–30).

OVERVIEW

Epilogue II (Pericope 13: Jdg 19:1–30 and Pericope 14: Jdg 20:1—21:25), like Prologue I (Pericope 1: Jdg 1:1—2:5), deals with the socio-political situation of the Israelites.

Judges 1	Socio-political decline (Foreign wars: חֶרֶם, *kherem*; 1:17) (Judah to go first in battle: 1:1–2) (Treatment of women: 1:11–15)	Prologue I
Judges 2	Religious decline	Prologue II
Judges 3–16	Major and minor judges	Body
Judges 17–18	Religious collapse	Epilogue I
Judges 19–21	Socio-political collapse (Domestic wars: חֶרֶם; 21:11) (Judah to go first in battle: 20:18) (Treatment of women: 19:1–21:25)	Epilogue II

There is חֵרֶם in Prologue I (1:17), but these holy wars were divinely sanctioned undertakings against foreign enemies, and women were treated respectfully (1:12–16); in Epilogue II, חֵרֶם is humanly initiated against fellow Israelites (21:11) and women are treated disdainfully.[1] That both Epilogue I (Pericope 12: Jdg 17:1—18:31) and Epilogue II (Pericopes 13 and 14) deal with Levites who initiate action (17:3–5; 19:1—20:7) that subsequently involves the broader populace of tribe/nation is telling. The moral downfall has affected even the very institution responsible for the upkeep of the cult of Yahweh; the consequences for the nation are disastrous.

Both the Levites involved in these Epilogues leave Bethlehem for a place to stay—both are "sojourners" (17:7; and 19:1)—and they are the catalysts for the dire complications of their respective stories (17:7–8; and 19:10)[2]; both Epilogues bemoan the absence of a king in Israel (17:6; 18:1; and 19:1; 21:25); and both have narrative analogies to a prior historic event (Epilogue I to Numbers 12–14 [see Pericope 12]; Epilogue II to Genesis 19 [see below]).[3]

Every character in this pericope is anonymous—the Levite, his concubine, his father-in-law, his servant, and his Gibeahite host. In the next pericope, Pericope 14 (Jdg 20:1—21:25), too, except for Phinehas the priest in 20:28 (and that only a mention), no one else has a name. In a book that often names even its minor characters,[4] this namelessness in Epilogue II (Pericopes 13 and 14) is unsettling.[5] "The technique of namelessness illustrates the disintegration and dehumanization of society while it universalizes the characters in this sordid story. The Levite, the father, the old host, and the men of Gibeah are paradigmatic perpetrators, unforgivable, earning and deserving the contempt of history. And the nameless woman, immortalized, represents every victim—man, woman, or child—of the tyranny

---

1. These are the only two instances of חֵרֶם in the book.

2. The Levite in Judges 19 goes to Bethlehem (19:1–3); the other Levite came from Bethlehem (17:7).

3. O'Connell, *The Rhetoric of the Book of Judges*, 264–65. Other similarities between the two Epilogues include: priestly functionaries employing mantic devices to procure an oracle from God (18:5–6; and 20:17–28); a military contingent of six hundred men (18:11, 16, 17; and 20:47); holy wars, or something quite similar (18:27; and 20:48; 21:10–11); references to Shiloh (18:31; and 21:12, 19, 21); and violations of Deuteronomic legislations: Epilogue I ends with an illegitimate shrine set up by the Danites, Jdg 18:30–31 (see Deut 12:5, 11, 13–14, 18, 21, 26), and Epilogue II ends with the illegitimate rebuilding of cities by Benjamin, Jdg 21:23 (see Deut 13:16).

4. Even the servant of Gideon is named: Purah (7:10). Also see 1:10, 11; 4:2, 11; 7:25; 8:20; 11:1; etc.

5. Epilogue I (Pericope 12: Jdg 17:1—18:31) is also notable for a pervading sense of namelessness; except for Micah, one of the protagonists, and Jonathan, the Levite (his name merits only a fleeting mention in 18:30), the rest of the characters are anonymous.

of the strong over the weak."[6] Not only does this anonymity universalize "everyone" who did "what was right in his own eyes" (21:25), the narratival dehumanization is a powerful statement of how the value of human life and individual morality, particularly relating to women, has hit rock bottom in Canaanized Israel.

This first pericope of Epilogue II (Pericope 13: Jdg 19:1–30) describes the rape and murder of one Israelite woman—viewed by the nation as a crime. The second pericope of Epilogue II (Pericope 14: Jdg 20:1—21:25) describes two separate rapes/seizures, of four hundred and of two hundred Israelite women, respectively—but now viewed by the nation as acceptable. Nothing that has happened as a national response to the violent crime and abuse in Judges 19 has made the status of women any better or the situation in the nation any safer in Judges 20–21. Indeed, things have only gotten worse.[7] Appropriately enough, Epilogue II is bounded on either side by the dire remark of the narrator: "there was no king in Israel" (19:1; 21:25), not to mention the twofold repetition in Epilogue I of the same lament (17:6; 18:1).

17:6	"no king in Israel"; "every man did what was right in his eyes"
18:1	"no king in Israel"
19:1	"no king in Israel"
21:25	"no king in Israel"; "every man did what was right in his eyes"

Here in Pericope 13: Jdg 19:1–30, besides the namelessness of its characters, deity is also completely absent, mentioned neither as Yahweh nor even as אֱלֹהִים (ʾelohim, "God"): he is never referred to, either by the protagonists or even by the narrator. Even when he is present in Pericope 14: Jdg 20:1—21:25,[8] there is a strange reticence about Yahweh and a reserved distance that he maintains from his people, as he permits them to suffer the consequences of their folly and sacrilegious behavior.

13.1. Judges 19:1–10

THEOLOGICAL FOCUS 13.1

13.1 A lack of concern and care for the weak and defenseless marks a godless and leaderless community (19:1–10).

---

6. Reis, "The Levite's Concubine," 146.
7. Satterthwaite, "'No King in Israel,'" 85.
8. See 20:1, 2, 18, 23, 27–28; 21:1, 3, 5, 7–8.

NOTES 13.1

13.1 A lack of concern and care for the weak and defenseless marks a godless and leaderless community.

Once again, a Levite is involved in the initial matters of a pericope (19:1; see 17:7). After the nefarious activities of the Levite in the preceding pericope, we are immediately suspicious: What is this one going to do? And the last time we encountered a concubine in Judges (8:31), things got unstable very quickly (the story of Abimelech in Pericope 8: Jdg 8:33—10:5). Tragedy is, no doubt, looming on this horizon as well.

The Levite maintains a concubine (19:1), but it is unclear whether he had a wife, too, though it sounds unlikely. Perhaps he maintained only a concubine "for purposes of sexual gratification or housekeeping (or both), possibly because he could not afford the bride price of a wife."[9] His "taking her for himself" (19:1) suggests she is more property than partner. But the fact that the narrator calls her father the Levite's "father-in-law" (19:4, 7, 9) gives the relationship between the couple a certain degree of legitimacy.

What exactly the concubine did—"play the harlot"—and why she left the Levite to go to her father's house have been cruxes in this narrative (19:2). The phrase זנה (*znh*) + עַל (*'al*) + 3rd person masculine singular suffix (19:2, usually translated: "play the harlot against him") is unusual. Elsewhere the violated party in harlotry is never indicated with the preposition עַל; rather the victim is denoted with the prepositions מִן (*min*, Ps 73:27), מֵאַחֲרֵי (*me'akhare*, Hos 1:2), מִתַּחַת (*mitakhat*, Hos 4:12), or מֵעַל (*me'al*, Hos 9:1).[10] If in fact "she [the concubine] played the harlot against him [the Levite]," it seems unlikely she would have then gone away to her father's house.[11] Instead of harlotry, the LXX^A has ὠργίσθη αὐτῷ, *ōrgisthē autō*, "she was angry with him"; the LXX^B has ἐπορεύθη ἀπ' αὐτοῦ, *eporeuthē ap' autou*, "she went away from him." But these still do not explain why exactly she was being angry with him or rejecting him.

---

9. Klein, *The Triumph of Irony*, 162–63. Abraham's wife, Keturah, is labeled both "wife" (Gen 25:1) and "concubine" (1 Chr 1:32). The Levite's concubine becomes his "maidservant" in Jdg 19:19. Another instance of a concubine being called a maidservant is in 9:18 (see with 8:31).

10. See Chisholm, *Judges and Ruth*, 489 n.76. The syntax of Jdg 19:2 does occur in Ezek 16:16, but it is obvious there that the harlotry was being committed "*upon* [עַל]" the high places, not *against* any individual.

11. Adultery would have been punishable by death (Lev 20:10; Deut 22:22) though, of course, no one was following the law in those days; rather, "every man was doing what was right in his own eyes" (Jdg 17:6; 21:25).

Reis reads עַל + the masculine suffix as "for/on account of/because of/ on behalf of . . . him"; thus וַתִּזְנֶה עָלָיו (*wattizneh ʿalayw*) is: "and she was prostituting *for* him [the Levite]." She adds that whatever the status of the concubine, prostitution was out of bounds, and so the exploited woman was within her rights to abandon her husband and leave for her father's home. Such a reading has the advantage of explaining why the Levite chose to go to her only four months later (19:2), perhaps when he was in need of more ill-gotten gains; he may have expected her to have cooled off a bit by then.[12] And it would also fit his plan to "speak to her heart," to smooth-talk her into returning with him (19:3).

But quite strangely, the "girl's father" seems to have been *glad* to see the Levite (19:3), when one would have expected him to have been outraged by the treatment meted out to his daughter (as Samson's father-in-law was, 15:1–2). The term "father of the young woman," אֲבִי הַנַּעֲרָה, *ʾabi hannaʿarah*, is found elsewhere in the OT only in Deuteronomy 22. This text of the Torah deals with charges of non-virginity brought against his wife by a newlywed husband (22:13–14). If the charges were found to be true, she was to be stoned (22:20–21). On the other hand, if the charges were deemed false, with "the young woman's father" (אֲבִי הַנַּעֲרָה ×3, in 22:15, 16, 19) and mother producing evidence substantiating the innocence of their daughter (22:15–17), she was to be freed and her husband whipped and fined (22:18–19).[13] Reis suspects that the author of Judges specifically echoed the unique אֲבִי הַנַּעֲרָה to contrast that protective father in Deuteronomy 22 who zealously guards his daughter, with this nonchalant father in Judges 19 who does not. The least the latter could have done was return the bride-price and redeem his daughter from the Levite's sex-slavery.[14] To emphasize this contrast between the responsible father of the bride in the Torah and the irresponsible one in Judges, אֲבִי הַנַּעֲרָה resounds six times in seven verses (19:3, 4, 5, 6, 8, 9). In fact, often the term is redundant; that man could simply have been called "her father" (אָבִיהָ, *ʾabiha*) as in 19:2, 3. Indeed, twice "father-in-law" and "the young woman's father" occur in apposition (19:4, 9)—unduly repetitive—bookending the scenes at the father's house (19:4–9).[15] "He is her

---

12. Reis, "The Levite's Concubine," 129, 131. Schneider thinks that in a day without the benefit of modern diagnostic techniques, the four months may have had to do with ensuring she was not pregnant (*Judges*, 253).

13. Ostensibly the evidence was "bloodstained sheets resulting from a ruptured hymen" (see Deut 22:17) (Merrill, *Deuteronomy*, 302–3).

14. Reis, "The Levite's Concubine," 132.

15. Similar repeats of relationships between protagonists—specifically to emphasize those relationships as integral to the theological thrust of the narrative—are also found in the story of the fratricide in Genesis 4, where "brother" is mentioned six times

father, father, father, father, father, father, but he does not act like a father. The stress on his kinship and her peril bares the heinousness of the father's indifference to his daughter's plight, and the reader recognizes that it is not the woman, but rather her father, whom the author denigrates."[16] He is the one who is *glad* to see the abuser of his daughter (19:3)![17]

Notice Jdg 19:6: "and they sat and they ate, *the two together*, and they drank." Reis observes that in the OT, "there are only four instances in which an extraneous word or phrase ['and' or 'not,' or the content of what is eaten or drunk, or parallelisms[18]] separates eat from drink and the verb drink also occupies the end of the sentence or clause, a position of emphasis in Hebrew syntax. Each of the four occurrences displaying these two linguistic elements bears a suggestion of alcoholic excess" (Gen 27:25; Ruth 3:7–8; Jdg 19:6; 1 Sam 1:9). Here in Jdg 19:6, "[t]he author cues by vocabulary ('two of them together'), distinguishes by rarity, and reinforces by syntax, so that the reader suspects drinking to excess": "and they sat and they ate, the two [of them] together, and they drank."[19]

Even the invitations to eat are directed exclusively to the Levite: "sustain yourself [with a piece of bread]" (19:5, 8) is a masculine *singular* imperative. While we can be hopeful that "*they* ate and drank" in 19:4 included the woman, that is certainly not the case in 19:6 ("and they ate, the *two* [of them] together, and they drank") and 19:8 ("and they ate, the *two* [of them]")—"two" indicating only the Levite and his host, the father-in-law. We wonder if the woman is eating at all! In any case, there are multiple bouts of such consuming and imbibing, sufficient to make the heart merry (19:4, 6, 9).[20] That the woman is somewhere in the background is hinted at in 19:8,

---

in 4:8 (×2), 9 (×2), 10, 11; in the account of a father commanded to sacrifice his son in Genesis 22, where "father" and/or "son" are mentioned fifteen times in 22:2 (×2), 3, 6, 7 (×3), 8, 9, 10, 12 (×2), 13, 16 (×2); and in the narrative of incest in 2 Samuel 13, where "brother" and/or "sister" are mentioned twenty-one times in 13:1, 2, 3, 4 (×2), 5, 6, 7, 8, 10, 11, 12, 20 (×5), 22, 26, 32 (×2). Incidentally, the only other "father-in-law," חֹתֵן, *khoten*, ever mentioned in the OT is Moses's father-in-law (Jdg 1:16; 4:11; besides Exod 3:1; 4:18; and several instances in Exodus 18; and Num 10:29).

16. Ibid., 133.

17. Incidentally, there is another father-in-law in Judges, though he is not labeled as such: the father of Samson's Philistine wife. This non-Israelite father-in-law is far more protective of and concerned for his daughter (15:1–2) than the Israelite specimen thereof in this pericope.

18. E.g., 2 Sam 12:3: "ate from his morsel and drank from his cup."

19. Ibid., 134.

20. Notice that on the fifth day, "they ate" (19:8), and then the father-in-law urges the Levite to remain "that your heart may be merry" (19:9). Thus far, they had eaten *and* drunk (19:4, 6). This pairing suggests that the "eating" in 19:8 goes with "making your heart merry [i.e., *by drinking*]" in 19:9.

where the verb "wait," is a masculine *plural*, even though the verse begins by referring only to the Levite (*"he* awoke early"), and though the host's other imperative in the same verse, "sustain yourself," is masculine singular. Also, later when the party leaves the house of the young woman's father, *"he* arose, and *he* departed, and *he* came" to the precincts of Jebus (19:10). Somewhere in the cracks is the young woman, wraithlike and unreal—at least in the eyes of the men in her life.[21] Strikingly—or perhaps *not* strikingly!—the woman utters not a word and no one ever talks to her in this pericope (at least not while she is alive; see 19:28 when her corpse is addressed by the Levite).

Also notice the number of time-stamps given: in 19:4 ("three days"); in 19:5 ("fourth day," "awoke early," "morning"); in 19:8 ("fifth day," "awoke early," "morning," "stretching/declining of the day" [i.e., "afternoon"]); and in 19:9 ("day is sinking," "evening," "spend the night," "day has declined," "spend the night," "awake early," "tomorrow"). The narrator wants us to be aware of the clock ticking and the male merrymaking going on hour after hour, as the woman, silent and still, invisible and defenseless, suffers ignored.

The "young woman's father" is obsequious in his urging the Levite to stay, wanting to continue the festivities: 19:6 ("*please* be willing"); 19:8 ("*please* sustain yourself"); 19:9 ("behold, *please*" and "*please* spend the night").[22] All of this shows the callousness of the אֲבִי הַנַּעֲרָה and his utter lack of concern for his daughter's plight of being pimped by the Levite. And to add insult to injury, finally the father permits his daughter to be taken by her abuser (19:10). All throughout, not a word from the woman. "Now the concubine has nowhere to run. Her father will not safeguard her; he will just return her to her husband, and in this lawless land, a woman under no man's protection would be every man's prey. She does not know that her violent and agonized death will soon bring an end to the lifetime of wretchedness she sees before her."[23] This was an utter lack of concern for the weak and defenseless.

---

21. While 19:15 has "no man took *them* [Levite + concubine + servant] into the house," notice the number of instances where the woman is rendered invisible: "and *he* came and *he* sat in the square of the city" (19:15); "a man, a traveler" (19:17); "no man will take *me* into his house" (19:18); and "and he took *him* into his house" (19:21)—all referring to the Levite alone. Yes, the male servant in the party (see 19:11–13) is also excluded in these statements, but servants are not generally integral family members; besides, the servant in this case has not been referred to in the prior journey of the Levite (19:3) and his stay at his father-in-law's place; and, at best, this equates the concubine, the unofficial wife, with a servant—not a mark of respect, I daresay.

22. The particle נָא, *na*, indicates the interjection.

23. Ibid., 136.

13.2. Judges 19:10–30

> **THEOLOGICAL FOCUS 13.2**
>
> 13.2   A lack of morality marks a godless and leaderless community (19:10–30).

NOTES 13.2

13.2   A lack of morality marks a godless and leaderless community.

The Levite's party decides not go into Jebusite land because it was foreign (19:11–12), but instead arrives at an Israelite town, Gibeah of Benjamin (19:13, 16). The journey of 19:11–14 is structured as an *inclusio*[24]:

A   Narrative: Bethlehem → Jebus (19:11a): "day was almost gone"
   B   Dialogue: servant (19:11b): "come"; "spend the night"
      C   Dialogue: master (19:12): "city of foreigners" vs. "sons of Israel"
   B'   Dialogue: master (19:13): "come"; "spend the night"
A'   Narrative: Jebus → Gibeah (19:14): "sun went in"

The speeches in B and B' have the same structure: imperative of הלך (*hlk*, "come") + cohortative ("let us turn aside" or "let us draw near") + place ("city of the Jebusites" or "one of these places") + "and spend the night" + ב (*b*, "in") + place ("it" or "Gibeah or Ramah"). The speech in C is the center of this *inclusio*: it reveals the fateful decision of the Levite to avoid the city of foreigners and to stay in a town of the sons of Israel (19:12). Disastrously, the "sons of Israel" turn out to be no better than the "foreigners," and are arguably even worse. The Canaanization of Israel will be manifest soon!

The caravan turns in to Gibeah of Benjamin but no one takes them in (19:14–15), until an old man, himself a "sojourner" from Ephraim and an alien, offers the travelers hospitality for the night (19:16).[25] In fact, the old man's insistence that the travelers not spend the night in the square (19:20) indicates that he was aware of the dangers lurking at night in Gibeah.

The Levite claims he is going to the "house of Yahweh" (in the LXX, it is "my house," 19:18, followed in most English translations). It is unclear if this is a sanctuary in his home (as it was in Micah's, 17:5–13), or if he was hinting that he was a priest. In any case, this is the first time Yahweh shows

---

24. From Fokkelman, *Reading Biblical Narrative*, 109.

25. That he does not entirely belong in Gibeah is further hinted at by the fact that he does "his work" in "*the* field"—ostensibly not his, for he is not local (19:16).

up in this episode, and it seems to be an attempt by the Levite to put a glossy sheen on events: it would not have done for him to confess that he had gone to pick up his concubine to resume his abuse of her in sex-trafficking. So the Levite, in character, appears to be deceptive in his responses to his host, "a mere façade of piety, offered for the consumption of the old man to make the Levite appear more sympathetic." The Levite declares, "No man will take *me* into his house" (19:18), but the narrator had noted earlier that "no man took *them* into the house" (19:15). Lapsley thinks this is part of the narrator's depiction of the Levite as "one who cares more for himself then he does for those in his care."[26] Well, we already knew that!

At any rate, the hospitality of the old man in Gibeah resembles that of the young woman's father: both involve male conviviality—"eating and drinking" (19:4, 6, 8 and 19:21), and "making merry" (19:6, 9 and 19:22). That this bout of carousing ends in a horrific sexual assault (see below), with both old man and Levite at least partially culpable, leads us to an inescapable conclusion: "Working back from the end to the beginning, we see that the crime, for which he and his host are partly responsible in a hardly fathomable but certainly visible way, is by virtue of the structure linked to the callousness of the two men, which casts a backward shadow. We now understand what value label we should attach to the extensive boozing in Bethlehem: self-indulgence and materialism."[27] If this second round of festivity and gaiety ended in tragedy, besmirching the two men's nonchalant fellowship, then that earlier sequence of revelry must be seen as equally unseemly and unwarranted.

That night, while the Levite and his host are making merry, the traveling party is attacked by the townsfolk who should have shown them benevolence (19:22). The ruffians involved are "men, the sons of Belial" (19:22 and 20:13), and they desire to engage in homosexual gang rape.[28] "That he

---

26. *Whispering the Word*, 43. The disjunctive clause that concludes 19:15 is also premonitory ("and no man was taking them to the house to spend the night"): something was wrong in this Israelite township, where even routine hospitality to travelers, an integral part of ancient Near Eastern culture, was missing.

27. Fokkelman, *Reading Biblical Narrative*, 109–10.

28. "Belial," "death," and "Sheol" are synonymously parallel in Ps 18:4–5. Perhaps this is why Belial, in intertestamental, rabbinic, and early Christian literature (1QM 13:11, 16; 15.3; *Jub* 1.20; *T. Reuben* 2:2; 2 Cor 6:15; etc.), refers to an evil supernatural being. Here in Jdg 19:22, the "sons of Belial" describes people who reflect the horribly depraved state of society in Gibeah and, indeed, in all Israel (Webb, *Judges*, 466). Elsewhere in the OT the term describes the obnoxious rabble and vile predators parasitic on society and rebellious against God, causing havoc and creating chaos: Deut 13:13; 1 Sam 2:12; 10:27; 25:17; 30:22; 2 Sam 23:6; 1 Kgs 21:10, 13; Prov 6:12; 16:27; etc. "To know" (Jdg 19:22; as also in Gen 4:1; 19:5, 8; Num 31:17; 1 Kgs 1:4) means to have carnal knowledge.

[the Gibeahite host] should volunteer his own daughter is one thing; that he should volunteer the Levite's concubine is another; but that he volunteer either is unimaginable. But then, he is only doing what is right in his own eyes!"[29] The subsequent ignominy and barbarity stretches from dusk in 19:14 to dawn in 19:26.

There are some very ominous tones sounded in the similarities between the episode in Jdg 19:11–30 and that in Genesis 19 (the Sodom and Gomorrah story); there are both thematic and linguistic parallels, portraying the utter depravity of Israel at the end of the book of Judges[30]:

Elements	Genesis 19:1–11	Judges 19:11–30
"Evening"	19:1	19:16
"Sat in the gate/square"	19:1	19:15
"Turning aside"	19:2	19:15
"Spend the night in the square"	19:2	19:20
Host, a "sojourner"	19:9	19:16
"Entering house"	19:3	19:21
"Washing feet"	19:2	19:21
"Eating" and "drinking"	19:3 (מִשְׁתֶּה, *mishteh*, "feast")	19:21 (שתה, *shth*, "drink")
"Men of the city"	19:4	19:22
"Surrounded the house"	19:4	19:22
Call to "bring out" guest	19:5	19:22
Threat "to know" (rape)	19:5, 8	19:22
Host "goes out"	19:6	19:23
Host protests "wickedness"	19:7–8	19:23
Host offers two women	19:8	19:24
Offers to "bring them out"	19:8	19:24
Permits rape: "Do to them …"	19:9	19:24
"… what is good in your eyes"	19:9	19:24
"But do not do anything …"	19:9	19:24
Consequence (Lot/concubine)	19:9–11 (escape)	19:25–28 (death)
Aftermath: ruin	19:12–29	19:29–21:24

All of these similarities between Genesis 19 and Judges 19 "depict the inverted moral condition of Israel, the utter perversity to which the Israelites have sunk, at the conclusion of the period of the judges."[31] Indeed, Israel had become Canaan!

---

29. Younger, *Judges, Ruth*, 357.

30. See O'Connell, *The Rhetoric of the Book of Judges*, 250–52; and Block, *Judges, Ruth*, 532–33.

31. Klein, *The Triumph of Irony*, 172. Other links include: "rise early and go on your way" (Gen 19:2; Jdg 19:9); "wait" (Gen 19:16; Jdg 19:8); "urge strongly/pressed" (Gen

These stories are not about hospitality. They are about the brutish depths to which people sink when God's laws are flouted and no civil authority legislates their observance. Withholding hospitality is a minor measure of the inhumane behavior to which Genesis 19 and Judges 19 bear witness. I propose that the far more appalling expressions of humankind's descent into savagery are a cowardly parent offering his children to a howling mob and a callous husband offering his wife. . . . For the Levite from Ephraim, the father-in-law from Bethlehem, the old host, and the citizens of Gibeah to match and surpass the Sodomites in wrongdoing shows the thorough and pervasive regression of the congregation of Israel. The biblical author holds up the mirror of Sodom, and the reader sees Israel reflected.[32]

It is not insignificant that in the accounts of the only three rapes in the OT, נְבָלָה (*nabalah*, "folly/disgrace") is mentioned: Gen 34:7 (the rape of Dinah by Shechem); Jdg 19:23, 24; 20:6, 10 (the rape of the Levite's concubine by the vermin of Gibeah); and 2 Sam 13:12 (the rape of Tamar by Amnon). Elsewhere, the word, used often of sexual trespass, describes actions that warrant terminal punishment on occasion (see Deut 22:21; Jdg 20:6, 10; Jer 19:23–24; etc.). All of this is tacit finger-pointing by the narrator at a despicable incident that has taken place in Israel. "Although the text is remarkably free of the narrator's own evaluative comments, the negative picture of Israel is fleshed out with the author's skillful portrayal of the characters. By these and other literary means the reader is drawn into one of the darkest pictures of Israelite life in the entire Old Testament. But the narrator leaves it to the reader to draw the implications from the conversations and the events themselves."[33] Canaanization, indeed!

It is striking that the host abhors the "*doing* of evil" (19:23) and the "*doing* of folly/disgrace" (19:23, 24) against the male (guest), but permits the wicked Gibeahites' "*doing* what is good in your own eyes" to the females (guest and daughter; 19:24). He even prefaces this invitation with an exhortation to the rapacious mob to "ravish/afflict" (or "abuse," ענה, '*nh*[34]) the two women he was offering! Such an encouragement was something even

---

19:3, 19; Jdg 19:7); "dawn rising" (Gen 19:15; Jdg 19:25); "rise" (Gen 19:14, 15; Jdg 19:28). Block notes that every element in Genesis 19 has its counterpart in Judges 19. In fact, if each instance of a direct object marker (את, '*et*) and the following substantive is counted as a single word, the total in each text is identical—sixty-nine words (*Judges, Ruth*, 534).

32. Reis, "The Levite's Concubine," 140.

33. Block, *Judges, Ruth*, 520–21.

34. The *piel* of this verb often indicates rape: Gen 34:2; Deut 22:29; 2 Sam 13:12, 14, 22, 32; Lam 5:11.

Lot in Sodom did not lower himself to, in Genesis 19. Gibeah, thus, had "out-sodomed" Sodom! But that was the underlying problem in those days, with every man "doing what was right in his eyes" (Jdg 17:6; 21:25).[35] The tenets of hospitality and the norms of sexuality were being grossly violated in this episode. Host, guest, and the rabid rabble are not very different. All are "enmeshed in the same evil, and symptomatic of the same basic, moral sickness."[36]

Upon the evildoers' refusal to accept the female alternatives (19:25a), it seems the host was in a quandary, for the next thing we see is the Levite, without any further ado, seizing his concubine and thrusting her outside (19:25b)—he was in no way going to be humiliated or abused himself.[37] The rest of the harrowing scene is thankfully not detailed, but simply summed up in three verbs: "they raped her, and they abused her . . . , and they let her go" (19:25c).[38] And this went on "all night"!

One wonders where the rest of Gibeah was that night. Should those "sons of Israel" (19:12) not have arrived to protect the travelers from the malevolence and abuse of these "sons of Belial"? Clearly there is collective responsibility here, intensified later in the entire tribe of Benjamin extending protection to the guilty (20:13).[39]

At dawn the woman "comes" and "falls" at the door of the old man's house (19:26): this is the first and only time the woman becomes the subject of active verbs—and it would be her last series of actions in life. Too weak to go further, too weak to knock, too weak to call out, the unfortunate woman collapses at the door with her hand on the threshold (19:27). "The image of safety and rest inside the door stands in marked contrast to the image of suffering and abandonment outside the door. . . . This detail describing the disposition of the woman's hands functions like a zoom lens, mercilessly drawing the reader toward an excruciating vision of the woman's agony and

---

35. The corresponding "*doing* evil in the eyes of Yahweh" is a common theme in Judges (2:11; 3:7, 12; 4:1; 6:1; 10:6; 13:1).

36. Webb, *Judges*, 468.

37. This is the easiest reading, to assume that "the man" in 19:25b is the Levite, since it is the concubine, not the virgin daughter of the host, who is delivered to the gangsters of Gibeah. Besides, the old man, it appears, is still outside the house, having gone to plead with the attackers (19:23a). Having heard the negotiations (19:23b–24), the Levite, from inside the house, ejects his concubine (19:25). Chisholm also notes a syntactical parallel in 2 Sam 1:11 ("and David seized [חזק, *khzq*] his clothes"), where David is both the subject of the verb ויחזק, *wayyakhazeq* (the same verb in the same form as in Jdg 19:25), and the antecedent of the pronominal suffix (*Judges and Ruth*, 493n87).

38. Why the savages finally accepted the concubine when they had demanded the Levite is unclear.

39. See Pericope 14: Jdg 20:1—21:25.

the horror of the suffering she endured."[40] One cannot imagine a more poignant scene!

The narrator's specification of the Levite as "her *master*" (19:26) is doubtless pejorative, for that term does not indicate a normal marital relationship; even a union with a concubine was worthy of more respect.[41] Instead, the affiliation between Levite and concubine is depicted as that between master and slave, reflecting the callous disposal by the "master" of his "slave" to the whims of a marauding horde for abuse. Besides, the woman's desperate (but vain) attempt to return to "where her master was" (19:26) points to the security of her master *inside* the dwelling, while she, his concubine, was being brutally abused *outside*.

Here, in 19:26, for the first time the concubine is referred to simply as "a woman." Till now she was "a woman, a concubine" (19:1), "concubine" (19:2, 9, 24, 25), or "a young woman" (19:3, 4, 5, 6, 8, 9—always in connection with her father), or a "maidservant" (19:19). The only time the concubine is referred to without relation to her male relatives is here, as she lies raped and dying, discarded by all . . . and she is called "a woman!" Prostituted by her husband, abandoned by her father, and now brutally raped and left for dead by hoodlums, the woman's suffering paints a horrific picture of the situation in Israel at the time of the judges. Canaanization!

The unusually frequent references to time of day in first episode of this pericope was noted earlier in relation to the extended merrymaking of the Levite and his father-in-law (19:4, 5, 8, 9). There are even more such notices in the second episode of this pericope. Altogether, the time-stamps in this pericope are remarkable for the number of them that relate to darkness or near darkness: "awoke early in the morning" (19:5, 8, 9), "spend the night" (19:6, 7, 9 [×2], 10, 11, 13, 15, 20), "stretching/declining of the day" (19:8), "day is sinking into the evening" (19:9), "day has declined" (19:9), "day was almost gone" (19:11), "sun went in" (19:14), "evening" (19:16), "all night" (19:25), "until morning" (19:25), "ascent of dawn" (19:25), and "turning of the morning" (19:26). This dreadful and dark sequence concludes only

---

40. Lapsley, *Whispering the Word*, 47–48.

41. The Levite is identified as a Levite only at the beginning and towards the end of the story, in the first and last scenes in which he makes an appearance in Judges (19:1; 20:4). But he is "master" to the servant accompanying him (19:11, 12), and now he is "master" of his concubine, as well (19:26). And the first time (and the only time in Judges 19) that the Levite refers to the woman, he calls her a "maidservant" (19:19). In that same verse he also calls his "servant" (the male attendant labeled by the narrator as a "servant," 19:11, 13), a "young man." Apparently, in the Levite's eyes the male servant had become a young man, and his young woman had become a maidservant: a switching of roles. Even the servant, it seems, was held by the Levite in higher standing than he did his concubine!

when we are told that the woman lay at the door of the old man's house "until light" (19:26). "With these chronological notes the narrator has given his verdict on the spiritual and moral state of Israel. The light of the knowledge of Yahweh and 'doing what is right in his eyes' have been eclipsed by the depravity of the human soul expressed in 'doing what is good in one's own eyes.'"[42] The darkness of Canaanization has taken over Israel—its land, its people, and their souls.

The next morning, the Levite "*arises*" and opens the doors, for the express purpose of departing Gibeah ("to *go* on his way," 19:27), not to see what happened the night before or to check on his concubine or to seek justice for the perpetrators of the abuse or anything of the sort. That "her master arose in the morning" (19:27)—"chilling in what it implies by its sheer ordinariness"—tells us he slept well that night![43] He has no complaint, no indignation, no remorse, no concern, no questions. All that happened the night before might just as well have been a bad dream as far as the Levite was concerned. And in the morning, he just wants to be off, to "*arise*" and "*go*," taking over where he had left off the night before. But then—"behold!" (19:27)—he sees the tragedy on the threshold (almost trips over the victim, we suppose) and callously tells the dying (already dead?) woman, "*Arise*, and let us *go*" (19:28), the same verbs that described the man's actions upon waking (19:27).[44] There is no answer from the victim, so he puts her on his donkey, "*arises*" again and "*goes*" home (the third instance of this pair of collocated verbs in 19:27–28). It is almost as if the woman lying in front of the door was an interruption to his routine of *arising* and *going*. There is no emotion on his part, no attempt to check on the woman (forget any effort to revive her), no responsibility and no care in the world, apparently—a microcosm of the calloused state of the Israelites towards evil, towards their fellowmen, and towards Yahweh: Canaanization!

At the beginning of the story, the Levite was "her husband/man" (אִישָׁהּ, '*ishah*, 19:3); after being labeled "her master[s]" in 19:26–27 (אֲדֹנֶיהָ, '*adoneha*), he finally ends up as "the man" (הָאִישׁ, *ha'ish*, 19:28). He has now been stripped—perhaps it is better to say he has stripped himself—of any obligation to the raped woman. "His relationship with her is now defined purely in terms of rule and power. He takes her home because she is his property,

---

42. Block, *Judges, Ruth*, 540. That the terms, "stretching/declining of the day" (19:8), "day is sinking into the evening" (19:9), and "turning of the morning" (19:26) are relatively rare, underscores the symbolic force of pervading darkness in the narrative.

43. Webb, *Judges*, 469.

44. As was noted, this is the first and only time the Levite addresses his concubine in the entire narrative, though, of course, she is now presumably dead. After his initial intention "to speak to her heart," 19:2, he now speaks to her corpse!

nothing more, and because, dead or alive, he still has some use for her, or at least what's left of her."⁴⁵ The Levite "seizes" (חזק, *hzq*) his concubine, cuts her up, and "sends" (שׁלח, *shlkh*) her throughout Israel (19:29). Both verbs have already occurred together in 19:25, where the Levite "seized" his concubine, thrust her out to the mob which, after abusing her, "sent" her away. This repetition of verbs in the pattern "seize"-abuse-"sent" (19:25) and "seize"-cut-"sent" (19:29), seems to equate the Levite's action of dismemberment with the sexual abuse inflicted on the concubine by the rapists.

The cutting up of a body and sending out parts as a message to receivers is also seen in 1 Sam 11:7, though the dead bodies there are of a pair of oxen, signifying the kind of punishment that would come upon those who refused to follow Saul.⁴⁶ Perhaps that was the intention of the Levite as well: failing to execute justice for what had happened, this would be the kind of divine judgment that would befall the Israelites. Reis thinks that all twelve parts of the corpse were sent to every tribe, signifying the fragmentation of Israel's tribes. If sent singly to each tribe, Benjamin would hardly be open to receiving a part of the body it had a role in killing.⁴⁷

And so the woman dies, as silent as she has been throughout the narrative. "Of all the characters in scripture, she is the least. Appearing at the beginning and close of a story that rapes her, she is alone in a world of men. . . . She is property, object, tool, and literary device. Without name, speech, or power, she has no friends to aid her in life or mourn her in death. . . . Captured, betrayed, raped, tortured, murdered, dismembered, and scattered—this woman is the most sinned against."⁴⁸ One remarkable feature of this last scene is that the narrator never tells us exactly when the concubine died. In the case of Eglon and Sisera, when they "fell," they "fell" *dead* (Jdg 3:25; 4:22 and 5:27). Not here (19:26): the concubine falls, but there is no mention of her dying. We are only told that she made no response to the Levite's "Arise, and let us go" (19:28). Was she dead on the doorstep (19:26), or did she die upon dismemberment later (19:29)?⁴⁹ At the very least, by denying

---

45. Ibid., 470.

46. Block also notes the existence in the Mari archives, from a few centuries before the period of the judges, of a document (*ARM* 2.48) that mentions the dismembering of a prisoner's body and distributing the parts to various places as a warning to others (*Judges, Ruth*, 546).

47. Reis, "The Levite's Concubine," 143.

48. Trible, *Texts of Terror*, 80–81.

49. That the narrator describes her as being "murdered" in 20:4 is troubling. Why is she labeled thus when the primary intention of the Gibeahites had been raped and abuse? And how trustworthy is the Levite's recital there? His statement, "and she died" (וַתָּמֹת, *watamot* [*qal*], 20:5), is not as specific as it could have been: "and they killed her" (וַיְמִיתוּהָ, *waymituha* [*hiphil*]). Polzin wonders if the *qal* form of the verb, though not a

her a decent burial he had violated Deut 21:23. All things considered, it is most likely that the woman died when she collapsed with her hands on the threshold of the door; if she were not dead yet, that extra detail of the position of her hands, her terminal plea for help, would seem to be pointless.[50]

In sum, "[t]he Canaanization of Israel is complete. When the Israelites look in the mirror, what they see is a nation that may be ethnically distinct from the natives but which is indistinguishable from them with regard to morality, ethics, and social values. They have sunk to the level of those nations whom they were commanded to destroy and on whom the judgment of God hung."[51] Yet one is struck by the silence of Yahweh in the egregious events that transpired in Judges 19: "[T]he deity refrains from intervention in order to preserve the exercise of human freedom, even if that exercise results in innocent victims."[52]

SERMON FOCUS AND OUTLINES

THEOLOGICAL FOCUS OF PERICOPE 13 FOR PREACHING

13 An immoral lack of care for the weak and defenseless marks a godless and leaderless community (19:1–30).

The raped and murdered concubine is the exemplar of the weak and defenseless in society. In the story, even her blood relative, the one most responsible for her—her father—abandons her! The sermon should rightly focus on application that exhorts the people of God to care for such helpless elements—a mark of both godliness and godly leadership within the Christian community.

Possible Preaching Outlines for Pericope 11

I. Circumstances

---

lie, is a cover up by the Levite of his complicity in her demise, "if not by dismemberment then at least by a cowardly unconcern for her fate until he opened the door that morning and stumbled upon her prostrate form. . . . It may very well be that the ambiguity of the narrator is as deliberately orchestrated as that of the Levite himself" (*Moses and the Deuteronomist,* 201–202). Incidentally, the only other instance in the OT of "taking the knife" (Jdg 19:29) is in Gen 22:6, 10, where a human sacrifice is contemplated, adding to the suspicions aroused here in Judges 19 about the time and circumstances of the woman's death. What was the proximal cause of death—the violent rape or the dismemberment?

50. Reis, "The Levite's Concubine," 144.
51. Block, *Judges, Ruth,* 544.
52. Bowman, "Narrative Criticism," 41.

Leaderlessness: Downward spiral of leaders (3:7–16:31)[53]
Namelessness: Anonymity of characters
Godlessness: Absence of deity
Move-to-relevance: Circumstances of our day
II. Culpability
Culpability of the Levite: concubine and harlotry (19:1–2)
Culpability of the father-in-law (19:3–9)
Culpability of the host (19:22–24)
Culpability of the Levite (19:25–30)
Culpability of the Gibeahites: Judges 19:10–30 and Genesis 19:1–11
Move-to-relevance: Our culpability in neglecting the defenseless
III. *Care for the defenseless!*
Specifics on caring for the defenseless[54]

A more focused approach, dealing in turn with society, men, and the woman, may also work:

I. SOCIETY: Callous
Leaderlessness: Downward spiral of leaders (3:7–16:31)
Namelessness: Anonymity of characters
Godlessness: Absence of deity
Move-to-relevance: Circumstances of our day
II. MEN: Culpable
Culpability of the Levite: concubine and harlotry (19:1–2)
Culpability of the father-in-law (19:3–9)
Culpability of the host (19:22–24)
Culpability of the Levite (19:25–30)
Move-to-relevance: Reasons for our neglect of the defenseless
III. WOMAN: Crushed
Neglected by her husband
Neglected by her father
Neglected by her host
Neglected by society
Move-to-relevance: The neglected around us
IV. *Care for the defenseless!*
Specifics on caring for the defenseless

---

53. Of course, this recap should be quite brief.
54. This application may well comprise a church-wide corporate program directed to benefit society's powerless and disenfranchised. The power of a program grounded on a Scripture-based application, extended through a text-faithful sermon to the whole body of believers, cannot be understated.

PERICOPE 14

Israel vs. Israel

Judges 20:1–21:25

[Civil War and Decimation of Benjamin; Illicit Attempts
to Reconstitute the Tribe]

REVIEW, SUMMARY

Review of Pericope 13: In Jdg 19:1–30, the first part of Epilogue II (Jdg 19:1—21:25), there is complete anonymity of characters and universal absence of deity. The near-total breakdown of law and order and the lack of any concern for the weak and defenseless in society is reflected in the culpability of the raped and murdered woman's husband, her father, her host, and the Gibeahites—the horrific brutality of the latter rivaling those of Sodom and Gomorrah. This is the chaos of a godless and leaderless society.

Summary of Pericope 14: The fourteenth and final pericope of Judges (20:1—21:25) is a sequel to the previous pericope. Here an illicit holy war is undertaken by Israelites against Israelites, with such unity as was never seen in initiatives against foreigners anywhere in this book. To the end, the Israelites are rebellious and recalcitrant, even blaming God for what transpired: 65,000 killed, with a tribe almost decimated.

Their continued godlessness leads to more evildoing—kidnappings and rapes—in an attempt to find wives for the remnant of the tribe of Benjamin. Everyone was, indeed, doing what was right in his own eyes.

14. Judges 20:1–21:25

THEOLOGICAL FOCUS OF PERICOPE 14

14 Acts of revenge and attempts to remedy past misdeeds—without divine input—only lead to more horrific evildoing, havoc in the community, and a hopeless future (20:1—21:25).

  14.1 Acts of revenge, initiated without any consideration of God's desires, wreak havoc in the community (20:1–48).

  14.2 Attempts to remedy past misdeeds, without divine input, only lead to more horrific evildoing and a hopeless future (21:1–25).

OVERVIEW

Epilogue II (Pericope 13: Jdg 19:1–30 and Pericope 14: Jdg 20:1—21:25), like Prologue I (Pericope 1: Jdg 1:1—2:5), is concerned with the socio-political situation of the Israelites; both have חֵרֶם, *kherem*, "holy war" (as will be seen in this pericope).[1]

---

1. Indeed, חֵרֶם occurs only in 1:17 and in 21:11 in Judges. The Israelites were expected to "utterly destroy" the Canaanites and not give their sons and daughters in marital alliances to them (Deut 7:3; Jdg 3:6). The Israelites disobey on both counts. And, in this pericope, in a perverse turnaround, they "utterly destroy" the Benjaminites and refuse to give their daughters in marriage to them (Jdg 21:1, 7, 18). The verb עלה (*'lh*, a key word in Pericope 1, see 1:1, 2, 3, 4, 16, 22; 2:1) ostensibly reappears in 20:9: the verb form נַעֲלֶה (*na'aleh*, "we will go up") is absent here, likely omitted accidentally before עָלֶיהָ (*'aleha*, "against it"). There is also the return of "lot" in 20:9 (גּוֹרָל, *goral*, seen earlier in 1:3 [×2]), investing the current enterprise with some supposed heft. But, unlike in Pericope 1, there is no word from Yahweh here. Also, the Israelites "strike with the edge of the sword" Gibeah and the towns of Benjamin (20:27, 48); ironically, in Prologue I (Pericope 1: Jdg 1:1—2:5), this was the same decimating tactic the Israelites employed, but against *foreigners* (1:8, 25).

Judges 1	Socio-political decline (Foreign wars: חָרַם; 1:17) (Judah to go first in battle: 1:1–2) (Treatment of women: 1:11–15)	Prologue I
Judges 2	Religious decline	Prologue II
Judges 3–16	**Major and minor judges**	**Body**
Judges 17–18	Religious collapse	Epilogue I
Judges 19–21	Socio-political collapse (Domestic wars: חָרַם; 21:11) (Judah to go first in battle: 20:18) (Treatment of women: 19:1–21:25)	Epilogue II

In Prologue I, however, the holy war had divine sanction; here in Epilogue II, it commences as an entirely human initiative. Notice that in 1:1, "the sons of Israel," not particularly unified (see 1:3 and the individual tribes' campaigns in Judges 1), were preparing to fight foreigners. In 20:1, "*all* the sons of Israel," unified (excepting Benjamin, of course), are preparing to fight one of their own (the same descriptor, "all [you/the] sons of Israel," is found also in 20:7, 26). This term, "*all* the sons of Israel," as well as "*all* the tribes of Israel" (20:2, 10; 21:5), and "*all* the men of Israel" (20:11, 33), had never been used of any action taken by Israel thus far in Judges.[2] In fact, no other military transaction in the entire book had been conducted by a unified Israel.[3] But here, they gather "from Dan to Beersheba" (the first use of the phrase in Scripture, 20:1, indicating the comprehensive breadth of Israel from north to south), including Gilead, assembling "as one man to Yahweh" (20:1; also in 20:8, 11)—to fight one of their own![4] This was a unique undertaking. All this tells the reader how far and how low Israel has fallen, when the greatest exhibition of their unity is to fight against *Israelites*! This is what happens when everyone does what is "right in their own eyes" (21:25).[5] Both Epilogues deal with the moral downfall of the nation—and even of the order of Levites guarding the cult of Yahweh. The consequences are catastrophic.

---

2. "All the sons of Israel" appears in 2:4 and 10:8, but there they are the objects of actions taken by others.

3. Indeed, Judges 5 particularly excoriates tribes that refused to participate in maneuvers against a Canaanite enemy (see Pericope 5: Jdg 5:1–31).

4. Also note "all the people" in 20:2, 8, 26.

5. Polzin labels this section "Israel's Moral (Dis-)solution"—clever . . . and accurate (*Moses and the Deuteronomist*, 200).

Pericope 14: Judges 20:1–21:25   287

The Levite from the previous pericope shows up briefly in this one, in 20:4–7, and then disappears from the scene. As was noted, Phinehas is the only named individual in Epilogue II (in 20:28, but meriting only a quick mention). This almost universal anonymity of actants is striking in a book that often names even minor characters. Human life has been devalued in an Israel that has rapidly become Canaanized.

The first part of Epilogue II (Pericope 13: Jdg 19:1–30) described the rape and murder of one Israelite woman—viewed by the nation as a crime. The last part of Epilogue II, the current pericope (Pericope 14: Jdg 20:1–21:25), describes two separate kidnaps/rapes, of four hundred and two hundred Israelite women, respectively—viewed by the nation as acceptable. Chaos reigns and, in the end, the nation spirals into a horrific civil war. Appropriately, Epilogue II is bounded on either side by the dire remark of the narrator: "there was no king in Israel" (19:1; 21:25). In sum, this pericope addresses the primary issue of this book, leadership, depicting what happens when there is a dearth of godly leaders with every person doing "what was right in his own eyes" (21:25). The Epilogues are also a lesson on how the deficiencies of leaders (depicted in the Body: Jdg 3:7—16:31) become the distinctives of the people (Epilogues I and II: Jdg 17:1—20:25). As go the leaders, so go the people!

In this pericope, the Israelites seem eager to interact with God: they assemble before Yahweh in Mizpah (20:1) as the people of God (20:2); they ask his advice at Bethel (20:18, 23, 27–28); they weep before him at the same place (21:2), bemoan to Yahweh the loss of a tribe (21:3), and perform sacrifices to him (21:4). They also drop his name in 21:5, 7–8, as they discuss amongst themselves plans to replenish the depleted tribe of Benjamin. But all of this seeming piety towards Yahweh does not negate the ungodliness and tragic consequences of their actions.

War and preparations for war take up a sizable chunk of Judges 20: mustering of troops (20:14, 15, 17, 19, 22, 29, 32), seeking of oracle (20:18, 23, 26–28), response of deity (20:18, 23, 28), moving to battle (20:20, 21, 24, 25, 30, 31), the battle proper (20:25, 31, 33, 34, 35, 36–37, 39), and its aftermath (20:39–48).[6] After war has been decided upon and Israel gathers to fight Benjamin (20:11), there is a curious alternation in 20:12–14 between mentions of Israel and Benjamin:

---

6. Niditch, *Judges*, 203.

>   Tribes of Israel (20:12a)
>   Tribes of Benjamin (20:12b)
>   Israel (20:13a)
>   Sons of Benjamin (20:13bα)
>   Sons of Israel (20:13bβ)
>   Sons of Benjamin (20:14a)
>   Sons of Israel (20:14b)

The intertribal civil war is thus literarily depicted with the two parties intertwined, added emphasis coming from the description of the sons of Israel as the "brothers" of the sons of Benjamin (20:13, 23, 28).[7] The question of 1:1, "Who shall go up first for us against the Canaanites, to fight against them?" had become, in 20:18, "Who shall go up first for us to fight against the sons of Benjamin?"—almost identical, but diametrically opposed in direction: fighting foreigners in one vs. fighting brothers in the other.

And it it is the height of irony that the precipitating factor of this wholesale mustering for war was an anonymous Levite—a pimp, selfish, callous, and heartless. Not even Deborah and Barak accomplished what this character succeeded in doing. It is this nefarious individual who gets going the greatest assemblage of Israelites for battle in the entire book of Judges—a parody of a judge, an "anti-judge." "Ironically, the Levite sacrificed his concubine to save himself and now is willing to sacrifice the sons of Israel to get his personal revenge on the Gibeahites."[8] After the Levite's accusations are heard, no other witnesses are sought, no investigations are made as to the veracity of the his story, and no attempt is made to hear from the other side (20:4–11). And, worst of all, no input from deity is solicited, despite all the outward piety exhibited.

And ultimately, no one wins this war. Yahweh punishes both parties, the Benjaminites and the rest of the Israelites: 65,000 perish (40,000 Israelites: 20:21, 25; and 25,000 Benjaminites: 20:46). So it is clear that just as the chaos of the Samson saga was under Yahweh's sovereign control (14:4, 14; 15:14; 16:28–30), so also were the calamities and disasters of this pericope (20:28, 35; and possibly 21:15).

> The Epilogue thus confirms and intensifies the emerging portrait of God in Judges, one in which the deity refrains from intervention in order to preserve the exercise of human freedom, even if that exercise results in innocent victims. It also confirms and intensifies the emerging portrayal of human beings as

---

7. Satterthwaite, "'No King in Israel,'" 79.
8. Coogan, et al., *The New Oxford Annotated Bible*, 386.

flawed in the exercise of their freedom. The narrator's portrayals stress human responsibility, not divine accountability, and emphasize responsible human interaction, not responsive divine intervention.[9]

There may have been no "king" acknowledged by the Israelites (17:6; 21:25), but there certainly was a King sovereignly in charge of their affairs.

14.1. Judges 20:1–48

THEOLOGICAL FOCUS 14.1

14.1 Acts of revenge, initiated without any consideration of God's desires, wreak havoc in the community (20:1–48).

NOTES 14.1

14.1 Acts of revenge, initiated without any consideration of God's desires, wreak havoc in the community.

Judges 20:1–48 has essentially two scenes: preparation for war (20:1–17), and execution of war (20:18–48). While we are hopeful that the gathering of the Israelites in 20:1 is a spiritual occasion—after all, it is an "assembly" (20:1, 2; 21:5, 8, often used of religious gatherings: Num 16:3; 20:4; Deut 23:2–3; etc.), and a "congregation" (Jdg 20:1; 21:10, 15, 16; usually used of God's community as in Josh 22:12), it is a convention of "the people of God" (20:2), it is "to Yahweh" (Jdg 20:1), and it is in Mizpah (20:1).[10] But our expectations are dashed: this is not a spiritual event, but a martial one—they are bound for war against one of their own. This would turn out to be another instance of revenge killing in the book of Judges, though the scale is far broader and more extensive than that initiated by Gideon, Jephthah, Samson, or even that despotic tyrant of an avenger, Abimelech.

The assembly of the Israelites in 20:1 would have been the ideal occasion for Israel to seek Yahweh's judgment on the matter of the Levite's concubine and the Gibeahites. Unfortunately, the Israelites are not interested in divine opinion: The Levite challenges the *sons of Israel* (19:30), but *all the sons of Israel* assemble as *one man* (20:1), and the chiefs of *all the people*, of *all the tribes of Israel*, prepare for war (20:2). After the Levite's testimony to *all you sons of Israel* (20:7), *all the people* arise as *one man* (20:8) pledging

---

9. Bowman, "Narrative Criticism," 41.
10. Not the Mizpah east of the Jordan (10:17), but the one north of Jerusalem.

themselves to battle. Then *all the men of Israel* gather, united as *one man* (20:11), from *all the tribes of Israel* (20:10). The human decision had already been made. God had been excluded from this discussion. In Genesis 19, it was God who judged Sodom and Gomorrah for the evil they had perpetrated, and it was God who executed punishment on those evil cities. But here, after the similar (worse?) atrocities of Judges 19, it is man who judges Benjamin and it is man who delivers punishment.[11]

The Levite's account in 20:4–6 is skewed: he accuses the "*baʿals* [leaders] of Gibeah" as the perpetrators of the crime, magnifying its seriousness; in actuality, it was only the "sons of Belial" in Gibeah who were guilty (19:22).[12] And the Levite also attributes to the Gibeahites an intention to kill him that is inaccurate; he fails to mention their homosexual tendencies; he does not include his own role in his concubine's abuse, selfishly thrusting her out the door; no details are given of his discovering the woman at the door the next morning; his account of the concubine's death is somewhat ambiguous ("and she died"); and there is no mention of the other witness to the whole matter, the old man, the Levite's host in Gibeah. Of course, the Levite also completely avoids the reason for his journey to Bethlehem and for his being in Gibeah in the first place: the sex-trafficking of his concubine, her leaving him, and his pursuit of her. And now with his mention of sending her body parts "throughout the land of Israel's inheritance," the Levite seems to be taking the high road of protecting the sanctity of the nation.[13]

Entirely in keeping with what we know of his character—his sole interest was self-preservation as he sacrificed his concubine to the mob—the Levite is careful to protect himself here, too, with no concern whatsoever about what he was initiating, a war that would call for the sacrifice of many in the tribes of Israel. No wonder, then, that the Levite's story is loaded with first-person references; 20:4–6 literally reads: "*I* came to Gibeah which is of Benjamin to spend the night—*I* and *my* concubine. But the *baʿals* of Gibeah rose up against *me*, and surrounded the house at night against *me*. *Me* they intended to kill, and *my* concubine they abused, and she died. And *I* seized *my* concubine, and *I* cut her in pieces, and *I* sent her to all the lands of the

11. See Pericope 13 (Jdg 19:1–30), for a comparison between the events of Genesis 19 and those of Judges 19.

12. But the Israelites seem to have figured that out, for they later demand the "sons of Belial" be handed over for punishment (20:13).

13. One then wonders whence came the Levite's sense of outrage, if he did not really care for his concubine. Perhaps it was all mercenary in origin. While the man's pride had been wounded and he had likely been traumatized by the dreadful events of Judges 19, one cannot forget that his source of income—the concubine he had been prostituting—had also just evaporated. Some of his outrage may also have been manufactured in an attempt to cover up his own misdeeds.

inheritance of Israel, because they did wicked and disgraceful acts in Israel." All this is nothing but "a self-centered apologia."[14] But the narrator is clear as to the Levite's responsibility, labeling him the "husband" of the murdered woman (20:4). Whatever the Levite thought of his concubine (he never calls her his "wife" or refers to himself as her "husband," instead always designating her as his "concubine" [20:4, 5, 6]), and whatever the nature of their relationship, there is no doubt that the storyteller sees the man as the one who should have been responsible for his wife—her "husband." In sum, this is the story of

> a nation that disregards God's laws, tramples social justice, and turns wives into whores. Israelites, like Sodomites, show senseless hatred toward the stranger and try to rape and humiliate him. A husband saves himself by flinging his wife to the rabble. And, with no deference to the Israelite laws concerning reverence for the human corpse, chops her to pieces after she dies of his cowardice and neglect. Rather than doing what is right in the sight of God, the Levite and all Israel have done what is right in their own eyes. They have strayed so far from God's word that they have become no better than Sodomites—the lowest example of ethically objectionable citizenry the Bible has chronicled thus far. Israel's rejection of God leads to an even lower descent, resulting in the atrocious cruelty of the Levite, the old host, and the base fellows of Gibeah. Their punishment, recounted in the remainder of Judges, will be a vicious civil war that rips an already unraveling nation apart.[15]

Canaanization!

Upon being asked by the tribes of Israel to deliver the culprits (the "sons of Belial"), the Benjaminites refuse: the narrator employs the same phrase ("they did not agree . . . to listen," 20:13) that described the refusal of those selfsame sons of Belial to listen to the pleas of the old man ("they did not . . . agree to listen," 19:25). The subsequent punitive process against Benjamin undertaken by the Israelite assembly appears to be that of חרם, *kherem*, the "ban" described in Deut 13:12–18 against idolatry—the consequence of behavior contrary to Yahwistic covenantal principles. It is no coincidence that that passage from the Torah also describes the offenders as "sons of Belial" (13:13). But here in Judges 20 there is no "investigation," "searching out," or "inquiring thoroughly," as demanded by Deut 13:14:

---

14. Block, *Judges, Ruth*, 554. Reis remarks wryly: "What a narrow escape! If his concubine had not somehow gotten herself gang-raped, he might have been killed!' ("The Levite's Concubine," 145).

15. Ibid., 145.

action was to be taken only "if it is true, the matter established, that this abomination is done among you." Not so here. Unsanctioned by deity, based on faulty testimony, sustained without appropriate investigation, and decided upon by a leaderless assembly, the resulting civil war was the gruesome consequence of disregard for God, and a grotesque parody of divinely ordained modes of justice.

Webb calculates that the pre-conquest numbers of Israel had declined by about thirty percent in the Joshua-Judges period (assuming the textual numbers to be reliable, with all men qualified for military duty called up).

Men Able to Fight	Numbers 26	Judges 20:2, 15–17
Tribe of Benjamin	45,600	26,700
Rest of Israel	556,130	400,000
Total	**601,730**	**426,700**

Israel has clearly not prospered in the conquest era, as they were warned about in Deut 28:15–68. The losses they would suffer in the current civil war in Judges 20 would decimate them further: this is what happens when leadership collapses and everyone does "what is right in one's own eyes" (Jdg 17:6; 21:25).[16] Canaanization has dire results.

The first involvement of deity in the proceedings comes only *after* the Israelites have decided to fight. They had already decided on a course of action—war—and had committed themselves to it, determining the offensive by lot, mustering troops, and making provisions (20:8-13, 17). Now that they had arrogated for themselves the exclusive authority to judge and decide, the inquiry made of God in 20:18 seems an afterthought, merely a mechanical procedure following the pattern set in 1:1, not so much a sincere desire to comprehend Yahweh's will. Perhaps that is exactly why Yahweh replies with a laconic: "Judah first" (20:18).[17] In fact, the narrator notes that here they inquired of אֱלֹהִים, *ʾelohim* ("God," 20:18), not "Yahweh" as in 1:1.[18]

The war scene (20:18-48) can be divided into three parallel panels corresponding to the three battles fought (20:18-21, 22-25, and 26-48)[19]:

---

16. Webb, *Judges*, 481.

17. The reason for selecting Judah to go first may have been because the victim of the atrocity, the concubine, hailed from Bethlehem, in Judah (19:2). But after this, Judah is not in the picture any more.

18. And, strikingly unlike in 1:1, there is no divine promise of victory at the outset; that is given only later in 20:28.

19. Modified from Block, *Judges, Ruth*, 558.

First Battle (20:18–21)
Preparation: went up to Bethel (20:18a)
   Inquiry of אֱלֹהִים ("Who shall go up first ...?") (20:18b)
      Answer ("Judah first") (20:18c; no verb)
         Attack (20:19–20)
            Severe defeat (20:21)

Second Battle (20:22–25)
Preparation: encouraged themselves; went up; wept (20:22–23a)
   Inquiry of Yahweh ("Shall we again draw near ...?") (20:23b)
      Answer ("Go up against him") (20:23c; verb)
         Attack (20:24)
            Less severe defeat (20:25)

Third Battle (20:26–48)
Preparation: went up; came to Bethel; wept; fasted; sacrificed (20:26)
   Inquiry of Yahweh ("Shall I again go out ... or shall I cease?") (20:27–28a)
      Answer ("Go up ... I will ...") (20:28b; verb and promise)
         Attack (20:29–30)
            Victory (20:31–36a; details: 20:36b–48)

For each of the three battles in Judges 20 there is: preparation, inquiry of אֱלֹהִים/Yahweh, divine answer, the attack, and an outcome (20:21—severe defeat; 20:25—less severe defeat; 20:31–48—victory).[20] Overall, the three battle preparations get progressively more intense, and the three inquiries made of Yahweh become increasingly tentative. The only instance of fasting in the book, as well as the only appearance of the ark in Judges,[21] are in the third inquiry (20:26–28a).[22] And it is this last inquiry that is conducted by Phinehas the priest (20:28a).[23] The Israelites are apparently coming to their

---

20. Interestingly, in the first two battles, there are no reports of Benjaminite casualties; only Israelites seem to have suffered losses (20:21, 25).

21. It is not clear how the ark of the covenant happened to be at Bethel (20:26–27), when other texts tell us it was located at Shiloh (Josh 18:1; 22:12–13; Jdg 18:31; 1 Sam 4:4). One cannot rule out movement of the central shrine (and the ark) between Shiloh and Bethel.

22. Also, the first two inquiries made of deity are by the "sons of Israel" (20:18, 23); it is when they are rendered helpless and hopeless that "all the sons of Israel and all the people" inquire of Yahweh (20:26). One also notes that the first inquiry regarded action against the "sons of Benjamin" (20:18); the last two dealt with what they should do with the "sons of my brother Benjamin" (20:23, 28).

23. This Phinehas, the son of Eleazar and the grandson of Aaron, had already figured in some remarkable incidents where he vigorously defended Yahweh's honor (Exod 6:25; Num 25:7–11; Josh 22:10–34). His presence on stage in Judges 20 places this entire incident early in the conquest, within decades of Joshua's passing, though

senses. And so deity's answers in each of those inquiries becomes more detailed: from a verbless response in 20:18c, to one with a verb in 20:23c, to an answer with a verb and a promise of victory in 20:28b.[24]

The narrator portrays both sides (the eleven Israelite tribes, and the tribe of Benjamin) as comprising "valiant fighters" and "men who draw the sword" (of the Israelites: 20:2, 17, 25; of the Benjaminites: 20:15, 35, 44, 46), clearly portraying a battle between brothers (and equals). The Israelites appear to be more willing to fight and defeat their own, than they are to overcome foreigners. They are more eager to "do what is right in their own eyes," than to "do what is right in Yahweh's eyes." Beyond the obvious calamity of an intertribal civil war that inflicts severe casualties, "[t]he tragedy is that these are all valuable soldiers whom Israel cannot afford to lose in their occupation of the land of Canaan—a task that seems all but forgotten": 65,000 perish.[25]

In any case, in the third and final battle, that involved an ambush (20:32–24, 36b–43), the Benjaminites recognize that "disaster/evil" (רעה, *rʿh*) has befallen them (20:34, 41), exactly what the Gibeahites had themselves perpetrated (רעה in 20:3, 12, 13; the verb, רעע, *rʿʿ*, is used in 19:23). And 20:45 describes the Benjaminites being chased and "caught" (עלל, *ʿll*); the only other occurrence of the verb in Judges is in 19:25, where it denoted the "abusing" of the concubine. The Benjaminites attempt to escape towards Gibeah, one of their home bases (20:43), but they find Gibeah torched (20:37–38): they have no escape. That this is similar to the attempt of the concubine to flee to the house of the old man (19:26) is obvious, but made even more so by the narrator's description of Gibeah here—"opposite Gibeah *where the sun rises*" (20:43). One is reminded of the number of allusions to sunrise in the earlier story, in 19:25–27: "until morning" (19:25), "ascent

---

the narrator would, of course, have us see the war in the context of his creation of the sequence of Judges—after all, authors *do* things with what they say.

24. The final response of Yahweh, "I will deliver them into your hand" (20:28) is quite similar to his promise to Israel in 1:1: "I have given the land into his [Judah's] hand."

25. Younger, *Judges, Ruth*, 375. Those who perished among Israel in the first battle were "all these [who] drew the sword" (20:25). On the other hands, the Benjaminites, who also did have swordsmen (20:15, 35, 46), also included seven hundred stone-slingers in their contingent. Chisholm (*Judges and Ruth*, 501 n.116) observes that these slings and stones were deadly weapons, shooting 8-ounce flint stones of 2–3 inches in diameter at speeds of over 100 miles an hour! See Introduction for the connection of this rather out-of-place comment about lefthanders in Epilogue II to an incident in the Body of Judges. Of note, 20:31–36a gives a condensed version of the final hostilities, with 20:36b–48 providing a more detailed account thereof, not all of it very clear. The details of the battle are not of particular interest for preaching purposes, beyond what has already been noted.

of dawn" (19:25), "turning of the morning" (19:26), "until light" (19:26), and "morning" (19:27).[26] Thus the Benjaminites are punished in like measure as their offences. The final act of retribution upon the Benjaminites was the "*sending* of fire" (שִׁלְּחוּ בָאֵשׁ, *shillkhu ba'esh*, 20:48), corresponding to the final act of abuse upon the concubine inflicted by the Gibeahites: "*sending* her away" (וַיְשַׁלְּחוּהָ, *wayshallkhuha*, 19:25)—two acts of שׁלח, *shlkh*, perpetrated by abusers upon victim in each case. There is also the "falling" of the woman at the door of the house (19:26), and the "falling" of the Benjaminite casualties (20:44, 46).[27]

Element	Rape of Concubine	War on Benjamin
Victim(s) "surrounded"	19:22	20:43
Victim(s) of "evil"	19:23; 20:3, 12, 13	20:34, 41
Sunrise imagery	19:25–27	20:43
Victim(s) subject to עלל, '*ll*	19:25 ("abused")	20:45 ("caught")
"Sent"	19:25 (of victim)	20:48 (of fire on victims)
Victim(s) "fall(s)"	19:26	20:44, 46
Demise at home base	19:26	20:43
Reflection on tragedy	20:12	20:48

Truly, evil had been punished with more evil! In sum, more than 25,000 Benjaminites end up dead (20:35; 20:46 is likely a rounding); six hundred escape (20:47; they will figure in Judges 21; see below). Perhaps the most involved Yahweh is in this entire pericope is in 20:35—he was the true victor, the one who defeated Benjamin; after all he was the one who promised to deliver the Benjaminites into the hand of Israel (20:28).

Wong notes several parallels between this third battle (an ambush, 20:29, 33, 36, 37, 38) and Israel's attack on Ai (also an ambush, Josh 8:2, 4, 7, 9, 12, 14, 19, 21). Indeed, it appears that Israel, here, had treated one of their own tribes, as they had Canaanites: indeed, they killed more Benjaminites than Canaanites (25,000 warriors in Jdg 20:35, 46, not counting noncombatants; but only 12,000 fatalities, including men and women, in Josh 8:25); here they burned all the Benjaminite towns, not just the offending city (Jdg 20:48; Josh 8:28); and they even killed the animals of the Benjaminites, a level of carnage not seen in the earlier battle (Jdg 20:48; Josh 8:27).[28] In the

26. See Pericope 13 (Jdg 19:1–30).

27. Table below from Berman, *Narrative Analogy,* 74. For details see ibid., 60–61, 66–67.

28. *Compositional Strategy,* 57–70. Also similar: הפך, *hpk,* in Josh 8:20 and Jdg 20:41 (the ambushed "turning back"); and נבלה, *nblh* ("folly") in Josh 7:15 and Jdg 19:23, 24; 20:6, 10 (the only instances of this word in either book). The Joshua story is one of

end, after the victory at Ai, the Israelites celebrated covenant renewal (Josh 8:30–35); but after the civil war in Judges 20, they mourned the near-total loss of a tribe (Jdg 21:2–3, 6). These contrasts lend support to the suspicion that though Yahweh sanctioned (and helped in) the defeat of the Benjaminites—"I will deliver them into your hand" (20:28; and see 20:35; and possibly 21:15)—the subsequent deracination of that tribe almost into non-existence was an act that went far beyond their commission from God. The "striking . . . with the edge of the sword" (20:27, 48) is clearly an application of חֵרֶם, but the only such permitted engagements against fellow Israelites were for idolatrous activities (Exod 22:19; Deut 7:26; 13:12–19; Josh 6:18), not relevant in this case.[29] Israel's actions were obviously inappropriate and immoderate. "God said the most you could do was an eye for an eye, a tooth for a tooth. The Levite sought to destroy a tribe for the crimes of a few town ruffians. This was not justice. This was not divine. This was human rage. This was human revenge conceived totally apart from divine law, divine word, divine oracle, or divine presence."[30] Canaanization at its worst!

14.2. Judges 21:1–25

THEOLOGICAL FOCUS 14.2

14.2 Attempts to remedy past misdeeds, without divine input, only lead to more horrific evildoing and a hopeless future (21:1–25).

NOTES 14.2

14.2 Attempts to remedy past misdeeds, without divine input, only lead to more horrific evildoing and a hopeless future.

It is only at the conclusion of this bloody civil war that the Israelite victors consider the repercussions of their brutality. Once again they congregate at Bethel and weep (Jdg 21:2; see 20:18, 23, 26). One notices that this time they have assembled before אֱלֹהִים, not Yahweh: all is still not right here, despite the grief. Indeed, 21:2–3 is not even a request, but rather a howl of protest and an attempt to absolve themselves of any blame and, instead, to pile it

---

success, with Yahweh intimately involved; the Judges story, on the other hand, is one of failure, with Yahweh only peripherally involved, if at all.

29. In Deut 13:12–18 the destruction of Israelite cities by incineration was effectively a whole burnt offering unto Yahweh (13:16; see Jdg 20:38, 40, 48). For חֵרֶם and the "ban" practiced upon Canaanite cities, see Deut 7:1–2; 20:16–18.

30. Butler, *Judges*, 450.

all on God! The "God of *Israel*" is interrogated as to why this happened "in *Israel*" so that one tribe is missing "in *Israel*"—a clear attribution of fault to Israel's deity. Yahweh, they allege, has failed in his status as patron of the nation. But it was they themselves who had decided to fight Benjamin—without input from deity. It was *they* who had carried out the post-battle carnage—without specific instructions from God.[31] Yahweh does not deign to reply to Israel's query in 21:3. The question that the Israelites ought to have been asking was: "How did we get to this point?"[32] Attempting to rouse Yahweh, the Israelites redo the combo of "burnt offerings and peace offerings" (21:4). Earlier all these maneuvers had been successful (20:26), but now Yahweh refuses to take the bait.

After Benjamin was routed, only six hundred males were left in the tribe for whom wives needed to be found if the tribe were to survive (20:47), since the rest of the Israelites had sworn not to give their daughters in marriage to any Benjaminite (21:1).[33] So Israel adopts a couple of fraudulent sidestepping tactics. In the first cunning strategy, they discover that Jabesh-gilead has not participated in the assembly at Mizpah (and thus it was not a

---

31. The verb "cut/hacked off" in 21:6 is the only occurrence of the root גדע, *gdʿ*, in Judges (the name "Gideon," is derived from the same verb). This connotes a violent action such as the chopping of human arms (1 Sam 2:31), tree limbs (Isa 10:33), animal horns (Lam 2:3), etc. The passive voice of the verb here—"has been cut off" (*niphal*)—is suspicious: Are the Israelites blaming Yahweh again? See Block, *Judges, Ruth*, 572. The narrator's comment in 21:15 is ambiguous as to the cause of the loss of a tribe. It is unclear whether this is the Israelites' wrong interpretation of the "breach"—blaming God, as in 21:3, 6—or the narrator's theological assessment—affirming God's sovereignty over all events (see 20:28, 35).

32. Ibid., 571. This "lifting up their voices and weeping bitterly" happened once before in Judges, in 2:4 at Bokim, when the angel of Yahweh indicted the Israelites for their failure to maintain covenant fealty. The book of Judges is thus functionally a journey from Bokim to Bethel, from tears to tears—a book of lament! But in Bochim, Yahweh did speak to his people, so there was hope. Here in Bethel, deity is silent, and all is hopeless, bleak, and desolate.

33. The events of 21:1 (at Bethel) are tied in to those in 20:8 (at Mizpah): the gathering of all the Israelites "as one *man*" at Mizpah, declaring that "no *man*" will go to his tent and "no *man*" will turn back to his house (20:8), is linked to "the *man* of Israel" (i.e., all the men of Israel) swearing not to give his daughter to a Benjaminite (21:1). In 21:18, we find out that this oath also came with a curse upon those who *did* give wives to Benjamin. A second oath seems to have been made at the same time, also prior to the battle: those who did not muster for battle would be put to death (21:5). Such oaths could have been condoned if taken in the heat of battle, particularly in the context of the heavy losses incurred by the Israelites in the first two conflicts (20:21, 25). But these vows at Mizpah were made *before* any martial engagement, making them premeditated and all the more reprehensible, with the extinction of a tribe a distinct possibility as a result (21:3, 6). See Younger, *Judges, Ruth*, 379.

party to the vow) or the war against Benjamin (21:8-9).³⁴ The Israelites decide to consign the town to the "ban," and conduct חֵרֶם against it (21:8-11). It is astonishing that between the commencement of the book of Judges and now there has been a wholesale reluctance on the part of the Israelites to implement this holy war policy against the Canaanites. But, lo and behold, here they are at the end of the book, employing it with abandon against their own kith and kin!³⁵

Interestingly, there is no account of an actual fight or of any slaughter though, of course, there must have been significant casualties. From the resolve of the congregation to go to battle against Jabesh-gilead (21:10-11), the narrator moves immediately to the aftermath—the salvaging of virgins (21:12). This conservation of virgins is suspicious. The Israelites clearly did not care to save the *Benjaminite* virgins (assumed to have all been slain; see 20:47-48); therefore, this saving of the marriageable-age women of Jabesh-gilead reveals itself to be purely a matter of expediency.³⁶ The Israelites' oath to deal חֵרֶם upon Jabesh-gilead is not one reflecting moral outrage but Machiavellian opportunism. Curiously, the notation of Shiloh being "in the land of Canaan" (21:12) is entirely redundant. Perhaps the mention has the rhetorical purpose of asserting that not only did Israel live in an alien land, she also behaved like the aliens in whose land she lived. And all this is conducted with the concurrence of the "whole congregation" (21:13). Never was anything done with such catholicity in Judges!³⁷

The attack on Jabesh-gilead "procured" only four hundred virgins for the six hundred male Benjaminite remnant. So for the second sneaky tactic, the Israelites permitted the remaining two hundred Benjaminite bachelors to abduct the daughters of Shiloh while they were dancing at a

---

34. The reason for the absence of Jabesh-gilead from the war council is not given.

35. The only other time the word חֵרֶם shows up in Judges is in 1:17 where Judah and Simeon exterminated the Canaanites at Zephath and renamed the place "Hormah," from חרם. Also notable is that "strike . . . with the edge of the sword" in 21:10 and 20:37, 48 are the only times this tactic is employed by Israelites against Israelites; elsewhere in Judges it is exclusively applied against foreigners (1:8, 25; 4:15, 16; 18:27). The systematic wiping out of all things living and the burning of cities (20:48) is also suggestive of חֵרֶם. See Deut 7:1-5; 13:16-17; 20:16-18; Josh 6:21, 24. Plus, as was noted, the similarities between the current anti-Benjamin campaign and the anti-Ai exercise of Joshua 8 make the links between prior events and the current undertakings in Judges 21 stronger, with the latter a travesty of חֵרֶם.

36. Such a selective application of חֵרֶם is also seen in Num 31:17-18, where virgins are spared, with the significant difference that there it was by Moses's prophetic command (presumably endorsed by Yahweh); here, in Jdg 21:10-11, only human voices are heard.

37. Also, other than 21:16 that has "elders of the congregation," the only mention of national elders is in 2:8. Elders of a particular tribe are found in 11:5, 7, 8, 9, 10, 11.

Yahwistic feast (21:19–23).³⁸ The problem besetting the Israelites in 21:6–7 seems to have been repeated in 21:15–18: both sections have the Israelites "sorry" for Benjamin; both raise the question "What shall we do for wives for those who are left?"; both seek solutions that involve kidnapping women (21:12, 19–23): "catch" and "carry away."³⁹ The Benjaminites, once defeated by an ambush (20:29, 33, 36, 37, 38), are now advised to set one up themselves (21:20), in order to shanghai two hundred unsuspecting women of the "daughters of Shiloh" (21:21). And so the narrative comes around full circle, with the "elders" (from זקן, *zqn*, 21:16) advocating exactly what the "old man" (זקן, 19:16) had done in Judges 19, facilitating kidnapping and rape, crimes worthy of the death penalty (Exod 21:16; Deut 22:55–57; 24:7). Besides, "Israel now sanctions the same crime of forced sexual rape against the maidens of Shiloh as Benjamin had earlier sanctioned against the Levite's concubine. The license that Benjamin gave the Gibeahites, Israel now gives Benjamin."⁴⁰ Slaughter, kidnap, and rape become the Israelites' modus operandi to clean up the horrific messes created by an ungodly, wanton war.

The rationalization of all this, as explained to the complaining fathers of the kidnapped women (Jdg 21:22), is bizarre, if not devious. The parents had every right to lodge a formal complaint against the kidnap and rape of their daughters, as did the Levite in response to the same atrocities against his concubine. But the Israelites in this case, with arguments that are pure sophistry, warn the fathers to cease creating trouble (21:22). It substantiates our view of the Israelites' "logic" as specious mumbo jumbo: the women are being taken, not being "given," and therefore their fathers are innocent of any violation of the earlier oath not to "give" their daughters to Benjamin (21:3, 18), and since there is nothing they can do, they should do nothing, but "*give* them to us voluntarily"! What a fallacious rationalization of violence—nothing but "a repeat on a mass scale the crimes they found so abhorrent in the men of Gibeah."⁴¹

The irony of all these undertakings is great: to ameliorate the brutal consequences of one war (20:15–48), Israel engages in another equally

---

38. The nature of this "feast of Yahweh" (21:19) is unclear. The hideout of the Benjaminites, in the vineyards (21:20, 21), suggests that it was related to the grape harvest.

39. "Catch" (חטף, *khtp*, 21:21) is used only twice more in the OT, both times in Ps 10:9, for an evildoer's ambush of an innocent person, comparing it to a lurking lion's capture of its prey. "Carried away" (גזל, *gzl*, Jdg 21:23) is found only once more in Judges, in 9:25, to describe robbery (as elsewhere: Lev 6:2, 4; Deut 28:29, 31; etc.). With the significantly negative connotations of these words, what the Israelites sanctioned and what the Benjaminite remnant executed would certainly qualify as violent kidnap.

40. O'Connell, *The Rhetoric of the Book of Judges*, 263.

41. Exum, "The Centre Cannot Hold," 430–31.

bloody one, only this time against a city, Jabesh-gilead, rather than a whole tribe (21:1-12). One must not forget that all the Benjaminite women had been slaughtered in the first war (20:15-48), leaving only six hundred *men*. Thus the Benjaminite women suffered the same fate as did the Levite's concubine: death. Equally ironic was the subjection of the daughters of Shiloh to kidnap and rape to furnish brides for the Benjaminites, who thereby themselves become guilty of the crime that had initiated the civil war in the first place (21:13-25). One woman's rape led to six hundred others being raped, to mention nothing of the slaughter of thousands of both men and women in between![42]

> **A** Rape of the Levite's concubine (19:1-30)
>   **B** Holy war against Benjamin (20:1-48)
>   **C** Problem: Benjamin threatened with extinction (21:1-6)
>   **B'** Holy war against Jabesh-gilead (and rape) (21:7-14)
> **A'** Rape (with kidnap) of the daughters of Shiloh (21:15-24)

The story ends with the rebuilding of Benjaminite cities (21:23), another violation of the rules of חֵרֶם: Deut 13:17 specifically prohibited such rebuilding projects after the imposition of חֵרֶם. Justice, thereby, has been totally perverted on every side and on every count, with everyone doing "what was right in his own eyes" (21:25).

> This civil war stands out in Judges because it was not sanctioned by the deity, was based on the testimony of a man whose actions in the whole episode have been dubious, was decided on by a group acting in the absence of a leader, whose decisions repeatedly caused larger problems. All of this is tied to the question of leadership, which is fitting since the whole book focuses on the search for a leader, the relationship of the leaders to the deity, and the reasons and motivations of leaders. Here there was no leader and the entire nation rallied together and made a decision as a group. Their motives were immediate and personal, not based on the commandments of their deity or on Israel's relationship to their deity.... The final judgment of the book is clarified in this episode; while a system of government dependent on the judges did not work for Israel, the concept of group leadership was even worse.[43]

The Canaanization of Israel is complete! "When the Israelites look in the mirror, what they see is a nation that may be ethnically distinct from the

---

42. Table below modified from Webb, *Judges*, 507.
43. Schneider, *Judges*, 271-72.

natives but which is indistinguishable from them with regard to morality, ethics, and social values. They have sunk to the level of those nations whom they were commanded to destroy and on whom the judgment of God hung. And in the words of Moses in Deut 8:19–20, when Israelites act like Canaanites, they may expect the same fate."[44]

The book of Joshua had concluded with Joshua "sending" the Israelites, "every man to his own inheritance" (אִישׁ לְנַחֲלָתוֹ, *'ish lnakhalato*, Josh 24:28) after *renewing* their covenant relationship with Yahweh (24:1–27). Now the book of Judges ends similarly with the sons of Israel "returning," "every man to his own inheritance" (אִישׁ לְנַחֲלָתוֹ, Jdg 21:24), after *rending* their covenant relationship with Yahweh (Jdg 19:1—21:22). This pericope (and the Epilogues and the entire book) concludes with a dire statement, already encountered in 17:6, a grievous commentary on all that has taken place: Israel had no king, no morals (21:25). "Wickedness is democratized; everyone does what is right in his own eyes, and the results are disastrous."[45] The book that commenced with weeping (2:4) ends with weeping (20:23, 26; 21:2). "Ultimately, what the people are weeping about is the reality that they and their leaders—the judges or 'bringers of justice' . . . —have failed miserably to serve and obey God alone."[46] To the end of the book, the "land of Canaan" has not become the "land of Israel." Israel ends exactly where it began: no progress had been made. Landless, leaderless, feckless, godless. Indeed, the situation at the end of Judges is *worse*: at the conclusion of Joshua the people had agreed to live in accordance with the demands of Yahweh. No such agreement is found in the conclusion of Judges. They have no leader, no commitment, no future! And, of course, without God's ultimate leadership, there can be no godly human leadership. And without godly human leadership, there can be no godly people. As go the leaders, so go the people.

SERMON FOCUS AND OUTLINES

THEOLOGICAL FOCUS OF PERICOPE 14 FOR PREACHING

14 Ungodly acts of revenge and attempts to remedy past misdeeds lead to more evildoing, wreaking havoc in the community (20:1—21:25).

This last pericope brings the book of Judges to an end: Israel has spiraled into an abyss of godlessness and leaderlessness, and the consequences are plainly laid out here. The focus of the sermon should be upon God's people

---

44. Block, *Judges, Ruth*, 544.
45. Ibid., 583.
46. McCann, *Judges*, 31.

ignoring him in an age of everyone doing right in his own eyes; application then ought to be upon our involving God in everything.

Possible Preaching Outlines for Pericope 11

I. Absurdity of War[47]
    Human initiative for war (20:1–14)
    Intertribal (20:12–14), between "brothers" (20:13, 23, 28)
    Unified war of Israelites (20:1, 2, 7, 8, 10, 11, 33; 21:5)
    Realization of misdeeds as battle progresses (20:18–48)
    Protest about losses of war (21:1–3)
    Refusal to give daughters in marriage (21:1, 5)
    Rationalization of kidnappings and rapes (21:1–23)
    Move-to-relevance: Inutility of humanly conceived initiatives

II. Aftermath of War
    Yahweh's punishment of both parties: 65,000 killed (20:21, 25, 46)
    Benjaminites' punishment commensurate with culpability of Gibeahites
    Move-to-relevance: Consequences for humanly conceived actions

III. *Accommodate God in every facet of life!*
    How specifically to involve God in everything[48]

This is another instance where a "single-move" could be successfully pulled off:

I. Ignoring God
    Human initiative for war (20:1–14)
    Intertribal (20:12–14), between "brothers" (20:13, 23, 28)
    Unified war of Israelites (20:1, 2, 7, 8, 10, 11, 33; 21:5)
    Realization of misdeeds as battle progresses (20:18–48)
    Protest about losses of war (21:1–3)
    Refusal to give daughters in marriage (21:1, 5)
    Rationalization of kidnappings and rapes (21:1–23)
    Yahweh's punishment of both parties: 65,000 killed (20:21, 25, 46)
    Move-to-relevance: Consequences for humanly conceived actions

II. Involving God: *Accommodate God in every facet of life!*
    How specifically to involve God in everything

---

47. "War" here includes all of the events in this pericope, in both Judges 20 and Judges 21.

48. Or, as suggested elsewhere, one way to involve God in everything. Often the concrete application given will be a "significance"—a creative, concrete, and compelling first step to accomplishing what the text/theology/general application calls for. It is such ritual practices that lead to radical passions.

CONCLUSION

*"In those days there was no king in Israel;
everyone did what was right in his eyes."*

Judges 17:6; 21:25

WHEN PREACHING JUDGES, IT does help to realize that the world now is as brutal, godless, and immoral as it was then: everyone doing right in his/her own eyes! Nonetheless, despite the similarity of situation, it is, indeed, a remarkable predication that from such an ancient text as Judges truth may be discerned and preached—not just truth that informs, but truth that transforms: truth that is applicable and that changes lives into Christlikeness, for the glory of God, by the power of the Spirit. The lot of the homiletician is not easy, neither is the responsibility of such a one minimal: each week, the preacher has to negotiate this formidable passage from ancient text to modern audience to expound, with authority and relevance, a specific biblical pericope for the faithful. But how may this august responsibility be discharged?

Unfortunately, commentaries, generally written by biblical scholars not particularly acquainted with preaching, have tended towards with what I call "a hermeneutic of excavation"—the exegetical turning over of tons of earth, debris, rock, boulder, and gravel: a style of interpretation that yields an overload of biblical and Bible-related information, most of it unfortunately not of any particular use for one seeking to preach a relevant message from a specific text. Karl Barth's indictment is appropriate:

> My complaint is that recent commentators confine themselves to an interpretation of the text which seems to me to be no commentary at all, but merely the first step toward a commentary.

> Recent commentaries contain no more than a reconstruction of the text, a rendering of the Greek words and phrases by their precise equivalents, a number of additional notes in which archaeological and philological material is gathered together, and a more or less plausible arrangement of the subject matter in such a manner that it may be made historically and psychologically intelligible from the standpoint of pure pragmatism.[1]

I have given heed to Barth, and attempted to go beyond the "first step toward a commentary," to deliver not so much what the author was *saying* in comprehensible fashion, but also the nuggets—clues from the text as to what the author was *doing* with what he was saying: the theology of the pericope. With an abiding interest in preaching, I come to this task of commentary writing with the hope of providing preachers what they can profitably use to create sermons. In other words, *Judges: A Theological Commentary for Preachers* is one small attempt in a larger endeavor to help the preacher move safely, accurately, and effectively across the gulf between text and application. Thereby, this intrepid soul, aided by the Holy Spirit, becomes the pastoral agent of the life-transforming truths of Scripture.[2]

Judges, like any other book of the Bible, is designed to "seduce" its readers to change their lives in thought, in feeling, and in action, to comply with the priorities, principles, and practices of God's world (i.e., the theology of the pericope) that is displayed in, with, and through the inspired writing. All this so that pericope by pericope, God's people would be moved towards Christlikeness—a *christiconic* mode of interpreting Scripture.[3]

That is to say—again!—that the author/editor/redactor of Judges is *doing* something with what he is saying. This theological agenda of the writer mandates that interpreters, particularly those who interpret for preaching and application purposes, attend not only to what is being said, but also to what is being *done* with what is said. In aiding the preacher, this commentary has approached Judges in a unique fashion, undertaking a form of

---

1. Barth, "Preface to the Second Edition," 6.

2. See Kuruvilla, *A Vision for Preaching*. It bears repeating that the commentaries in this current series are only "theological" commentaries, not "preaching" commentaries. They take the preacher only part of the way to a sermon, from text to theology (the hermeneutical step). It remains the preacher's burden to complete the crossing by moving from theology to application, i.e., making concrete application that is specific for the particular audience, and presenting all of this in sermon that is powerful and persuasive (the rhetorical step).

3. See Kuruvilla, *Privilege the Text!* 238–69; and idem, "Christiconic Interpretation."

exegesis geared towards discerning the theology of the pericope—*theological* exegesis.[4]

It is a foundational conviction of this work that valid application of a pericope of Scripture may be arrived at only via this critical intermediary between text and praxis, pericopal theology.[5] The hermeneutical philosophy behind this commentary also holds that such valid application to change lives for the glory of God is the appropriate goal of every sermon. And so the task of the preacher with a pastoral heart ought to include the delineation of specific ways in which the theological focus of the pericope may be translated into the real life of real people.

So here again is the broad theological focus of the entire book of Judges:

> *Maintenance of godly traditional values, personal experience of God* (Prologues), *and manifesting virtues of godly leadership* (Body)—*integrity in life* (Ehud), *fearless faith* (Barak), *participation in the endeavors of God* (Song of Deborah), *giving God credit for his work* (Gideon-1), *rejection of self-glorifying pursuits* (Gideon-2) *and the thirst for power* (Abimelech), *avoiding manipulation of God* (Jephthah), *maintaining devotion to God and his interests* (Samson-1), *faithfully cleaving to one's call* (Samson-2)—*result in a godly society and provide hope for the future* (Epilogues).

As is obvious from this statement, and as has hopefully been evident in the commentary, the larger thrust of Judges deals with what godly leadership looks like. However, in a sense, all of God's people are called to be leaders—in some arena or another, in some fashion or another, to some degree or another. Therefore this book is relevant for all God's children, teaching us all how to lead in the spheres he has placed us, faithfully, uncompromisingly, steadfastly. The consequences of *un*godly leadership are amply demonstrated in Judges.

It is this larger focus on leadership that drives the book, with each pericope of Judges contributing a slice or a quantum of theology to its broad theological thrust: uncompromising faithfulness to God, maintenance of godly traditional values, and reliance on divine strategies for success results in divine blessing (Pericope 1: Jdg 1:1—2:5 [Prologue I]); personal

---

4. See Introduction; Kuruvilla, *Privilege the Text!* 33–65; idem, *Text to Praxis*, 142–90; and idem, "Pericopal Theology," 265–83, for details on this hermeneutical entity, pericopal theology, and its value in the homiletical process.

5. In the commentary, a crystallization of pericopal theology shows up as the "Theological Focus."

experience of God produces unwavering commitment to him (Pericope 2: Jdg 2:6—3:11 [Prologue 1; Othniel]); integrity in life, driven by reverence for God and reliance upon him, receives divine approbation (Pericope 3: Jdg 3:12-31 [Ehud]); reverencing of God by fearless faith characterizes godly leadership (Pericope 4: Jdg 4:1-24 [Barak]); participation in the endeavors of God, with God, keeps one in the realm of his blessing (Pericope 5: Jdg 5:1-31 [Song of Deborah]); refusal to take prideful credit for divine action results in blessing (Pericope 6: Jdg 6:1—7:22 [Gideon-1]); godliness is expressed in the rejection of self-glorifying pursuits (Pericope 7: Jdg 7:23—8:32 [Gideon-2]); an illicit thirst for power brings about the fitting retribution of God (Pericope 8: Jdg 8:33—10:5 [Abimelech]); ungodly manipulation of God for selfish purposes can lead to tragic loss of blessing (Pericope 9: Jdg 10:6—12:15 [Jephthah]); rejection of Yahweh's interests in favor of selfish passions leads only to trouble (Pericope 10: Jdg 13:1—14:20 [Samson-1]); disdaining of one's divine calling can lead to destruction (Pericope 11: Jdg 15:1-16:31 [Samson-2]); godless leadership brings about godlessness in society (Pericope 12: Jdg 17:1—18:31 [Epilogue I]); immoral unconcern for the weak and defenseless marks a godless and leaderless community (Pericope 13: Jdg 19:1-30 [Epilogue II-1]); continued ungodliness only leads to more evildoing, greater havoc, and a hopeless future (Pericope 14: Jdg 20:1—21:25 [Epilogue II-2]).

In preaching the book of Judges, then, week by week and pericope by pericope, preachers are called to fulfill the solemn responsibility, helped by the Holy Spirit, to align themselves and their listeners closer to the divine goal of instituting godly leadership in and among God's people. Inasmuch as the application propounded by homileticians in each sermon is faithfully assimilated into listeners' lives, creating Christian dispositions and forming Christlike character, the people of God will have aligned themselves to the will of God for the glory of God—the goal of preaching. Text will have become praxis, the people of God will have experienced and enjoyed divine blessings, and Christlikeness will have been inculcated in God's children. Here, in Judges, one important aspect of such Christlikeness is the godliness of God's leaders, in any and every situation and circumstance. And as God's people develop into godly leaders, one can say that the kingdom of God is near!

BIBLIOGRAPHY

Ackerman, Susan. *Warrior, Dancer, Seductress, Queen: Women in Judges and Biblical Israel*. New York: Doubleday, 1998.
Albright, W. F. "The Song of Deborah in the Light of Archaeology." *Bulletin of the American Schools of Oriental Research* 62 (1936) 26–31.
Alter, Robert. *The Art of Biblical Narrative*. Revised and updated. New York: Basic Books, 2011.
———. *The Art of Biblical Poetry*. New York: Basic, 1985.
———. "Samson Without Folklore." *Text and Tradition: The Hebrew Bible and Folklore*, edited by Susan Niditch, 47–56. Atlanta: Scholars, 1990.
Amit, Yairah. *Hidden Polemics in Biblical Narrative*. Biblical Interpretation Series 25. Translated by Jonathan Chipman. Leiden: Brill, 2000.
Assis, Elie. *Self-Interest or Communal Interest: An Ideology of Leadership in the Gideon, Abimelech and Jephthah Narratives (Judg 6–12)*. Vetus Testamentum Supplement 106. Translated by Stephanie Nakache. Leiden: Brill, 2005.
Bal, Mieke. *Murder and Difference: Gender, Genre, and Scholarship on Sisera's Death*. Translated by Matthew Gumpert. Bloomington: Indiana University Press, 1988.
Barré, Michael L. "The Meaning of PRŠDN in Judges III 22." *Vetus Testamentum* 41 (1991) 1–11.
Barth, Karl. "Preface to the Second Edition." In *The Epistle to the Romans*, translated by Edwyn C. Hoskyns, 2–15. 6th ed. London: Oxford University Press, 1933.
Bauer, Uwe F. W. "Judges 18 as an Anti-Spy Story in the Context of an Anti-Conquest Story: the Creative Usage of Literary Genres." *Journal for the Study of the Old Testament* 88 (2000) 37–47.
Beem, Beverly. "The Minor Judges: A Literary Reading of Some Very Short Stories." In *The Biblical Canon in Comparative Perspective: Scripture in Context IV*, edited by K. Lawson Younger, Jr., William W. Hallo, and Bernard F. Batto, 147–72. Ancient Near Eastern Texts and Studies 11. Lewiston, NY: Edwin Mellen, 1991.
Berman, Joshua A. *Narrative Analogy in the Hebrew Bible: Battle Stories and Their Equivalent Non-battle Narratives*. Vetus Testamentum Supplement 103. Leiden: Brill, 2004.
———. "The 'Sword of Mouths' (Jud. iii 16; Ps. cxlix 6; Prov. v 5): A Metaphor and Its Ancient Near Eastern Context." *Vetus Testamentum* 52 (2002) 291–303.
Berra, Yogi. *The Yogi Book*. New York: Workman, 1998.
Best, Ernest. "The Reading and Writing of Commentaries." *Expository Times* 107 (1996) 358–62.

Bibliography

Block, Daniel I. "Deborah among the Judges: The Perspective of the Hebrew Historian." In *Faith, Tradition, and History: Old Testament Historiography in Its Near Eastern Context,* edited by A. R. Millard, James K. Hoffmeier, and David W. Baker, 229–53. Winona Lake, IN: Eisenbrauns, 1994.

———. "Echo Narrative Technique in Hebrew Literature: A Study in Judges 19." *Westminster Theological Journal* 52 (1990) 325–41.

———. *Judges, Ruth.* New American Commentary 6. Nashville: Broadman & Holman, 1999.

———. "Will the Real Gideon Please Stand Up? Narrative Style and Intention in Judges 6–9." *Journal of the Evangelical Theological Society* 40 (1997) 353–66.

Bluedorn, Wolfgang. *Yahweh Versus Baalism: A Theological Reading of the Gideon-Abimelech Narrative.* Journal for the Study of the Old Testament Supplement 329. Sheffield: Sheffield Academic Press, 2001.

Boling, Robert G. *Judges: Introduction, Translation and Commentary.* Anchor Bible 6A. Garden City, NY: Doubleday, 1975.

Boogaart, T. A. "Stone for Stone: Retribution in the Story of Abimelech and Shechem." *Journal for the Study of the Old Testament* 32 (1985) 45–56.

Bowman, Richard G. "Narrative Criticism: Human Purpose in Conflict with Divine Presence." In *Judges and Method: New Approaches in Biblical Studies,* edited by Gale A. Yee, 17–44. Minneapolis: Fortress, 1995.

Brensinger, Terry L. *Judges.* Believers Church Bible Commentary. Scottdale, PA: Herald, 1999.

Butler, Trent C. *Judges.* Word Biblical Commentary 8. Nashville: Thomas Nelson, 2009.

Chisholm, Robert B., Jr. "The Chronology of the Judges: A Linguistic Clue to Solving a Pesky Problem." *Journal of the Evangelical Theological Society* 52 (2009) 247–55.

———. *A Commentary on Judges and Ruth.* Kregel Exegetical Library. Grand Rapids: Kregel, 2013.

———. "Ehud: Assessing an Assassin." *Bibliotheca sacra* 168 (2011) 274–82.

Claassens, L. J. M. "Notes on the Characterisation in the Jephtah Narrative." *Journal of Northwest Semitic Languages* 22 (1996) 107–15.

Coogan, Michael D. "A Structural and Literary Analysis of the Song of Deborah." *Catholic Biblical Quarterly* 40 (1978) 143–66.

Coogan, Michael D., Marc Z. Brettler, Carol A. Newsom, and Pheme Perkins. *The New Oxford Annotated Bible.* 3rd ed. New York: Oxford University Press, 2001.

Danelius, Eva. "Shamgar Ben 'Anath." *Journal of Near Eastern Studies* 22 (1963) 191–93.

Davis, Dale Ralph. "Comic Literature—Tragic Theology: A Study of Judges 17–18." *Westminster Theological Journal* 46 (1984) 156–63.

———. *Such a Great Salvation: Expositions on the Book of Judges.* Grand Rapids: Baker, 1991.

Day, J. *Yahweh and The Gods and Goddesses of Canaan.* Sheffield: Sheffield Academic Press, 2000.

Dorsey, David A. *The Literary Structure of the Old Testament: A Commentary on Genesis–Malachi.* Grand Rapids: Baker, 1999.

Drews, Robert. "The 'Chariots of Iron' of Joshua and Judges." *Journal for the Study of the Old Testament* 45 (1989) 15–23.

Endris, Vince. "Yahweh versus Baal: A Narrative-Critical Reading of the Gideon/Abimelech Narrative." *Journal for the Study of the Old Testament* 33 (2008) 173–95.

Exum, J. Cheryl. "The Centre Cannot Hold: Thematic and Textual Instabilities in Judges." *Catholic Biblical Quarterly* 52 (1990) 410–29

Fewell, Danna Nolan, and David M. Gunn. "Controlling Perspectives: Women, Men, and the Authority of Violence in Judges 4 & 5." *Journal of the American Academy of Religion* 58 (1990) 389–411.

Fokkelman, J. P. *Reading Biblical Narrative: An Introductory Guide*. Louisville: Westminster John Knox, 1999.

———. "The Song of Deborah and Barak: Its Prosodic Levels and Structure." In *Pomegranates and Golden Bells: Studies in Biblical, Jewish, and Near Eastern Ritual, Law, and Literature in Honor of Jacob Milgrom*, edited by David P. Wright, David Noel Freedman, and Avi Hurvitz, 595–628. Winona Lake, IN: Eisenbrauns, 1995.

———. "Structural Remarks on Judges 9 and 19." In *"Sha'arei Talmon": Studies in the Bible, Qumran, and the Ancient Near East Presented to Shemaryahu Talmon*, edited by Michael Fishbane and Emanuel Tov, 33–45. Winona Lake, IN: Eisenbrauns, 1992.

Frolov, Serge, and Alexander Frolov. "Sisera Unfastened: On the Meaning of Judges 4:21 ab–g." *Biblische Notizen* 165 (2015) 55–61.

Gillmayr-Bucher, Susanne. "Framework and Discourse in the Book of Judges." *Journal of Biblical Literature* 128 (2009) 687–702.

Gitin, Seymour, and Mordechai Cogan. "A New Type of Dedicatory Inscription from Ekron." *Israel Exploration Journal* 49 (1999) 193–202.

Gooding, D. W. "The Composition of the Book of Judges." *Eretz Israel* 16 (1982) 70–79.

Green, Alberto R. W. *The Storm-God in the Ancient Near East*. Biblical and Judaic Studies 8. Winona Lake, IN: Eisenbrauns, 2003.

Greenspahn, Frederick E. "The Theology of the Framework of Judges." *Vetus Testamentum* 36 (1986) 385–96.

Grottanelli, Cristiano. *Kings and Prophets: Monarchic Power, Inspired Leadership, and Sacred Text in Biblical Narrative*. New York: Oxford University Press, 1999.

Halpern, Baruch. "The Assassination of Eglon: The First Locked-Room Murder Mystery." *Biblical Research* 4.6 (1988) 33–44.

Hamilton, Victor P. *Handbook on the Historical Books*. Grand Rapids: Baker, 2001.

Hasel, Gerhard. "זָעַק, zā'aq." In *Theological Dictionary of the Old Testament, Volume 4*, edited by G. Johannes Botterweck, Heinz-Josef Fabry, and Helmer Ringgren, 115. Grand Rapids: Eerdmans, 1981.

Hauser, Alan J. "Two Songs of Victory: Exodus 15 and Judges 5." In *Directions in Biblical Hebrew Poetry*, edited by Elaine R. Follis, 265–84. Journal for the Study of the Old Testament Supplement 40. Sheffield: JSOT Press, 1987.

Janzen, David. "Why the Deuteronomist Told about the Sacrifice of Jephthah's Daughter." *Journal for the Study of the Old Testament* 29 (2005) 339–57.

Kellerman, D. "גּוּר gûr." In *Theological Dictionary of the Old Testament, Volume II*, translated by John T. Willis, 439–49. Grand Rapids: Eerdmans, 1975.

Kim, Jichan. *The Structure of the Samson Cycle*. Kampen, Netherlands: Kok Pharos, 1993.

Klein, Lillian R. *The Triumph of Irony in the Book of Judges*. Journal for the Study of the Old Testament Supplement Series 68. Bible and Literature Series 14. Sheffield: Almond Press, 1988.

Koehler, L., W. Baumgartner, and J. J. Stamm. "*פַּרְדֹן." In *Hebrew and Aramaic Lexicon of the Old Testament, Volume 3*. Leiden: Brill, 1996.

Kuruvilla, Abraham. "Christiconic Interpretation," *Bibliotheca sacra* 173 (2016) 131–46.
———. *Genesis: A Theological Commentary for Preachers*. Eugene, OR: Resource Publications, 2014.
———. "Pericopal Theology," *Bibliotheca sacra* 173 (2016) 3–17.
———. *Privilege the Text! A Theological Hermeneutic for Preaching*. Chicago: Moody, 2013.
———. *Text to Praxis: Hermeneutics and Homiletics in Dialogue*. Library of New Testament Studies 393. London: T. & T. Clark, 2009.
———. *A Vision for Preaching: Understanding the Heart of Pastoral Ministry*. Grand Rapids: Baker, 2015.
Lapsley, Jacqueline E. *Whispering the Word: Hearing Women's Stories in the Old Testament*. Louisville: Westminster John Knox, 2005.
Lewis, Theodore J. "The Identity and Function of El/Baal Berith." *Journal of Biblical Literature* 115 (1996) 401–23.
Lindars, Barnabas. "Deborah's Song: Women in the Old Testament." *Bulletin of the John Rylands Library* 65 (1983) 158–75.
———. *Judges 1–5*. London: T. & T. Clark, 1994.
Marais, Jacobus. *Representation in Old Testament Narrative Texts*. Biblical Interpretation Series 36. Leiden: Brill, 1998.
Matthews, Victor H. *Judges and Ruth*. New Cambridge Bible Commentaries. Cambridge: Cambridge University Press, 2004.
McCann, J. Clinton. *Judges*. Louisville: Westminster John Knox, 2011.
Merrill, Eugene H. *Deuteronomy*. New American Commentary 4. Nashville: Broadman and Holman, 1994.
Miller, Geoffrey P. "Verbal Feud in the Hebrew Bible: Judges 3:12–30 and 19–21." *Journal of Near Eastern Studies* 55 (1996) 105–117.
Mobley, Gregory. *The Empty Men: The Heroic Tradition of Ancient Israel*. New York: Doubleday, 2005.
Murray, D. F. "Narrative Structure and Technique in the Deborah-Barak Story (Judges IV 4–22)." In *Studies in the Historical Books of the Old Testament*, edited by J. A. Emerton, 155–89. Vetus Testamentum Supplement 30. Leiden: Brill 1979.
Nelson, Richard D. "Ideology, Geography, and the List of Minor Judges." *Journal for the Study of the Old Testament* 31 (2007) 347–64.
Niditch, Susan. "Eroticism and Death in the Tale of Jael." In *Gender and Difference in Ancient Israel*, edited by Peggy L. Day, 43–57. Minneapolis: Fortress, 1989.
———. *Judges*. Old Testament Literature. Louisville: Westminster John Knox, 2008.
O'Connell, Robert H. *The Rhetoric of the Book of Judges*. Vetus Testamentum Supplement 63. Leiden: Brill, 1996.
Olson, Dennis T. "The Book of Judges: Introduction, Commentary, Reflections." In *The New Interpreter's Bible, Volume II*, edited by Leander Keck and David Petersen, 721–888. Nashville: Abingdon, 1998.
Pardee, Dennis "Ugaritic Science." In *The World of the Aramaeans III: Studies in Language and Literature in Honour of Paul-Eugène Dion*, edited by P. M. Michèle Daviau, John W. Wevers, and Michael Weigl, 223–54. Journal for the Study of the Old Testament Supplement 326. Sheffield: Sheffield Academic Press, 2001.
Polzin, Robert. *Moses and the Deuteronomist: A Literary Study of Deuteronomic History: Part One: Deuteronomy, Joshua, Judges*. New York: Seabury, 1980.

Pritchard, J. B. *Ancient Near Eastern Texts Relating to the Old Testament.* 3rd ed. Princeton: Princeton University Press, 1969.
Ramban Nachmanides. *Commentary on the Torah: Leviticus.* Translated by Charles B. Chavel. New York: Shilo, 1974.
Rashi Yitzhaki. *Judges: A New English Translation.* Translated by Avrohom Fishelis and Shmuel Fishelis. New York: Judaica, 1991.
Reis, Pamela Tamarkin. "The Levite's Concubine: New Light on a Dark Story." *Scandinavian Journal of Theology* 20 (2006) 125–46.
———. "Uncovering Jael and Sisera: A New Reading." *Scandinavian Journal of the Old Testament* 19 (2005) 24–47.
Sasson, Jack M. *Judges 1–12: A New Translation with Introduction and Commentary.* Anchor Yale Bible 6D. New Haven: Yale University Press, 2014.
———. "Who Cut Samson's Hair? (And Other Trifling Issues Raised by Judges 16)." *Prooftexts* 8 (1988) 333–46.
Satterthwaite, Philip. "'No King in Israel': Narrative Criticism and Judges 17–21." *Tyndale Bullletin* 44 (1993) 75–88.
Schneider, Tammi J. *Judges.* Berit Olam: Studies in Hebrew Narrative and Poetry. Collegeville, MN: Liturgical, 2000.
Schwemer, Daniel. "The Storm-gods of The Ancient Near East: Summary, Synthesis, Recent Studies Part II." *Journal of Ancient Near Eastern Religions* 8 (2008) 1–44.
Sharon, Diane M. "Echoes of Gideon's Ephod: An Intertexual Reading." *Journal of the Ancient Near Eastern Society* 30 (2006) 89–102.
Smith, Mark S., and Wayne T. Pitard. *The Ugaritic Baal Cycle Volume II: Introduction with Text, Translation and Commentary of KTU/CAT 1.3–1.4.* Leiden: Brill, 2009.
Smith, Michael J. "The Failure of the Family in Judges, Part 1: Jephthah." *Bibliotheca sacra* 162 (2005) 279–98.
Sodon, John M. "Samson: The Image of Israel's Loyalties in Judges." *Evangelical Journal* 26 (2008) 65–78.
Spronk, Klaas. "A Story to Weep About: Some Remarks on Judges 2:1–5 and Its Context." In *Unless Someone Guide Me . . . : Festschrift for Karel A. Deurloo.* Amsterdamse Cahiers voor Exegese van de Bijbel en zijn Tradities Supplement Series 2. Maastricht, Netherlands: Uitgeverij Shaker, 2001.
Sternberg, Meir. *The Poetics of Biblical Narrative: Ideological Literature and the Drama of Reading.* Bloomington: Indiana University Press, 1987.
Trible, Phyllis. *Texts of Terror: Literary-Feminist Readings of Biblical Narratives.* Philadelphia: Fortress, 1984.
van Wolde, Ellen. "Ya'el in Judges 4." *Zeitschrift für die alttestamentliche Wissenschaft* 107 (1995) 240–46.
Webb, Barry G. *The Book of Judges.* New International Commentary on the Old Testament. Grand Rapids: Eerdmans, 2012.
Wharton, James A. "The Secret of Yahweh: Story and Affirmation in Judges 13–16." *Interpretation* 27 (1973) 48–66.
Williams, Jay G. "The Structure of Judges 2:6—16:31." *Journal for the Study of the Old Testament* 49 (1991) 77–85.
Wong, Gregory T. K. *Compositional Strategy of the Book of Judges: An Inductive, Rhetorical Study.* Vetus Testamentum Supplement 111. Netherlands: Leiden, 2006.

———. "Gideon: A New Moses?" In *Reflection and Refraction: Studies in Biblical Historiography in Honour of A. Graeme Auld,* edited by Robert Rezetko, Timothy H. Lim, and W. Brian Aucker, 529–44. Leiden: Brill, 2007.
———. "Ehud and Joab: Separated at Birth?" *Vetus Testamentum* (2006) 399–412.
———. "Song of Deborah as Polemic." *Biblica* 88 (2007) 1–22.
Younger K. Lawson, Jr. *Judges, Ruth*. New International Version Application Commentary. Grand Rapids: Zondervan, 2001.

INDEX OF ANCIENT SOURCES

1QM (War Scroll)
13:11	275n28
13:16	275n28
15.3	275n28

Aqhat Legend
A, 34–35	178n30
C, 42–46	137n25

Archives royales de Mari
2.48	281n46

Aristophanes, Ecclesiazusae
1020	99n33

Augustine, De doctrina christiana
4.27.59	5

b. Yebamot
103a	99n33

b. Nazir
23b	99n33

b. Megillah
14b	90n6

b. Sanhedrin
101a	253n18

Jubilees
1.20	275n28

Liber antiquitatum biblicarum
31:3	99n33

Sirach
21:3	75
44:1—45:26	5
46:11–12	5

Tertullian, Apology
39	2n4

Testament of Reuben
2:2	275n28

INDEX OF MODERN AUTHORS

Ackerman, Susan, 90
Albright, W. F., 110n10
Alter, Robert, 120n36, 215n10, 235
Amit, Yairah, 42n41, 253n18, 261
Assis, Elie, 136, 142, 150, 160n35, 162, 175, 177, 190

Bal, Mieke, 99
Barré, Michael L., 80
Barth, Karl, 303–4
Bauer, Uwe F. W., 262
Beem, Beverly, 8, 182, 183
Berman, Joshua A., 75, 295
Berra, Yogi, 237
Best, Ernest, 4
Block, Daniel I., 5n9, 6–7, 11, 11n24, 13, 17, 30, 31, 41, 42n41, 51, 57n28, 67, 74, 82n46, 89, 91, 101n37, 107n1, 108, 112, 120n36, 133, 142, 156, 159, 160, 161, 170n11, 179n33, 189, 194, 194n14, 195, 221n23, 234, 241, 254, 256, 257, 260, 276, 277, 277n31, 280, 281n46, 282, 291, 292, 297n31, 301
Bluedorn, Wolfgang, 127n3, 135n15, 136, 138, 141, 152, 152n10, 154, 160, 167, 170, 171, 178
Boling, Robert G., 5n9, 229
Boogaart, T. A., 177
Bowman, Richard G., 3, 282, 289
Brensinger, Terry L., 116
Brettler, Marc Z., 288
Burns, Robert, 179n34

Butler, Trent C., 5, 5n9, 50n7, 57n28, 60, 62, 135, 180, 182, 228, 251, 296

Chisholm, Robert B., Jr., 5n9, 11, 12n26, 14n33, 16n37, 34n18, 37n26, 43, 48n4, 53n16, 54, 58, 61, 74n22, 76n28, 78n3390, 116, 121, 135, 138n25, 168, 180n38, 212n4, 234n12, 236n20, 237n20, 260, 261, 263, 270, 278n37, 294n25
Claassens, L. J. M., 189n5
Cogan, Mordechai, 143n39
Coogan, Michael D., 110, 288

Danelius, Eva, 82
Davis, Dale Ralph, 86, 261, 263n47
Day, J., 82n46
Dorsey, David A., 67
Drews, Robert, 33n14

Endris, Vince, 170
Exum, J. Cheryl, 56, 299

Fewell, Danna Nolan, 121, 121n39
Fokkelman, J. P., 107n1, 121, 140, 158, 180, 274, 275,
Frolov, Alexander, 101–2
Frolov, Serge, 101–2

Gillmayr-Bucher, Susanne, 52–53, 55
Gitin, Seymour, 143n39
Gooding, D. W., 148, 181
Green, Alberto R. W., 110n11
Greenspahn, Frederick E., 52–53, 56
Grottanelli, Cristiano, 100

INDEX OF MODERN AUTHORS

Gunn, David M., 121, 121n39

Halpern, Baruch, 72n14
Hamilton, Victor P., 63
Harrison, George, 203n34
Hasel, Gerhard, 56

Janzen, David, 198

Kellerman, D., 254n21
Kim, Jichan, 227, 228n1, 241n35
Klein, Lillian R., 33, 39, 60n37, 80, 89n5, 143, 154, 161n38, 171, 251, 252, 252n15, 259, 270, 276
Kuruvilla, Abraham, 1, 2, 2n5, 2n6, 12, 41n38, 44n47, 64n46, 103n43, 304, 305

Lapsley, Jacqueline E., 275, 279
Lewis, Theodore J., 169n9
Lindars, Barnabas, 99n33, 107n3

Marais, Jacobus, 32, 107n3, 108, 128, 260, 263
Matthews, Victor H., 141
McCann, J. Clinton, 255, 301
Merrill, Eugene H., 271n13
Miller, Geoffrey P., 72
Mobley, Gregory, 70
Murray, D. F., 92, 99, 100

Nelson, Richard D., 182n46
Newsom, Carol A., 288
Niditch, Susan, 41n39, 99n33, 120n36, 121, 173n17, 220, 287

O'Connell, Robert H., 15, 29, 48, 70–71, 73, 75, 76, 80n34, 96, 103, 107, 113, 119, 131, 138, 162, 181, 241n37, 250, 256, 268, 276, 299
Olson, Dennis T., 35, 250

Pardee, Dennis, 197n21
Perkins, Pheme, 288
Pitard, Wayne T., 116n25

Polzin, Robert, 28, 48, 61, 148, 167, 232, 259, 281n49, 286n5

Ramban (Nachmanides), 201n32
Rashi (Yitzhaki), 263n46
Reis, Pamela Tamarkin, 120n37, 269, 271, 272, 277, 281, 282, 291n14

Sasson, Jack M., 54n19, 57n29, 110n9, 153, 196, 240n34
Satterthwaite, Philip, 248, 269, 288
Schneider, Tammi J., 5n9, 16, 138n27, 162, 174, 236, 252n14, 271n12, 300
Schwemer, Daniel, 110
Sharon, Diane M., 159
Smith, Mark S., 116n25
Smith, Michael J., 204
Sodon, John M., 227
Spronk, Klaas, 42n41
Sternberg, Meir, 103

Trible, Phyllis, 200, 281

van Wolde, Ellen, 100

Webb, Barry G., 5n9, 12, 15, 15n33, 34, 40, 51, 54n19, 58, 80n36, 115n23, 117, 132, 135n15, 138n26, 153, 154, 156n19, 163, 175, 179, 180, 181, 195, 198, 213, 221, 236, 237, 238, 244, 253n19, 263, 275n28, 278, 280, 292, 300
Wharton, James A., 213, 238
Williams, Jay G., 8–9, 9n21
Wong, Gregory T. K., 7n15, 18, 23n65, 37n23, 40, 41n37, 72, 75, 77, 91, 109, 111, 114n21, 117, 127n3, 156n17, 159, 169, 249n4, 260, 295

Younger, K. Lawson, Jr., 5n9, 10, 33n13, 43, 48, 57n28, 61, 115, 120, 135n17, 173, 176–77, 237n23, 238, 276, 294, 297n33

INDEX OF SCRIPTURE

OLD TESTAMENT
Genesis

1:20	222	19:9–11	276
1:24	222	19:9	276
1:30	222	19:12–29	276
2:7	222	19:14	277n31
3:13	41n39	19:15	277n31
4	271n15	19:16	276n31
4:1	51, 275n28	19:19	277n31
4:8	272n15	19:32	120n36, 236
4:9	272n15	19:34	120n36, 236
4:10	272n15	19:35	120n36
9:12	222	21:2	212
9:15–16	222	21:21	220n19
9:15	222	22	272n15
12:18	41n39	22:2	272n15
14:13	169n9	22:3	272n15
15:2–3	214	22:6	272n15, 282n49
15:15	162	22:7	272n15
15:19	38	22:8	272n15
16:1–4	214	22:9	272n15
16:1–2	214	22:10	272n15, 282n49
16:2	229n3	22:12	271n15
18:19	51	22:13	272n15
19	268, 276, 278, 290	22:16–18	41n38
19:1	276	22:16	272n15
19:2	276, 276n31	22:17	189n3
19:3	276, 277n31	24	220n19
19:4	276	24:7	41n38
19:5	275n28, 276	24:41	252n15
19:6	276	24:61	107n1
19:7–8	276	25:1	270n9
19:8	275n28, 276	25:2–4	130n7

Genesis (continued)

Reference	Page
25:8	162
25:19	214
25:21	212, 214
25:26	214
26:3	41n38
26:10	41n39
26:28	252n15
26:30	221n23
27:25	272
27:39	116n25
28:17	253n18
28:22	253n18
29:21	229n3
29:25	41n39
30:1–2	214
30:3	229n3
30:14–15	214
30:23	212
31:14	107n1
31:19–35	252n13
33:5	189n3
34	167, 168
34:2	277n34
34:7	277
35:8	42n41
35:29	189n3
36:11	38
36:15	38
36:42	38
37:25–36	130n7
38:8	229n3
41:2	80n36
41:4	80n36
41:5	80n36
41:7	80n36
41:18	80n36
41:20	80n36
41:50–52	31n9
45:8	254n24
49:11	183n49
49:13–14	115n23
49:33	189n3
50:12–13	189n3
50:23	114n21

Exodus

Reference	Page
1:11–14	127
1:15–21	101n38
1:21	101n38
2:14	96
2:23–24	127
3:1	127, 127n3, 272n15
3:2–7	127
3:2–3	127
3:10	127
3:11	127
3:12	127
3:14	127
3:15	127
3:16–17	127
3:20	127
4:1–7	127
4:10	127
4:13	127
4:18–20	127
4:18	272n15
4:21	69
4:29–30	127
6:11	127
6:18–20	254n21
6:25	127, 263n46, 293
9:12	69
10:4	127
10:12	127
10:13	127
10:14	127, 127n2
10:19	127
10:20	69
10:27	69
11:10	69
12:35–36	159
13:2	200
13:5	41n38
13:11	41n38
13:13	200
14–15	107
14	96
14:1–4	96
14:4	69, 96
14:5	96
14:6	96

14:7	96	18:22	6
14:8	69, 96	18:26	6
14:9	96	19:6	249
14:10–12	96	20:4–5	251n13
14:11	41n39	20:4	261
14:13	96	20:6	122, 169
14:17	69, 96	21:16	299
14:18	96	21:34	37n23
14:21	96	22:19	296
14:23–28	33n14	23:32–33	43
14:23	96	23:32	98
14:24–25	96	24:13	32
14:24	96	26:35	258
14:25–27	96n23	28:4–31	159n29
14:25	96	28:6–14	252n13
14:27	96	28:41	253n19
14:28	96	29:9	253n19
14:30–31	127	29:20	72n15
14:30	96	29:29	253n19
14:31	51	29:33	253n19
15	87, 96, 141	29:35	253n19
15:1	96, 107	32:1–8	159
15:4	33n14, 107	32:1–6	127n4
15:5	107	32:1	159
15:6	107	32:2–3	159
15:9	107	32:4	80n36, 159, 251n13, 254
15:10	107		
15:11	216n12	32:8	57n29, 80n36, 252n13, 254
15:13–18	249		
15:13	169	32:13	41n38
15:19	107	32:19	80n36
15:20–21	106n1, 107	32:20	80n36, 159
15:20	90n7, 106n1	32:24	80n36
15:25	56n26	32:25–29	254
15:26	220, 249	32:35	80n36
16:33	133	33:1	41n38
16:34	133	33:2	41n37
17:4	56n26	33:20	216
17:8–9	96	34:6	169
18	272n15	34:7	169
18:1	127n3	34:11–15	43
18:13–16	91, 96	34:13	135n18
18:13–14	90	34:15–16	57n28, 161n37
18:13	6	34:16	38n29, 58, 219n17
18:15	258	34:17	252n13
18:21–26	91n12	39:2–22	159n29
18:21–22	90n7	40:24	258

Leviticus

1:1–15	81n40
2:1–15	81n39
2:1–14	81n40
2:8	133
3:3–17	81n42
4:8	81n42
4:9	81n42
4:19	81n42
4:26	81n42
4:31	81n42
4:35	81n42
5:13	81n39
6:2	299n39
6:4	299n39
6:7–16	81n39
7:32	72n15
8:23	72n15
10:19	249
11:24–25	222
11:39–40	222
14:7	81n41
14:53	81n41
16:10	81n41
16:21	81n41
16:22	81n41
16:26	81n41
17:7	57n28
18:22	236
19:4	252n13
19:24	178n30
20:5–6	57n28
20:10	270n11
26:1	251n13
26:42–44	41n38
27:1–8	200

Numbers

3:10	254n21
6	218n15
6:1–21	217
6:3	221
10:29–32	98
10:29	272n15
11:2	56n26
11:28	32
12–14	256, 257, 268
12:1	107n1
12:8	51
13:1–2	257
13:2–33	257
13:2–17	257
13:7	257
13:20	80n36
13:21	257
13:30	257
14:1–4	257
14:7–8	257
14:9	257
14:10	257
14:18	169
14:19	169
14:24	257
14:26–37	257
14:30–31	257
14:36	257
14:38	257
14:39	257
14:40–45	257
16:3	289
16:30	199n28
16:32	199n28
17:7	133
18:1–7	254n21
18:15	200
20:4	289
21	34n18
21:4	192n8
21:13	197n22
21:29	196n18
23:21	249
23:27	220
24:21	96
25:7–11	293
25:7	263n46
25:11	263n46
26	292
26:29	114n21
27:18	32
30:2	23n65
31:6	263n46
31:17–18	298n36
31:17	275n28
32:12	32, 38

32:24	197n22	8:19–20	301
32:39–40	111n21	9:12	57n29, 252n13
33:55	43	9:16	57n29, 252n13
35:12–28	156n19	9:18	55, 250
34:2	256n29	9:23	259
		10:1	70
		10:3	70

Deuteronomy

		10:11	259
1:8	259	11:1	122
1:16–17	91n12	11:8	259
2:3–9	198	11:10–17	138n25
2:19–23	198	11:29	167
2:24–36	198	11:31	259
2:34	33n13	12	250
3:6	33n13	12:1–32	250
3:12–17	198	12:1–4	190n6
3:15	114n21	12:2–3	250
4:16	71, 241n13,	12:3	71, 135n18,
4:23	71, 251n13		136n20
4:25	55, 71, 250, 251n13	12:4–27	253
5:8–9	251n13	12:4–18	250
5:8	71	12:5	263, 268n3
5:10	122	12:8	220, 250
6:5	122	12:11	263, 268n3
6:10	41n38	12:12	250
6:12	61	12:13–14	268n3
6:14–15	55n23	12:18	250, 263, 268n3
6:18	41n38, 220, 249, 259	12:19	250
		12:21	268n3
7:1–5	32n10, 42, 298n35	12:25	220, 249
7:1–3	219n17	12:26–27	250
7:1–2	34n19, 296n29	12:26	268n3
7:2	33n13, 39, 98	12:28	220, 249
7:3–4	38n29, 58, 161n37	12:29–31	190n6
7:4	55n23	12:31	200
7:4–5	35, 135n18, 136n20	13:12–19	296
		13:12–18	262n45, 291, 296n29
7:5	71		
7:6	190	13:13	275n28, 291
7:9	122	13:14	291
7:16	32n10, 42, 43	13:16–17	298n35
7:25–26	32n10, 35, 42	13:16	268n3, 296n29
7:25	71	13:17	300
7:26	296	13:18	249
8:1	259	13:19	220
8:11	61	14:2	190
8:17–18	143n40	16:18–20	91n12
8:18	168	16:18	6

Deuteronomy (continued)

17:2–3	55
17:2	250
17:8–13	91n12
17:9	6, 248
17:12	6
17:14–20	162
17:17	161
17:18	248, 254n21
18:1–5	254n22
18:10	200
18:16–21	91n12
19:4–6	156n19
19:11–13	156n19
19:17–18	6
20:1–20	262n45
20:10–15	260
20:11	34n19
20:12–14	260
20:16–18	34n19, 296n29, 298n35
20:17	33n13
21:2	6
21:5	254n21
21:9	220
21:23	282
22	271
22:13–14	271
22:15–17	271
22:15	271
22:16	271
22:17	271n13
22:18–19	271
22:19	271
22:20–21	271
22:21	277
22:22	270n11
22:29	277n34
22:55–57	299
23:2–3	289
24:7	299
24:8	248
25:1–3	91n12
25:1–2	6
26:4	133
26:7	192n8
26:10	133
27:9	248
27:14	248
27:15	71, 251n13, 252n13
28:15–68	292
28:15–37	55n23
28:29	299n39
28:31	299n39
28:57	80n36, 120n36
29:12	252n15
29:14	252n15
29:23	179n33
30:20	122
31:11	263
31:16–21	55n23
31:16	57n28
31:29	55, 250
32:16	55
32:21	55
32:26–27	143n40
32:35	230, 243n40
32:41	37n23
32:42	75n26
33:5	249
33:13	116n25
34:2	69n5
34:5	51
34:9	32
34:10	32, 96

Joshua

1:1	28, 30, 32, 51
1:7–8	54n18
1:11	69n6, 259
1:15	69n6
2	40, 257, 258
2:1	40, 258
2:3–5	101
2:9–13	40, 258
2:10	33n13
2:12	40n33
2:13–14	40
2:13	258
2:14	40n33
2:15–21	40
2:19	197n22
3:10	41n37, 69n6

INDEX OF SCRIPTURE 323

4:1–24	42	11:4–9	33n14
5:9	42	11:5	231n7
6:1–21	40	11:6	51
6:2	51	11:10	156n17
6:4	142	11:12	156n17
6:8	142	11:17	54n19, 156n17
6:9	142	11:21–22	37n25
6:13	142	11:23	259
6:16	142	13:6	69n6
6:17–21	33n13	13:31	114n21
6:18	296	14–15	37n25
6:20	142	14:6–15	34, 37
6:21	40n34, 298n35	14:6	38
6:22–25	40	14:14	38
6:23	40n34	14:15	259
6:24	298n35	15:7	258
6:25	40	15:8	34
6:26	40	15:13	37
6:27	40	15:14–15	37
7:15	295n28	15:17	60n35
7:24–26	199n27	15:18	102
8	298n35	17:1	114n21
8:2	295	18:1	293
8:4	295	18:5	31n9
8:7	69n6, 295	18:17	258
8:9	295	18:28	34
8:11	231n7	19:1–9	32n12
8:12	295	19:40–48	256
8:14	295	19:40–46	19
8:19	295	19:47	259
8:20	295n28	20:4	156n19
8:21	295	21:4–5	254n21
8:23	156n17	21:20–26	254n21
8:25	295	22–24	27
8:27	295	22:5	122
8:28	295	22:10–34	293
8:29	156n17	22:12–13	293
8:30–35	296	22:12	289
10:5	231n7	22:30–32	263n46
10:8	51	23:5	69n6
10:16–18	156n17	23:6–8	54n18
10:22–28	156n17	23:9	69n6
10:29	156n17	23:11	122
10:34	231n7	23:12–13	58
10:36–37	37n25	23:12	38n29
10:36	156n17	23:13	43
11	93	23:14–16	54n18
11:1–11	93, 93n17	24	168

Joshua (continued)

24:1–27	301
24:1	167
24:18	41n37
24:26–27	54n18
24:28–31	49, 50n6
24:28	48, 50, 301
24:29	50, 51
24:30	50
24:31	50
24:32	167

Judges

(Also see within the appropriate chapter for particular verses of a pericope.)

1–9	182
1:1—3:6	16, 47, 93n18
1:1—2:5	7, 7n14, 18n47, 19, 24, 46, 47, 58, 168n6, 267, 285, 285n1, 305
1	7, 248, 267, 286
1:1–2	48, 233, 267, 286
1:1	193, 285n1, 288, 292, 292n18, 294n24
1:2–36	19
1:2	18, 74n21, 285n1
1:3	285n1, 286
1:4–7	169
1:4	14, 94, 285n1
1:5	14
1:6	14n32, 152, 169
1:7	18, 149n5, 156, 169
1:8	14, 18, 75, 285n1, 298n35
1:9–10	14
1:11—3:6	18
1:11–15	18, 267, 286
1:12–16	268
1:12–15	10, 220n19
1:12	18n49, 86
1:14	102
1:15	18n49
1:16	18, 98, 272n15, 285n1
1:17	14, 267, 268, 285n1, 286, 298n35
1:18–36	13
1:18	14, 148
1:19	69, 93n16, 121, 223n26
1:20	69, 223n26
1:21–36	82
1:21	12, 18, 69, 223n26
1:22	18, 285n1
1:23	18
1:25	14, 18, 75, 285n1, 298n35
1:26	12, 170
1:27	69, 223n26
1:28	69, 223n26
1:29	69, 223n26
1:30	69, 223n26
1:31	69, 223n26
1:32	69, 223n26
1:33	69, 223n26
1:34–36	256
1:34	115n23
2	7, 248, 267, 286
2:1–23	28n2
2:1–3	15, 16, 19n51, 20
2:1–2	129, 130, 168
2:1	13, 18, 160n31, 285n1
2:2	18, 70, 218, 219n17
2:3	13, 160
2:4	15, 18, 118, 286n2, 297n32, 301
2:5	130, 170
2:6—3:11	8, 19, 24, 26, 27n1, 29, 65, 88, 103, 306
2:6—3:10	41
2:6—3:6	7, 7n14, 16, 19, 27, 28, 28n2, 255
2:6–23	41
2:6–10	17
2:6–9	28
2:6	69, 223n26
2:7—16:31	7n14
2:7	196n17

2:8	32, 298n37	3:6	17, 18n49, 38, 70, 82, 161, 161n37, 219n17, 248n2, 285n1
2:10—3:6	248n2		
2:10–19	248n2		
2:10	13, 17, 196n17		
2:11–19	8, 13, 15, 16, 19, 19n51, 66, 87, 91, 93, 106, 128, 160, 166, 175, 209	3:7—16:31	7, 11, 17, 19, 20n53, 27, 35, 49n5, 247, 247n1, 248, 250, 287
2:11–13	13, 70, 250n7	3:7–31	88, 95n21
2:11	13, 19, 67, 88, 129, 188, 210, 250, 278n35	3:7–11	7n14, 27n1, 28n2, 38, 66, 88, 92
		3:7–8	131
2:12	13, 21n56, 141, 196n17	3:7	11, 13, 15, 17, 67, 166, 167n3, 190, 196n17, 250, 250n7, 278n35
2:13	21n55, 21n56		
2:14	19, 67, 88, 129, 188, 210		
		3:8	10, 11n24, 55, 67, 88, 88n2, 94, 167n3, 190, 192
2:15	55n23, 249n4		
2:16–17	6		
2:16	6n12, 13, 19, 67, 88, 90, 111n12, 129, 188, 210	3:9–10	13, 94
		3:9	6n12, 20n55, 67, 89, 90, 93, 94, 111n12, 161, 166, 167n3
2:17–19	16		
2:17	6n12, 13, 70, 141, 160, 196n17		
		3:10–11	11, 147n1, 234
2:18	6n12, 13, 19, 67, 88, 111n12, 129, 188, 210	3:10	6 n12, 14, 67, 70, 91, 92, 143, 149n5, 156, 166, 175, 176, 198, 212, 219, 224
2:19	6n12, 13, 19, 20, 67, 70, 88, 129, 141, 188, 196n17, 210	3:11	9, 10, 11n24, 67, 122, 166, 175, 203, 259
2:20—3:6	15	3:12–31	22, 24, 47, 85, 113, 306
2:20–22	28n2		
2:20	13, 18, 160n31, 196n17	3:12–14	131
		3:12–13	192
2:21	21n56, 41, 69, 223n26	3:12	11, 13, 53, 59, 166, 167n3, 190, 196n17, 250, 250n7, 278n35
2:22	13, 69, 137, 223n26		
2:28	142, 143		
3–16	7, 27, 47, 248, 251, 267, 286	3:14	10, 11n24, 53, 88, 88n2, 111n12, 167n3
3	101		
3:1	137	3:15–26	100n37
3:4	13, 137	3:15	6n12, 13, 20n55
3:5–6	168	3:16	48n4, 58n31, 166
3:5	18	3:19–20	9n21
3:6–7	13	3:19	88

Judges (continued)

Reference	Pages
3:20	88, 198
3:21–25	14
3:21–22	14n32, 149n5, 156
3:21	100n37
3:24–25	100n37
3:24	88, 120n36
3:25	88, 101n37, 102, 281
3:26	58n31
3:27–29	100n37
3:27	6, 9n21, 100n37
3:28	94, 100n37, 140, 152
3:29–30	147n1
3:29	14, 94, 100n37
3:30	9, 10, 11, 11n24, 14, 53, 100n37, 161, 175, 198, 203, 259
3:31	6n12, 62, 88, 111, 118, 183, 190
4–5	68n4, 120n37, 157
4	7n15, 96n22, 107, 108, 113
4:1–24	6n11, 24, 66, 74n20, 79n33, 105, 106, 107n4, 120n36, 123, 134n13, 144, 180, 306
4:1–3	131
4:1	11, 13, 53, 57, 59, 122, 166, 167n3, 196n17, 250, 250n7, 278n35
4:2	53, 108, 116, 120n37, 166, 175, 190n7, 192
4:3–24	147n1
4:3	10, 20n55, 33, 52n15, 53, 113, 121, 167n3, 209
4:4–14	38n27
4:4–7	20n55
4:4–5	108
4:4	6n11, 6n12, 53, 106n1, 129, 166
4:5	7, 18
4:6–9	108
4:6–7	13, 53, 57
4:6	53, 113, 114, 166
4:7	120n37, 175, 213
4:9	53, 111n12, 119
4:10	6, 113, 114, 115n24, 166
4:11	108, 272n15
4:12–14	108
4:13	33, 121
4:14	52n15, 74, 111n12, 120n37, 122, 142, 143
4:15–17	108
4:15–16	14
4:15	33, 75, 115n24, 198n26, 298n35
4:16	75, 108, 115n24, 116, 152, 298n35
4:17–22	38n27, 111
4:18–20	108
4:18	122
4:21–22	149n5
4:21	14, 14n32, 79n33, 99n33, 108, 120n37, 156, 238
4:22	99n33, 101n37, 106, 108, 122, 140, 152, 281
4:23–24	108, 161
4:23	11, 13, 53, 70, 108, 116, 167n3, 198, 203
4:24	14, 108, 116, 120n37, 153, 167n3
4:25	79n33
4:27	119
5	6, 96, 108, 141, 147n1, 233, 286n3
5:1–31	10n23, 24, 86, 98n30, 100, 103, 125, 286n3, 306
5:1–31a	87
5:1	48n4

INDEX OF SCRIPTURE   327

5:2	212n5	6:13	13, 149
5:3	96	6:14	6n12, 13, 53, 57, 62, 90, 148, 158
5:5	13		
5:6	81, 183	6:15	6n12, 62, 149, 156, 158, 213
5:7–10	20n55		
5:7	244n43	6:16	13, 53, 57, 148
5:9	212n5	6:17–22	149
5:10	183n49	6:19	171
5:11–24	20n55	6:20–21	170
5:15	97n27, 175	6:20	148, 154
5:15b–17	13, 20n54	6:21	149n5
5:23	13, 20n54	6:23	12, 148, 156
5:24–27	98	6:24	170
5:24	101, 212n5	6:25–32	13, 148n2, 160, 173
5:26–27	156	6:25–27	170, 171, 173
5:27	97n27, 100, 140, 281	6:25–26	15, 170
		6:25	10, 58n31, 148, 163
5:30	158	6:27	149, 156
5:31	1, 9, 10, 11, 11n24, 53, 153, 198, 203, 259	6:28–32	171
		6:28–30	13
		6:28	154
5:31b	87, 147n1, 161, 175	6:31	154
6:1—9:57	126	6:32	154, 161, 170
6–8	131	6:33	231n7
6:1—7:22	24, 106, 146, 148, 161n36, 163, 183, 213, 306	6:34–35	6, 171, 197
		6:34	13, 53, 166, 176, 193, 212, 219, 224
6	154	6:35	148, 150, 193
6:1	10, 11, 11n24, 13, 53, 59, 166, 167n3, 171, 190n7, 192, 196n17, 250, 250n7, 278n35	6:36–40	149, 154
		6:36–37	158
		6:36	6n12
		6:37	6n12
		6:38	13
6:2	167n3	6:40	13
6:4	231n7	7–8	68n4
6:6	20n55, 53, 167n3	7:1–8	149
6:7–10	15	7:1	155, 231n7
6:7	53, 171	7:2–3	148
6:8–10	148, 171	7:2	13, 149, 151, 158
6:8	13	7:3	155
6:11—7:14	156, 163	7:4–8	6
6:11–24	149n5	7:4	148
6:11–12	13	7:5	148
6:11	149n5, 151, 154, 166, 171	7:6	89
		7:7	6n12, 13, 52n15, 148, 158
6:12–24	154		
6:12–16	171	7:8	13, 74n21, 111n12, 149n4
6:12	57, 148		

INDEX OF SCRIPTURE

Judges (continued)

7:9–14	154
7:9–11	148, 154
7:9	149
7:10	156
7:13	149
7:14–15	74
7:14	52n15, 154, 158
7:15–23	163
7:15–16	166
7:15	52n15, 94
7:16	171
7:17	171
7:18	159
7:19–22	155, 155n16
7:20–22	151
7:20	89, 158n25, 159
7:21	149
7:22	13, 14, 75, 147, 151, 193
7:23—8:32	21, 23, 24, 126, 126n1, 142n39, 144, 165, 183, 306
7:24—8:32	171
7:24—8:21	163
7:24—8:13	202
7:24	6, 150, 171, 193
7:25	14, 48n4, 160n35, 171, 17
7:29	48n4
8:1–4	202
8:1–3	6, 20n54
8:1	41n39
8:3	52n15, 175
8:4–9	10, 20n54
8:4	48n4
8:6	175
8:7	52n15
8:10	14, 139, 142
8:12	14
8:13–17	10, 20n54
8:14–16	171
8:14	175
8:17	14, 23, 75, 171
8:19	23, 171
8:20	75
8:21	14, 14n32, 127n4
8:22–32	171
8:22	6n12, 62, 90, 127, 175n22, 198n26
8:23	175n22, 249
8:24–27	127, 127n4
8:24	130n7
8:27	13, 15, 21, 58n31, 255
8:28	9, 10, 11, 11n24, 53, 129, 175, 193, 203, 234, 259
8:31	193, 270, 270n9
8:32	53, 129, 234
8:33—10:5	24, 37n23, 147, 156, 160n34, 186, 270, 306
8:33—9:57	160
8:33	13, 54n19, 122, 148n2, 161, 162
9:1–6	193
9:2	161
9:4	54n19, 161, 193
9:5	14, 35
9:6	36n22, 193
9:8–17	161
9:16–17	128n5
9:18	270n9
9:21	187
9:22	10, 11n24
9:23–24	128n5, 162
9:23	212
9:24	37
9:25	299n39
9:26–57	193
9:30	175
9:33—10:5	249n4
9:40	152
9:42	48n4
9:43	14
9:46	161
9:49	14
9:50–57	193
9:53–54	38n27, 14, 100
9:53	14n32
9:54–55	122
9:56–57	15, 37n23, 128n5, 162
9:56	37

INDEX OF SCRIPTURE

10–12	68n4	11:21	52n15
10:1–5	9, 188	11:23	41n37, 63
10:1	6n12, 62, 111n12	11:26	12n26
10:2	6n12, 10, 11n24, 91, 122, 234	11:27	6n12, 91
10:3	6n12, 7n13, 10, 11n24, 91, 111n12	11:29	6, 13, 53, 212, 219, 224
10:4	188	11:30–31	255
10:5	122, 234	11:30	52n15
10:6—23:15	12n26	11:31	13
10:6—12:15	23, 24, 24n67, 37, 166, 184, 207, 306	11:32	14, 53
		11:33	11, 53
10:6—12:7	9	11:34	23, 106n1
10:6–16	13, 15	11:35	23
10:6–14	34	11:36	23n65
10:6–8	58n31, 131, 196n17	11:37	23, 42n42
		11:38	23
10:6	11, 13, 21n55, 53, 55, 57, 59, 167n3, 250, 278n35	11:39	14, 14n32, 23, 122, 255
		11:40	23
10:7	53, 55	12:1–6	9n 21, 10, 20n54, 23
10:8	10, 11n24, 53, 167n3	12:1	6, 193
		12:2–6	6
10:9	48n4, 249n4	12:2	90
10:10	20n55, 167n3	12:4	14, 48n4
10:11–14	20n55, 211	12:6	14
10:11–12	14, 17	12:7	6n12, 9, 10, 11n24, 53, 91, 122, 234
10:11	82, 82n47	12:8–15	9
10:12	6n12	12:8–9	7n13
10:13	6n12, 127	12:8	6n 12, 91
10:14	17, 249n4	12:9–10	234
10:17	231n7	12:9	6n12, 10, 11n24, 91
10:18	175	12:10	122
10:29	176	12:11–12	234
10:30–31	15	12:11	6n12, 7n13, 10, 91, 122
10:39	15	12:13	6n12, 7n13, 91
11:1	10, 57n28	12:14–15	234
11:2	213	12:14	6n12, 7n13, 10 11n24, 91
11:4	48n4	12:15	122
11:5	298n37	13–16	68n4
11:7	298n37	13:1—14:20	20, 21, 24, 187, 226, 228, 229, 230, 234n16, 306
11:8	298n37		
11:9	298n37		
11:10	298n37		
11:11	298n37		
11:12–28	23		
11:12–14	9n21		
11:20	231n7		

Judges (continued)

13:1	10, 11, 13, 21n55, 53, 57, 59, 131, 167n3, 190, 192, 250, 250n7, 278n35
13:2–25	53
13:2	10, 22, 235n17, 238, 252n14
13:3–5	13, 57
13:5	6n12, 62, 90, 230, 240, 242, 243
13:18	18n44
13:24	170
13:25	9, 13, 22, 53, 176, 228, 242, 252n14
14	227, 228
14:1–4	21, 228
14:1	15, 22, 228, 235, 235n17, 238, 243
14:2–3	229
14:2	22, 228
14:3	22, 228, 229, 239, 242, 243
14:4	175n22, 228, 288
14:5–6	228
14:5	21, 197n22, 228, 233
14:6	9, 13, 53, 176, 228, 233
14:7–9	228
14:7	15, 228, 229, 239, 242, 243
14:8–9	15, 21
14:9	176
14:10–20	228
14:10–18	21
14:10	21, 228, 237
14:12–18	228
14:12–14	232
14:14	288
14:15	63, 228, 229, 230, 232, 237n21
14:16–18	228, 232
14:16	42n42, 229n5, 237n21
14:17	237n21
14:18	80n36
14:19–20	21
14:19	9, 13, 14, 21, 53, 227n1, 228, 229, 230, 232
14:19a	228
14:19b	228
14:20	227n1, 228n1, 229
15:1—16:31	20, 21, 24, 208, 210n2, 214n9, 224n28, 246, 306
15:1	15, 22, 211, 212n3
15:1–8	221
15:1–2	272n17
15:3	10, 22
15:4	89
15:5	89
15:6	22
15:7–8	10
15:7	22
15:8	14, 21
15:9–13	10
15:10–13	20
15:11–13	13
15:11	41n39, 175n22
15:12	52n15
15:14–20	210
15:14	9, 13, 53, 176, 211, 212, 288
15:15	14, 21
15:17	171
15:18	52n15, 52n18, 90, 213
15:19	12, 13, 171
15:20	6n12, 10, 91, 210
16:1–31	210
16:1	21, 22, 57n28, 99n33, 211, 212n3, 243
16:3	48n4
16:4–20	252
16:4	21, 211, 218
16:5	252
16:7–12	218
16:15–22	218
16:16	192n8, 223n27
16:17	15, 21, 218, 222
16:19	209n1

16:20	209n1, 213	18:12	12, 22
16:21	14n32, 243	18:14–31	13
16:27	14	18:14–20	13
16:28–30	211, 288	18:14	21, 70n8
16:28	213, 243	18:16	268n3
16:30–31	122	18:17	21, 70n8, 268n3
16:30	14, 53, 210, 218	18:18	21, 70n8
16:31	6n12, 22, 91, 210, 252n14	18:20	21
		18:22	193
17:1—21:25	17	18:23	193
17–18	7, 27, 47, 58n31, 267, 286	18:27	14, 18, 75, 250, 298n35
17:1—18:31	7, 7n14, 12, 18, 20n53, 21, 24, 27, 27n1, 47, 227, 266, 268, 268n5, 306	18:30–31	268n3
		18:30	12, 13, 20n53, 21
		18:31	15, 18, 268n3, 293
		19–21	6, 7, 27, 38, 47, 248
17:1–13	13, 15	19:1—21:25	7, 7n14, 27, 163, 247, 248, 290n11, 299
17:1	24		
17:2	212n5	19	
17:3–5	268	19:1–30	7n14, 10, 12, 13, 18, 22, 24, 27n1, 38, 39n31, 47, 72n13, 247, 251, 269, 284, 285, 287, 290n11, 306
17:3	70n8		
17:4	70n8		
17:5–13	274		
17:5	21, 159		
17:6	12, 22, 22n60, 55, 67n4, 268, 269, 270n11, 278, 288, 292, 301, 303		
		19:1–2	22, 248
		19:1	12, 22n60, 167n4, 248, 249, 287
17:7–8	268	19:2–3	22
17:7	21, 268, 268n2, 270	19:2	57n28, 292n17
17:8	21	19:3–5	161n37
17:9	21	19:10	18, 258
17:10–12	21	19:11	18
17:10	238	19:16	22, 299
17:20	70n8	19:22–27	15
17:30	70n8	19:22–25	250
17:31	70n8	19:22	290, 295
18:1–31	19	19:23	295, 295n28
18:1	12, 22n60, 167n4, 268, 269	19:24	295n28
		19:25–27	294, 295
18:2	22	19:25	291, 294, 295
18:4	21	19:26–29	250
18:5–6	268n3	19:26	294, 295
18:5	18n44	19:27	14, 22, 295
18:7	22	19:29—20:7	22
18:8	22	19:29	14n32
18:9	22	19:30	289
18:11	22, 268n3	20–21	42n41, 249 n4, 269

Judges (continued)

20:1—21:25	7n14, 10, 12, 13, 18n42, 20n53, 22, 24, 24n67, 27n1, 29, 38, 42n41, 47, 72n14, 247, 251, 267, 268, 269, 278n39, 306
20:1–7	250
20:1	269n8
20:2	269n8
20:4	161n37, 281n49
20:5	281n49
20:6	277
20:10	15n33, 277
20:13	175, 278
20:15	22n62
20:16	22, 72
20:17–28	268n3
20:17	22n62
20:18	18, 18n44, 29, 267, 269n8
20:19	231n7
20:21	14
20:23	15, 18, 18n44, 23, 42n42, 269n8
20:25	14, 22n62
20:26–28	263n46
20:26	15, 18, 42n41, 42n42
20:27–28	248, 269n8
20:27	18, 18n44
20:28	23, 251, 268
20:31	18
20:35	14, 15n33, 22n62, 48n4
20:37	18, 22n62, 75
20:43	152, 258
20:46	22n62
20:47	268n3
20:48	18, 22n62, 75, 295
21:1–25	18
21:1–24	18n49
21:1–23	15
21:1	18, 23, 38, 269n8
21:2	15, 18, 42
21:3	269n8
21:5	269n8
21:6	23, 48n4
21:7–8	269n8
21:7	18, 23, 38
21:8–24	250
21:8	23
21:10	14, 75, 250
21:11	267, 268
21:12	18, 23, 248, 268n3
21:18	18, 18n49, 38
21:19–23	248
21:19	18, 255, 268n3
21:21	18, 23, 268n3
21:23	23n66, 268n3
21:24	48n4
21:25	12, 16, 22n60, 24, 55, 167n4, 221, 249, 250, 268, 269, 270n11, 278, 303

Ruth

3:7–8	272
3:7	99n33
4:13	99n33

1 Samuel

1:9	272
1:11	217
1:24–28	217
2:12	275n28
2:28	159
2:31	297n31
4:4	293
4:18	6
7:6	6
7:15–17	6
9:9	258
10:25	133
10:27	275n28
11:7	281
12:9–11	20n53
12:11	16n37, 90, 162, 172
12:12	249
13:19	252n16
15:8–9	156n17
15:23	156n17, 252n13

15:33–34	173	13:7	272n15
16:14	176n24	13:8	272n15
17:26	74n22	13:10	272n15
17:36–37	74n22	13:11	120n36, 272n15
17:45–47	74n22	13:12	272n15, 277, 277n34
17:47	74n22		
17:49	74n22	13:14	277n34
18:6–7	106n1	13:20	272n15
18:6	197n22	13:22	272n15, 277n34
18:10	176n24	13:23	54n19
19:9	176n24	13:26	272n15
19:13	252n13	13:29	183n49
19:16	252n13	13:32	272n15, 277n34
22:15	258	15:4	6
22:18	252n13	15:21	143n39
23:6–12	252n13	18:9	183n49
24:3	120n36	20:8–10	78
24:12	243n40	20:8	78
25:17	275n28	20:9	78
25:36	221n23	20:10	78
30:22	275n28	23:6	275n28
		24:1	176n24

2 Samuel

1 Kings

1:1	28	1:4	275n28
1:11	278n37	1:33	183n49
2:21	224	2:5–6	78
2:26	75n26	2:10	161
3:27	78	2:31–32	78
3:28–39	78	2:32	78
4:12	36	3:3	122
5:18	231n7	3:9	6
5:22	231n7	3:28	6
6:17	160n32	4:23	80n36
11:4	120n36	11:5	196n18
11:14	120n36	11:7	196n18
11:21	180	11:33	196n18, 249n5
11:25	75n26	11:38	249n5
12:3	272n18	11:43	161
12:14	99n33	12:26–33	253n18
12:24	120n36	12:31–32	253n18
13	272n15	12:31	12
13:1	272n15	13:1–3	42n41
13:2	272n15	13:33	253n18
13:3	272n15	14:8	249n5
13:4	272n15	14:31	161
13:5	272n15	15:5	249n5
13:6	272n15		

1 Kings (continued)

15:8	161
15:11	249n5
15:24	161
15:26	250n6
15:34	250n6
16:25	250n6
16:30	250n6
17:1	138n25
20:29–43	156n17
21:10	275n28
22:22	176n24
22:43	249n5

2 Kings

2:1–3	143n39
3:2	250n6
6:21	254n24
8:9	254n24
8:18	250n6
8:27	250n6
10:29	253n18, 263
10:30	249n5
12:2	249n5
13:2	250n6
13:11	250n6
13:14	254n24
14:3	249n5
14:24	250n6
15:3	249n5
15:5	6
15:9	250n6
15:18	250n6
15:24	250n6
15:28	250n6
15:29	263
15:34	249n5
16:2	249n5
16:3	200n30
17:2	250n6
17:17	200n30
17:41	71n11
18:3	249n5
19:1–4	12
19:7	176n24

21:1–18	13, 263n46
21:2	250n6
21:3	13
21:4–5	13
21:6	13, 14, 200n30
21:9	14
21:10–15	14
21:20	250n6
22:2	249n5
22:14–20	90n7
23:1–20	12
23:7	54n19
23:13	196n18
23:15–20	42n41
23:24	252n13
23:32	250n6
23:37	250n6
24:9	250n6
24:19	250n6

1 Chronicles

1:32	270n9
5:15	160 n31
21:1	176n24
23:12–15	254n21
23:16	263n46
26:24	263n46
29:28	162

2 Chronicles

14:3	136n20
15:3–6	249n4
15:4	249n4
15:5	249n4
18:21	176n24
28:15	69n5
31:1	136n20
33:1	13
33:19	71n11
33:22	71n11
34:3	71n11
34:4	71n11, 136n20
34:7	71n11, 136n20
34:22–28	90n7

Nehemiah

6:14	90n7
9:27–28	8n17

Esther

1:5–10	221n23
1:6	159n30
5:5–14	221n23
6:14	221n23
7:2–8	221n23
8:15	159n30

Job

1:4	221n23
21:4	192n8
39:21	197n22

Psalms

2:4	161
9:7	161
18:4–5	275n28
25:6	243
25:18	192n8
29:10	161
31:23	122
37:14	75n26
44:3	41n37
55:19	161
57:5	75n26
61:7	161
68:7–9	111n16
73:27	57n28, 270
74:18	243
77:11	216n12
77:14	216n12
78:12	216n12
78:58	71n11
80:9	41n37
88:10	216n12
88:12	216n12
89:50	243
90:10	192n8
102:12	161
106:4	243
106:39	57n28, 160n31
107:34	179n33
119:129	216n12
127:3–5	189n3
132:1	243
132:2	23n65
137:7	243
149:6	75n26

Proverbs

5:4	75n26
5:15	99n33
5:16	99n33
12:15	221
6:12	275n28
9:17	99n33
16:27	275n28
24:2	192n8

Songs

4:15	99n33

Isaiah

2:12–13	174
3:18–19	158n24
5:2	237
7:20	80n36, 120n36
8:3	90n7
9:4	128n5
9:6	216n12
10:1	192n8
10:26	128n5
10:33	297n31
14:18–20	189n3
14:31	56n26
16:5	90n7
19:14	176n24
19:20	56n26
19:22	56n26
25:1	216n12
25:6	221n23
29:10	176n24
29:14	216n12
30:2	174
31:8	75n26

Isaiah (continued)

34:5	75n26
49:2	75n26
56:6	122
65:14	56n26

Jeremiah

2:21	237
4:15	263
4:30	120n36
5:6	197n22
7:31	200
10:9	159n30
11:4–5	41n38
12:12	75n26
15:15	243n40
16:4	189n3
16:8	221n23
17:6	179n33
19:23–24	277
20:18	192n8
25:34	56n26
46:10	75n26
46:14	75n26
51:39	221n23

Lamentations

1:9	216n12
2:3	297n31
2:18	56n26
5:11	277n34
5:19	161

Ezekiel

2:8	199n28
3:2	199n28
6:9	57n28
16:16	270n10
16:20–21	200
16:25	120n36
21:26	252n13
21:33	75n26
23:39	200
27:7	159n30
27:16	159n30
31:6	174
31:12	174
31:17	174
33:15	37n23
34:20	80n36
37:15	31n9
37:19	31n9
38:10–11	260
47:14	256n29
47:18	256n29
47:22	256n29

Daniel

1:16	221n23
12:6	216n12

Hosea

1:2	270
3:4	159, 252n13
4:2	270
4:15	42n41
9:1	270
14:5–8	138n25

Joel

2:28–29	90n7
3:4	37n23
3:12	90n7

Amos

1–2	54n17
4:4	42n41
4:15	42n41
5:5	42n41
5:25	133
7:10–17	42n41
8:14	263

Nahum

3:15	75n26

Habakkuk

1:13	192n8
2:11	103

Zephaniah

2:9	179n33

Haggai

1:10–11	138n25

Zechariah

9:9	183n49
10:2	252n13
10:6	31n9
11:8	192n8
11:16	80n36

Malachi

3:3	133, 161
2:12	133
2:13–16	51

NEW TESTAMENT

Matthew

21:5	183n49

Luke

19:30	183n49
19:40	103

Romans

8:4	3
8:29	3, 103

2 Corinthians

6:15	275

Hebrews

11:32	16n37, 20n53, 90, 128n5, 162, 172
11:33–34	16n37

Revelation

1:16	75
2:12	75

www.ingramcontent.com/pod-product-compliance
Lightning Source LLC
Chambersburg PA
CBHW020109010526
44115CB00008B/763